SPHERES OF INFLUENCE

SPHERES OF INFLUENCE

The Social Ecology of Racial and Class Inequality

Douglas S. Massey
and
Stefanie Brodmann

Russell Sage Foundation • New York

The Russell Sage Foundation

The Russell Sage Foundation, one of the oldest of America's general purpose foundations, was established in 1907 by Mrs. Margaret Olivia Sage for "the improvement of social and living conditions in the United States." The Foundation seeks to fulfill this mandate by fostering the development and dissemination of knowledge about the country's political, social, and economic problems. While the Foundation endeavors to assure the accuracy and objectivity of each book it publishes, the conclusions and interpretations in Russell Sage Foundation publications are those of the authors and not of the Foundation, its Trustees, or its staff. Publication by Russell Sage, therefore, does not imply Foundation endorsement.

Library of Congress Cataloging-in-Publication Data

Massey, Douglas S.
   Spheres of influence : the social ecology of racial and class inequality / Douglas S. Massey and Stefanie Brodmann.
      pages cm
   Includes bibliographical references and index.
   ISBN 978-0-87154-643-2 (pbk. : alk. paper) — ISBN 978-1-61044-822-2 (ebook)
   1. Equality.   2. Race.   3. Social classes.   I. Brodmann, Stefanie.   II. Title.
   HM821.M38 2014
   305—dc23   2013041413

Text design by Suzanne Nichols.

RUSSELL SAGE FOUNDATION
112 East 64th Street, New York, New York 10065
10 9 8 7 6 5 4 3 2 1

CONTENTS

TABLES AND FIGURES

ABOUT THE AUTHORS

Douglas S. Massey is Henry G. Bryant Professor of Sociology and Public Affairs at the Woodrow Wilson School of Princeton University.

Stefanie Brodmann is an economist at the Social Protection and Labor Unit of the World Bank.

ACKNOWLEDGMENTS

This book was made possible by grant R01 HD053731 with additional support from grant R24 HD047879, both from the Eunice Kennedy Shriver National Institute of Child Health and Human Development whose support is gratefully acknowledged. We also thank Robert J. Sampson for his valuable comments and suggestions for revision.

CHAPTER 1

The Social Ecology of Human Development

The characteristics and behavior of all living organisms arise from a complex interaction between genes and the environment. This gene-environment interaction occurs not only within the genome of any species across historical time, but also within the lifetime of any particular organism. Among species, random mutations inevitably occur in the process of DNA replication and over time regularly introduce changes into its genome. These genetic changes may increase, decrease, or have no effect on an organism's ability to survive and reproduce. Those changes that enhance the odds of survival and reproduction are likely to be passed on and be retained in the genome. Those that reduce survival and reproduction are not passed on and over time disappear. Mutations that have no effect on survival or reproduction remain, though generally at lower frequencies.

This interaction between genes and the environment constitutes the core mechanism of evolution and has been recognized since the time of Charles Darwin (1859). The realization that genes interact with the environment within the lifetimes of individual organisms is much more recent. For many years, scientists had a rather static view of genetic inheritance, in which specific genes were passed on by parents and duly inherited and expressed by their progeny, irrespective of environmental conditions. Genes were invariably revealed biologically and the principal debate was over which was more important—genes or the environment—in accounting for observed traits and behaviors in the phenotypes of living organisms (Ceci and Williams 2000).

In recent years, however, this static view has given way to a more dynamic model in which the environment itself determines whether and how specific genes are expressed (Ridley 2004), a phenomenon known as epigenetics (Allis et al. 2007). As a result, current scientific debates tend not to be over which is more important—genes or the environment—but about how genes and the environment interact to bring about the expression of certain inherited proclivities. The focus of current work in both the biological and behavioral sciences has thus shifted to gene-environment interactions (Rutter 2006). The environment not only shapes behavior through learning and physiological conditioning, but also by determining which certain genes get turned on or off, and hence, expressed or not (Costa and Eaton 2006). Scientists have now documented instances where the environment has changed an organism's genetic structure to create a new genotype that is passed on to progeny through a process known as methylation (Suzuki and Bird 2008; Champagne 2012).

Environmental circumstances are especially important in understanding outcomes among human beings, given the complexity of their genome and the importance of learning in shaping their behavior. Unlike most organisms, however, the critical environment for human beings is not physical, but social. Since the emergence of *Homo sapiens* around two hundred thousand years ago, human adaptation has primarily been through culture rather than through genetics (Massey 2005a). Prior to the advent of the genus *Homo*, our ancestors occupied a very restricted environment both geographically and climatically, one essentially confined to the savannahs of East Africa. With the arrival of *Homo sapiens*, however, culture became the primary mechanism of adaptation and human beings quickly came to occupy virtually every ecological niche in the globe (Cavalli-Sforza, Menozzi, and Piazza 1994).

Human beings do not interact directly with the physical environment, but through the intervening filters of culture and society; and since cultural practices and societal institutions are socially transmitted, the critical environments for understanding the expression of human traits and behaviors are thus social. It is within specific social contexts that learning occurs and human proclivities play out. In order to explain human outcomes, therefore, one must consider the social ecology of development—the series of social environments that people come to inhabit at different stages of the life cycle (Bronfenbrenner 1979).

Everyone is born into a kinship system, of course, and the family is the first social environment all human beings occupy. Newborn babies are help-less and would quickly perish without constant attention from family mem-bers, mostly the mother, but also the father, siblings, grandparents, and sometimes even more distant relatives. As children age and approach adult-hood, they grow progressively less dependent on the family and more depen-dent on other social spheres such as neighborhoods, schools, and peers (Bron-fenbrenner 1973). As adults, of course, humans face a social environment defined by a variety of macro social structures—governments, corporations, and other major social institutions—but the capabilities that humans deploy in adapting to contingencies in the macro social environment are largely de-termined before adulthood through interactions that play out within micro social spheres.

The social settings experienced during childhood and adolescence are espe-cially powerful in shaping the physical, cognitive, and social capacities of human beings (Eliot 1999). In contemporary postindustrial societies, the key social settings for human growth and development are the family, the school, the neighborhood, and the peer group (Bronfenbrenner 1979). Together they are the four fundamental social contexts within which human capabilities are nurtured and ultimately expressed (Bronfenbrenner 2001). In addition, human beings have created an additional sphere, one in which they may or may not spend significant amounts of time while coming of age: religion, whether a church, a temple, or a mosque. The experience of interacting so-cially with coreligionists may offset or exacerbate the positive and negative effects of growing up in the four other settings.

SPHERES OF SOCIAL INFLUENCE

To grow, develop, and survive, all organisms must extract resources from the environments they experience. If human children are to grow, develop, and reach full adult potential, the social spheres they progressively inhabit—fami-lies, neighborhoods, schools, peers, and sometimes religious congregations—must provide access to key material, emotional, and symbolic resources (Kelly 1995; Gamble 1999). The critical material resources for developing human capabilities in contemporary societies are wealth and income, which deter-mine access to food, clothing, shelter, medicine, recreation, and education. The key emotional resources are warmth, affection, and physical contact, which social scientists have long shown to be fundamental to healthy social maturation (Harlow and Harlow 1986; Montague 1971; Davis 1999). Symbolic resources include markers of status, prestige, social standing, and esteem, constructs that though intangible nonetheless have powerful effects on well-being across a variety of dimensions and developmental transitions (Link et al. 1997; Rosenfield 1997; Zittoun 2006).

Access to necessary and sufficient resources is particularly important during phases of the life cycle when humans are biologically programmed to undergo specific developmental changes (Heckman 2006). Physical growth does not occur linearly from birth to adulthood, for example, but in distinct phases concentrated at ages zero to four and twelve to eighteen (Stützle et al. 1980). Although insufficient nutrition slows growth at any age, if it occurs during one of these critical developmental phases severe stunting typically results, and the shortfall in growth cannot be undone after the developmental window has closed, even if food later becomes abundant (Mann and Truswell 1998). The same is true for cognitive growth, except that in addition to nutrition and other physical resources, cognitive growth depends critically on the richness of the social environment (Doyle et al. 2009).

Unfortunately, as in the physical environment, resources in the social environment are not distributed equally; and to the extent that critical resources are deficient in any of the social spheres inhabited by human beings while growing up, we can expect their growth, development, and overall well-being to be compromised. Differences in access to material, emotional, and symbolic resources within families, schools, neighborhoods, peers, and religious settings translate directly into differences in human capabilities and well-being. In the United States, sharp inequalities in access to resources are well documented across all five of the foregoing social spheres.

Among families, for example, inequalities in wealth and income have risen dramatically since the mid-1970s (Keister 2000; Picketty and Saez 2003; Thompson 2012). These are quite strongly linked to disparities in the amount of parental attention devoted to children (Bianchi, Robinson, and Milkie 2006; Kendig and Bianchi 2008) as well to the quality and nature of that attention (Kohn 1989; Lareau 2003). Access to symbolic resources also varies systematically by family economic status, with markers that signal material disadvantage tending to trigger reactions of contempt, disgust, and avoidance by other social actors (Fiske et al. 2002; Cuddy et al. 2009).

Schools likewise differ dramatically in terms of the material resources at their disposal (Coleman 1966; Kozol 1991; Reimers 2001) and these differences are, in turn, associated with differences in proximate educational factors such as student-teacher ratios (Card and Krueger 1996; Darling-Hammond 1999; Finn and Achilles 1999; Rothstein 2004) and quality of instruction (Bowles and Gintis 1976; Willis 1977; Bourdieu and Passeron 1990). As with schools, moreover, neighborhoods also vary dramatically by economic status (Jargowsky 1997; Sampson, Morenoff, and Gannon-Rowley 2002) and this variation is similarly associated with differences in access to social support (Sampson and Graef 2009), security and safety (Sampson and Morenoff 2004), social efficacy (Sampson, Morenoff, and Earls 1999), civic action (Sampson et al. 2005), esteem (Sampson and Raudenbush 2004), and public order (Sampson and Raudenbush 1999). Indeed, indicators of neighborhood disadvantage display a very strong and persistent ecological correlation so that "bad" neighborhoods are characterized by multiple sources of disadvantage whereas "good" neighborhoods are typified by multiple sources of advantage, thus reifying the lines of stratification (Peterson and Krivo 2010; Sampson 2012; Sharkey 2013).

Although closely connected to schools and neighborhoods, peer networks are not necessarily coincident with either sphere, but like them vary widely with respect to social and economic composition to influence a variety of socioeconomic and health outcomes (Christakis and Fowler 2009; Small 2009; Martin 2009; Christakis and Fowler 2009). Finally, unlike the four fundamental spheres that virtually all people experience, religious congregations are voluntary and are thus more socioeconomically diverse (Schwadel 2009) than schools or neighborhoods, thus potentially offering low-status congregants a bridge to the material resources of higher status coreligionists, in addition to whatever emotional and symbolic resources church membership itself provides.

In the United States, access to critical material, emotional, and symbolic resources within different social spheres is not only structured by class, of course, but also by race and ethnicity. Among Hispanics and blacks, for example, rates of unwed childbearing and marital dissolution are significantly higher than among whites and Asians and rates of marriage are lower, yielding pronounced differences in the amount of parental time and resources potentially available to children (McLanahan and Sandefur 1994; Casper and Bianchi 2001; McLanahan 2004; Bianchi, Robinson, and Milkie 2006). Parenting styles also differ by race as well as class (Lareau 2000, 2003; Massey et al. 2003) and given continuing high levels of segregation in the United States, the quality of schools and neighborhoods also varies markedly by racial and ethnic group (Massey and Denton 1993; Orfield and Eaton 1996; Sampson 2008, 2012). There is also considerable segregation among interpersonal networks on the basis of both class and race-ethnicity (McPherson, Smith-Lovin, and Cook 2001) and the high degree of racial segregation among American religious congregations is well documented (Emerson and Smith 2000; Haynes 2012), despite their relative economic diversity (Schwadel 2009).

Race historically has served as a "master status" in the United States, dominating class and other social dimensions in defining the status and welfare of groups and individuals within American society; but the hegemony of race over class began to shift in the latter half of the twentieth century (Wilson 1978). In part, this shift stemmed from a revolution in attitudes. Before the 1960s, a clear majority of white Americans were principled racists. Before the civil rights era, for example, two-thirds of whites favored racial segregation in schools, 60 percent endorsed segregation in neighborhoods, 55 percent supported segregation in employment, and 54 percent backed segregation in transportation. By the 1990s, however, white support for segregation had all but evaporated, levels of support for segregation in these venues falling to just 4 percent, 13 percent, 3 percent, and 12 percent, respectively (Schuman et al. 1998). Moreover, whereas before 1964 two-thirds of whites said they would not vote for a black political candidate, in 2008 Americans elected a black president with significant, though hardly universal, white support.

Accompanying this revolution in attitudes were two ancillary social transformations that also helped change the relative balance between race and class in determining social outcomes, one demographic and the other economic. After 1965, the revival of mass immigration radically altered the demographic structure of the United States. In 1950, 88 percent of all Americans were white and non-Hispanic and 10 percent were African American. By 2010, only 65 percent of Americans were non-Hispanic and white, 17 percent were Hispanic, 13 percent were African American, and 5 percent were Asian.

Over the same period, a political realignment brought about economic changes that undid the equalizing policies of the New Deal to usher in an era of rising inequality (McCarty, Poole, and Rosenthal 2006). As a result, the Gini index for household income inequality went from 0.386 in 1968 to 0.466 in 2008, a remarkable 21 percent increase over four decades (U.S. Census Bureau 2009). Inequalities of wealth are even more extreme than inequalities of income (Keister 2000; Wolff 2002; Frank 2007a), and recent research clearly indicates that elected representatives are much more likely to act on the priorities of the affluent and wealthy than of the poor and middle class (Bartels 2008; Gilens 2012). As a result, the United States by 2010 was vastly more unequal than at any time since the 1920s.

In sum, because of immigration race was transformed from a dichotomy defined by a bright black-white color line to a more blurred continuum populated by a variety of groups of different hues, and through political realignment class was increasingly defined by a skewed distribution of income and wealth that produced bright boundaries between rich and poor (McCarty, Poole, and Rosenthal 2006; Frank 2007b). The changing meaning of race and the rising importance of class have necessarily increased the importance of race-class interactions in American society. With respect to neighborhood segregation, for example, black-white segregation steadily declined from 1970 to 2010 while Asian and Latino segregation held steady despite mass immigration, though given the large increase in the number and proportion of Latinos within urban areas, however, their isolation within neighborhoods rose sharply (Rugh and Massey 2013). Over the same period, segregation on the basis of socioeconomic status generally rose (Massey, Rothwell, and Domina 2009; Reardon and Bischoff 2011). As a result, some race-class groups, such as poor blacks, remain as spatially isolated as ever, whereas other groups (affluent blacks, for example) have become more integrated (Iceland and Wilkes 2006; Sampson 2012).

In considering the distribution of advantage and disadvantage across families, schools, neighborhoods, peers, and congregations, we therefore focus on race and class as key structuring factors. Put simply, we seek to determine how exposure to advantage and disadvantage within social spheres varies by race-ethnicity and social class simultaneously, and how this variation affects critical indicators of human development and well-being. We define race-ethnicity in terms of four broad groups that make up the prevailing taxonomy currently in use by government, industry, and the public: non-Hispanic whites, non-Hispanic blacks, non-Hispanic Asians, and Hispanics, henceforth simply whites, blacks, Asians, and Hispanics. We define class on the basis of household income quartiles, yielding four categories corresponding to the lower, lower middle, upper middle, and upper classes. Cross-classifying race-ethnicity by class yields a sixteen-cell social space we henceforth label the race-class distribution.

The fact that access to resources within social spheres varies by race and class and that this variation affects human outcomes and behaviors is hardly news. As noted, many studies have documented socioeconomic differentials between families, schools, neighborhoods, and peers. The influence of material resources on human well-being is so well established that indicators of family socioeconomic background are routinely included in statistical models used to study and predict developmental and behavioral outcomes, either as control variables or as theoretically specified determinants. It is also increasingly well documented that the socioeconomic composition of schools, neighborhoods, and peers exert independent influences on developmental outcomes (Wilkinson et al. 2000; Small and Newman 2001; Sampson, Morenoff, and Gannon-Rowley 2002; Sellström and Bremberg 2006).

Although considerable attention has been devoted to studying material inequalities across various social spheres, less attention has been paid to inequalities in access to emotional and symbolic resources, though these are also relevant to human growth and development. Here we endeavor, to the extent possible, to develop indicators of access to resources other than those that are material, working to define measures of access to emotional and social support as well as their opposite: exposure to disorder, violence, instability, and stigma.

In addition to broadening the measurement of inequality to incorporate nonmaterial features of the social environment, we also build on prior work by seeking to measure and study the interactive effects of inequality across different social spheres. It is not enough, we argue, simply to acknowledge the detrimental effects of exposure to disadvantage in families, schools, neighborhoods, and networks as main effects. Rather, to fully appreciate the effects of disadvantage experienced across multiple spheres simultaneously, we must consider potential interactive effects. Some groups are likely to experience high levels of disadvantage across all social spheres simultaneously, whereas others experience disadvantage in some but not all. It is well documented, for example, that poor whites are unlikely to live in neighborhoods characterized by high concentrations of poverty, whereas poor blacks are (Massey and Eggers 1990; Massey and Fischer 2003; Sampson and Sharkey 2008; Sampson 2012; Sharkey 2013). As a result, interactive measures must be incorporated into studies of the social ecology of human development. The full effect of disadvantages experienced in multiple spheres simultaneously is quite possibly much more than a simple sum of main effects.

STUDYING SOCIAL ECOLOGY

The ideal data needed to study the social ecology of human development would consist of a longitudinal survey that compiled detailed information on individuals and the various social environments they experienced at regular intervals from birth through childhood, adolescence, and into adulthood. If analyses exploring the additive and interactive effects of race and class are to be undertaken, moreover, the data would have to include oversamples of minority groups. Such a survey would require many years and a great deal of money to put together, of course, and the absence of such data explains the lack of a systematic account of the comparative social ecology of human development in the literature to date, despite the fact that the ecological model has been around for at least three decades (see Bronfenbrenner 1979).

Several contemporary surveys do enable investigators to follow subjects for certain portions of the life cycle—birth to childhood, childhood to adolescence, and adolescence to adulthood; but most of the sample sizes are not large enough to enable detailed analysis by race and class. One survey, however, follows a large number of subjects from adolescence into young adulthood and is based on a sample of sufficient size and complexity to allow reliable identification of detailed race-class groups, one that includes an unusual wealth of social, economic, and even biological data compiled at different levels of analysis. It thus provides an empirical foundation for a systematic analysis of the social ecology of racial and class inequality during a critical phase of human development: the adolescent transition to adulthood.

The Adolescent Health Survey, known popularly as Add Health, began with a baseline national sample compiled in 1994 and 1995, when respondents were age twelve to eighteen, and has so far carried out follow-up surveys one, two, seven, and thirteen years after the baseline. At the time we began this research, data from the most recent survey wave were not yet available and thus we conduct most of our ecological analyses using data from the first three waves. By the time the study was nearing completion, however, data from the fourth wave were released, and in the final chapter we use this information to analyze the final transition to adulthood, when most respondents were twenty-five or older. Specifically, we consider how variation in social ecological conditions experienced before Wave 3, and social and health outcomes attained by Wave 3, condition the transition to adulthood as measured in Wave 4, when the youngest respondents were twenty-four years old.

A detailed description of the Adolescent Health Survey is provided in appendix A. Briefly, the initial wave was implemented over 1994 and 1995 and focused on students attending grades seven through twelve, when most respondents were age twelve to eighteen. The school-based sample was designed to be nationally representative of adolescents attending middle schools and high schools in the United States during the 1994–1995 school year. The Wave 1 data come from five sources: an in-school survey of all students attending sampled schools; a more detailed in-home survey of a random subsample of these students; a survey of the latter's parents; a survey of administrators from sampled schools, and census tract data matched to the address of the adolescent's in-home interview. The second wave occurred a year later, in 1996, and consisted of an in-home survey of students interviewed in Wave 1 along with a telephone survey of school administrators. The third wave once again surveyed students included in Wave 1 using an in-home interview fielded in 2001 and 2002 when most respondents were age nineteen to twenty-six, and the fourth wave was carried out in 2007 and 2008 when they were age twenty-four to thirty-two.

In the Add Health Survey, African American, Latino, and Asians students were oversampled, yielding sample sizes large enough for detailed analysis by race and class. As described in the appendix, the study design called for oversampling black students having a parent with a college degree, as well as Chinese students, Cuban students, and Puerto Rican students, in addition to the black, Latino, and Asian students who were identified and interviewed in the core sample. The core sample itself contained more than 1,500 students of Mexican origin in addition to Cubans, Puerto Ricans, and others. In general, then, Add Health does a fairly good job representing the black and Latino student populations, but the Asian population is likely to be dominated by the experience of the Chinese, who were oversampled despite being the largest component of the Asian population, and less representative of South Asians, such as Indians or Pakistanis.

The Add Health data are not ideal for studying ecological effects on development, of course, since the panel begins in adolescence rather than birth or early childhood. Given that ages zero to four are critical for children's physical, cognitive, and social development, a survey that begins in adolescence will not be able to capture many important ecological effects, especially family influences on infant and preschool development. Nonetheless, in addition to early childhood, adolescence constitutes the other critical phase of human

Figure 1.1   Conceptual Diagram for Analyzing Social Ecology of Inequality

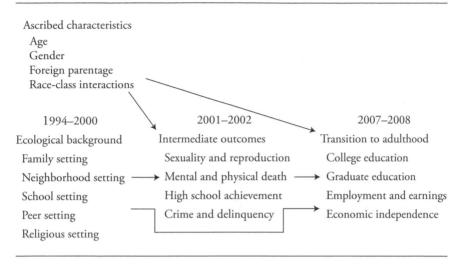

Source: Authors' compilation.

growth and development (Stützle et al. 1980). Moreover, to the extent that social environments experienced in childhood are correlated with those experienced later in adolescence, as seems to be the case (Sharkey 2013), then the Adolescent Health Survey is likely to capture some share of the socially-induced variation in developmental outcomes introduced during earlier phases of the life cycle.

The basic design of our analysis is summarized in figure 1.1. We take as exogenous the ecological circumstances that respondents experience in adolescence, mostly around the time of Waves 1 and 2, when they were thirteen to nineteen, but in the case of neighborhoods including average characteristics experienced between Waves 1 and 3. In the next two chapters, we develop indices of the material, symbolic, and emotional resources respondents were exposed to in their families, neighborhoods, schools, peer networks, and religious congregations before Wave 3. We also take as exogenous the ascribed characteristics of age, gender, foreign parentage, race, and class, the latter two of which we measure interactively. We then consider how the foregoing factors influence development and well-being expressed at Wave 3, when respondents were age roughly nineteen to twenty-six, focusing in par-

ticular on outcomes related to reproduction, health, human capital formation, crime, and delinquency. Finally, conditioned on these intermediate outcomes, we consider the effect of ecological circumstances and ascribed
characteristics on the transition to adulthood by Wave 4, which we define in
terms of relative success in education and employment, and the consequent
achievement of personal economic independence.

ARGUMENT AND ORGANIZATION

The ensuing chapters basically follow the conceptual diagram laid out in figure 1.1. Our core argument is that the United States is moving from a regime
of powerful binary racial effects and weak class effects to one characterized by
increasingly powerful class effects and diminishing though still very potent
racial effects, which increasingly are expressed along a continuum rather than
a dichotomy. As a result, both race and class need to be taken into account in
characterizing the social environments experienced by Americans today. Because the pace of change with respect to race and class differs across racial
groups and social spheres, moreover, class standing confers different sets of
advantages and disadvantages to incumbents of different racial groups and
different social settings. In other words, race-class interactions are often complex, and at present no single pattern of class privilege or penalty is invariant
with respect to race or social context.

This book is data intensive, containing many complicated statistical models and detailed analyses. As a result, reading it straight through is a bit of a
slog and readers may be overcome with data fatigue. One way around this
difficulty might be to read chapters 1, 2, and 3 and then read the conclusions
of chapters 4 through 8 and finish up by reading the whole of chapters 9 and
10. This exercise will convey the big picture of the book's basic arguments
and findings without getting the reader bogged down in the minutia of data
and analysis. Those readers interested in the gory details of multivariate analysis can then go back and read chapters 4 through 8 in their entirety, though
doing so in one sitting is not recommended.

The chapters follow the logic summarized in figure 1.1. In chapter 2, we
describe differences in access to material, symbolic, and emotional resources
within the family sphere, first examining differences across major racial
groups and then assessing this social sphere by race and class simultaneously.
In general, taking class as well as race into account greatly increases the observed range of intergroup variation in access to resources. With respect to

average income, for example, the range across major racial categories is from $28,400 for black families to $50,800 for Asian families, white and Hispanic families falling between at $48,500 and $35,200, respectively. Taking into account class, however, the range increases by a factor of nearly four, going from an average of only $9,300 for lower-class blacks up to $97,000 for upper-class Hispanics.

Adult time and attention are obviously critical resources for the healthy development of children and adolescents, and our analysis reveals large differences by race and even greater variation by race and class. The key structural feature of family life that determines access to adult time, as well as other resources, is the presence or absence of a biological father. The share of adolescents whose father was never present between Waves 1 and 3 ranged from 15 percent among Asians to 61 percent among blacks, but taking into account class as well as race increased the range from 12 percent among upper-middle-class Asians to 76 percent among lower-class blacks. In the remainder of the book, we thus focus on race-class differences in access to resources.

The remainder of chapter 2 focuses on the family sphere and considers differences in access to material, symbolic, and emotional resources among white, black, Latino, and Asian adolescents who are lower class, lower middle class, upper middle class, and upper class, yielding a total of sixteen discrete race-class categories. Our principal method is to rank order these categories with respect to the resource in question and array them in a bar chart going from smallest to largest. Before examining actual race-class distributions in access to resources, however, we describe idealized bar charts of what the distributions would look like if they were determined purely by race with no class effects or purely by class with no race effects.

Access to some family resources (such as paternal absence) show relatively strong racial effects whereas others (income obviously) show relatively strong class effects. In most cases, however, we observe complex interactions between race and class that make it difficult to generalize about the simple effects of race and class taken by themselves. To characterize the family environment experienced by adolescents in America today, one thus needs to consider race and class simultaneously; and as noted earlier, doing so generally yields a much larger range of variation in access to resources than is visible when either variable is considered by itself. Often the race-class differences are huge. As noted, we observe a tenfold difference in adolescents' access to income within the family sphere, the range going from $9,300 among lower-class blacks to \$97,000 among upper-class Hispanics. Likewise, the range in access to another material resource, health insurance, was also quite large, going from 46 percent among lower-class Hispanics to 80 percent among upper-class Asians. With respect to symbolic resources, the lowest level of prestige was observed among lower-class Hispanics, whose parental occupational status averaged just 26.1; the highest was for upper-class whites, whose average parental status was 47.1, 80 percent higher. Among symbolic resources, the gap was even greater in terms of access to human capital. Whereas 72 percent of upper-class adolescents had a college-educated parent, the share for lower-class Hispanic adolescents was just 15 percent, a gap of nearly 5 to 1.

We also observe stark contrasts in the degree of access to emotional resources. In addition to the huge spread in father absence already noted, we also observe a large range in child-to-adult ratios within the household, which go from 0.87 among upper-class blacks to 1.54 among lower-class blacks. The emotional burdens that inevitably come with family life are also borne unequally. Whereas only 1 percent of upper-middle-class Asian adolescents and 4 percent of upper-class white adolescents experienced a death in their immediate family before age eighteen, the figure was 13 percent for lower-class blacks and 14 percent for those in the lower middle class. Likewise, only 1.5 percent of upper-middle-class Asian fathers had ever been incarcerated by Wave 1, whereas the figure was 27 percent among lower-middle-class blacks. Families also differed significantly, though less sharply, with respect to their emotional tenor. On our scale of family sternness lower-class Asians stood out with a high value of 19.9 compared with 15.9 among lower-class blacks. Lower-class Asians also stood out for their lower access to family mentors, only 16 percent saying that an adult family member had made a difference in their lives, versus 37 percent of lower-class blacks.

As these statistics indicate, the Add Health Survey offers a great wealth of information about conditions in the family sphere; but it also includes an impressive amount of data on circumstances in other ecological settings. Chapter 3 uses these data to characterize the neighborhood, school, peer, and religious environments inhabited by adolescents in different race-class categories. In these environments, as well, we uncover a great deal of variation in access to material, symbolic, and emotional resources. In terms of material resources, the least privileged race-class group experienced 4.2 times more neighborhood disadvantage than the most privileged group and 1.5 times more school disadvantage. In terms of emotional resources, the least advantaged race-class category experienced 1.7 times more neighborhood inefficacy than the most advantaged category, 1.3 times more school inefficacy, 1.2 times more school disorder, and 2.4 times more peer violence. They were likewise 76 percent less likely to report a neighborhood mentor, 66 percent less likely to report a school mentor, and 50 percent less likely to report a peer mentor, but nine times more likely to have a suicidal friend.

These extremes were not evenly distributed among adolescents, but were concentrated in certain race-class categories, leading to the accumulation of advantages and disadvantages across social spheres. In general, lower-class blacks tended to be at the bottom and upper-class whites at the top with respect to most ecological resources. In twenty-five specific comparisons of indices across five social spheres, poor blacks displayed the most disadvantaged score in five cases, and in sixteen of twenty-five cases scored within 20 percent of the least privileged group. In contrast, in six comparisons, upper-class whites evinced the most advantaged score and in fifteen of twenty-five cases they were within the top 20 percent.

Having documented how race and class condition exposure to advantages and disadvantages across social spheres in early waves of the Adolescent Health Survey, the next four chapters assess how unequal ecological circumstances affect adolescent decision-making at the time of Wave 3, around 2001 and 2002, when respondents were age nineteen to twenty-six and just moving into young adulthood. Chapter 4 focuses on sexuality and family formation, studying how circumstances experienced in different family, neighborhood, school, peer, and religious environments affect sexual activity and partnering, paying particular attention to reproduction that prior research has shown to be socially risky in terms of its socioeconomic consequences, namely teenage and unwed childbearing.

We found that African American reproduction is characterized by a high likelihood of early sexual debut, a young age at first intercourse, and a relatively low likelihood of union formation, either through cohabitation or marriage. The low probability of marriage and cohabitation combined with high rates of sexual activity means that most sex among African Americans occurs outside stable unions, and the early age at first intercourse and the extremely low probability of marriage means that black women experience a prolonged risk of unwed childbearing, one that is not strongly affected by class or explained by ecological circumstances. Although the greater likelihood of teenage childbearing and the higher likelihood and earlier age of first intercourse among black women disappear once ecological circumstances and other background variables are controlled, the high likelihood of nonmarital childbearing is not, despite the fact that black women are more likely than others to use contraception. It is the virtual disappearance of marriage as a viable social institution and the rarity even of cohabitation in the black community, combined with the early initiation of young African American women into sex, that explain high rates of unwed childbearing across all classes of young black women in the United States.

At the other extreme are Asians, who display a low likelihood and late age of entry into first intercourse, a high likelihood of contraception use, and a low probability of cohabitation, which together yield extremely low rates of unwed and teenage childbearing. As with blacks this distinct pattern of reproduction does not vary systematically by class and is not explained away by controlling for ecological conditions. Blacks and Asians, it seems, have evolved two very different patterns for socializing people into sex, union formation, and childbearing.

Whites and Hispanics generally exhibit patterns of sexual activity, union formation, and childbearing that lie between the two extremes established by blacks and Asians, with Hispanics tending toward the former and whites the latter, except that both groups display a clear class gradient, such that the likelihood of first intercourse drops, the age of first intercourse rises, and the probability of cohabitation falls as class standing increases, yielding a similar class gradient with respect to risky childbearing. Thus the odds of nonmarital and teenage childbearing are greatest in the lower class, less in the lower middle class, less still in the upper middle class, and least in the upper class.

In general, family socioeconomic status does not play a major role in conditioning the process of reproduction, and material circumstances in schools and neighborhoods also carry relatively little weight. Sexuality, union formation, and childbearing among young Americans are more tightly connected to emotional resources in the family sphere. Women who grew up in an emotionally distant, cold, and stern family environment were less likely to initiate sex, do so at a later age, and are more likely to use contraception. They were also less likely to marry or cohabit, or to have children under any social auspices, either inside or outside marriage or before or after the age of eighteen.

Experiencing the death of a parent or sibling is a traumatic emotional burden that significantly lowers the odds of childbearing. Coming from an inefficacious neighborhood characterized by a low level of trust and mutual support also acts strongly to increase the age of first intercourse and depress childbearing. Social inefficacy in the school setting likewise lowers the odds of unwed fertility among young women, though it does increase the likelihood of cohabitation and sexual debut. In general, however, coming of age in an emotionally austere family and anomic neighborhoods and schools discourages formation of sexual unions, entry into either formal or informal romantic partnerships, and childbearing.

Chapter 5 takes up the issue of health, considering how ecological circumstances get "under the skin" to influence the mental and physical well-being young men and women. We begin by considering how the incidence of various risky health behaviors differs by race and class. Contrary to common stereotypes, we found that the likelihood of consuming controlled substances with well-known negative health effects—cigarettes, alcohol, and hard drugs—is greatest among whites and least among blacks, with Hispanics and Asians falling between. Although social class influences the likelihood of substance abuse, it acts in different ways for different substances and varies by racial group. The odds of smoking, for example, fall with increasing social class among whites but rise among Hispanics, and class has no systematic influence on the smoking behavior of blacks and Asians. The likelihood of abusing alcohol and hard drugs, however, generally rises with class among whites, Asians, and Hispanics, but displays no consistent class pattern among blacks.

Although African Americans are least likely to abuse controlled substances, they are most likely to eat fast food and to engage in risky sexual practices that increase the risk of sexually transmitted disease (STD) infection, such as paying for sex or having intercourse with known drug users. Asians are generally least likely to engage in such behavior, and whites and Hispanics fall between Asians and blacks. Once again, however, class operates differently for different risk behaviors in different racial groups. Thus, fast food consumption falls with rising social class among whites, Asians, and Hispanics, but varies little by class among African Americans. Moreover, whereas risky sex becomes less likely as class standing rises among blacks, Hispanics, and whites, it displays no class pattern among Asians.

Although respondents to the Adolescent Health Survey were in the prime of early adulthood at the time of the third wave and generally in good health, we nonetheless found that the likelihood of engaging in risky health behaviors was connected to poor health outcomes. Regular smoking, for example, increased the likelihood of reporting a limitation on physical activity and decreased self-reported health, and drug use reduced mental health and was associated with higher levels of depression. Having sex with a risky partner was also associated with greater likelihood of physical disability, greater body mass, and not surprisingly, STD infection.

Whereas blacks were least likely to report a limitation in physical activity and generally rated their health as better than other groups, they were also most likely to evince a high body mass index, to report ever having an STD, to be more depressed, and to expect an early death. Moreover, these health effects varied less by class for blacks than for other groups. Among whites and Hispanics, the incidence of negative health conditions generally fell as class standing rose but Asians often evinced a u-shaped pattern, with extreme values in the lower and upper classes and moderate levels in the middle classes.

The distinctive behavioral patterns of African Americans with respect to health are generally not attributable to their ecological circumstances. If anything, taking account of the generally more disadvantaged ecological circumstances experienced by blacks tends to accentuate the distinctiveness of black behavioral patterns, both positively (not abusing drugs, alcohol, or cigarettes) and negatively (eating fast food and engaging in risky sex). Although the health-related behaviors of blacks may be independent of their social context, however, their actual health outcomes are not. Once ecological conditions are controlled, their physical condition and self-assessed mental and physical health are no different than those of other groups. The one exception is the likelihood of STD infection, which tends to be quite high in the upper middle and upper classes even after the application of controls.

Hispanics, likewise, are less prone to smoke than whites even after taking ecological circumstances into account, but most of the other race-class effects on health behaviors and outcomes are reduced to marginal significance or disappear entirely once ecological circumstances are controlled. Although Asians display no greater tendency toward risky health behaviors once ecological differences are controlled, upper and lower-class Asians nonetheless are still more likely to report a physical disability and display a stronger tendency toward depression, whereas lower and middle-class Asians rate their health more poorly, even after controls. Among whites, however, the various class gradients observed in basic tabulations generally disappear, fall to marginal significance, or reverse sign in the presence of ecological controls.

Among ecological circumstances, we found that material and symbolic resources within the family sphere generally had weak or nonexistent effects on health behaviors and outcomes, with the notable exception of access to health insurance, which lowered the likelihood of smoking, raised the age at which smoking begins, reduced the likelihood of hard drug use, increased the incidence of physical disabilities, and mitigated poor health, depression, and the perception of low life chances. Growing up with a stepparent increased the likelihood of smoking, and coming of age with a single parent raised the odds of drug abuse, but other effects of family composition were marginal or absent. The only effect of income is to increase the age at which smoking begins and lower the tendency to expect an early death. Higher parental occupational status actually increased the risk of drug abuse.

Aside from access to insurance, health behaviors and outcomes are more strongly connected to emotional than to material circumstances within the family, family sternness and paternal incarceration having particularly strong and ubiquitous effects. The more remote and stern the emotional style in the family of origin, the lower the likelihood of smoking, alcohol abuse, drug taking, and risky sex, and the less likely respondents are to report an STD, poor health, symptoms of depression, and the prospect of an early death. Independent of family emotional style, paternal incarceration raises the odds of smoking, alcohol abuse, hard drug use, fast food consumption, and obesity while increasing body mass. The mass incarceration of black men thus has strong health implications for their children, and other family members were no substitute for absent fathers. Young people who said they relied on another mentor in the family were more likely to abuse alcohol, eat fast food, evince a physical limitation, and rate their health as poor.

A second critical sphere of influence in terms of health was peer setting. Exposure to peer violence greatly increased the odds of smoking, drug abuse, and having risky sex and raised the perceived likelihood of an early death. The emotional blow of a friend's suicide attempt also increased the likelihood of smoking, abusing alcohol, using hard drugs, engaging in risky sex, having a physical disability, and evincing obesity. Not surprisingly, therefore, having a suicidal friend also increased the tendency of respondents to rate their health as poor, report depressive symptoms, and perceive a low chance of making it to middle age. Reliance on a peer mentor increased the risk of smoking, alcohol abuse, and physical disability.

Although not as consistently strong or significant as conditions in the family emotional and peer environments, neighborhoods and schools also displayed a number of powerful effects. Material disadvantage within neighborhoods was associated with greater body mass, a higher expectation of early death, and a higher rate of obesity, and an elevated risk of STD infection. However, contrary to prevailing perceptions, neighborhood disadvantage lowered the relative likelihood of alcohol and drug abuse and reduced the degree of depression. Material disadvantage within schools likewise lowered the odds of smoking and alcohol abuse, but social inefficacy within neighborhoods did act to increase physical disability, depression, and expectation of an early death, and inefficacy within schools raised the odds of smoking, drug use, and STD infection and increased perceptions of poor health and a likely early death.

In general, the religious sphere had only modest effects on respondent health behaviors and outcomes. Religious involvement lowered the likelihood of smoking and alcohol abuse and increased health and perceived survival chances. Having a religious mentor, meanwhile, reduced the rate of smoking and alcohol abuse. Religiosity itself was associated with greater depression, however. This association does not necessarily mean that religiosity causes depression. Indeed, it is quite likely that depressed people seek solace in religion. The accumulation of multiple disadvantages across social spheres increases the likelihood of fast food consumption, lowered self-assessed health, and increased depression.

All in all, our results suggest that young people's health is driven primarily by family emotional circumstances and conditions in the peer environment, and show strong effects also in the school and neighborhood settings, weaker effects in the religious sphere, and, with the exception of access to health insurance, relatively weak effects with respect to family composition, material resources, and symbolic resources. In chapter 6, we took the foregoing health outcomes as predetermined and considered their effects on human capital formation along with the effects of family, school, neighborhood, peer, and religious circumstances, focusing on the production of cognitive skills and high school achievement.

An important input into learning and cognitive skill formation is a young person's degree of focus and attention. Consequently, its absence, a syndrome known as Attention Deficit and Hyperactivity Disorder (ADHD) has become the focus of increasing research in cognitive science. In our analyses, we found that the expression of ADHD was most strongly predicted by conditions in the peer environment. Exposure to peer violence, having a suicidal friend, and relying on a peer mentor all act to increase ADHD. The expression of ADHD is also influenced by conditions in the neighborhood and family spheres. Relying on a neighborhood mentor is associated with greater ADHD, as is reliance on mentors in the family and peer settings. In terms of attention deficit and hyperactivity, relying on a peer, family, or neighborhood mentor thus yields a worse outcome than having a school-based mentor or no mentor at all. Within the family sphere, growing up in a stepparent household is also associated with greater ADHD, but ADHD is sharply reduced by access to health insurance.

Cognitive skill formation is very strongly affected by ecological conditions within all the social spheres. We measured cognitive skills using the Peabody Picture Vocabulary Test (PVT) and found that within the family sphere, PVT scores are increased by access to health insurance, by access to the symbolic resources of parental education and prestige, and by the experience of a death in the family, but are reduced by a stern emotional style. Exposure to material disadvantage within schools and neighborhoods and the accumulation of disadvantages across spheres also act strongly to reduce PVT scores. In contrast, social inefficacy in schools and neighborhoods appears to increase verbal intelligence, as does a relative scarcity of young single males in the neighborhood. We interpret these findings to mean that limited opportunities for socializing translate into fewer distractions and greater cognitive skill. Socializing is a competing use of adolescent time and energy and detracts from cognitive skill formation. We also found that having a mentor improves verbal intelligence, whether the mentor originates in the family, neighborhood, school, peer, or religious spheres. PVT scores improve with greater religious involvement but not religiosity per se. It is thus social capital rather than spiritual capital from the religious sphere that is implicated in cognitive development.

Grade performance in high school is not surprisingly enhanced by having a high status, college-educated parent and coming from a two-parent household with health insurance, but grade point average (GPA) is unrelated to emotional resources within the family. Within the family, academic performance is more tied to symbolic and material resources. GPA is strongly improved by having a school or religious mentor and by greater religious involvement. As with verbal intelligence, grades are enhanced by social inefficacy and a relative absence of young unattached males in the neighborhood, again suggesting that socializing and learning are competing activities for most adolescents. Unlike the PVT score, however, GPA is reduced by social inefficacy at school, suggesting that warmth, caring, and support in this social sphere are central to academic achievement. Grade achievement is also sharply lowered by exposure to peer violence and by exposure to multiple disadvantages across spheres.

Another important educational outcome is the proportion of courses that were failed in high school. The risk of course failure is generally predicted by the same family characteristics as GPA, being greater for respondents from single-parent families and lower for those having a college-educated parent and access to health insurance. The risk of course failure is also raised by exposure to material disadvantage within schools and neighborhoods and to violence in the peer network, and is negatively predicted by access to a mentor within the school or religious sphere, and by greater religiosity and involvement in the religious sphere, again underscoring the salience of social over spiritual capital in the formation of human capital.

We found that in terms of the likelihood of high school graduation, ecological effects are mostly indirect, operating through the proportion of courses failed, which unsurprisingly quite strongly predicts the odds of graduation. The strongest direct ecological effects on high school completion are the positive effect of access to health insurance and the negative effect of exposure to peer violence. Thus access to health insurance stands out as a remarkably important determinant of cognitive skill formation and scholastic achievement, with very strong and highly significant effects for all of the cognitive and academic outcomes we considered. The recent health-care reform, if it indeed succeeds in expanding coverage, may thus yield important societal benefits by raising the rate of human capital formation in the United States. Social capital also plays an important role, effects consistently significant not only in the religious sphere but also in the peer environment. We found that exposure to peer violence, which one might consider to constitute negative instance of social capital, impedes the formation of human capital among adolescents by increasing ADHD, reducing GPA, raising the rate of course failure, and reducing the odds of graduation.

Holding constant ecological and mediating circumstances largely eliminates the performance gap displayed by African Americans of all classes with respect to indicators of high school achievement, but does not eradicate their consistently lower scores they earn on either the PVT or the ADHD index.

Much the same pattern prevails among Hispanics. Among Asians, taking into account ecological circumstances does not account for the lower ADHD and PVT scores and higher GPAs they generally exhibit. Only among whites does controlling for ecological conditions and mediating circumstances tend to eliminate class differences with respect to cognitive skill formation and high school achievement.

Chapter 7 completes our analysis of social and economic factors that mediate the transition to adulthood by considering the tendency of different race-class groups to engage in criminal behaviors and degree of criminal justice involvement. Proclivities for crime and delinquency are not spread evenly within most populations, of course, but are heavily concentrated among certain demographic groups—specifically males age twelve to twenty-nine with a peak in criminality in the late teens and early twenties (Steffensmeier et al. 1989). Although for biological reasons young men are at greatest risk of exhibiting antisocial and criminal behaviors, not all young men succumb to the elevated risks associated with high levels of testosterone and delayed development of the prefrontal cortex and the actual expression of crime and delinquency over the life cycle is substantially under social control.

Simple tabulations of levels of involvement in violent and nonviolent criminal activities and criminal justice reveal that Asians generally show lower levels of both violent and nonviolent crime and lower-class Asians exhibit lower levels of contact with the criminal justice system. Apart from these generalizations, however, few systematic patterns emerge. Baseline statistical models predicting nonviolent criminal involvement show that most other race-class groups exhibit the same degree of involvement as upper-class whites, with certain nonsystematic exceptions—such as lower- and upper-middle-class whites, lower-middle- and upper-class Hispanics, and lower-class blacks—all of whom exhibit lower proclivities toward violent crime. With respect to violent crime, the differences are even fewer, with the exception of the higher rates of violent criminal behavior exhibited by lower- and lower-middle-class African Americans. In terms of criminal justice involvement, the only significant difference is for lower-class Asians, who display lower levels of involvement than everyone else.

Once ecological and mediating circumstances are taken into account, race-class differences with respect to the degree of violent and nonviolent criminal involvement diminish even further. Other things equal, upper-class Asians and Hispanics display less involvement in nonviolent criminal activities, but these are the only significant race-class effects. Among the ecological determinants of criminal involvement, conditions in the peer environment have the strongest and most consistent effects. Our models show that exposure to violence among peers very sharply increases the expression of both violent and nonviolent crime as well as criminal justice involvement. In addition, having a suicidal friend also increases the propensity to engage in both kinds of criminal activities, and relying on a peer mentor increases the degree of criminal justice involvement.

Outside the peer group, the next most consistent effects occur within the family sphere. Although family sternness is modestly associated with lower levels of involvement in nonviolent crime, it has no effect on the tendency toward violent crime or criminal justice involvement. Not surprisingly, a strong predictor of criminality is paternal incarceration. Having a father who has been imprisoned or jailed increases the expression of both violent and nonviolent criminal behaviors, suggesting that mass incarceration may increase rather than reduce the intergenerational transmission of criminal behavior by removing an important authority figure from the household. Moreover, turning to other family members does not seem to help, in that reliance on a family mentor is also associated with a higher degree of contact with the criminal justice system.

We observe few strong or consistent effects in social spheres outside the family. Social inefficacy in the school setting is generally associated with greater involvement in nonviolent crime, having a school-based mentor is associated with higher levels of criminal justice involvement, and greater religious involvement lowers the degree of contact with the criminal justice system. In the end, however, expressions of violent and nonviolent crime are most strongly connected to conditions in the peer and family spheres.

Although controlling for ecological and mediating circumstances decreases the degree of race-class variation in the expression of criminal behaviors, it accentuates differences in the degree of criminal justice involvement. Other things equal, most race-class groups exhibit the same proclivity toward violent and nonviolent crime as upper-class whites, and absent any adjustment for ecological or mediating conditions, they also display the same level of criminal justice involvement. Once ecological circumstances and mediating conditions are taken into account statistically, however, whites below the upper class display significantly lower levels of criminal justice involvement, as do lower-, lower-middle-, and upper-middle-class Hispanics, and lower-class blacks and Asians. Put another way, if upper-class whites did not enjoy so many ecological advantages, they would exhibit far higher rates of criminal justice involvement. We conclude that white skin color and upper-class status continue to confer privileges in American society by reducing the likelihood of entanglement with the nation's judicial system.

Chapter 8 shifts ahead to 2007 and 2008, when Wave 4 of the Adolescent Health Survey provides information on respondents age twenty-four to thirty-two and most had completed the transition to early adulthood. In assessing this transition, we focus on the likelihood of completing college and graduate education as well as achieving gainful employment. We define a successful transition to adulthood as achieving economic independence by the time of the fourth wave. We predict the likelihood of college completion, employment, and dependency from ecological circumstances experienced before Wave 3 and intermediate outcomes achieve at Wave 3. In doing so, we are able to measure the long-term direct effects of exposure to circumstances in family, neighborhood, school, peer, and religious settings on the odds of achieving a successful transition to adulthood, as well as the indirect effect of ecological conditions through their influence on intervening conditions such as unwed parenthood, health, education, and delinquency.

In terms of direct ecological effects, a successful transition to adulthood is most powerfully and consistently predicted not by income or composition within one's family of origin, but by access to health insurance. Full access to health insurance while growing up increases the likelihood of graduating from college, earning a graduate degree, and being employed even as it significantly boosts earnings and lowers the likelihood of receiving public transfers. Other ecological factors are important in determining specific adult outcomes, but none have the same across-the-board effects as access to health insurance. Thus parental prestige, parental college attainment, neighborhood inefficacy, and school disorder increase the odds of college graduation, as do having a family or school-based mentor, but these factors do not have consistent influences across other domains of adult independence. Having a father incarcerated before Wave 1 decreases the odds of college graduation and increases the likelihood of adult dependence. The probability of receiving public transfers in adulthood is also strongly predicted by experiencing multiple disadvantages across social spheres during adolescence. Once ecological circumstances and mediating variables are held constant, few race-class differences in economic independence remain, with the main exceptions being the greater proclivity of lower-middle- and upper-middle-class blacks to work part time and the greater proclivity of lower-class and upper-middle-class blacks to receive public transfers.

Chapter 9 summarizes results from the preceding chapters by assessing the cumulative influence of ecological advantages disadvantages across social spheres and modeling their effects as they operate both directly and indirectly through mediating outcomes to determine the likelihood of making a successful transition to economic independence. We accomplish this task by undertaking a counterfactual analysis. After observing what happens to lower-class blacks and upper-class whites as they grow up subject to the influences of their respective social ecologies, we ask what would happen if each were to grow up experiencing the social ecology of the other.

We find in all cases that switching ecological exposures in this fashion yields substantially improved outcomes for lower-class blacks and more deleterious outcomes for upper-class whites. The overall pattern of results indicates that the gap in well-being between blacks at the lower end of the income hierarchy and whites at the top of the hierarchy would mostly be eliminated if conditions within family, school, neighborhood, peer, and religious spheres could somehow be equalized, essentially eliminating differentials with respect to health, cognition, education, criminality, delinquency, and college graduation. Notable exceptions to this generalization occur with respect to unwed and teenage childbearing, where strong racial differentials persist despite taking into account differences in ecological circumstances and intervening developmental outcomes. Moreover, given this persistent racial gap in nonmarital and early childbearing, the gap in welfare dependency, though substantially reduced, is by no means eliminated.

By way of summary, the final chapter offers a broad justification and rationale for the ecological approach we have adopted and for its use in attempting to understand how race and class interact within America's social ecology to generate inequality in the contemporary United States. After summarizing the huge range in exposure to ecological advantages and disadvantages that adolescents face in American society, and how this variation in exposure is structured simultaneously by race and class, we go on to identify those ecologies that are most critical in promoting human growth development and thereby ensuring a successful transition to adulthood. Finally, we outline the most important ecological mechanisms that contribute to the creation and perpetuation of racial and ethnic inequalities in the United States today.

CHAPTER 2

Divergent Family Spheres

The family is the basic social unit of all human societies. All people are embedded in a web of consanguineous relationships at birth, and some subset of this network is culturally defined to be the family of procreation—the group of people responsible for the bearing and raising of children through infancy, childhood, adolescence, and into independent adulthood, however that is defined in a particular social setting. How kinship is labeled and what caregiving responsibilities are assigned to which people vary by place, time, and culture, of course (see Aries 1965; Fox 1984). Virtually all human societies, however, assign primary responsibility for child rearing to the biological mother, with ancillary duties allocated to fathers and other family members depending on specific cultural traditions (Parkin and Stone 2004). In some cultures, especially those in resource-constrained environments, fictive kinship categories may be invented to garner additional support for mothers and children beyond what is potentially available from actual relatives (Lomnitz 1977; Chatters, Taylor, and Jayakody 1994).

Whatever its configuration, the family is almost always the primary unit responsible for providing young people with the material resources they need for physical growth and development—food, clothing, and shelter at a minimum, but also other resources. The family provides children with critical emotional resources necessary for social development and psychological well-being, such as physical contact, warmth, comfort, and affection—the basic elements of parental love (Harlow 1964; Harlow and Harlow 1986). As children age, the family also plays a central role in conferring more intangible, symbolic resources that enhance well-being, such as status and prestige, which bring deference and regard from others.

In contemporary societies, families typically occupy a dwelling unit of some sort, yielding a social institution known as the household. *Family households* are those in which a dwelling's occupants are related to one another by blood or marriage and these may be grouped into two basic subdivisions: nuclear (containing parents and their offspring) and extended (including other relatives as well). *Nonfamily households* are those where residents are not related to one another by blood or marriage. Although nonfamily households have become increasingly common in developed societies, they are not of primary interest here since the vast majority of them are not involved in raising children. Most are composed of single persons, various configurations of roommates, or cohabiting sexual partners who are childless and not formally married. If any member of the latter configurations should come to bear a child, of course, the resulting collective would automatically become a family household, by definition, because of the consanguineous mother-child relationship.

In the United States, the rearing of human beings has historically occurred within family households, and nuclear family households currently predominate in American society, although other family arrangements have been more common at different times and places and are still more common among some social groups than others (Mintz and Kellog 1988). Within nuclear families, the tasks of household production and reproduction are divided between husbands, wives, and older children, typically in a gendered fashion that assigns mothers disproportionate responsibility for household labor and fathers or male partners greater responsibility for work outside the household (Bittman et al. 2003). Even when fathers and mothers contribute equally to work outside the household, "caring labor" within the household tends to fall most heavily on women, though the balance has shifted to become somewhat more egalitarian in recent years (Bianchi 2000).

Although older children may assist in housework within larger families, most domestic work done in American households today, including the core tasks of child rearing and housekeeping, are divided between husbands and wives, or more generally between women and their adult partners, though not without contestation (England and Shafer 2009). As a result, the most important single determinant of the quantity, if not the quality, of material, emotional, and symbolic resources available to children is the presence or absence of a second parental figure, in most but certainly not all cases a husband or cohabiting male. Although male contributions to household labor continue to be quite asymmetric, the presence of a second adult nonetheless means that additional time and effort are at least theoretically available for household chores and child rearing activities; and of course male earnings outside the household contribute directly to the material resources available to household members.

Building on this logic, Daniel Patrick Moynihan (1965) argued in a well-known report that the rise of unwed childbearing and single-parent families during the 1960s constituted a serious threat to children's well-being and was becoming a key link in the reproduction of poverty over time and across generations, particularly among African Americans. At the time he prepared his controversial report, Moynihan was assistant secretary of labor in the administration of President Lyndon Johnson and his primary focus was on the black family, which he argued was being systematically destabilized by high rates of black male joblessness and underemployment, which made black men less desirable as marital partners (Rainwater and Yancey 1967). Moynihan made this argument to justify a federal jobs program that would guarantee employment to all able-bodied adult males, but especially African Americans (Wilson 2009). The report, however, set off a firestorm of protest in which Moynihan was accused of maligning the black family, patronizing black women, emasculating black men, and generally "blaming the victim" (Massey and Sampson 2009).

Despite the controversy, subsequent research has generally confirmed that, on average, growing up with two parents is better for children than growing up with one parent and that there are clear and persistent differences in access to material, emotional, and symbolic resources available to children in one- and two-parent households (McLanahan and Sandefur 1994; Haskins 2009). Although remaining in a dysfunctional marriage characterized by domestic violence, substance abuse, or sexual predation is not advisable, absent clear negatives two-parent families generally offer children more resources than one-parent families, at least given the current institutional configuration of American society, which provides little for children outside of families (Furstenberg 2009; McLanahan 2009). In this chapter, therefore, we consider differences in the composition of the family sphere by race and class, and document how the presence or absence of fathers condition access to key material, emotional, and symbolic resources.

ACCESS TO ADULT TIME AND ATTENTION

We begin by considering the living arrangements experienced by adolescents in the four racial-ethnic groups identified by the Adolescent Health Survey, focusing on the degree to which adult authority figures are present and thus potentially available within the family to contribute to the tasks of child rearing and housekeeping and resource accumulation. As described in appendix A, we combine data from students, parents, and school administrators across multiple waves of the Add Health survey, which results in some loss of data through list-wise deletion to produce a total sample of 8,998 cases, though the precise number shifts from tabulation to tabulation owing to variation in item non-response.

The top panel of table 2.1 examines the presence or absence of biological parents within the family spheres occupied by white, Asian, Hispanic, and black respondents to the Adolescent Health Survey. As can be seen, the rather large total number breaks down into much smaller subpopulations when the data are subdivided by race and ethnicity, despite Add Health's oversampling of minority populations. As expected, the largest sample size is that of whites (5,039), who still constituted by far the majority of adolescents in 1994. Although much smaller than the white sample, the sizes of the black and Latino samples (1,894 and 1,482, respectively) are nonetheless large enough to yield robust estimates for most purposes, thanks to oversampling (see appendix A). The sample size for Asians (629) is most problematic, in that it is the smallest of the four groups and only one of its many constituent groups (the Chinese) was oversampled. In general, then, we can expect considerably greater instability in estimates for Asians compared with the other groups and for Asian findings to disproportionately represent the experience of Chinese adolescents.

The first line in the table shows the presence of biological mothers at the time of first wave of the survey in 1994 and 1995. It is immediately obvious that little heterogeneity exists between groups in terms of access to mothers. In keeping with deeply ingrained and genetically rooted social traditions, biological mothers are almost universally present in the lives of adolescents, the share essentially fixed across all groups at around 93 percent or 94 percent. What varies substantially between groups is the presence of biological fathers, and here the percentage diverges quite dramatically by race, ranging from a

Table 2.1   Living Circumstances

Variable	Whites	Asians	Hispanics	Blacks
Biological parents				
Mother present at Wave 1	93.1	93.3	93.2	94.2
Father present at Wave 1	69.5	80.1	63.9	36.1
Father never present	23.4	15.2	25.7	60.7
Relative number of adults				
Average number of adults	2.1	2.5	2.4	2.0
Average number of children	2.2	2.4	2.8	2.6
Child-adult ratio	1.06	0.98	1.18	1.32
Number of cases	5,039	629	1,482	1,894

Source: Authors' calculations based on data set described in Harris and Udry (2008).
Note: Adults are eighteen and older; children are younger than eighteen.

low of 36 percent among African Americans to a high of 80 percent among Asians, whites and Hispanics falling in between at 70 percent and 64 percent, respectively.

In terms of sheer access to time and attention from biological parents, therefore, we observe a very clear intergroup gradient. Under any realistic scenario, African American children have much less access to parental time and resources than other children because so many of them (indeed the majority) lack access to a residential father. The last line in the top panel shows the percentage of adolescents who never had a live-in biological father during the six years between Waves 1 and 3 of the survey. Whereas these circumstances only befell a distinct minority of white, Asian, and Hispanic adolescents (with respective figures of 23 percent, 15 percent, and 26 percent), it characterized the living situation experienced by a clear majority of black adolescents (61 percent).

Fathers are not the only adults capable of providing time and attention to children, of course. Stepfathers, live-in boyfriends, same-sex partners, older siblings, aunts and uncles, grandparents, and various other relatives might also be present and available to lend assistance with the tasks of housework and child rearing. The first two lines of the second panel therefore show the number of adults and children within households occupied by adolescents in each group. As can be seen, the average number of adults present in the household ranges from 2.0 among African Americans to 2.5 among Asians, and the relative number of children present ranges from 2.2 among whites to 2.8 among Latinos.

Dividing these two series of numbers into one another yields the number of children per adult in the household. Very clearly, even when all household members age eighteen or older are taken into account, the same intergroup gradient emerges with respect to children's access to adult time and attention. Whereas each white and Asian child could count on the attention of roughly one adult (with child-adult ratios of 1.06 and 0.98, respectively), the relative number of children per adult was much greater for other groups: 1.18 for Hispanics and 1.32 for African Americans. Put a different way, black adolescents had a potential claim on adult time that was 25 percent less than Asian adolescents, 19 percent less than white adolescents, and 10 percent less than Hispanic adolescents.

ACCESS TO OTHER RESOURCES

Table 2.2 continues our analysis of the family sphere by considering other kinds of resources accessible to children within the family environment—material, symbolic, and emotional. Income is obviously a key material resource for child well-being. Our measure thus includes parents' self-reported pre-tax income in 1994 as well as the incomes of others in the household plus income from welfare benefits, dividends, and other sources. To keep sample attrition within reasonable limits, we imputed income for the 22 percent of households that had missing data. We based our imputation on child's race-ethnicity, immigration status, age and education of primary caregiver, family type, employment status (full-time, part-time, and not employed) and disability status of primary and secondary caregivers, whether a public assistance recipient lives in household, median income for household's race/ethnicity in census tract, school ID, and community ID.

With respect to income, once again we see very clear differences between groups. Whereas households occupied by white and Asian adolescents enjoyed average annual incomes of $48,500 and $50,800, respectively, those inhabited by Latino and black adolescents displayed respective values of just $35,200 and $28,400. In other words, Asian young people enjoyed a 5 percent income premium relative to whites, whereas Hispanic and African American adolescents suffered respective income deficits of 27 percent and 41 percent.

Table 2.2   Access to Resources Within Family

Variable	Whites	Asians	Hispanics	Blacks
Material resources				
Household income	48.5	50.8	35.2	28.4
Full year health insurance	64.2	69.5	53.6	59.7
Ever received welfare	7.3	9.3	17.4	22.2
Received a housing subsidy	2.2	2.7	3.6	11.7
Not enough money for bills	13.3	15.3	25.2	30.7
Symbolic resources				
Average occupational prestige	41.6	39.3	33.3	34.3
Parental education				
Less than high school	11.3	28.3	50.3	23.0
High school graduate	34.5	17.3	21.6	33.3
Some college	30.5	13.0	18.5	27.1
College graduate	15.4	31.9	6.4	11.0
Postgraduate studies	8.2	9.5	3.1	5.7
Emotional resources				
Family sternness scale ($\alpha = 0.90$)	17.4	18.8	17.8	16.4
Death in family	5.8	7.3	7.8	12.1
Father incarcerated	12.9	5.1	17.0	20.3
Family mentor named	26.0	19.3	23.8	34.1
Number of cases	5,039	629	1,482	1,894

Source: Authors' calculations based on data set described in Harris and Udry (2008).
Note: Household income in thousands of dollars. Occupational score numeric. Sternness as indicated. All other numbers are percentages.

The United States historically has historically lacked a system of guaranteed health insurance, meaning that lower-income families often have fewer resources to invest in the maintenance or enhancement of physical and emotional health (National Research Council 2003). Moreover, in the absence of access to health insurance, a sudden medical emergency can quickly undermine a family's material well-being (Hadley 2002). Indeed, unexpected medical expenses are a principal cause of bankruptcy in the United States (Sullivan, Warren, and Westbrook 1989, 2000). Unfortunately, access to this critical resource is also unequally distributed across groups. The second line in the table shows the percentage of respondents who were fully covered by health insurance during the twelve months prior to Wave 3 of the Add Health Survey. As can be seen, Hispanics experienced the least protection from unexpected health-care expenses, with just 54 percent of respondents being covered, compared with nearly 70 percent of Asians, 64 percent of whites, and 60 percent of African Americans.

The foregoing variation in access to material resources is mirrored in other economic indicators shown at the bottom of the top panel. For example, whereas just 7 percent of white families and 9 percent of Asian families ever received welfare, 17 percent of Latino and 22 percent of black families did. The same ordering prevails when we consider receipt of a housing subsidy (living in a project or receiving a rent voucher), the share rising from 2 percent among whites and 3 percent among Asians to 4 percent among Latinos and 12 percent among African Americans. The relative paucity of material resources was noticed by the survey respondents themselves. Around 13 percent of white adolescents said there was not enough money available in their household to pay bills, some 15 percent of Asian adolescents, but 25 percent of Hispanics and nearly 33 percent of African Americans.

Money cannot buy some advantages, of course (see Mayer 1997), and in turning to symbolic resources, we note that in postindustrial societies the principal means of garnering status and prestige comes from participating in the labor force. Being able to support oneself through work confers dignity and supports a claim to public respect and social regard, especially in the United States (Lamont 2000). Yet among those who work, occupations vary greatly in terms of the prestige they carry, and to measure variation in prestige the sociologist Otis Dudley Duncan (1961) developed a quantitative index of occupational status. He assigned each occupational category defined by the U.S. census a socioeconomic indicator (SEI) based on the social and economic characteristics of the occupation's incumbents, yielding a widely used 100-point scale of prestige that allocated single-digit values to unskilled workers of various sorts and values in the 1990s to workers in highly skilled professions.

As the nature of work has changed over time, these SEI scores have periodically been recalibrated (Hauser and Warren 1997) and they have also been adapted for international comparisons (Ganzeboom and Treiman 1996). We computed average SEI scores for the parents of adolescents using the Hauser-Warren update. To compute these values, we assigned the SEI score for the occupation of whomever the respondent designated as his or her main parent. If this person reported no occupation, we assigned the SEI score for the occupation held by the spouse or partner. If no parent or partner was present or working, we assigned a value of zero (indicating no access to parental occupational status). The resulting averages are reported by race in the panel labeled symbolic resources in table 2.2.

These results suggest that in addition to differences in access to material resources such as income, adolescents from different groups also experience differential access to the symbolic resource of prestige. White parents, for example, displayed an average occupational status score of around 42, whereas that for Asian parents was only slightly lower at 39; but the average prestige score for blacks stood at just 34 and that for Hispanics was only 33. Compared with white adolescents, in other words, black and Hispanic adolescents had access to around 20 percent less in the way of prestige.

Postindustrial societies generate wealth by creating knowledge and manipulating information, and in such an economy the most critical symbolic resource a person brings to the workforce is what economists call human capital—skills, training, expertise, and, centrally, education (Becker 1994). Education not only signals status and prestige in a globalized, high-tech economy; it translates directly into material resources through labor force participation and entrepreneurship (Harmon, Walker, and Westergard-Nielsen 2001; Goldin and Katz 2008). Indeed, the earnings premium for college education and advanced degrees has risen sharply in recent decades (Golden and Katz 1999; Card and Lemieux 2001) and education has become ever more important in determining one's location in the postindustrial stratification system (Massey 2007).

Parental education is also critical as an input into children's cognitive development (McLoyd 1998; Rowe et al. 1999; Davis-Kean 2005) and it appears to have strong effects on their social development as well (Phillips, McCartney, and Scarr 1987). The middle panel of table 2.2 presents parental education by race. In the vast majority of cases, the figures refer to the education of mothers. In the few cases when a mother was not present, the father's educational attainment was substituted. In the United States today, a high school diploma is the minimum educational credential required for a reasonable chance at socioeconomic stability; yet even on this minimum threshold, we observe large intergroup differences.

Hispanic adolescents, in particular, come of age within families characterized by the extremely low levels of access to human capital. Half of all Latino parents have not finished high school and just 22 percent hold a high school diploma. Only 19 percent of Latino parents report any college experience and just 6 percent have a college degree, some 3 percent reporting postgraduate education. These low educational levels reflect the fact that many Hispanic parents are immigrants from Mexico, which is characterized by low average levels of schooling (Santibáñez, Vernez, and Razquin 2005). However, low levels of parental education also reflect the stagnation of educational progress across generations of Mexicans within the United States (Telles and Ortiz 2008).

Like Hispanics, Asian parents are also substantially of immigrant origins, but a large share of immigrants from Asia, especially East Asia, enter through occupational preferences that favor the entry of skilled professionals, yielding levels of parental education higher even than those of whites. Whereas 32 percent of Asian parents are college graduates and 10 percent hold advanced degrees, the corresponding figures for whites are just 15 percent and 8 percent. Although many Asian immigrants enter the country with skills and education, in truth the distribution is bimodal, and Asian parents also contain more high school dropouts than whites. Whereas only 11 percent of white parents lacked a high school diploma, 28 percent of Asian parents did. Likewise, whereas 35 percent of white parents had finished high school, only 17 percent of Asian parents had done so.

Compared with their white and especially Asian counterparts, African American parents display relatively low levels of education, though not as low as Hispanic parents. Nearly a quarter of all black parents (23 percent) have not finished high school and just 11 percent have completed college, with 6 percent reporting a postgraduate degree. Most African American parents fall within the middle of the educational distribution, with a third holding a high school degree and 27 percent reporting some college-level work.

The bottom panel of table 2.2 shows indicators of relative exposure to emotional resources within the family. As noted earlier, studies generally show that children benefit developmentally if they grow up in family environments characterized by high levels of warmth and caring. To assess the emotional tenor of the family environment, we drew on a series of questions about family warmth and caring posed to respondents on Waves 1 and 2 of the Add Health Survey. The details of the construction of this and other indices used throughout this book are presented in appendix B. Briefly, ten items asked adolescents to rate their family with respect to specific measures: how much adults cared about them, how much parents cared about them, how much family members understood them, how much the respondent wanted to leave home, how much fun the family had together, how much attention the family paid to the respondent, the degree to which the mother was warm and loving, the degree to which the mother talked to the respondent to understand them, respondent's satisfaction with this maternal communication, and respondent's satisfaction with the maternal relationship.

All responses were scaled on a 4-point continuum that we reverse-coded so that higher scores indicated less access to a warm, caring, and supportive family environment and greater exposure to an emotionally distant environment, yielding a very reliable 80-point scale of family sternness ($\alpha = .90$) when the ten items were combined across the first two waves. As can be seen, Asians tend to experience a more emotionally remote family environment compared with other groups, with an average sternness rating of 18.8, compared with 17.8 for Latinos, 17.4 for whites, and 16.4 for African Americans.

The death of a family member is among the most stressful life events a person can experience (see Holmes and Rahe 1967) and such a loss can generally be expected to have serious consequences for individual well-being (Harris 1995; Agid et al. 1999; Luecken 1998, 2000). As discussed in appendix B, the Adolescent Health Survey determined whether respondents had experienced the death of a parent or sibling before the age of eighteen, and these data are summarized in the second line of the third panel. At the high end, 12.1 percent of black adolescents experienced the death of an immediate family member by the age of eighteen; the figure for whites stood at just 5.8 percent, for Asians 7.3 percent, and Latinos 7.8 percent.

Death is not the only way a child can lose a family member, of course. In addition, family members may be removed through incarceration, and in the United States mass imprisonment has come to play an important role in the lives of low-income and minority families (Alexander 2010), yielding sharp intergroup differences in the emotional burdens imposed by incarceration (Tonry 1996). At any point in time, around 12 percent of black men of prime working age are in prison or jail, but among those without a college degree the figure rises to 17 percent and among those without a high school degree it reaches 33 percent (Western 2006). These cross-sectional rates yield huge cumulative risks of incarceration over the male life cycle. Among black men born between 1965 and 1969, for example, the cumulative risk of incarceration by age thirty-five was 21 percent, whereas for those who were high school dropouts it was 59 percent (Western 2006).

Such high probabilities of imprisonment impose very significant social and economic costs on the spouses, children, and partners of convicted men (Edin, Nelson, and Parnal 2004; Johnson and Waldfogel 2004; Western, Lopoo, and McLanahan 2004). The third line in the bottom panel confirms the inequality of this emotional burden by showing the proportion of respondents whose biological father had been incarcerated by the time of the first wave of the survey. Whereas only 5 percent of Asian fathers had ever been incarcerated, at 20 percent the figure was four times greater for black fathers, compared with 13 percent for white fathers and 17 percent for Hispanic fathers.

To some extent, the emotional burdens of marital disruption, family mortality, and paternal incarceration may be offset by turning to another trusted adult family member. In a special series of questions on mentors, Wave 3 respondents were asked the following question: "other than your parents or stepparents, has an adult made an important and the positive difference in your life at any time since you were fourteen years old?" If the answer was yes, respondents were asked how that person was related to them and the last line shows the percentage who reported some family member as their adult mentor. As can be seen, African Americans were most likely to report having a family mentor, 34 percent identifying a relative as having made a positive difference in their life, followed by 26 percent for whites, 24 percent for Hispanics, and 19 percent for Asians. The extent to which the greater frequency of mentors within black families mitigates the negative effects of parental absence through death, incarceration, divorce, and unwed childbearing is an empirical question we explore in subsequent chapters.

To this point, we have argued that the presence or absence of fathers is a major factor structuring access to resources within the family sphere. Table 2.3 confirms this hypothesis by showing the distribution of resources for adolescents in families where the father was present or absent during Wave 1 of the survey (results differ little when we factor in the father's absence on other waves). Without exception, families where the father is present contain more abundant access to material resources than those in which the father is absent. Adolescents living with both parents enjoy a household income that averages $53,300 for whites, $52,500 for Asians, $41,000 for blacks, and $36,800 for Latinos, whereas those inhabiting in families without fathers display respective averages of just $38,300, $42,200, $33,300, and $22,500. In keeping with these income differentials, only 10 percent to 11 percent of white and Asian adolescents, and 22 percent to 23 percent of black and La-

Table 2.3   Access to Resources, by Presence or Absence of Father

Variable	Whites	Asians	Hispanics	Blacks
Father present Wave 1				
Material resources				
Household income	53.3	52.5	36.8	41.0
Ever received welfare	4.0	7.5	10.5	12.2
Received a housing subsidy	0.9	1.9	1.2	4.7
Not enough money for bills	10.2	11.5	22.4	22.7
Full year health insurance	69.5	71.7	57.4	67.6
Symbolic resources				
Occupational prestige score	42.8	39.2	33.3	42.8
Parental education				
Less than high school	9.1	29.6	52.0	14.6
High school graduate	35.2	18.4	19.6	31.1
Some college	29.8	10.9	19.4	28.4
College graduate	16.7	31.2	5.5	3.6
Postgraduate studies	9.2	9.9	3.6	9.3
Emotional resources				
Death in family	3.7	1.8	3.6	6.0
Father incarcerated	7.5	4.7	9.2	9.3
Family sternness scale ($\alpha = 0.90$)	16.6	18.7	16.4	15.5
Family mentor named	25.8	19.2	23.6	33.0
Father absent Wave 1				
Material resources				
Household income	38.3	42.2	33.3	22.5
Ever received welfare	14.8	15.7	30.5	29.1
Received a housing subsidy	5.2	5.6	7.4	15.2
Not enough money for bills	20.5	30.0	30.6	34.8
Full year health insurance	53.3	63.8	47.5	56.1
Symbolic resources				
Occupational prestige score	39.6	41.6	33.1	30.9
Parental education				
Less than high school	14.7	25.9	45.3	24.5
High school graduate	31.9	13.7	26.8	34.8
Some college	33.5	21.4	17.8	27.8
College graduate	13.5	31.8	7.2	8.6
Postgraduate studies	6.4	7.2	2.9	4.4
Emotional resources				
Death in family	8.9	25.6	12.5	12.1
Father incarcerated	25.4	7.6	32.7	26.2
Family sternness scale	19.4	18.8	20.4	17.1
Family mentor named	26.1	18.3	24.0	33.8
Number of cases	5,039	629	1,482	1,894

Source: Authors' calculations based on data set described in Harris and Udry (2008).

Note: Household income in thousands of dollars. Occupational score numeric. Sternness as indicated. All other numbers are percentages.

tino adolescents in father-present families said there was not enough money to meet family bills. Among father-absent families, however, the percentage jumped to 21 percent for whites, 30 percent for Asians, 31 percent for Latinos, and 35 percent for African Americans.

The intergroup contrasts are less clear cut with respect to the symbolic resources of occupational prestige and education. Although the mean SEI score associated with father-present households is greater than that associated with father-absent households for whites and blacks, the difference is quite small for white families. Moreover, there is no difference in average occupational prestige between the two household types among Hispanics, and among Asians father-absent households display a higher average level of prestige. Likewise, differences are inconsistent and generally small when contrasting the percentage of college graduates and postgraduates between father-present and father-absent households.

Sharper contrasts are observed with respect to emotional resources, where family sternness, paternal incarceration, and familial mortality are generally greater, and often much greater, in father-absent families. Thus among father-present families, the share experiencing a death ranges from around 2 percent to 6 percent, whereas among father-absent families it ranges from 9 percent to 26 percent. Likewise, incarceration is more extensive in father-absent families, with the share of fathers ever incarcerated ranging from 8 percent to 33 percent, compared with 5 percent to 9 percent among father-present families. Obviously, two major reasons for a father's absence are death and incarceration, so this contrast is hardly surprising. Nonetheless, on the family sternness scale, we observe a similar, though less extreme contrast, with the range of sternness going from 17.1 to 20.4 among father-absent families but from 15.5 to 18.7 among those with a father present. The prevalence of family mentors, however, is remarkably similar across the two family types.

RESOURCES BY RACE AND CLASS

As noted in the opening chapter, race historically has been a "master status" in the United States, carrying disproportionate weight relative to class in determining access to societal resources and its continuing importance has just been confirmed in the foregoing section. In recent years, however, the black-white color line has been transformed into a more diverse continuum because of immigration from Asia, Africa, and Latin America (Bean et al. 2009; Lee and Bean 2010); and white racial attitudes toward blacks have moderated and become more complex and variegated (Bobo and Charles 2009). At the same time, inequalities of income and wealth have risen to record levels not seen since the laissez faire days of the 1920s (Keister 2000; Piketty and Saez 2003). As a result of these intertwined trends, access to resources within American society is increasingly determined by a complex interplay of class and race and the main effects of these variables have declined in relative importance (see Massey 2007; Massey, Rothwell, and Domina 2009).

Class may be defined with considerable complexity if one seeks to take into account a person's autonomy, authority, and relation to the means of production (see Wright 1997). However, for the sake of simplicity here, we simply create class categories by placing families into one of four ranked groups depending on their position in the distribution of household income. Those in the bottom quartile of the total income distribution we define as lower class, whereas those in the top quartile we label upper class. Families in the second and third income quartiles are classified as the lower middle class and upper middle class, respectively.

Cross-referencing class with the four major race-ethnic groups yields a social space of sixteen cells, to which we assign three-letter mnemonic codes to indicate the specific race and class combination, with the first letter referring to the racial group and the next two letters to the social class. Thus BLO refers to the black lower class, BLM the black lower middle class, BUM the black upper middle class, and BUP the black upper class. The other codes are produced by substituting W, A, and H for B to indicate class categories for whites, Asians, and Hispanics, yielding for the latter group the mnemonic tags of HLO, HLM, HUM, HUP. For ease of exposition, we refer to this sixteen-category classification scheme as the race-class distribution, even though Hispanics are more properly defined as an ethnic group that is itself multiracial.

As noted, estimation is generally quite reliable for whites given their large sample size and reasonably reliable for Hispanics and blacks given their status as the nation's two largest minority groups. When the groups are broken down into specific race-class categories, however, some of the resulting cells become rather small. Given their numerical dominance in the sample, cell sizes for whites are generally sufficient. When the sample's 5,039 whites are classified by quartile in the overall income distribution, for example, the resulting cell sizes are 925 for the lower class, 1,149 for the lower middle class, 1,148 for the upper middle class, and 1,537 for the upper class.

The subdivision of 1,894 black and 1,482 Hispanic respondents by class also yields reasonable cell sizes, though obviously not as large as for whites. Among blacks, we get 739 in the lower class, 443 in the lower middle class, 361 in the upper middle class, and 303 in the upper class, and among Hispanics the corresponding cell sizes are 568, 411, 304, and 199. The most limited cell sizes naturally occur for Asians, who make up a relatively small share of the Add Health sample. Subdividing the survey's 629 Asians by class yields more problematic cell sizes of 83, 147, 164, and 235, respectively, moving from lower to upper class, meaning that class-specific estimates for Asians may exhibit considerable sampling variability and much less reliability, a fact that should be borne in mind when making comparisons between them and the other groups (see appendix A).

Our methodological approach in studying race-class interactions is to rank the sixteen race-class categories in order of ascending disadvantage to observe at which point along the continuum of disadvantage different race-class combinations fall. Figure 2.1 illustrates this approach by showing two idealized distributions. The top chart shows a stylized ordering of race-class groups in which race but not class determines exposure to disadvantage. In this case, whites are all in the lowest quadrant of disadvantage irrespective of class and blacks are in the highest, again irrespective of class. The bottom panel, in contrast, shows a pure class effect, with the top quadrant being occupied by lower classes of all races and the bottom quadrant occupied by upper-class members of all races. Upper-middle-class members and lower-middle-class members of each of the four groups occupy the second and third quadrants of disadvantage, respectively.

These two stylized charts depict stratification systems characterized by main effects for race and class with no race-class interaction. To the extent that race and class interact in conditioning access to resources within families, the various race-class groupings will be scattered irregularly over the four quadrants and disadvantage will vary systematically by class within as well as between racial groups. Access to material resources such as income varies by class, of course, by definition, and to the extent that black and Hispanic families are positioned lower in the class distribution than white and Asian families, they naturally will enjoy less access to income and wealth and the things they buy. Although differentials with respect to race have been well documented for a variety of socioeconomic variables (Krysan and Lewis 2004; Neckerman 2004; Katz and Stern 2006; Lin and Harris 2008), figure

Figure 2.1   Pure Race and Class Effects

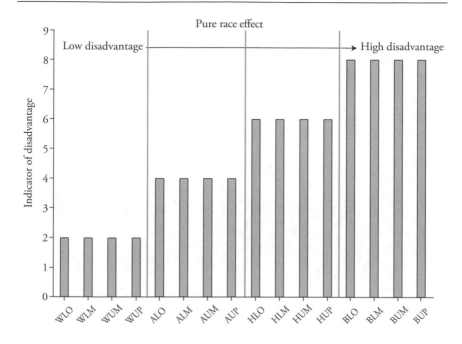

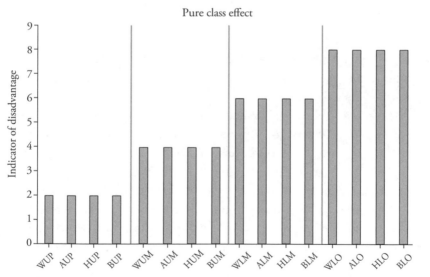

Source: Authors' calculations.

Figure 2.2   Average Household Income

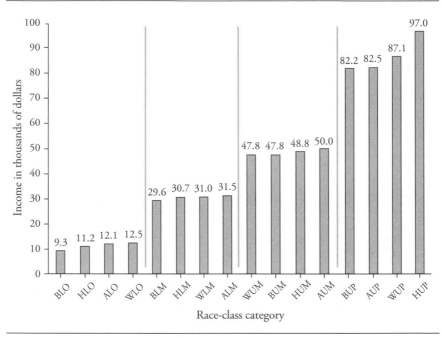

Source: Authors' calculations based on Harris and Udry (2008).

2.2 shows the full distribution of average household income by race and class to indicate the entire range of material deprivation experienced by adolescents in the United States.

As one would expect, the distribution of income is quite close to the idealized class pattern described in figure 2.1. Irrespective of race, lower-class group members are in the lowest quadrant and upper-class members are in the highest quadrant, while lower-middle-class group members occupy the next-to-lowest quadrant and upper-middle-class members the next-to-highest quadrant of the race-class distribution. Nonetheless, there are some indications of race-class interactions, as African Americans always occupy the lowest position within each quadrant. Thus low-income black families had an average household income of just $9,300 compared with $12,500 for low-income white families (the highest in that quadrant). At the other end of the spectrum, upper-class black families had an average income of $82,200 compared with $97,000 for Hispanics (the highest group in that quadrant). In

Figure 2.3   Health Insurance Coverage

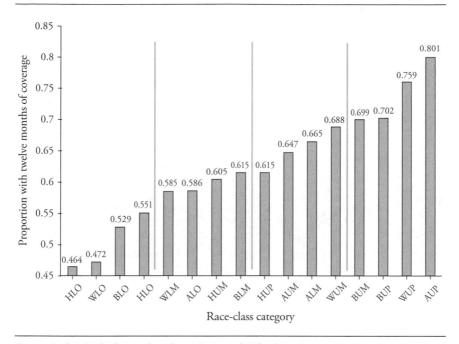

Source: Authors' calculations based on Harris and Udry (2008).

the next-to-lowest quadrant, black families earn $29,600 against $31,500 for Asians, and in the next-to-highest quadrant $47,800 against $50,000 for Asians. Although these within-class differences are not very large, they nonetheless illustrate the continuing influence of race as a stratifying variable within classes.

Although the race-class distribution naturally yields something approaching an idealized main effect for class, the distribution of access to health insurance, shown in figure 2.3, suggests much more of an interaction between race and class. Whereas the greatest access to health insurance is not surprisingly experienced by upper-class Asians and whites, the percentage of respondents covered being 80 percent and 76 percent, respectively, upper-class African Americans are less likely to be covered at 70 percent and upper-class Hispanics are much lower still at 62 percent. Likewise, although lower-class Hispanics, whites, and blacks display the three lowest rates of insurance coverage at 46 percent, 47 percent, and 53 percent, respectively, lower-class

Asians enjoy significantly greater coverage at 59 percent, almost the same percentage as upper-class Hispanics. Although class clearly matters in determining access to health care, so does race, with Hispanics and blacks generally in the bottom half of the access distribution of class, and whites and Asians disproportionately in the upper half.

Figure 2.4 shows the race-class distribution of average SEI scores for parental occupation. As with income, the distribution of access to symbolic resources closely resembles the idealized class pattern described in figure 2.1. Lower-class members of each racial group are generally in the lowest quadrant, and upper-class members typically in the upper quadrant of the status distribution. Although figure 2.4 is dominated by a class effect, we once again observe some race-class interactions. Three of the eight positions in the two most disadvantaged quadrants are occupied by Hispanics, compared with just one position occupied by white families. At the other end of the spectrum, two of the four positions in the most advantaged quadrant are occupied by whites. With a score of only 27.4, African American families rank close to Hispanic families in the lowest quadrant of occupational prestige. In the two most advantaged quadrants, the prestige score for black families is quite close to that of white families. Asian families rank high within the lowest two quadrants, but with a score of only about 40, Asian upper-middle- and upper-class families occupy a similar rank as white lower-middle-class families in the second most advantaged quadrant. Although the distribution of prestige is dominated by a class effect, there are nonetheless clear racial effects, Hispanic families ranking lowest and white families highest.

A more critical symbolic resource is access to a college education, which has become increasingly salient as the gateway to a middle-class lifestyle. Figure 2.5 displays the percentage of families containing a college-educated parent by race and class and this distribution again displays a strong main effect of class. The top quadrant is composed primarily of upper-class families from each group and the bottom quadrant of lower-class families, whereas lower-middle-class families and upper-middle-class families predominate in the second and third quadrants. The principal departure from a pure class distribution is that Hispanics are situated lower than one might expect on the basis of class alone and Asians are located higher. Thus Hispanics hold two of the positions in the lowest quadrant and none of the positions in the highest, and Asians hold two positions in the highest quadrant and just one in the lowest. In absolute terms, the range in access to parental education is very large.

Figure 2.4   Parental Occupational Status

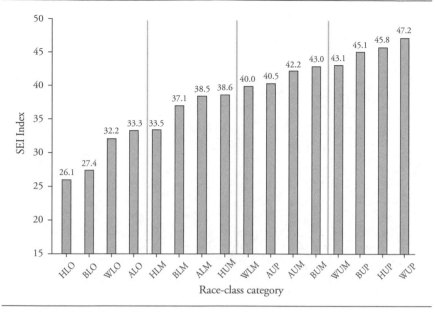

Source: Authors' calculations based on Harris and Udry (2008).

Figure 2.5   Parent College-Educated

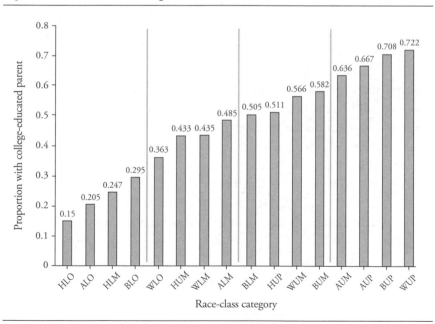

Source: Authors' calculations based on Harris and Udry (2008).

Figure 2.6   Father Never Present

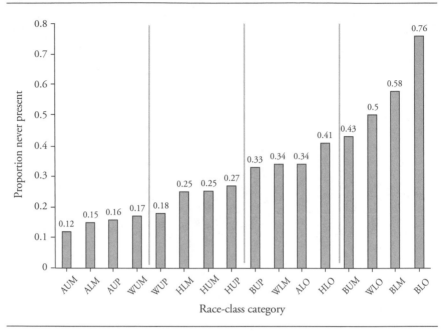

Source: Authors' calculations based on Harris and Udry (2008).

Whereas only 15 percent of lower-class Hispanic families include a parent with a college education, 72 percent of white upper-class families do.

Given that material resources naturally vary by class and access to symbolic resources is closely linked to material wealth, we are more interested in other class differences in the family sphere that carry weight in the development process, such as access to adult time and attention. To begin, figure 2.6 shows the race-class distribution of father absence. As in our idealized figure, the sixteen race-class categories are arranged in ascending order of disadvantage by showing the share of families in each group that never experienced the presence of the biological father in the family between Waves 1 and 3. As can be seen, dividing adolescents into these more detailed race-class categories greatly increases the range of variation over racial groups alone. The percentage without fathers ranged from 23 percent to 61 percent across racial groups, but the range is from 12 percent to 76 percent when class is also taken into account.

Although there is some evidence of a race-class interaction with respect to father absence, figure 2.6 is nonetheless dominated by powerful race effects. Three of the four positions in the most disadvantaged quadrant are occupied by African Americans, whereas three of the four positions in the least disadvantaged are occupied by Asians. A remarkable 76 percent of lower-class black adolescents came of age in a fatherless family, versus 58 percent of their lower-middle-class and 43 percent of upper-middle-class counterparts. In contrast, only 12 percent of upper-middle-class Asian adolescents experienced a fatherless family, versus 15 percent of lower-middle-class Asians and 16 percent of upper-class Asians.

The remainder of the upper half of the disadvantage distribution is occupied by lower-class whites, lower-class Hispanics, and lower-class Asians, with the respective fatherless shares being 50 percent, 41 percent, and 34 percent. The lower half of the distribution is filled out by white upper-middle-class and white upper-class adolescents, with respective fatherless shares of 17 percent and 18 percent. The middle range of the distribution goes from 25 percent fatherless to 34 percent fatherless and is occupied by upper-middle-class Hispanic adolescents and upper-class black adolescents. Thus upper-class black families are about as likely to be without fathers as lower-class Asians and lower-middle-class whites and more likely to be without fathers than lower middle and upper-middle-class Hispanic adolescents.

Figure 2.7 continues the analysis by considering relative access to adult time and attention within the family. The more children per adult in the household, the less undivided adult time each child can expect to enjoy within the family sphere. This figure reveals more of a race-class interaction than the distribution of father absence, owing to differential patterns of fertility by race and class. Paradoxically, African Americans exhibit both the highest and the lowest child-to-adult ratios, the highest in lower-class households (1.54) and the lowest in upper-class families (0.87). Although upper-class black families are less likely to have a father or other adult present in the household than other upper-class families, they also tend to have many fewer children, which gives them low average child-adult ratios. This finding is consistent with the minority group status and fertility hypothesis, which argues that upwardly mobile minority group members reduce childbearing to offset other disadvantages they experience in society (see Goldscheider and Uhlenberg 1969).

In general, upper-class families display child-adult ratios below 1.0, as do Asian upper-middle-class families. Lower-middle-class Asian families and

Figure 2.7   Child-Adult Ratio

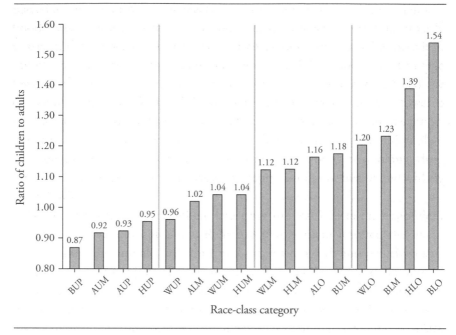

Source: Authors' calculations based on Harris and Udry (2008).

upper-middle-class white and Hispanic families display ratios just above 1.0 (1.02 to 1.04). Thus, within upper-class and upper-middle-class families, children can count on the undivided attention of at least one adult, on average. In contrast, lower-middle and lower-class families generally had ratios above 1.12 irrespective of race. Next to lower-class blacks, lower-class Hispanics were highest with a child-adult ratio of 1.39, followed by lower-class whites (1.2), upper-middle-class blacks (1.18), lower-class Asians (1.16), and lower-middle-class white and Hispanic families (1.12 each). Considering the entire range of variation, the most advantaged race-class combination commanded potentially 77 percent more adult time than the least advantage combination.

As noted, one of the greatest disruptions a young person can experience while growing up is the death of a family member. Figure 2.8 shows how this disadvantageous event is distributed by race and class. Once again we observe a huge range in the risk of family mortality, with black lower-middle-class adolescents experiencing a probability of family death (0.143) fourteen

Figure 2.8   Family Mortality

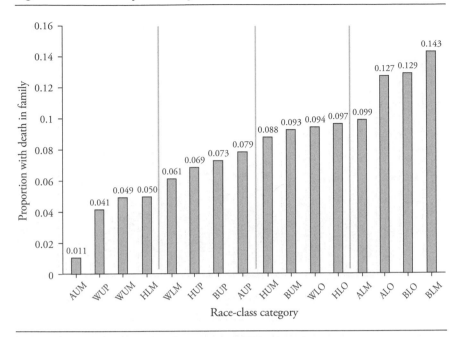

Source: Authors' calculations based on Harris and Udry (2008).

times that experienced by Asian upper-middle-class adolescents (0.011). In addition to adolescents from black lower-middle-class families, those in lower-class black families also display a very high risk of experiencing family mortality (0.129), followed by lower-class Asian families (0.127), lower-middle-class Asian families (0.099), lower-class Hispanic families (0.097), lower-class white families (0.094) and upper-middle-class black families (0.093). At the other end of the continuum, adolescents from upper-class white families, upper-middle-class white families, and lower-middle-class Hispanic families all experience a risk of family mortality of 0.05 or less. Very clearly, then, the burden of experiencing a family death falls disproportionately on members of the lower classes, especially blacks.

Figure 2.9 considers the emotional resources of warmth, caring, and support by arraying race-class groups in ascending order of family sternness. Again we observe a substantial range, with the highest index being about 25 percent greater than the lowest. Three of the four positions in the lowest quadrant of family sternness are occupied by African Americans, with lower-

Figure 2.9   Family Sternness

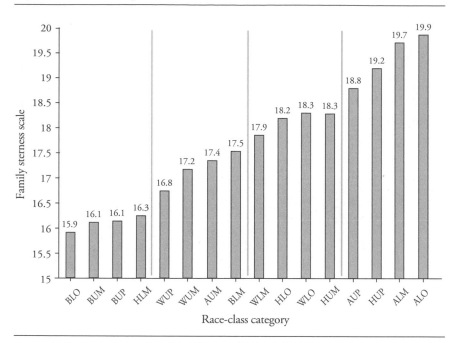

Source: Authors' calculations based on Harris and Udry (2008).

class black families displaying an index of 15.9 and upper-middle-class and upper-class black families both evincing indices of 16.1. Also quite low at 16.3 are lower-middle-class Hispanic families. At the other end of the spectrum, three of the four positions in the highest coldness quadrant are occupied by Asians, lower-class Asians the highest at 19.9 followed by lower-middle-class Asians at 19.7, upper-class Hispanic families at 19.2, and upper-class Asians at 18.8. In general, then, black families tend toward a warm style of child rearing and Asian families toward a colder and more distant emotional style. Hispanic and white families tend to fall in the middle. But where coldness generally increases with rising social class among Hispanics, it decreases with rising social class among whites, indicating a rather complex race-class interaction for these groups, compared with the strong main effect of race for Asians and African Americans.

The degree of inequality in experiencing the emotional burdens of parental incarceration among adolescents is the subject of figure 2.10. Whereas

Figure 2.10   Father Ever Incarcerated

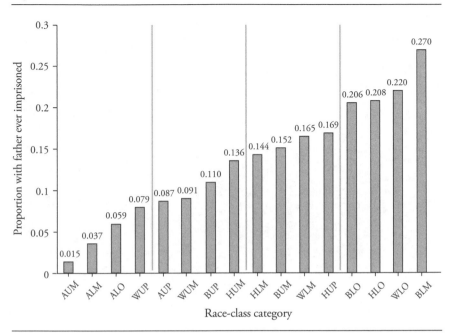

Source: Authors' calculations based on Harris and Udry (2008).

only 1.5 percent of Asian upper-middle-class adolescents had experienced the incarceration of their father by Wave 1, 27 percent of black lower-middle-class adolescents had done so. In general, whites and Asians are clustered at the lower end of the distribution and blacks and Hispanics at the top. The five lowest rates of paternal incarceration are all observed for Asian or white groups. The five highest are all black or Hispanic, with one exception. Indeed, black upper-class adolescents evince higher rates of paternal incarceration than Asians of any class background. Likewise, upper-class Hispanics experience higher rates of paternal incarceration than Asians of all class origins and whites of all class origins save the lowest. Whites generally show the strongest class effect, the rate of paternal incarceration rising from 8 percent among upper-class whites to 14 percent and 17 percent among the lower classes.

It is thus quite obvious that black families suffer disproportionately from the emotional burdens of family mortality and paternal incarceration. Al-

Figure 2.11   Family Mentorship

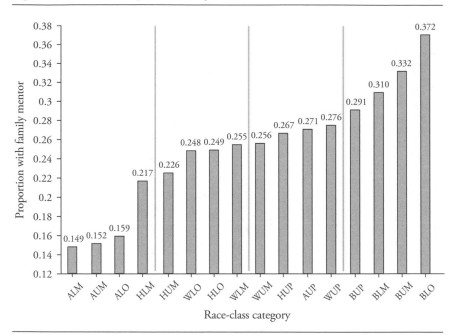

Source: Authors' calculations based on Harris and Udry (2008).

though these burdens are greatest for lower-class African Americans, to a greater extent than other groups they are also borne by adolescents in all black families regardless of class. Figure 2.11 suggests that higher levels of father absence among blacks are offset to some degree by the substitution of family mentors. This figure is obviously characterized by very strong racial effects, all four positions in the highest quadrant of family mentoring held by African Americans and three of the four positions in the lowest quadrant occupied by Asians, whites and Hispanics being scattered across the second and third quadrants. At the top of the distribution, among black adolescents, 37 percent of the lower-class sample reported having an adult mentor who was a family member, followed by 33 percent of the upper-middle-class sample, 31 percent of the lower-middle-class sample, and 29 percent of the upper-class group. At the other end of the distribution, fewer than 16 percent of lower-class, lower-middle-class, and upper-middle-class Asians reported having a family mentor. The various classes of white and Hispanic adolescents generally reported having family mentors in the range of 20 percent to 28 percent.

INEQUALITIES IN THE FAMILY SPHERE

This chapter has uncovered substantial variation by race and class in access to resources within the family spheres occupied by American adolescents. A key resource in human development is access to adult time and attention, and the main dimension of variability here is the presence or absence of the biological father. On this important dimension, African American families fare quite poorly, especially those of lower class. More than 75 percent of adolescents living in lower-class black families did not have access to a residential biological father throughout adolescence. Lower-class adolescents in other groups also experienced relatively high levels of persistent fatherlessness, 50 percent among lower-class whites, 41 percent among lower-class Hispanics, and 34 percent among lower-class Asians.

The importance of race in structuring access to adult time and attention is underscored by the fact that even upper-class black adolescents experience a relatively high rate of fatherlessness (33 percent), compared with upper-class Asian families (16 percent) or upper-class white families (18 percent). We observe, however, that upper-class black women compensate for the absence of fathers by having fewer children, yielding a low ratio of children to adults (0.87), which is comparable to that observed in other upper-class families. The ratio was 0.93 among Asian families, 0.95 among Hispanic, and 0.96 among white families. Upper-middle-class families in all groups generally experienced ratios close to 1.0, meaning that each child got the attention of around one adult.

The least access to adult time and attention generally occurred within lower- and lower-middle-class families, especially lower-class black families. The latter evidenced a rather extreme child-adult ratio of 1.54, followed by lower-class Hispanic families at 1.39, lower-class white families at 1.20, and lower-class Asian families at 1.16. Adolescents in these race-class categories were also more likely to experience the trauma of losing an immediate family member through death. Whereas only 4 percent of upper-class white adolescents experienced a family death before the age of eighteen, the figure was 13 percent for lower-class black adolescents. The rate of family mortality was likewise relatively low for upper-class blacks and Hispanics (around 7 percent) and upper-class Asians (around 8 percent) but relatively high for lower-class Asians (13 percent), Hispanics (10 percent), and whites (9 percent).

The emotional burden of having a father incarcerated also fell disproportionately on the poor, the share having an imprisoned father being 21 percent among lower-class blacks and Hispanics and 22 percent among lower-class whites. Race also played an important role, however, as the highest rate of paternal incarceration (27 percent) was observed for lower-middle-class blacks (27 percent), though upper-middle-class blacks also showed a fairly high rate of 15 percent. In contrast, the lowest rates were generally observed for Asian adolescents, with paternal incarceration running at 1.5 percent for those in the upper middle class, 3.7 percent in the lower middle class, 5.9 percent in the upper middle class, and 8.7 percent in the upper class, versus 7.9 percent among upper-class whites.

Whether achieved through mortality, marital dissolution, imprisonment, or unwed child bearing, the absence of fathers within the family sphere was always associated with a reduction in access to material resources, and in many cases to symbolic resources and emotional resources as well. Considering all of the indicators of material, symbolic, and emotional resources developed in this chapter, the gap between the most and least advantaged race-class group is often quite substantial. Compared with the most advantaged race-class configuration, those in the least advantaged category encounter 10.4 times more income deprivation, 83 percent less occupational prestige, 6.3 times more father absence, 1.8 times fewer adults per children, 13 times more exposure to family mortality, 18 times more paternal imprisonment, 40 percent less mentoring, and 25 percent less warmth and support within the family.

Even if adolescents experienced no other disadvantages, therefore, inequalities in family social ecology can generally be expected to produce substantial variation in developmental outcomes among adolescents. Unfortunately, as we shall see, inequalities in the family sphere are not the only ones that American adolescents experience, for differences are also dramatic in access to resources within school, neighborhood, peer, and religious environments, which also generally operate to allocate life chances unequally by race and class. Unfortunately, as Sampson (2012) has noted, "things go together" ecologically in American society, and disadvantages across the different social spheres tend to be highly intercorrelated. It is to these other social spheres that we turn in the next chapter.

CHAPTER 3

Other Spheres of Influence

Human beings have been on earth for at least 150 millennia, and throughout this time the family has served as the primary unit for the bearing and rearing of children. Indeed, for 95 percent of humanity's existence, kinship was the only meaningful form of social organization and the family was solely responsible for the cultivation of human capabilities. Until roughly ten thousand years ago, all human beings survived as foragers, living together in small mobile bands (Massey 2005a). Although the size of foraging communities varied with the material abundance provided by the local ecology, they rarely exceeded one thousand persons and averaged only around 150 (Kelly 1995). Within such communities, there was little social division of space. Dwellings were temporary and primarily used for sleeping and cooking and were not segmented into different functional areas as in contemporary homes. Most social life unfolded in communal space outside the household.

Babies born into this world were raised by a family of procreation through infancy and then by a wider circle of extended kin as toddlers. Moving into childhood they would bond with same-age peers, but most of these people would also be blood relatives such as cousins, aunts, or uncles. As children aged, they would interact more widely with other members of the community, but most of these people would also be related by blood or marriage. At all stages of the life cycle, the number of social actors people encountered was quite limited. In a foraging community of 150 persons, for example, the average newborn would enter a cohort of just eighteen individuals age zero to five, which by age fifteen would have been reduced to fourteen by mortality; and by the end of childbearing only around eight peers would remain (Massey 2005a). In such a social setting, there were no strangers (Diamond 2012).

Other ecological contexts began to emerge around ten thousand years ago when the first cities appeared in the wake of the agricultural revolution, which by generating a food surplus made permanent settlements and higher population densities possible (Massey 2005a). The first cities emerged in Mesopotamia between the Tigris and Euphrates rivers and were quite small by today's standards—only around twenty-five thousand to thirty thousand persons (Chandler and Fox 1974). Nonetheless, they created a new social sphere to influence human growth and development beyond families and peers—the neighborhood, which may be defined as a spatially delimited segment of the urban landscape whose character is defined by the people and infrastructure it contains. The advent of neighborhoods created the potential for residential segregation and preindustrial cities were indeed differentiated spatially on the basis of power, wealth, religion, occupation, and ethnicity (Sjoberg 1960).

Cities also created the social and economic conditions for the accumulation of knowledge and the acceleration of learning, leading to the emergence of systems of writing and mathematics about five thousand years ago (Harris 1995). The new symbolic systems were too complex and complicated to be imparted informally by oral tradition within families, so yet another social setting emerged to affect human growth and development—schools—which are socially defined, physically delimited spaces in which formal instruction occurs. Whereas all residents of preindustrial cities inhabited neighborhoods, however, only a tiny elite attended schools, and so the various forms of human, social, and cultural capital they imparted became key markers distinguishing the elite from the masses (Sjoberg 1960).

Preindustrial cities defined urbanity for around ten thousand years, and throughout this time the number and size of urban agglomerations varied mainly with the geographic size of the agrarian empires that they controlled (Massey 2005a). Very large empires, such as those of the Romans, the Chinese, the Byzantines, or the Ottomans, supported a large number of sizeable cities by accumulating a huge food surplus over an immense geographic area and concentrating it at specific locations. Nonetheless, given the limits of agricultural productivity using preindustrial technologies, relatively few people could live in urban areas at any time. Prior to 1800, city populations rarely reached five hundred thousand persons and no more than 5 percent of any society was ever urbanized, however large the empire. During the long era of agrarian urbanism that defined civilization for ten thousand years, most human beings inhabited small peasant villages that were, in fact, little different from foraging communities in terms of size, scale, and social organization (Laslett 1971).

All this changed around two hundred years ago, when human beings began to substitute inanimate for animate sources of power in the production of goods and services (Levy 1972), making possible a new division of labor, massive increases in human productivity, unprecedented accumulations of wealth, and the extension of material well-being beyond a tiny elite (Maddison 2001). It also made possible a vast increase in the number and scale of cities (United Nations 1980). Whereas only 5 percent of the human population was urbanized in 1800, by 1950 some 28 percent was, and in industrialized nations 53 percent. Although in 1800, only six cities contained more than five hundred thousand inhabitants, by 1950 the number had reached 176, and of these seventy-seven boasted populations of one million or more (Massey 2005a). At present, all industrialized nations are highly urbanized, 80 percent or more of all inhabitants living in urban areas.

After 1950, urbanization spread increasingly to the developing world. Although levels of urbanization continue to lag behind those in the developed world, developing nation cities are nonetheless proliferating and growing at a very rapid pace. From a level of just 18 percent in 1950, urbanization in the developing world reached 30 percent in 1980, 40 percent in 2000, and 45 percent in 2010. As a result, by 2010 more than 50 percent of all human beings lived in cities for the first time in history, meaning that from this point onward a growing majority of human beings will undergo growth, development, and socialization within neighborhoods and schools as well as families and peer groups (United Nations 2010).

In developed countries such as the United States, of course, people have long been exposed to school and neighborhood environments. In addition, the peer networks in contemporary postindustrial urban societies are generally not composed of people related by blood or marriage, but mainly of friends and acquaintances who do not share kinship (Fischer 1982). The degree of exposure to the fundamental spheres of human ecology also varies across the life cycle. Infants exist almost entirely within the family sphere, neighborhood circumstances affecting them only indirectly insofar as they influence the behavior and attitudes of the adults who care for them (Furstenberg et al. 1999). As young people move into childhood, however, they begin to spend more and more time in school settings, and as they grow older still they become more deeply embedded within their neighborhoods, drawing on friends and acquaintances from both settings to construct an evolving network of peers (Coleman 1963). As human beings age, therefore, the balance of ecological influence tilts away from the family and toward schools, neighborhoods, and peers (Harris 1998). This development makes education, and particularly early childhood education, increasingly important as a mechanism for either ameliorating or exacerbating whatever inequalities exist in a society (Heckman and Masterov 2007).

Supernatural beliefs are likely as old as humanity itself. This said, with the emergence of cities, religion was transformed from a set of mythic beliefs informally transmitted between people through a shared oral tradition into a formal institution anchored in holy texts and transmitted to a lay public by a professional priesthood (Sjoberg 1960; Stark 2007; Wright 2009). The institutionalization of religion led inevitably to the creation of houses of worship and congregations, and hence yet another setting for human socialization. Although generations of intellectuals, philosophers, and scientists have forecast imminent demise of religion, it has steadfastly persisted as a basic feature of human society. Indeed, now more people than ever hold traditional religious beliefs. Religion continues to play a prominent role not only in the spiritual realm, but in the social, economic, and political realms as well (Norris and Inglehart 2004; Berger 1999).

Compared with other developed nations, the United States exhibits an unusually high degree of religious belief and affiliation (Baker 2004). According to the 2008 American Religious Identification Survey, 85 percent of all Americans profess adherence to some religion, 76 percent labeling themselves as Christians, 70 percent professing a faith in a personal God, and 34 percent considering themselves to be "born again" (Kosmin and Keysar 2009a). As with the other social spheres we have considered, religious exposure varies by race and class. Some 27 percent of Asians profess no religion, 16 percent of non-Hispanic whites, 12 percent of Hispanics, and 11 percent of blacks. Likewise, and among those who do not subscribe to any religion, 31 percent are college graduates against just 26 percent in the general population (Kosmin and Keysar 2009b). Religious settings are thus likely also to be stratified and characterized by varying degrees of access to material, emotional, and symbolic resources.

However, unlike the other spheres of influence we have discussed, participation in the religious sphere is to a greater extent voluntary. People are born into a religious context, of course, and most initially follow the religion of their parents; to this extent, religious spheres may be said to be inherited rather than chosen. Yet many parents do not expose their children to religion in any meaningful way, and even the children of religious parents may rebel and over time move into new religious spheres or abandon religion altogether. As a result, whereas nearly everyone experiences a family, school, neighborhood, and peer setting, not everyone experiences a religious setting.

THE NEIGHBORHOOD NEXUS

Although the importance of neighborhoods in human affairs was recognized early on by sociologists of the Chicago School (see Burgess 1925; Park 1926), for a time social scientists seemed to forget about the neighborhood as a critical context for human interaction and development (Small and Newman 2001; Sampson 2001). In the 1960s particularly, the advent of mainframe computers allowed investigators to harness the power of statistical sampling theory with advances in the methodology of questionnaire construction to create a new wave of large-scale social science surveys (Massey 2001). The proliferation of cross-sectional and later longitudinal surveys seemingly offered something to everyone. They enabled economists to analyze individual determinants of economic outcomes such as wages (Mincer 1974) and political scientists to study the influence of personal characteristics on values, attitudes, and opinions (Inglehart 1977). Following Peter Blau and Otis Duncan (1967), sociologists leapt into the fray by emphasizing the role of family background in constraining individual achievements, a perspective that rose to prominence under the rubric of the status attainment model (Duncan, Featherman, and Duncan 1972; Hauser and Featherman 1977).

Over time, data sets grew larger, richer, and increasingly complex as statistical methods became more powerful, precise, and sophisticated. Nonetheless, throughout the 1960s and 1970s analyses were done almost exclusively at the individual and household levels. It was not until William Julius Wilson (1987) pointed out the rising concentration of poverty in urban areas and the potentially powerful effects of spatially concentrated poverty in constraining opportunities among the poor that neighborhoods reentered mainstream social science as a key analytic category, instigating a burgeoning research literature on "neighborhood effects" (Jencks and Mayer 1990; Small and Newman

2001; Sampson, Morenoff, and Gannon-Rowley 2002; Clampet-Lundquist and Massey 2008).

In retrospect, it seems hard to believe that neighborhoods were ever elided as a key nexus for human development. Where one lives not only confers prestige (or lack, see Suttles 1968; Hunter 1975; Sampson and Raudenbush 2004), but neighborhoods directly influence access to key material resources such as jobs, transportation, wealth, income, education, and health (Massey, Condran, and Denton 1987; Massey and Fong 1990; Chen and Paterson 2006; Sampson 2008, 2012; Sharkey 2013). Residential location also determines access to emotional resources such as safety, security, trust, and social support (Sampson, Raudenbush, and Earls 1997; Sampson, Morenoff, and Earls 1999; Morenoff, Sampson, and Raudenbush 2001; Sampson 2003, 2004, 2012; Peterson and Krivo 2010). For these and other reasons, neighborhoods and the social processes that segregate them have been labeled the linchpin in the American system of stratification (Pettigrew 1979; Bobo 1989; Massey and Denton 1993; Massey 2007; Sampson 2012; Sharkey 2013).

In the United States especially, socioeconomic and residential mobility have always been very closely interconnected (Massey and Denton 1985; Massey, Gross, and Shibuya 1994; Crowder and South 2005; Crowder, South, and Chavez 2006; Sampson and Sharkey 2008). Indeed, spatial mobility is part and parcel of the broader process of socioeconomic mobility. Historically poor workers have arrived in urban areas from overseas or from rural sending areas in the United States. Upon arrival, they typically entered the bottom rung of the occupational ladder, taking whatever housing they could find no matter how disadvantaged the neighborhood. Over time, they advanced economically, securing better jobs with higher pay and greater stability. These material advances, in turn, enabled them to advance residentially, moving to a better home in a better neighborhood and thereby gaining access to lower crime rates, better schools, higher property values, more supportive peer networks, and better services. Access to these ecological resources, in turn, further enhanced the family's prospects for socioeconomic mobility and later moves up the socioeconomic ladder were again followed by additional moves up the residential ladder (Massey 1985). By converting socioeconomic attainments into residential attainments and vice versa, families were able to ratchet themselves up the status hierarchy over time and across generations (Massey and Mullan 1984).

In this sense, residential mobility is a fundamental component of economic advancement in the United States, and in a very real and concrete way barriers to spatial mobility are barriers to social mobility. Historically, of course, the path of residential mobility was substantially blocked for African Americans by rampant discrimination and segregation (Massey and Denton 1993). Although the barriers to Hispanic spatial mobility were never as severe as those blocking black residential achievement, they were nonetheless significant, especially for dark-skinned Hispanics of African ancestry (Massey and Bitterman 1985; Denton and Massey 1989), and they appear to be worsening in recent years (Rugh and Massey 2013).

In the years since the passage of the Fair Housing Act (1968), the Equal Credit Opportunity Act (1974), and the Community Reinvestment Act (1977), barriers to minority residential mobility have moderated in the United States but by no means have disappeared (Yinger 1995; Ross and Yinger 2002; Squires 2004; Choi, Ondrich, and Yinger 2005). Although African Americans and Hispanics may no longer be denied access to homes and credit openly, studies reveal that traditional discriminatory practices continue surreptitiously (Squires 1994; Turner et al. 2002; Charles 2003; Ross and Turner 2004). Moreover, even as old forms of discrimination persist in clandestine fashion, new and more subtle forms of discrimination have been invented (Massey 2005b). Among them are linguistic profiling (Purnell, Idsardi, and Baugh 1999; Massey and Lundy 2001; Fischer and Massey 2004; Squires and Chadwick 2006), predatory lending (Lord 2004; Squires 2004), reverse redlining (Smith and DeLair 1999; Turner et al. 2002; Friedman and Squires 2005; Williams, Nesiba, and McConnell 2005; Brescia 2009; Rugh and Massey 2010), and restrictive zoning (Rothwell and Massey 2009, 2010; Rugh and Massey 2013; Massey et al. 2013).

As a result of these diverse influences, levels of black residential segregation have fallen steadily, on average, but progress toward integration has been quite uneven. Desegregation has occurred mostly in places with small minority populations, larger stocks of newer housing, military bases, college campuses, and less restrictive zoning regimes (Rothwell and Massey 2009; Farley and Frey 1994; Charles 2003). Segregation, meanwhile, has remained high and changed little in the nation's largest urban black populations and continues to be strongly predicted by racist sentiment (Rugh and Massey 2013).

Among Asians and Hispanics, mass immigration since 1970 has bolstered segregation and increased spatial isolation (Charles 2003; Massey, Rothwell, and Domina 2009; Rugh and Massey 2013). The spatial isolation of Latinos, in particular, has risen quite dramatically in many metropolitan areas, leading to their hypersegregation in Los Angeles and New York by 2000 (Wilkes and Iceland 2004). Variation in Hispanic residential segregation and spatial isolation is increasingly related to prejudice against Latinos as "illegal aliens" (Rugh and Massey 2013).

The degree of class segregation has also risen substantially in the United States, especially during the 1980s and 2000s (Massey and Eggers 1990, 1993; Massey and Fischer 2003; Fischer et al. 2004; Massey, Rothwell, and Domina 2009; Reardon and Bischoff 2011), paralleling the overall increase in income and wealth inequality since 1970 (Keister 2000; Piketty and Saez 2003; Smeeding 2005). As noted, this combination of rising class segregation and continued racial segregation has made race-class interactions more important in determining the exposure of U.S. adolescents to disadvantaged ecological settings (Wilson 2009; Massey, Rothwell, and Domina 2009).

We thus begin our assessment of nonfamily spheres by considering exposure to socioeconomic disadvantage within neighborhoods among respondents to the Adolescent Health Survey. Specifically, we consider the census tracts inhabited by respondents in Waves 1 and 3. Following Robert Sampson and his colleagues (Sampson 2008; Sampson and Sharkey 2008; Sampson, Sharkey, and Raudenbush 2008; Sampson 2012), we performed a principal components factor analysis of five variables—the percentage of families receiving welfare, the tract poverty rate, the tract unemployment rate, the percentage of female-headed households, and the percentage African American. After rotating the factor matrix to improve fit, we used the factor loadings as weights to compute a weighted average of the five variables as our index of neighborhood disadvantage ($\alpha = 0.79$, details in appendix B).

The black percentage is included in the index because black neighborhoods suffer distinct social and economic disadvantages not captured fully by poverty levels, welfare dependency, unemployment rates, or the proportion of female-headed families (Sampson 2012). Holding these variables constant, for example, black tracts are more likely to have been subject to historical processes of public and private disinvestment as well as political marginalization. Holding constant the influence of socioeconomic status, black neighborhoods generally have poorer public services, fewer supermarkets, fewer banks, fewer retail outlets, less access to health medical care, and more exposure to environmental hazards, owing to historical processes of public dis-

Figure 3.1   Neighborhood Disadvantage

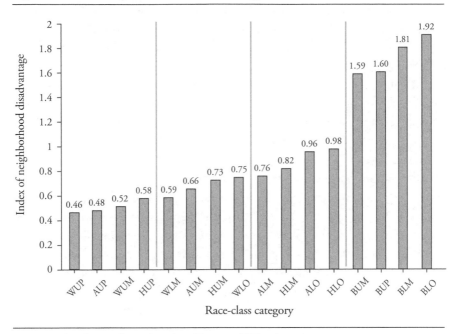

Source: Authors' compilation based on Harris and Udry (2008).

crimination and private disinvestment (Massey and Denton 1993; Peterson and Krivo 2010; Sampson 2012; Sharkey 2013). In addition, the scale reliability is significantly less reliable when percentage black is excluded ($\alpha = 0.69$).

Our index captures the average level of neighborhood disadvantage experienced by Add Health respondents between 1994 and 2001. Figure 3.1 shows values of the disadvantage scale computed for different race-class groups. It is immediately and quite starkly apparent that exposure to neighborhood disadvantage is highly structured by race, as others have also found (Sampson 2012; Sharkey 2013). For African Americans, at least, race largely trumps class in determining exposure to neighborhood disadvantage. All four positions in the top quadrant of neighborhood disadvantage are occupied by blacks, with a relatively small within-group gradient by class. With an index value of 1.92, exposure to neighborhood disadvantage is greatest for lower-class African Americans, followed closely by their lower-middle-class counterparts at 1.81. Higher class status does confer some protection from disadvantaged neighborhood circumstances, but not much. Although black upper-middle-class and black upper-class respondents have indices of 1.59 and 1.60, respectively, these values are 63 percent greater than the neighborhood disadvantage experienced by the next closest race-class group (lower-class Hispanics).

Indeed, upper-class African Americans are exposed to far more neighborhood disadvantage than the poor of any other group. For example, whereas upper-class African Americans inhabit neighborhoods with an average disadvantage index of 1.60, those occupied by poor Hispanics, poor Asians, and poor whites display index values of just 0.98, 0.96, and 0.74, respectively. Indeed, the gap between the most and least advantaged segments of the Hispanic, Asian, and white populations is but a fraction of the gap between blacks and everyone else. Whereas upper-class white respondents enjoy the most advantaged neighborhood environment (with disadvantage index of just 0.46) and lower-class Hispanic respondents experienced the least advantaged environment among nonblacks (index value of 0.98), this 0.52 point gap is smaller than the 0.63 point gap between lower-class Hispanics and upper-middle-class African Americans, the next closest black group.

Although high class status may not protect African Americans from disadvantaged neighborhood conditions, class does play an important role in structuring the exposure of whites, Asians, and Hispanics to detrimental neighborhood environments. The four positions in the lowest quadrant of neighborhood disadvantage, for example, are occupied by upper-class whites, upper-class Asians, upper-middle-class whites, and upper-class Hispanics. Likewise, the next-to-lowest quadrant is occupied by upper-middle-class Hispanics and Asians, along with lower-middle-class and lower-class whites, and the next-to-highest quadrant is populated by lower-class and lower-middle-class Hispanics and Asians. Whereas whiteness does confer clear advantages to adolescents in terms of exposure to disadvantaged neighborhood circumstances, class nonetheless remains a powerful influence, especially when compared with the situation of African Americans, for whom class matters far less.

The sharp disparities by race (between African Americans and everyone else) and class (among other groups), yield an extreme range of exposure to neighborhood disadvantage during the period of observation (the late 1990s). Compared with upper-class whites, low-income blacks experienced 4.2 times more neighborhood disadvantage while coming of age. Our results thus confirm that when it comes to neighborhood disadvantage, the distribution of exposure experienced by blacks really does not overlap with the distributions experienced by whites or even other minority groups (compare Sampson 2012; Sharkey 2013). Compared with other people in the United States, African Americans truly occupy "divergent social worlds" (Peterson and Krivo 2010).

Neighborhoods not only condition access to material resources, of course, but emotional resources as well, influencing outcomes such as safety, security, and social support. In addition to developing their index of neighborhood socioeconomic disadvantage, Sampson and colleagues also developed a measure of collective efficacy, which they defined as the relative ability of a neighborhood's residents to act collectively for the common good (Sampson 2004, 2005, 2006; Sampson, Raudenbush, and Earls 1997; Sampson, Morenoff, and Earls 1999). They based their measure on answers to survey items developed for the Project on Human Development in Chicago Neighborhoods, most of which were not included on the Adolescent Health Survey. Add Health nonetheless did contain other items that address the issue of collective efficacy in meaningful ways. For example, the survey asked respondents to report whether they knew most people in their neighborhood, whether in the past month they had stopped to talk to a neighbor on the street, whether they perceived people in the neighborhood to look out for one another, whether they felt safe in the neighborhood, and the degree to which they were happy with life in the neighborhood. These questions were asked at Wave 1 and repeated a year later in Wave 2. We coded the items so that higher values reflected less collective efficacy and combined the two waves to create a simple scale that varied from 0 to 16 with a high reliability coefficient ($\alpha = 0.70$, see appendix B).

This index captures the degree to which neighborhoods are perceived as inefficacious by respondents during the 1994 to 1996 period and mean values are shown by race and class in figure 3.2. As before, whites tend to occupy the most efficacious neighborhoods, but in this display the least efficacious quadrant is not inhabited by blacks but by Hispanics and Asians. Specifically the highest degree of collective inefficacy is observed in the neighborhoods occupied by lower-middle-class Asians (with a score of 5.59), followed by upper-middle-class Asians (5.17), lower-class Hispanics (4.85), and upper-middle-class Hispanics (4.61). The latter are, in turn, followed closely by lower-class Asians (just under 4.57) and upper-class Asians (4.48). Thus

Figure 3.2   Neighborhood Inefficacy

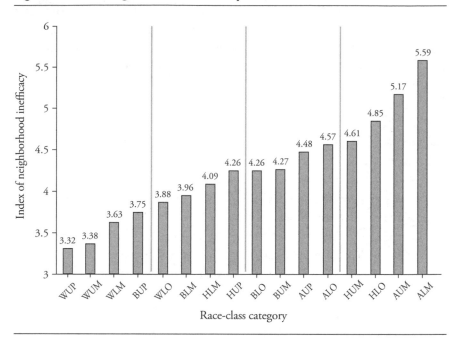

Source: Authors' compilation based on Harris and Udry (2008).

Asian and Hispanic adolescents appear to come of age in neighborhoods characterized by relatively low levels of public trust, where people do not know, look out for, or talk to one another and in which people feel neither happy nor safe.

In contrast, whites generally occupy neighborhoods with high overall levels of collective efficacy, or to put it in terms of our index, the least inefficacy. Thus three of the four positions in the lowest quadrant of neighborhood inefficacy are occupied by whites: upper-class whites (inefficacy index of only 3.32), upper-middle-class whites (3.38), and lower-middle-class whites (3.63). The last position in the most advantaged quadrant is occupied by upper-class African Americans, who have an inefficacy score of 3.75, which is only slightly below that of lower-class whites (3.88). Thus upper-class status seems to confer on African Americans about the same access to efficacious neighborhoods as whites, despite their greater exposure to material disadvantage. The middle ranges of the distribution of neighborhood efficacy are generally occupied by upper-class and upper-middle-class blacks, Hispanics, and Asians.

In his paradigm-shifting treatise on neighborhood effects, one of the conditions that Wilson (1987) identified as critical in understanding the life chances of community residents was the relative number of what he called "marriageable males," by which he meant young men in an economic position to form stable relationships and support families. He argued that the decline of marriage in poor black communities and the rise of unwed childbearing stemmed from a lack of steadily employed black males earning decent wages, owing to the structural transformation of the urban economy away from manufacturing and toward services, along with the suburbanization of employment.

Whereas Wilson focused on the social absence of males who possessed the wherewithal to support families, later work by Bruce Western (2006) pointed out that low-income black communities were also characterized by demographic deficits of young males. Owing to high rates of incarceration stemming from changes in the social organization of criminal justice during the 1970s and 1980s, black communities not only lacked employed males, they often lacked any males because so many young men were in jail or prison rather than in school or working. The demographic absence of young men within a community has clear implications for patterns of marriage and childbearing, generally lowering the odds that women will marry and increasing the likelihood that they will have children outside marriage. A skewed sex ratio among young adults also carries broader social and economic implications, implying a scarcity of male role models for effective socialization of boys, a disruption of social networks to inhibit social capital formation and attachment to jobs, and a lack of adult eyes and ears on the street to promote collective efficacy (Anderson 1999; Harding 2010).

To assess the effect of male scarcity within neighborhoods we computed the ratio of never-married females age twenty to twenty-four to never-married males age twenty to twenty-four within census tracts inhabited by Add Health respondents. The higher this ratio, the greater the relative supply of young males. We would have liked also to consider the relative presence or absence of employed or educated males at different ages, but these data were not available from the Add Health neighborhood files. Obviously, therefore, the index captures the demographic absence males more than the social absence of young males and this fact should be borne in mind when interpreting the data in figure 3.3, which shows the distribution of male scarcity within neighborhoods by race and class to reveal very strong racial effects.

Figure 3.3   Scarcity of Single Males in Neighborhoods

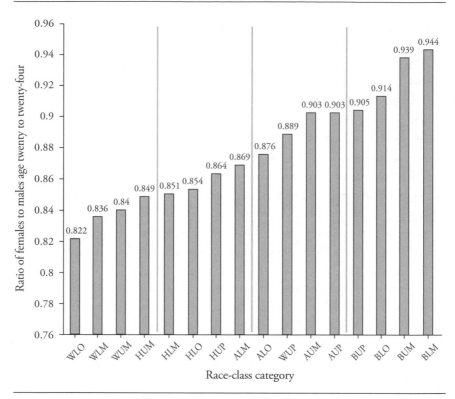

Source: Authors' compilation based on Harris and Udry (2008).

As Wilson (1987) and Western (2006) would predict, African Americans universally and without exception occupy the highest quadrant of male scarcity. Although upper-class blacks experience a relatively lower degree of male scarcity within neighborhoods than their counterparts of other social classes at 0.905, their ratio of single females to single males is still greater than the ratio of any other nonblack race-class group. The highest rates of male scarcity are experienced by lower-middle- and upper-middle-class African Americans, with respective ratios of 0.944 and 0.939, compared with 0.914 for lower-class blacks. Thus higher-class status does not appear to afford any clear or consistent advantage to African American women seeking partners or boys seeking role models, at least within the neighborhood sphere.

At the other extreme, the lowest levels of male scarcity are observed for whites and Hispanics in the middle and lower classes. The three lowest indices are observed for whites in the lower, lower middle, and upper middle classes, which have respective female-to-male ratios of 0.822, 0.836, and 0.840. They are followed closely by Hispanics in the upper middle, lower middle, and lower classes, which have ratios of 0.849, 0.851, and 0.854, respectively. Asians, along with upper-class Hispanics and whites, occupy positions between these two extremes, with indices that range from 0.864 to 0.903. In all cases, poor whites, Hispanics, and Asians experience lower scarcities of single males than their upper-class counterparts. The relatively high levels of male scarcity for upper-class groups likely reflect the fact that single males age twenty to twenty-four in upper-class neighborhoods are away at school. The high rates in black communities probably reflects the fact that they are in jail or the military or dead.

The relative absence of males and the greater concentration of disadvantage within black neighborhoods, along with the relative dearth of collective efficacy experienced in Hispanic and Asian neighborhoods, suggest that when it comes to the neighborhood sphere, minorities have considerably less access to resources than whites. To some extent, this deficit might be offset by greater access to other caring adults within the neighborhood; and indeed, when asked whether an adult other than a parent or stepparent had made an important difference in their lives, many respondents answered that a neighbor had done so. Older responsible adults in black neighborhoods have been labeled "old heads" by Elijah Anderson (1999), people who offer guidance and advice to adolescents who are "coming up," and historically male "old heads" have been particularly important in shaping the behavior of young black men.

Figure 3.4 shows the proportion of people naming a neighbor as a mentor by race and class. Asians are generally least likely to report being mentored by a neighbor, occupying three of the four positions in the lowest quadrant of the distribution. Only 3.7 percent of upper-class Asians reported a mentor from their neighborhood, followed by 4.8 percent among upper-middle-class Asians and 5.5 percent of lower-middle-class Asians. Lower-class Asians fell in the next lowest quadrant, only 6.6 percent reporting a mentor from the neighborhood. Black lower-class and lower-middle-class adolescents likewise reported little use of mentors from their neighborhoods, 4.8 percent and 6 percent respectively, as did lower-class whites at 6.2 percent.

At the other end of the spectrum, far above any other race category are

Figure 3.4   Neighborhood Mentorship

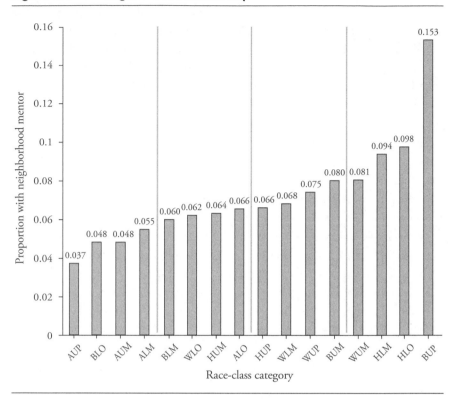

Source: Authors' compilation based on Harris and Udry (2008).

upper-class blacks, 15.3 percent of whom reported having a mentor who was a neighbor. At least for those in the upper classes, neighborhood mentors appear to offer a potential substitute for the lack of fathers. Next highest in the top quadrant were lower-class Hispanics, 9.8 percent of whom reported a neighbor as a mentor, followed by lower-middle-class Hispanics at 9.4 percent. Thus the greatest use of neighborhood mentors is paradoxically made by upper-class blacks and lower-class Hispanics. That high-status blacks rely on a social resource more often used by the lower classes of other groups underscores the scarcity of other resources in black neighborhoods.

The second highest quadrant in the distribution of access to neighborhood mentors includes upper-middle-class blacks, upper-class whites, lower-middle-class whites, and upper-class Hispanics. In general, we observe Asians and lower-class blacks to cluster at the bottom of the distribution and upper-class blacks and lower-class Hispanics to cluster at the top, other race-class categories falling in between. To some degree, therefore, one might hope that the disadvantages experienced by upper-class blacks with respect to neighborhood socioeconomic resources and the scarcity of males might be offset by greater access to neighborhood mentors. Unfortunately, neighborhood and family disadvantages are compounded by a lack of access to neighborhood mentors among lower-class African Americans. Likewise, the general concentration of Asians in low-efficacy neighborhoods is exacerbated by a lack of access to neighborhood mentors. However, the concentration of lower-class Hispanics in low-efficacy neighborhoods is offset by greater access to neighborhood mentors. Whether these offsetting and compounding potentialities actually function to produce advantage or disadvantage in terms of specific outcomes is a subject that we will, once again, address in subsequent chapters.

SCHOOL INFLUENCES

In the United States, the characteristics of schools and neighborhoods are strongly associated because students are assigned to specific schools based on their residence in surrounding geographic areas, at least in the public sector where the vast majority of adolescents are enrolled. As a result, high concentrations of poor minority students in neighborhoods yield high concentrations of the same students in the schools that serve them (Orfield 2002). It is no surprise, therefore, that high levels of residential segregation in the United States are paralleled by even higher levels of school segregation (Orfield and Eaton 1996). Schools tend to be more segregated than neighborhoods because those with the economic means to do so withdraw from the public sector of education and place their children in more costly, but also more advantaged private schools, yielding a selective migration of upper-class students out of the public sector, which only exacerbates inequalities built into the public sector by residential segregation (Kozol 1991, 2005).

To assess the quality of the school environment faced by adolescents in different race-class groups, we developed an index of school disadvantage drawing on responses to seven questions included on the Wave 1 survey administered to school administrators, combined with two items included on the Wave 1 in-school questionnaire filled out by the adolescents. The variables taken from the school administrator questionnaire include average daily attendance (which we grouped into five categories and coded 0 to 4); average class size (nine categories coded 0 to 8); the percentage of teachers at the school for at least five years (nine categories coded 0 to 8); the percentage of teachers with a master's degree or higher (nine categories coded 0 to 8); the percentage of students dropping out during the school year (seven categories coded 0 to 6); the percentage of students testing below grade level (five categories coded 0 to 4), and whether physical services were provided or referred (dichotomous 0–1). From the in-school questionnaire, we took the percentage of students who were nonwhite (five categories coded 0 to 4) and the percentage of students who participated in clubs, organizations, or teams (five categories coded 0–4). In each case the coding was done so that larger values indicated greater disadvantage (see appendix B), yielding a scale ranging from 0 to 42 with a good reliability coefficient ($\alpha = 0.70$). Again we include the black percentage to indicate special disadvantages built into schools by years of de facto and de jure segregation that go beyond simple economic conditions.

Average levels of school disadvantage are presented by race and class in figure 3.5 to reveal the clear legacy of white racial privilege in the United States. No matter what their class standing, whites are likely to attend the least disadvantaged schools, whites of all classes located in the lowest quadrant and displaying school disadvantage scores clustered tightly in the range from 18.4 for upper-class and upper-middle-class whites to 18.6 for lower-class whites and 18.8 for lower-middle-class whites. No other race-class group displayed a disadvantage index value less than 22.4, and perhaps surprisingly the most disadvantaged quadrant was occupied by Hispanics and Asians of the lower and lower middle classes and not African Americans. Thus, whereas lower-class whites had a school disadvantage index value of 18.6, that for lower-class Asians was 50 percent greater at 28.0 and that for lower-class Hispanics was 44 percent greater at 26.7. The indices for lower-middle-class Asians and Hispanics were 27.8 and 26.2, respectively.

African Americans tended to fall between these two extremes on the continuum of school disadvantage, mostly in the second lowest quadrant and in a relatively narrow range going from 22.6 among upper-class African Americans to 23.8 among lower-middle-class African Americans, black upper-middle and lower-class students falling between with values of 23.1 and 23.8, respectively. Upper-class Hispanics were exposed to roughly the same level of school disadvantage as upper-class blacks (22.4 versus 22.6). Although these values were significantly above the level of school disadvantage experienced

Figure 3.5   School Disadvantage

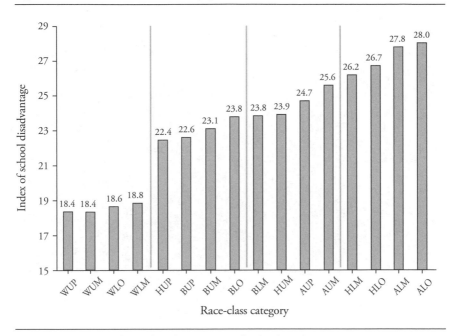

Source: Authors' compilation based on Harris and Udry (2008).

by upper-class whites (18.4) they were nonetheless well below the level faced by upper-class Asians (24.7). In general, therefore, Asians seem to attend the most materially disadvantaged schools, with some variance in exposure by social class, followed by Hispanics, and then blacks. As usual, whites enjoyed the least disadvantaged schools irrespective of social class.

Collective efficacy can be defined for schools as well as neighborhoods, and to accomplish this task we drew upon a series of items from the in-school questionnaire, which asked respondents to assess, on a five-point continuum, how much teachers cared about them; how close they felt to other people at school; how much they felt a part of the school they attended; how happy they were to be at that school; and the degree to which teachers treated students fairly. The same set of questions was asked in both Waves 1 and 2 and each item was coded 0 to 4 such that a higher score indicated less efficacy (see appendix B), yielding a basic index of school inefficacy that ranged from 0 to 40 with a high reliability ($\alpha = 0.81$). Average values are shown by race and class in figure 3.6.

Figure 3.6   School Inefficacy

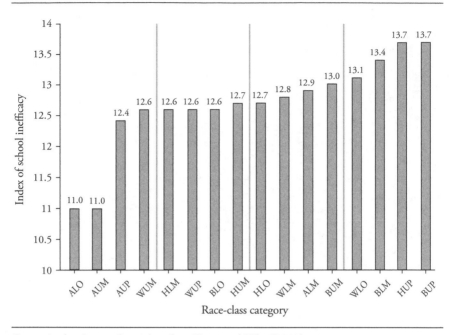

Source: Authors' compilation based on Harris and Udry (2008).

On this dimension, at least, we see little evidence of white privilege, the various white classes scattered across the middle range of the distribution and upper-class Hispanics and blacks generally reporting the greatest inefficacy in their schools (with an index value of 13.7) and Asian lower- and upper-middle-class students the least inefficacy (an index value around 11.0), which at first blush might seem surprising given the material deprivation that Asians generally experience in schools, a point we return to later. The school inefficacy index, however, displays relatively less variation than the other indices we have considered to this point, with the most disadvantaged race-class group being only 25 percent above the least disadvantaged. Nonetheless, three of the four positions in the lowest quadrant of inefficacy are occupied by Asians. In the top quadrant, however, the degree of school inefficacy experienced by upper-class blacks and Hispanics (13.7) is not much different from that reported by lower-class whites (13.1).

Perhaps the most fundamental emotional resource that a school can pro-

Figure 3.7   School Disorder

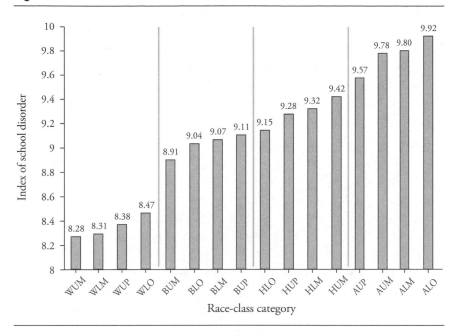

Source: Authors' compilation based on Harris and Udry (2008).

vide to young people is safety and security and shelter from disorder, a topic that is considered in figure 3.7 which shows average values for an index of school disorder by race and class. In Waves 1 and 2 respondents were asked to rate on a five-point scale how safe they felt at school. These items were combined with a set of Wave 2 items administered to administrators that asked about safety and security at their schools: whether a security or police officer was on duty (dichotomous 0–1); whether the school employed other safety or security measures (0–1); whether smoking, drug use, sexual harassment, vandalism, and stress or pressure were each not a problem, a problem, or a big problem (coded 0, 1, or 2). All items were again coded so that larger values indicated greater exposure to disorder, yielding a 0 to 20 point scale of school disorder of acceptable reliability (α = 0.60).

Once again, white privilege manifests itself in this figure, whites being clustered tightly in the lowest quadrant of school disorder and displaying relatively little variation by social class, index values ranging from 8.3 for upper- and lower-middle-class whites to 8.4 for upper-class whites to 8.5 for lower-class whites. In contrast to school efficacy, Asians are clustered in the upper quadrant of school disorder and violence, the lower class at 9.9, followed by the upper middle and lower middle class at 9.8, and the upper class at 9.6. The four Hispanic groups occupy the next highest quadrant and the four black groups the next highest after that. We thus observe a fairly clear racial ordering when considering exposure to social disorder within schools: whites experience the least disorder, followed in order by blacks, Hispanics, and Asians; and within groups disorder generally, though not always, rises as class standing falls. Moreover, in this case Asians display a relatively high degree of disadvantage that would seem to belie their reputation for academic advantage.

As in other spheres of social influence, disadvantages experienced because of greater exposure to disorder, inefficacy, and material deprivation might be compensated to some degree by greater access to a school-based mentor. Figure 3.8 thus shows the proportion of respondents who identified a teacher, guidance counselor, coach, or athletic director as the adult who made a positive difference in their lives after the age of fourteen. Although lower-class Asians experienced the highest levels of school disadvantage and disorder, they also experienced the highest rate of school-based mentoring, which possibly explains the high degree of success they achieve in otherwise materially deprived and chaotic school environments. Around 30 percent of lower-class Asian respondents reported having a school-based mentor. Relying on a school-based mentor was also common among upper-class and upper-middle-class Asians, 26.9 percent and 25.5 percent, respectively, identifying a mentor at school. Upper-class whites filled out the upper quadrant with a figure of 22.9 percent.

In contrast, the disadvantages that blacks and Hispanics experienced relative to whites in terms of material deprivation, disorder, and inefficacy within schools are clearly not offset by access to school-based mentors. Only 10 percent of lower-class Hispanics and 11.3 percent of lower-class blacks reported having an adult mentor at school. Among upper-class black adolescents, the figure rose only 12.3 percent. Among their upper-middle- and lower-middle-class counterparts, the figures were 16.7 percent and 17 percent, respectively. The percentage with school-based mentors was also quite low, at 13.5 percent, for lower-middle-class Hispanics and 14.5 percent for lower-middle-class Asians. In general, the share reporting access to educational mentors was

Figure 3.8   **School Mentorship**

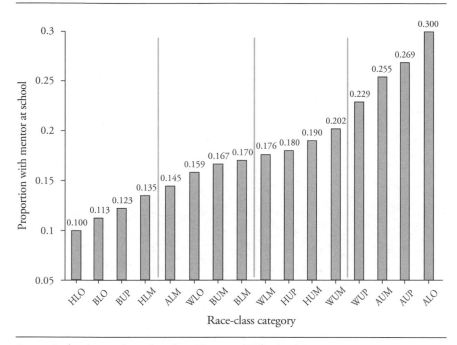

Source: Authors' compilation based on Harris and Udry (2008).

18 percent or greater for upper-middle- and upper-class whites and Hispanics and for all Asians except those in the lower middle class. The figure was 17 percent or less for lower- and lower-middle-class whites and Hispanics and all classes of African Americans. In the educational sphere, the standout group appears to be Asians, who attend materially deprived and socially disorganized schools but who nonetheless are able to establish strong relationships with an educational mentor and perceive a strong sense of efficacy in the schools they attend.

PEER PRESSURES

People in an adolescent's peer network might be neighbors or schoolmates, but they might also include people met in other social settings related to work, sports, or leisure. Both the Wave 1 and Wave 2 student questionnaires asked a detailed series of questions about exposure to interpersonal violence that were not tied explicitly to a school or neighborhood setting, but referred

Figure 3.9   Peer Violence

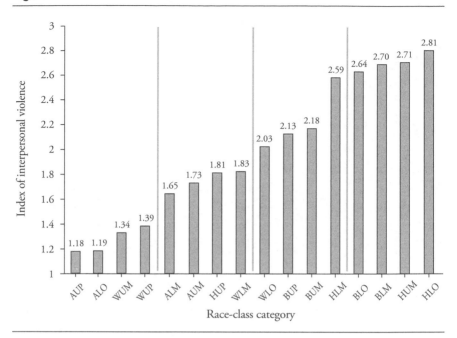

Source: Authors' compilation based on Harris and Udry (2008).

more generally to the social environment that spanned these and possibly other spheres. Both waves asked respondents how often, over the past twelve months, they had seen someone shoot or stab another person, had experienced a gun or knife being pulled on them, been stabbed, got into a physical fight, or been jumped (see appendix B). The possible responses in each case were never, once, and more than once, which we coded as 0, 1, and 2. The second wave survey also asked whether any of the respondent's romantic partners had called them names, insulted them, treated them disrespectfully, sworn at them, threatened them with violence, pushed or shoved them, or threw something at them to hurt them (all coded dichotomously 0–1). Combining these items produced a reliable 0–25 scale of exposure to interpersonal violence ($\alpha = 0.78$) that is shown by race and class in figure 3.9.

As can be seen, the resulting indices fall into four basic clusters that correspond closely but not entirely to the figure's four quadrants. At the top are index values of 2.6 or more, indicating significant exposure to violence in the lives of black and Hispanic adolescents, notably those of lower class background. Thus the index of peer violence stood at 2.59 for lower-middle-class Hispanics and 2.64 for lower-class blacks, 2.70 for lower-middle-class blacks, 2.71 for upper-middle-class Hispanics, and 2.81 for lower-class Hispanics. The second highest set of indices ranges closely from 2.0 to 2.2 and includes lower-class whites (2.03), upper-class blacks (2.13), and upper-middle-class blacks (2.18). In other words, blacks in all classes and Hispanics in all but the upper class generally experience greater exposure to interpersonal violence than even the poorest whites.

The third cluster down has index values that range from around 1.6 to around 1.8. and includes lower-middle-class whites (1.83), upper-class Hispanics (1.81), upper-middle-class Asians (17.3), and lower-middle-class Asians (1.65). The most advantaged respondents in terms of interpersonal violence display index values ranging from 1.2 to 1.4 and include upper- and upper-middle-class whites (1.39 and 1.34, respectively) and upper- and lower-class Asians (1.18 and 1.19, respectively). Thus the most disadvantaged group (poor Hispanics) experiences about 2.4 times the level of interpersonal violence as the least disadvantaged group (upper-class Asians).

Violence among adolescents may be self-directed as well as other-directed, and Wave 3 asked whether any of the respondent's friends had turned on themselves by attempting suicide in the previous twelve months, thereby indicating exposure to emotional turmoil and stress within the peer network. Figure 3.10 shows the proportion responding affirmatively by race and class. Exposure to this emotional burden appears to be structured substantially by class, at least among whites, blacks, and Hispanics. Suicide attempts by friends is greatest among upper-class and upper-middle-class Hispanics, of whom 13.6 percent and 10.6 percent reported an attempt, respectively, followed by upper-class blacks at 9.3 percent and upper-class whites at 8.9 percent, which is virtually the same as the 8.8 percent observed for upper- and lower-middle-class whites. Lower-middle-class Hispanics are close behind them at 8.4 percent.

Lower-class whites also display relatively high rates of peer suicide attempt, 8.2 percent reporting that a friend had tried to kill themselves in the past year, versus 7.5 percent for lower-class Asians and lower-class Hispanics. The lowest exposure to peer suicide occurs among the remaining Asian groups, just 1.5 percent among those in the lower middle class, 2.3 percent in the upper middle class, and 2.8 percent in the upper class. Lower-class and upper-middle-class blacks also display low levels of exposure to this source of

Figure 3.10   Friend's Suicide

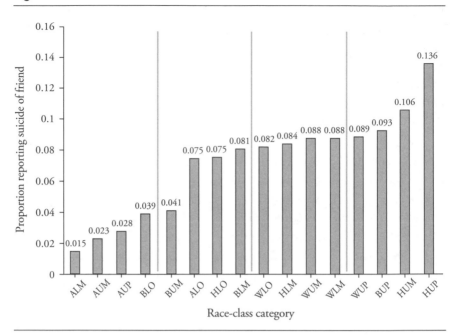

Source: Authors' compilation based on Harris and Udry (2008).

emotional distress, their respective percentages at 3.9 percent and 4.1 percent. Thus, poor black adolescents, who generally experience the harshest family, neighborhood, and school environments, and the highest levels of exposure to peer violence, are least likely to have friends who turn violence on themselves by attempting a suicide.

In addition to being a source of emotional stress, peers also provide social, material, and emotional support. In response to the question on mentors, a number of respondents identified a friend or coworker as the adult who had made a positive difference in their lives, and we coded these as peer mentors. As shown in figure 3.11, the share reporting peer mentors ranged from 13.4 percent among upper-middle-class blacks to 26.7 percent among upper-middle-class Asians, a substantial range of variation. Whites occupy the next highest positions in the race-class distribution of peer mentorship, the share reporting a peer mentor at 25 percent among upper-middle-class whites, 24 percent among lower-middle-class whites, 22.4 percent among lower-class whites, and 21.5 percent among upper-class whites. Asian lower-middle-class adolescents are next highest at 20.1 percent.

Figure 3.11   Peer Mentorship

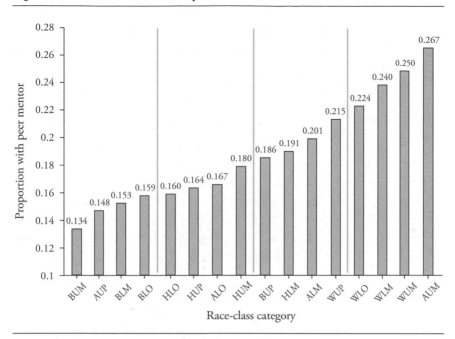

Source: Authors' compilation based on Harris and Udry (2008).

In sum, those adolescents most likely to report a peer mentor are whites and middle-class Asians. Those least likely are middle- and lower-class blacks and upper-class Asians. Only 13 percent of upper-middle-class black respondents reported having a peer mentor, followed by 14.8 percent of upper-class Asians, 15 percent of lower-middle-class blacks, and 15.9 percent of lower-class blacks. Also quite unlikely to report a peer mentor are Hispanics, whose frequencies ranged from 16 percent among those in the lower class to 16.4 percent in the upper class to 18 percent in the upper middle class. Asian lower-class members are also relatively low with 16.7 percent reporting a peer mentor. To the extent that peer mentors offer social capital to offset other disadvantages, therefore, they seem to be most accessible to whites and middle-class Asians and least accessible to blacks, lower-class Hispanics, and Asians in both the upper and lower classes.

THE RELIGIOUS OPTION

The accumulation of disadvantage across the four fundamental social spheres may be exacerbated or mitigated by conditions in a fifth sphere that individual actors may choose to inhabit. Although people are typically born into a religious tradition, not all parents are believers or practitioners, and people can and do change their religious beliefs and behaviors over time. In this sense, religious involvement is voluntary. Indeed, recent work in sociology has framed religious belief as a rational choice in which people make decisions about faith and participation not only to satisfy spiritual needs, but also to gain access to social and economic resources that come with religious affiliation (Stark and Bainbridge 1987; Warner 1993). David Smilde (2007) refers to the choice of religions as one of "imaginative rationality" in which forward-looking actors seek concrete returns through religious affiliation.

Religious behavior thus reflects instrumental decisions related to personal characteristics that indicate an individual's position in the social order (Iannaccone 1990); and Smilde (2007) argues that evangelical affiliation, in particular, often serves as a prophylactic measure chosen by poor people living in dangerous or threatening contexts to build and conserve positive social capital in an otherwise chaotic and threatening environment, offering poor people a practical path away from drugs, crime, gambling, alcohol, and other risks associated with disadvantaged families, neighborhoods, schools, and peers. Religion also potentially offers emotional support to help people cope with the hardships and setbacks of poverty and life in a poor community. Rodney Stark and Roger Finke (2000) refer to the mastery of religious knowledge and the psychological support, comfort, and esteem that it provides as "spiritual capital."

We measure participation in the religious domain using three indicators, the details of which are described in appendix B. To control for an individual's overall level of religious faith and devotion, we construct a measure of religiosity using items included on Waves 1 and 2 of the Add Health Survey: whether the respondent reports having a religion, whether he or she agrees that scripture is the word of God, the self-assessed importance of religion to the respondent (on a 0–4 scale), and the frequency with which the respondent prays (a 0–5 scale). When combined across the two waves, the eight items yield a 0–22 scale with a high degree of reliability ($\alpha = 0.84$). This scale measures overall religiosity or the spiritual capital dimension of religious participation.

Holding constant religiosity, we measure the intensity of religious involvement using two additional items also included on the first two survey waves: the frequency of service attendance (on a 0–4 scale) and the frequency of

Figure 3.12   Religiosity

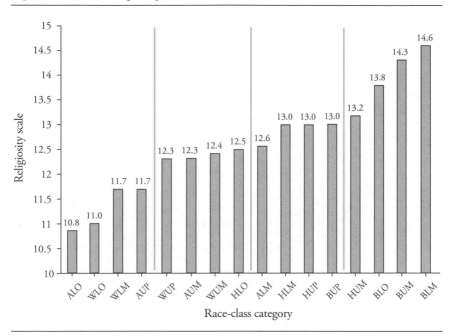

Source: Authors' compilation based on Harris and Udry (2008).

participation in religious youth activities (also a 0–4 scale), yielding a very reliable sixteen-point scale of religious involvement (α = 0.85). Finally, we define a dichotomous variable indicating whether the person identified as making a positive difference in the life of a respondent was a minister, priest, rabbi, or other religious leader, which we coded as having a religious mentor.

Figure 3.12 shows the distribution of religiosity by race and class to reveal fairly strong racial effects in terms of access to spiritual capital, with blacks and Hispanics displaying relatively high levels of religious faith compared with Asians and whites. The upper quadrant is dominated by African Americans, the top three spots being held by lower-middle-class blacks (14.6), upper-middle-class blacks (14.3), and lower-class blacks (13.8), who are closely followed by upper-middle-class Hispanics (13.2) and upper-class blacks (13.0). At the other extreme, the two lowest levels of religiosity are displayed by lower-class Asians (10.8) and lower-class whites (11.0), followed by lower-middle-class whites and upper-class Asians (with scale values of 11.7

Figure 3.13   Religious Involvement

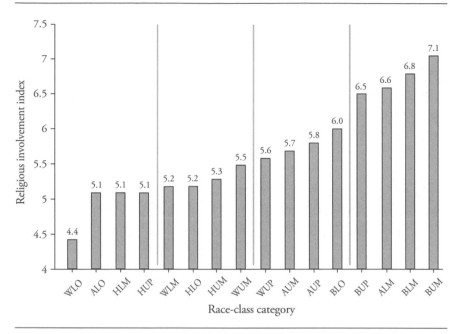

Source: Authors' compilation based on Harris and Udry (2008).

each). With one exception, the bottom two quadrants are filled by white and Asian class groups. The top two are occupied by blacks and Hispanics.

At the extremes, the pattern of religious involvement corresponds roughly to that of religiosity in general, as shown in figure 3.13. Again the two lowest levels of religious involvement are displayed by lower-class whites (4.4) and lower-class Asians (5.1) and the two highest positions are occupied by upper-middle and lower-middle-class blacks (at 7.1 and 6.8., respectively). Compared with their relatively low levels of self-assessed religiosity, however, Asians display a greater proclivity for religious involvement and affiliation, with index values of 6.5, 5.8, and 5.7 for lower-middle-class, upper-class, and upper-middle-class Asians, respectively, compared with 6.0 for lower-class blacks and 5.6 for upper-class whites. In general, Asian and black groups populate the upper half of the religious involvement distribution and whites and Hispanics the lower half.

Figure 3.14   Religious Mentorship

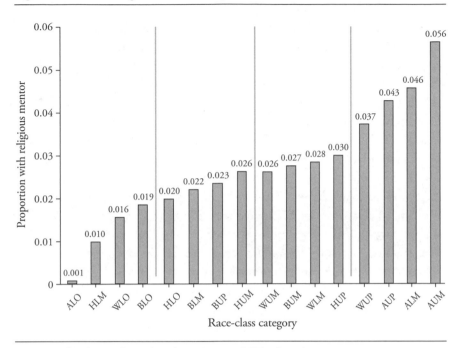

Source: Authors' compilation based on Harris and Udry (2008).

Despite the often high levels of religious faith and involvement reported in some race-class groups, relatively few respondents specified a religious mentor. As shown in figure 3.14, the three most frequent mentions of a religious mentor were by upper-middle-class Asians, lower-middle-class Asians, and upper-class Asians, their respective frequencies at 5.6 percent, 4.6 percent, and 4.3 percent. Paradoxically, Asians also occupied the lowest position, lower-class Asians naming almost no religious mentors. The lack of a religious mentor appears to be associated with lower-class status, as the bottom five positions are occupied by lower-class whites, blacks, Asians, and Hispanics, along with lower-middle-class Hispanics. Most of the positions in the upper half of the distribution are occupied by upper-class or upper-middle-class members of the various racial groups. To the extent that religious mentors make a positive difference in adolescents' lives, therefore, they would reinforce rather than mitigate class advantages and disadvantages.

CUMULATIVE DISADVANTAGES

To this point, we have examined the degree of disadvantage experienced by adolescents in four fundamental ecological spheres (families, schools, neighborhoods, and peers) and one voluntary sphere (religion), paying particular attention to differences in exposure to advantages and disadvantages by race and class. We have considered relative disadvantage in terms of material resources such as income and poverty, symbolic resources such as status and prestige, and emotional resources such as parental contact, emotional warmth, social efficacy, exposure to disorder and violence, and access to a mentor. In some cases, we found that exposure to disadvantage was structured more by race than by class (as with school and neighborhood material deprivation). In others, we discovered that disadvantage was structured more by class (as with income and prestige) and in still other cases exposure to disadvantage was determined by more complicated interactions between race and class (as with most other indicators).

Table 3.1 summarizes the pattern of ecological exposure to disadvantage that we have measured across social spheres to this point. The rows correspond to the twenty-three indices we have used to characterize conditions in the five social spheres, and the columns indicate the sixteen race-class groups. The resulting 316 cells show which quadrant in the distribution of disadvantage each race-class configuration fell with respect to each indicator. The quadrants are numbered 1 through 4, 1 indicating least disadvantage and 4 indicating the most disadvantaged.

If ecological circumstances were determined entirely by class, then the numbers for each group would decrease moving left to right. If ecological circumstances were determined totally by race, then all columns for each racial group would be the same. Departures from these two ideal types indicate race-class interactions. The only indicator to display the pure pattern for class is household income, which is hardly surprising since classes were defined on the basis of income. In each of the four groups we see a 4–3–2–1 progression. No indicator completely displays the pure configuration for race. The one that comes closest is scarcity of males, where all black class categories are coded 4, all Asian categories save one are coded 3, all Hispanic categories save one are coded 2, and all white categories save one are coded 1.

In general, the more high-numbered cells we observed in the columns for a particular racial group, the more it is disadvantaged on the basis of race rather than class. In addition to the index of male scarcity within neighborhoods, blacks are most disadvantaged in terms of father absence, family mortality, and paternal incarceration in the family sphere; material deprivation in the neighborhood sphere; inefficacy and access to mentors in the school sphere; violence and access to mentors in the peer network; and access to mentors in the religious sphere. The areas in which they are relatively advantaged are access to mentors in the family sphere and religiosity and religious involvement in the religious sphere. Among black adolescents, therefore, areas of disadvantage greatly outnumber areas of advantage to yield a social ecology of inequality.

In contrast, white adolescents display few areas of disadvantage and numerous areas of advantage. The only real areas of disadvantage are with respect to suicide of friends in the peer network and religiosity and religious involvement in the religious sphere. Within the family setting, the various ecological indicators tend to follow a basic class gradient, the numbers declining left to right. In the neighborhood, school, and peer settings, however, we observe multiple indications of advantage across indices, low numbers prevailing for indicators of material disadvantage, inefficacy, male scarcity, and access to mentors in the neighborhood sphere; low numbers for indicators of material disadvantage, disorder, and access to mentors in the school sphere; and a similar pattern for violence and access to mentors in the peer network.

Asians and Hispanics fall between these two extremes, Asians tending more toward white patterns and Hispanics to black patterns. Particular areas of Asian disadvantage are with respect to mortality, sternness, and mentors in the family sphere; inefficacy and access to mentors in the neighborhood sphere; access to mentors among peers; and religiosity in the religious sphere. Areas of Asian advantage include father absence and paternal incarceration in the family sphere; inefficacy and access to mentors in the school sphere; violence and suicide of friends in the peer setting; and involvement and access to mentors in the religious sphere.

In some ways, Hispanics experience a more daunting ecological environment than African Americans. Although Hispanics may not face the same kind of material deprivation and scarcity of males in the neighborhood sphere, in other spheres they generally experience as much or more disadvantage than African Americans. In the family sphere, for example, notable areas of disadvantage include access to health insurance, parental prestige, parental educa-

Table 3.1   Relative Disadvantage of Race-Class Groups in Different Spheres of Social Influence

	Whites				Asians	
	WLO	WLM	WUM	WUP	ALO	ALM
Family setting						
Household income	4	3	2	1	4	3
Health insurance	4	3	2	1	3	2
Parental prestige	4	2	1	1	4	3
Parent college graduate	3	3	2	1	4	3
Father absent	4	3	1	2	3	1
Family mortality	3	2	1	1	4	4
Family sternness	3	3	2	2	4	4
Father incarcerated	4	3	2	1	1	1
Family mentor	3	3	2	2	4	4
Neighborhood setting						
Disadvantage index	2	2	1	1	3	3
Inefficacy index	1	1	1	2	3	4
Scarcity of males	1	1	1	3	3	2
Neighborhood mentor	3	2	1	2	3	4
School setting						
Disadvantage index	1	1	1	1	4	4
Inefficacy index	4	3	1	2	1	1
Disorder index	1	1	1	1	4	4
School mentor	3	2	2	1	1	3
Peer setting						
Violence index	3	2	1	1	1	2
Friend attempted suicide	3	3	3	4	2	1
Peer mentor	1	1	1	2	3	2
Religious setting						
Religiosity scale	4	4	3	3	4	2
Involvement index	4	3	3	2	4	1
Had religious mentor	4	2	2	1	4	1

Source: Authors' calculations based on data set described in Harris and Udry (2008).
Note: Higher number indicates greater disadvantage

tion, family sternness, paternal incarceration, and access to mentors. They also experience relatively high levels of disadvantage in terms of inefficacy in the neighborhood sphere; material disadvantage, inefficacy, disorder, and access to mentors in the school sphere; violence, suicide, and access to mentors in peer settings; and involvement and access to mentors in the religious sphere. The

Asians		Hispanics				Blacks			
AUM	AUP	HLO	HLM	HUM	HUP	BLO	BLM	BUM	BUP
2	1	4	3	2	1	4	3	2	1
2	1	4	4	3	2	4	3	1	1
2	2	4	3	3	1	4	3	2	1
1	1	4	4	3	2	4	2	2	1
1	1	3	2	2	2	4	4	4	3
1	2	3	1	3	2	4	4	3	2
2	4	3	1	3	4	1	2	1	1
1	2	4	3	2	3	4	4	3	2
4	2	3	4	3	2	1	1	1	1
2	1	3	3	2	1	4	4	4	4
4	3	4	2	4	2	3	2	3	1
3	3	2	2	1	2	4	4	4	4
4	4	1	1	3	2	4	3	2	1
3	3	4	4	3	2	2	3	2	2
3	1	3	2	2	4	2	4	3	4
4	4	3	3	3	3	2	2	2	2
1	1	4	4	2	2	4	3	3	4
2	1	4	3	4	2	4	4	3	3
1	1	2	3	4	4	1	2	2	4
1	4	3	2	3	3	4	4	4	2
3	4	3	2	1	2	2	1	1	1
2	2	3	4	3	4	2	1	1	1
1	1	3	4	3	2	4	3	2	3

only real bright spot in the table is the relatively advantaged configuration of Hispanics in terms of access to neighborhood mentors.

In sum, when considering exposure to different sources of deprivation in different ecological settings, certain groups seem consistently to come up short whereas other groups generally come out ahead, yielding an accumulation of disadvantage across domains. Exposure to multiple sources of disadvantage is critical to understanding the situation of any group to the extent that disadvantages act cumulatively to undermine well-being. Coming from a poor family, living in a poor neighborhood, attending a poor school, and being exposed to a high degree of peer violence can each be expected to have negative consequences on individual well-being, but the negative effects may not be additive but multiplicative, leaving those who experience multiple disadvantages at the same time much worse off than others.

In subsequent chapters, we assess whether and how differences in access to resources across ecological spheres translate into differential well-being with respect to different outcomes. Here we assess the potential for nonadditive effects across settings by measuring the degree to which disadvantages accumulate across domains using twelve standardized indices of deprivation. Within the family sphere, we assess the degree of income deprivation, status deprivation, human capital deprivation, paternal deprivation, family mortality, and family sternness. Within neighborhoods, we consider the degree of material disadvantage and social inefficacy. Within schools, we measure exposure to material disadvantage, social inefficacy, and social disorder; and among peers we assess exposure to interpersonal violence. We do not include indicators of deprivation in the religious sphere because it is voluntary and some respondents do not participate at all. Rather we consider the degree to which advantages in the religious sphere offset individual and cumulative disadvantages experienced in the other spheres of influence.

Each disadvantage index was developed to range from 1 to 101, where 1 indicates minimum observed disadvantage with respect to the indicator and 101 indicates maximum observed disadvantage. In appendix B, we summarize the scaling operations we undertook to create the twelve indices of disadvantage. For each index, we selected a value to serve as a standard point of "no deprivation" and then measured the distance of each respondent from this value on a 0–100 scale, adding 1 to eliminate values of 0, which create obvious problems when computing multiplicative indices. In general, the point of no deprivation was the maximum observed value in the distribution, except for income where we used the value of income at the ninetieth percentile to create a more tractable distribution of index values.

Figure 3.15 summarizes the degree to which disadvantage cumulates across the various domains under consideration by computing the simple sum of disadvantage scores for each race-class group. As can be seen, the total disad-

Figure 3.15 Cumulative Disadvantage

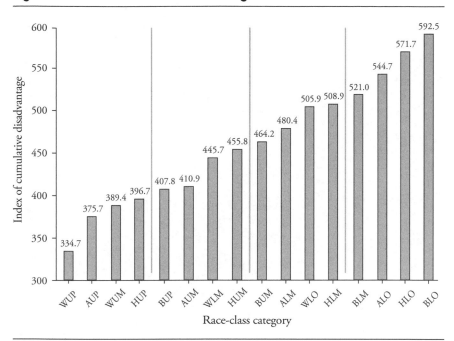

Source: Authors' compilation based on Harris and Udry (2008).

vantage experienced by lower-class blacks (592.5) is 77 percent greater than that experienced by upper-class whites (334.7). The next most privileged group is upper-class Asians, whose total score of 375.7 is 12 percent greater than that of upper-class whites. Moving from left to right, the index values generally move upward modestly over the next four positions, showing values of 389.4 for upper-middle-class whites, 396.7 for upper-class Hispanics, 407.8 for upper-class blacks, and 410.9 for upper-class Asians. Thus the most consistently advantaged groups are upper- and upper-middle-class whites and Asians, along with upper-class blacks and Hispanics. At this point in the distribution, there is a more marked shift upward. Whereas upper-middle-class Asians had a total disadvantage score of just 410.9, for the next closest group (lower-middle-class whites) the value was 445.7, a jump of 8.5 percent, and they are followed by upper-middle-class Hispanics at 455.8.

The top half of the cumulative disadvantage distribution is made up lower-class and lower-middle-class blacks and Hispanics, plus lower-class Asians

Figure 3.16 Interactive Disadvantage

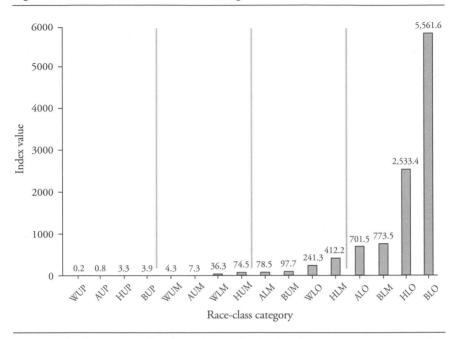

Source: Authors' compilation based on Harris and Udry (2008).

and whites. The most disadvantaged positions are occupied by lower-class blacks (with a total score of 592.5), lower-class Hispanics (571.7), and lower-class Asians (544.7). Nonetheless, lower-middle-class blacks and lower-middle-class Hispanics experience more cumulative disadvantage than lower-class whites, showing respective scores of 521.0 and 508.9 for the two minorities compared with 505.9 for lower-class whites. Obviously, then, disadvantage does accumulate across domains, and the accumulation tends to be greatest for lower-class and lower-middle-class blacks and Hispanics and least for upper- and upper-middle-class whites and Asians.

The foregoing figures presume, however, that the effects of disadvantage are additive rather than multiplicative. To assess the divergence between race-class groups when disadvantage across social spheres is experienced interactively, figure 3.16 shows indicators of accumulated disadvantage derived by multiplying rather than adding indices across the domains. Because the multiplication of twelve indices can yield very large numbers, we have divided the product by ten to the thirteenth power to produce more tractable indicators. As can easily be seen from the figure, if disadvantages are interactive rather than additive in their effects on human well-being, then outcomes for poor African Americans can be expected to differ by quanta compared with other groups. The interactive disadvantage index for poor blacks stands at 5,561.6, a value that is 2.2 times the value for poor Hispanics (2533.5), the next closest group, and 7.9 times that of lower-class Asians. Compared with lower-class whites, meanwhile, the interactive disadvantage index was twenty-three times greater. Compared with upper-class whites, it was 27,808. In subsequent analyses, we enter the natural log of this multiplicative index to test whether disadvantages experienced across the four fundamental social spheres functions interactively to determine well-being and outcomes across different dimensions of human development.

SPHERES OF ADVANTAGE AND DISADVANTAGE

This chapter and the preceding one have documented remarkable diversity in the social ecologies experienced by adolescents in the United States. Here social ecology is defined by twenty-three measures assessing circumstances in five social spheres that constitute the environment experienced by most U.S. residents, four fundamental spheres that virtually all adolescents experience (family, neighborhood, school, and peer) plus one elective sphere that young people may or may not inhabit (religion). Across all spheres, the principal dimensions structuring relative exposure to advantage or disadvantage are race and class, sometimes operating independently as main effects but more often interacting in complex ways to yield a highly variegated social ecology that can be expected to produce divergent social and economic outcomes.

The last chapter documented the sharpness of inequalities in the family sphere by comparing the most advantaged race-class configuration with the least advantaged, revealing that those at the top of the hierarchy earn ten times more than those at the bottom, garner 81 percent more prestige, enjoy 72 percent greater access to health insurance, and experience 84 percent less father absence, 92 percent less family mortality, 94 percent less paternal incarceration, and 60 percent greater access to a family mentor. In this chapter, we observed similar differences in other social spheres. Within neighborhoods, for example, the most advantaged race-class category faces 76 percent less neighborhood deprivation than the most disadvantaged category, 41 percent less social inefficacy, 13 percent less scarcity of young single males, and four times the likelihood of having a mentor. Likewise, within schools the most privileged group experiences 35 percent less disadvantage, 20 percent less social inefficacy, 17 percent less social disorder, and three times the likelihood of having a mentor; and among peers the most advantaged experience 58 percent less violence, an 89 percent lower likelihood of having a suicidal friend, and twice the likelihood of having a mentor. Finally, within the religious sphere, the most devout are 34 percent more religious than the least, 59 percent more involved, and seventy-four times more likely to have a mentor.

The distribution of advantages and disadvantages is not random by race and class, but highly patterned so that some race-class categories tend to accumulate disadvantages whereas others accumulate disadvantages as indicated by the indices of cumulative disadvantage just presented. In general, lower-class blacks constitute the most consistently disadvantaged group in American society, whereas upper-class whites are most consistently advantaged. How these large disparities in social ecology translate into varying life trajectories is an empirical question that we take up in the next four chapters, which examine ecological influences on outcomes having to do with reproduction, health, human capital formation, and crime and delinquency.

CHAPTER 4

Risky Reproduction

Like other living organisms, human beings exist biologically to reproduce and perpetuate the species. Compared with other mammals, however, the human transition to reproduction unfolds over a rather prolonged period. Among our closest living relatives, for example, chimpanzee females reach puberty at around age seven, begin mating at the age of eight or nine, and bear their first offspring at age ten or eleven (Estes 1991). In contrast, among young women in the United States today, the average age of menarche is 12.4 years (Chumlea et al. 2003), the average age of first intercourse is 17.2 years (Singh et al. 2000), the average age of first cohabitation is 21 years (Halle 2002), and the average age at first birth is 25 years (Mathews and Hamilton 2009). In the United States, the rise in nonmarital childbearing means that first marriage now occurs at about the same time as first birth, roughly 25.3 years, on average (U.S. Census Bureau 2010). Thus the typical American woman lives at least twelve years before acquiring even the minimal physical capacity to reproduce and then waits another five years before becoming sexually active and another eight years after that before becoming a wife and/or mother.

Variation is considerable around each of these milestones in the female life cycle, however, and within modern postindustrial societies the ages of entry into sexual activity and childbirth carry serious implications for the well-being of both mothers and children. Research shows that teenage mothers are less likely to graduate from high school and spend more years in poverty than those who delay childbearing (Hotz, McElroy, and Sanders 2008), and the negative effects of early childbearing appear to have increased over time (Hoffman 2008). Children born to teenage mothers have lower birth weights, display poorer health outcomes, and exhibit reduced cognitive skills compared with children born to older mothers, and when they grow up they are less likely to graduate from high school or go to college (Manlove et al. 2008).

Those born to teenage mothers are also more likely to exhibit chronic health problems and incur greater medical expenditures (Wolfe and Rivers 2008) and they are significantly more likely to exhibit externalizing behavioral problems ("acting out"), end up in foster care, and be subject to abuse or neglect (Hoffman 2002; Goerge, Harden, and Lee 2008). Sons born to teenage mothers are more likely to end up in jail or prison (Grogger 2008; Scher and Hoffman 2008), whereas daughters of teen mothers are more likely to become teenage mothers themselves (Haveman, Wolfe, and Peterson 2008; Hoffman and Scher 2008).

Whatever the age of the mother, it matters a great deal to children whether she is in a stable partnership or marriage during their infancy and childhood. Ample research confirms that unwed mothers have lower incomes, higher rates of poverty, and a higher likelihood of welfare dependency than married mothers (Naifeh 1998; Thomas and Sawhill 2002). Also, children born to unwed mothers go on to complete less schooling, attain lower occupational status, experience higher rates of unemployment, earn lower incomes, and display a higher rate of welfare dependency as adults, compared with women from two-parent families; they are also more likely later to have children outside of marriage (Astone and McLanahan 1991; Biblarz and Raftery 1993; McLanahan 1988; McLanahan and Sandefur 1994; Wu 1996).

Given the centrality of the family in the social ecology of human development, it is hardly surprising that family formation has emerged as a key nexus for the intertemporal and intergenerational transmission of poverty and disadvantage (Musick and Mare 2004, 2006; McLanahan and Percheski 2008). Other things equal, increasing the length of the transition to sexual intercourse, union formation, and childbearing can be expected to reduce the time that mothers will spend in poverty and promote better health and higher education for both themselves and their children. In this chapter, therefore, we consider the social ecology of reproduction to learn how exposure to contrasting circumstances in family, neighborhood, school, peer, and religious settings affects the transition of young men and women to sexual activity, cohabitation, marriage, and childbearing, paying particular attention to the differential likelihood of becoming an unwed or teenage mother by race and class.

SEXUAL DEBUT

In the United States today, the vast majority of young women experience menarche by the end of their thirteenth year (Chumlea et al. 2003). The next major transition in the path to human reproduction is the initiation of sexual activity, demarcated by first intercourse, or as it has been labeled in the social science literature, "sexual debut" (Cavazos-Rehg et al. 2009). Significant racial differences have been documented in the age of menarche, with the median age for black girls being about 12.1 years, for white girls 12.6, and for Mexican American girls 12.3 (Chumlea et al. 2003). These pubertal differences are, in turn, associated with differences in the timing of first intercourse, African Americans generally initiating sexual activity at younger ages than either whites or Hispanics (Moore 2001; Cavanagh 2004; Cavazos-Rehg et al. 2009; Cavazos-Rehg et al. 2010). An earlier sexual debut is associated, in turn, with a higher risk of subsequent delinquency (Armour and Haynie 2007), sexually transmitted infection (Kaestel et al. 2005; Shafii, Stovel, and Holmes 2007), unplanned pregnancy (Singh et al. 2000), and a lower likelihood of achieving postsecondary education (Spriggs and Halpern 2008).

Although racial and ethnic differences in the age of first intercourse have been well documented, up to this point race-class interactions have not been systematically explored. Figure 4.1 therefore plots the share of Add Health respondents who had experienced first intercourse by race and class at the time of the Wave 3 survey, when respondents ranged in age from eighteen to twenty-six years. Recall that dividing four racial groups into four class segments can yield cell sizes that are rather small. As noted earlier, we expect class patterns to be quite reliably depicted among whites, fairly reliably estimated among blacks and to a lesser extent Hispanics, and least reliably estimated among Asians, with the most problematic estimates being for the small numbers of Asians in the lower and lower middle classes. Bearing these caveats in mind, figure 4.1 reveals very clear and consistent racial differences in the odds of sexual debut, with black adolescents displaying the highest frequency of first intercourse, followed by Hispanics and whites, and then at some distance Asians.

The likelihood of first intercourse declines steadily with rising class status

Figure 4.1   First Intercourse

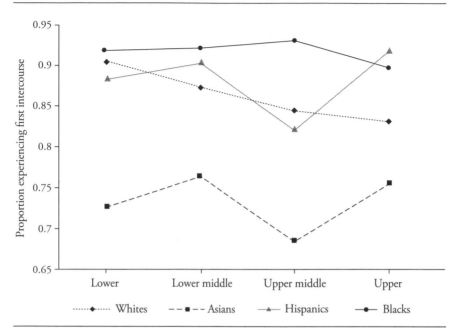

Source: Authors' compilation based on Harris and Udry (2008).

among white adolescents, falling from 91 percent in the lower class to around 84 percent in the upper class. Among African Americans, however, the proportion sexually active was fairly stable at around 92 percent to 93 percent in the lower, lower middle, and upper middle class, and dropped only slightly to 90 percent in the upper class. In contrast, a clear class pattern does not exist among Hispanics or Asians, possibly because of instability stemming from small cell sizes. Overall, the most consistent finding is the relatively low level of sexual activity reported by Asian respondents, with the share experiencing sexual debut by Wave 3 ranging from a low of 69 percent in the upper middle class to 76 percent in the lower middle class, well below the shares for any other race-class group.

Figure 4.2 shows the age of sexual debut for those who had begun sexual activity by Wave 3. The racial differentials observed in the likelihood of sexual debut persist in studying the age at which it occurred, blacks displaying the youngest average ages of first intercourse (15.7 to 16.0 years), followed by Hispanics (16.3 years to 16.5 years), whites (16.2 years to 16.6 years), and

Figure 4.2   Age at First Intercourse

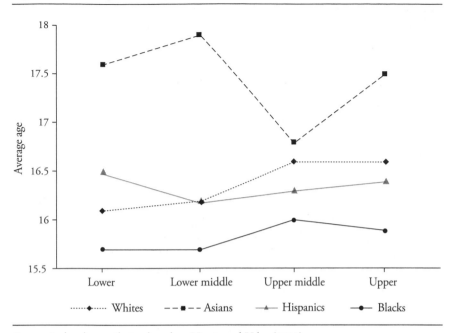

Source: Authors' compilation based on Harris and Udry (2008).

Asians (16.8 years to 17.8 years). Age of first intercourse generally rises with social class for whites and blacks, though the differentials are not large. Again, however, no clear class pattern is evident for Hispanics or Asians, who show considerable volatility, especially the latter, likely reflecting the small sample sizes.

If early entry into sexual activity increases the risk of experiencing undesirable social, economic, and physical outcomes, as prior research suggests, then blacks are clearly exposed to the greatest risk and Asians the least, with whites and Hispanics in between. To the extent that we observe class variation, risks seem to decrease with rising socioeconomic status, though this is true only for whites and African Americans. To explore race-class variation in the transition to sexual activity more formally, we turn to statistical models that predict the likelihood of initiating sex and, for those who have done so, the age at which the initiation occurred.

Our basic approach here and elsewhere throughout the book is to estimate a baseline model that includes dummy variables for the various race-class categories. Then, following the logic summarized in figure 1.1, we add ascribed characteristics and ecological circumstances, both to see how these controls influence observed race-class differentials and to understand how social ecological circumstances influence the outcome in question. Given that sexuality is socialized and enacted quite differently by gender, we estimated the models separately for males and females, but only report results for females here. The results for males are available in supplementary material posted online at the Russell Sage Foundation website (https://www.russellsage .org/publications/sphere-influence).

Table 4.1 begins by displaying two logistic regression equations estimated to predict the odds that a female respondent to the Adolescent Health Survey experienced first intercourse by the third wave. The left-hand columns show basic differences in the odds of experiencing first intercourse by race and class, with upper-class white women serving as the reference category. Consistent with what we saw in figure 4.1, young white women display a very clear class gradient in exposure to sexual intercourse, those in the lowest income class showing a significantly higher probability of initiating sexual activity than those in the upper class, followed in descending order by lower-middle-class women, and upper-middle-class women. The relative likelihood of first intercourse may be calculated by taking the natural exponent of coefficients associated with the variable in question. Thus the odds of first intercourse for lower class white women are 2.6 times greater than those for upper-class white women [Exp(0.957) = 2.604] and the odds for lower-middle-class white women are 1.4 times or 40 percent greater [Exp (0.334) = 1.397]. In contrast, the odds of sexual debut are about the same for upper-middle-class white women, given that the coefficient is not statistically significant.

The model also indicates the probability of first intercourse among Asian women is generally at or below that experienced by upper-class white women, though only the coefficient for upper-middle-class Asians is statistically significant, and then only at the 10 percent level. The odds of first intercourse among Hispanic women show the opposite class gradient, the greatest likelihood of intercourse occurring among upper-class females, whose odds of sexual debut are almost five times greater than those of upper-class whites. As one would expect from prior studies, the odds of first intercourse are greatest for young black women, particularly in the lower and lower middle classes, but they are also elevated in the upper middle class. In statistical terms, only

Table 4.1   Likelihood of Female Intercourse

Independent Variables	Group Effects		Full Model	
	B	SE	B	SE
Race-class group				
White lower	0.957***	0.248	−0.014	0.706
White lower middle	0.334+	0.174	−0.548	0.491
White upper middle	0.131	0.185	−0.209	0.304
White upper	—	—	—	—
Asian lower	0.786	0.644	0.286	1.101
Asian lower middle	−0.474	0.409	−0.492	0.602
Asian upper middle	−0.767+	0.450	−0.624	0.662
Asian upper	−0.626	0.411	−0.318	0.557
Hispanic lower	−0.109	0.187	−1.142	0.758
Hispanic lower middle	0.141	0.374	−0.402	0.555
Hispanic upper middle	−0.317	0.376	−0.878	0.398
Hispanic upper	1.596**	0.538	1.412*	0.597
Black lower	1.039**	0.324	−0.414	0.771
Black lower middle	1.292***	0.361	0.200	0.596
Black upper middle	0.842**	0.316	−0.142	0.421
Black upper	0.427	0.383	−0.416	0.456
Ascribed characteristics				
Age	—	—	0.225***	0.049
Parent foreign born	—	—	−0.387*	0.193
Ecological background				
Composition of origin family				
Two biological parents	—	—	—	—
Biological and stepparent	—	—	0.623+	0.346
One biological parent	—	—	0.181	0.170
No biological parent	—	—	−0.913	0.976
Family material resources				
Household income	—	—	−0.007	0.013
Access to health insurance				
No coverage	—	—	—	—
Coverage less than a year	—	—	0.132	0.258
Coverage a full year	—	—	−0.055	0.226
Family symbolic resources				
Parental prestige	—	—	0.001	0.004
Parent went to college	—	—	−0.197	0.302
Family emotional resources				
Experienced a death	—	—	−0.150	0.327
Family sternness	—	—	−0.009+	0.005

Table 4.1   *(continued)*

Independent Variables	Group Effects		Full Model	
	B	SE	B	SE
Father incarcerated	—	—	0.268	0.233
Had family mentor	—	—	0.009	0.184
Neighborhood setting				
Disadvantage index	—	—	0.292	0.183
Inefficacy index	—	—	−0.044	0.026
Scarcity of males	—	—	−0.177	0.140
Had neighborhood mentor	—	—	−0.109	0.324
School setting				
Disadvantage index	—	—	−0.011	0.011
Inefficacy index	—	—	0.034*	0.014
Disorder index	—	—	−0.048*	0.024
School mentor	—	—	−0.456+	0.221
Religious setting				
Religiosity scale	—	—	−0.071***	0.021
Involvement index	—	—	0.002	0.025
Had religious mentor	—	—	−0.980	0.366
Peer setting				
Violence index	—	—	0.111+	0.064
Friend attempted suicide	—	—	−0.017	0.245
Had peer mentor	—	—	−0.376+	0.224
Multiple disadvantages				
Log of interactive index	—	—	0.041	0.045
Intercept	1.571***	0.130	−1.362	2.047
N	4,718		3,738	
F-test	4.72***		4.55***	

Source: Authors' calculations based on data set described in Harris and Udry (2008).
+p < .10; *p < .05; **p < .01; ***p < .001

upper-class black women display the same odds of experiencing first inter-course as their white counterparts. The odds are 2.9 times greater for lower-class black women, 3.7 times greater for lower-middle-class black women, and 2.3 times greater for black women in the upper middle class.

Turning to the full model shown in the right-hand columns, we first consider the degree to which race-class variation in the odds of first intercourse can be accounted for by differences in the social environments to which young women are exposed. A technical problem in making such a comparison is that owing to missing data, the number of cases available for analysis in the full model is smaller than the number available in the baseline model. To ensure that shifts in the values and significance of race-class coefficients are not attributable to sample attrition, we re-estimated the baseline model for the reduced sample and compared the resulting coefficients with those shown in the left-hand columns of table 4.1 to confirm their stability. This operation is carried out systematically for all analyses done throughout the book in appendix C, which is included in the supplementary online material (https://www.russellsage.org/publications/sphere-influence). Unless indicated otherwise, readers can assume shifts in race-class effects are attributable to the addition of background controls and not artifacts of sample attrition.

Among white and black women, the significant class effects virtually disappear when the controls are applied, because positive signs for blacks are reversed and the coefficients themselves fall toward zero. This result implies that if we were somehow able to equalize ecological circumstances in the United States, sharp race-class differences in the odds of sexual debut would likely disappear for blacks and whites. In contrast, the application of ecological controls has little effect on Asian or Hispanic coefficients. Upper-class Hispanic women, in particular, display a much higher likelihood of making the transition to first sexual intercourse, their odds 4.1 times greater than that observed among upper-class white women. Thus, something in the circumstances of upper-class Hispanic women that is not captured in our model, perhaps having to do with cultural values or social norms, promotes early entry into sexual activity.

Of the two ascribed characteristics we consider, age naturally has a significant positive effect (the older a young woman is the more likely she is to have become sexually active), whereas being of immigrant origin has a negative effect (reducing the odds of first intercourse by around 32 percent). With respect to family ecology, growing up with a stepparent elevates the likelihood of first intercourse by around 86 percent compared with someone who grew up with two biological parents, but family sternness reduces it (by 0.9 percent per unit on the sternness scale, or a possible 90 percent over the observed range of the scale—see table A.1). Both effects, however, are only significant at the 10 percent level. Other marginally significant effects include exposure to peer violence (which raises the odds of sexual debut by around 12 percent per unit on the violence scale, for a total potential reduction of 240 percent over the range of the scale), having a school-based mentor (which reduces them by 37 percent), and having a peer mentor (reducing them by 31 percent).

Two features of the school setting have stronger and more significant effects. Exposure to greater social inefficacy at school raises the odds of first intercourse by 3.5 percent per unit on the inefficacy scale (140 percent over the range of the scale) and school disorder reduces the odds by around 5 percent per unit on the disorder scale (for a potential total of 96 percent). By far the most significant effect in the model is religiosity, which reduces the odds of sexual debut by 7 percent for each unit on the religiosity scale, yielding a total potential reduction of 126 percent over the scale's range). Holding the strength of religious belief constant, however, the degree of religious involvement and the degree of access to a religious mentor have no independent effects.

In sum, the ecological determinants of a young woman's entry into sexual activity appear to be, first, religiosity, followed by the degree of inefficacy and disorder experienced at school, and to a lesser extent the sternness of family discipline, exposure to peer violence, having peer and school mentors, and coming from a stepparent household. Table 4.2 continues our analysis of young women's sexual behavior by predicting the age of first intercourse among those who reported a sexual debut by Wave 3. Among whites, we once again observe a clear class gradient, as shown in the left-hand columns, with the age of first intercourse dropping steadily as one moves from upper class to lower class. According to the model, the average age of first intercourse was estimated to be 16.6 years for upper-class white women (calculated by adding together their coefficient with the intercept), 16.3 years for upper-middle-class white women, 16 years for lower-middle-class white women, and 15.9 for lower-class white women.

The age at first intercourse exhibited by upper-class and upper-middle-class black women does not differ statistically from upper-class white women, but black women in the lower and lower middle classes are significantly lower at 16 and 15.9 years, respectively. At the other extreme, lower-class and lower-middle-class Asian women display much greater ages of first intercourse, at 17.6 and 18.3 years, respectively, whereas upper-class Asian women are marginally higher at 17.2. Young Hispanic women appear to experience their sexual debut at about the same age as upper-class white women, whatever their social class.

Table 4.2   Age of First Female Intercourse

Independent Variables	Group Effects		Full Model	
	B	SE	B	SE
Race-class group				
White lower	−0.691***	0.152	−0.036	0.509
White lower middle	−0.599***	0.155	−0.186	0.367
White upper middle	−0.269	0.177	−0.108	0.237
White upper	—	—	—	—
Asian lower	1.009*	0.500	1.123	0.746
Asian lower middle	1.677*	0.563	1.225*	0.600
Asian upper middle	−0.339	0.830	−0.061	0.858
Asian upper	0.578+	0.336	0.156	0.445
Hispanic lower	0.267	0.456	0.594	0.548
Hispanic lower middle	0.006	0.422	0.103	0.489
Hispanic upper middle	−0.091	0.374	0.192	0.402
Hispanic upper	0.019	0.435	0.616	0.531
Black lower	−0.637***	0.175	0.049	0.539
Black lower middle	−0.713***	0.209	−0.096	0.424
Black upper middle	−0.243	0.293	−0.117	0.341
Black upper	−0.461	0.313	0.103	0.320
Ascribed characteristics				
Age at wave 3	—	—	0.239***	0.029
Parent foreign born	—	—	0.438**	0.144
Ecological background				
Composition of origin family				
Two biological parents	—	—	—	—
Biological and stepparent	—	—	−0.473**	0.169
One biological parent	—	—	−0.214+	0.118
No biological parent	—	—	0.823*	0.407
Family material resources				
Household income	—	—	−0.003	0.008
Access to health insurance				
No coverage	—	—	—	—
Coverage less than a year	—	—	0.092	0.153
Coverage a full year	—	—	0.191	0.145
Family symbolic resources				
Parental prestige	—	—	−0.006+	0.003
Parent went to college	—	—	−0.023	0.164
Family emotional resources				
Experienced a death	—	—	0.337	0.195
Family sternness	—	—	0.011***	0.003

Table 4.2   *(continued)*

Independent Variables	Group Effects		Full Model	
	B	SE	B	SE
Father incarcerated	—	—	−0.222+	0.135
Had family mentor	—	—	0.184	0.135
Neighborhood setting				
Disadvantage index	—	—	−0.108	0.103
Inefficacy index	—	—	0.037+	0.020
Scarcity of males	—	—	0.192*	0.079
Neighborhood mentor	—	—	−0.089	0.167
School setting				
Disadvantage index	—	—	0.006	0.008
Inefficacy index	—	—	−0.015+	0.009
Disorder index	—	—	−0.004	0.023
School mentor	—	—	0.161	0.136
Religious setting				
Religiosity scale	—	—	0.021+	0.012
Involvement index	—	—	0.071***	0.018
Had religious mentor	—	—	−0.476	0.359
Peer setting				
Violence index	—	—	−0.138***	0.033
Friend attempted suicide	—	—	0.001	0.136
Had peer mentor	—	—	−0.036	0.129
Multiple disadvantages				
Log of interactive index	—	—	−0.079**	0.026
Intercept	16.608***	0.120	12.594***	1.155
N	4,072		3,204	
F-test	4.59*		11.16***	
R^2	0.031		0.209	

Source: Authors' calculations based on data set described in Harris and Udry (2008).
$+p < .10$; $*p < .05$; $**p < .01$; $***p < .001$

As before, when age, foreign origins, and ecological circumstances are held constant, race-class differences in the age of first intercourse between blacks and whites disappear, while the Hispanic and Asian coefficients tend to persist. Hispanics experience the same average age of sexual debut as upper-class whites regardless of class, and lower-class and lower-middle-class Asians exhibit much older ages of first intercourse. Although the coefficient for lower-class Asians loses significance because the standard error rises with the addition of so many variables, the point estimate is higher than in the baseline model. Thus the late age of sexual debut in these two groups of Asian women appears not to be explained by ecological or ascribed characteristics.

As the right-hand columns show, age at first intercourse is positively related to age at the time of the Wave 3 interview, which implies that the age of sexual debut is dropping over time. Age of sexual debut also varies with immigrant status. Those with a foreign-born parent experience first intercourse about 0.4 years later than those with a native parent. Thus, not only are the children of immigrants less likely to initiate sexual activity, they also begin at older ages when they finally do initiate sex. Among ecological variables, age of first sex is quite strongly determined by family background. Compared with women who grew up in a household with two biological parents, those who came of age with a stepparent begin intercourse about 0.5 year earlier and those coming from a single-parent household begin 0.2 years earlier. In contrast, those who grew up without either biological parent began having sex an average of about 0.8 years later. Age of sexual debut is also increased by family sternness, rising by 0.011 years per scale unit but is decreased by having an incarcerated father (by 0.2 years, on average) and by having more prestigious parents (with age at debut falling by 0.006 years for each unit on the scale of occupation prestige, which has an observed range of 0 to 78).

Other facets of a young woman's social ecology also make a difference. Within neighborhoods, age of first intercourse is increased by a demographic scarcity of young males, as one would logically expect. The higher the ratio of young single women to young single men in the neighborhood, the older the age at which young women begin having sex. Age at sexual debut is also modestly reduced by greater social inefficacy within neighborhoods ($p < .10$), suggesting that in neighborhoods characterized by a lack of interpersonal trust and social solidarity, women begin sexual activity earlier. Within the religious sphere, the age of first intercourse is increased somewhat by greater religiosity ($p < .10$) but is more powerfully affected by religious involvement ($p < .001$). With each additional unit on the involvement scale, age of first intercourse rises by 0.071 years, for a potential increase of 0.85 years going from the minimum to maximum observed value. Greater religiosity thus reduces the odds of sexual debut and greater religious involvement delays the age of entry into sexual activity among those who do have sex.

Within the peer setting, exposure to higher levels of violence is strongly associated with earlier intercourse ($p < .001$), age of sexual debut decreasing by 0.14 years per unit on the peer violence scale. Age of sexual debut is also lowered by exposure to multiple disadvantages across family, school, neighborhood, and peer settings, each unit increase on the logarithmic scale lowering the age of first intercourse by around 0.08 years ($p < .01$). The age of sexual debut is also increased by exposure to greater inefficacy at school, though the effect is more modest ($p < .10$).

Generalizing from the foregoing results, the ecological circumstances that predict a higher likelihood and early age of first intercourse for a young woman are growing up in a step- or single-parent family that lacks a stern disciplinary style, experiencing low collective efficacy at school and a high interpersonal violence among peers, and coming of age in a neighborhood with a skewed sex ratio and relatively few young men. The accumulation of these conditions across social spheres also functions interactively to lower the age of first intercourse. The main ecological circumstances counterbalancing these tendencies toward early sexualization occur in the religious sphere. Among young women, greater religiosity strongly reduces the likelihood of first intercourse, whereas religiosity and especially greater religious involvement increases the age of the sexual debut.

In some ways, what is remarkable of this analysis of sexuality among young women in the United States is what is *not* significant in determining behavior. Neither the odds nor the age of first intercourse are related in any way to material circumstances in the family; household income and access to health insurance play no role. The entry into sexual experience is also largely unaffected by the symbolic resources parental education or occupational prestige. The former was never significant, and the latter only marginally significant in one of the four models considered. Rather than material or symbolic resources, the sexual behavior of young American women seems to be grounded more in family composition and family emotional resources, social efficacy in schools and neighborhoods, demographic imbalances within neighborhoods, exposure to violence among peers, and religious belief and practice.

UNPROTECTED SEX

Early transition into sexual intercourse entails a variety of risks reviewed at the outset of this chapter. But sexual activity need not carry risks to health and well-being if appropriate measures are taken. The use of condoms during sexual intercourse offers protection against sexually transmitted diseases as well as unwanted births, and the use of other forms of contraception such as birth

Figure 4.3   Sex Without Contraception

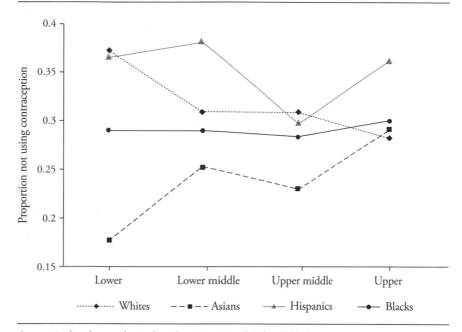

Source: Authors' compilation based on Harris and Udry (2008).

control pills, patches, or IUDs (intrauterine device) lower the likelihood of teenage or unwed pregnancy. Even if the latter methods do not protect against sexually transmitted diseases, childbearing is itself a serious health risk, especially for very young women. Also, as noted earlier, youthful childbearing generally has negative social and economic consequences for children.

The Adolescent Health Survey asked respondents whether they used contraception during their first sexual encounter, and figure 4.3 plots the frequency of those who said no by race and class. The percentage having unprotected sex displays a complicated pattern of variation by race and class. Among whites, we see a clear class gradient, the share having risky sex falling from around 37 percent in the lower class to 31 percent in the lower middle class and upper middle class, and then to 28 percent in the upper class. Blacks, by contrast, display no class gradient whatsoever. Across all classes, the share having unprotected sex is about the same as in the most advantaged white category, around 28 percent, except for the upper class itself, which is slightly higher at 30 percent. Asians, by contrast, display a rising propensity for unprotected sex as social class rises, from around 17 percent in the lower class, to 23 percent in the lower middle, to 25 percent in the upper middle classes, to 29 percent in the upper class. Hispanics display no strong class pattern but on average show the greatest proclivity to engage in unprotected sex (29 percent to 38 percent).

Table 4.3 considers patterns of racial and class variation in the likelihood that young women have unprotected sex at first intercourse and the degree to which this variation can be explained by differences in social ecology. The baseline model shown in left-hand columns confirm what we observed in the graph: that African Americans indeed display no class gradient, all classes statistically displaying the same propensity toward unprotected sex as upper-class whites. The same is true of Asian women, suggesting that the low probability of using contraception observed in figure 4.3 obtains for Asian men but not Asian women (confirmed by the analysis of male behavior included in the supplementary online material at https://www.russellsage.org/publications/sphere-influence).

Among Hispanics, the only significant effect is for lower-middle-class women, who display a higher likelihood of engaging in unprotected sex, but aside from this exception no class pattern is discernable, other classes of Hispanic women displaying the same likelihood as upper-class white women. Consistent with our visual inspection of figure 4.3, we do observe a significant class gradient among white women, the odds of having unprotected sex being about 60 percent greater in the lower class, 33 percent greater in the lower middle class, and 20 percent greater in the upper middle class, relative to upper-class white women.

The latter class gradient disappears entirely once ecological circumstances are controlled, however, as does the outlying positive effect of lower-middle-class status among Hispanic women. More striking is that all of the black coefficients become negative, three of four being statistically significant. Because conditions in the ecological settings occupied by African Americans are disadvantaged and tend to promote unprotected sex, blacks are actually revealed—when background conditions are equalized—to have a remarkably low propensity to initiate sex without contraception. Compared with upper-class white women, the odds unprotected sex among black women are 65 percent lower for the lower class, 73 percent lower for the lower middle class, 39 percent lower for the upper middle class, and 44 percent lower for the upper class. Holding ecological circumstances constant, in other words, we

Table 4.3   Likelihood of Not Using Contraception During First Female Intercourse

Independent Variables	Group Effects		Full Model	
	B	SE	B	SE
Race-class group				
White lower	0.467**	0.164	−0.669	0.527
White lower middle	0.285+	0.163	−0.578	0.373
White upper middle	0.186	0.155	−0.280	0.263
White upper	—	—	—	—
Asian lower	0.095	0.523	−0.868	0.813
Asian lower middle	0.335	0.429	−0.128	0.592
Asian upper middle	0.193	0.605	−0.467	0.472
Asian upper	0.303	0.307	0.126	0.451
Hispanic lower	0.378	0.259	−0.812	0.636
Hispanic lower middle	0.566*	0.248	−0.254	0.452
Hispanic upper middle	0.335	0.312	−0.481	0.414
Hispanic upper	0.383	0.314	0.192	0.412
Black lower	0.046	0.179	−1.060**	0.557
Black lower middle	−0.068	0.232	−1.297**	0.434
Black upper middle	0.055	0.231	−0.679+	0.382
Black upper	−0.190	0.309	−0.575	0.403
Ascribed characteristics				
Age at wave 3	—	—	0.042	0.038
Parent foreign born	—	—	−0.150	0.211
Mediating conditions				
Age at first intercourse	—	—	−0.157***	0.024
Ecological background				
Composition of origin family				
Two biological parents	—	—	—	—
Biological and stepparent	—	—	−0.276	0.174
One biological parent	—	—	−0.005	0.143
No biological parent	—	—	−0.941+	0.499
Family material resources				
Household income	—	—	−0.014	0.009
Access to health insurance				
No coverage	—	—	—	—
Coverage less than a year	—	—	−0.119	0.145
Coverage full year	—	—	−0.247+	0.138
Family symbolic resources				
Parental prestige	—	—	−0.002	0.003
Parent went to college	—	—	0.136	0.163

Table 4.3 *(continued)*

Independent Variables	Group Effects		Full Model	
	B	SE	B	SE
Family emotional resources				
Experienced a death	—	—	–0.246	0.246
Family sternness	—	—	–0.008*	0.003
Father incarcerated	—	—	–0.119	0.156
Had family mentor	—	—	–0.025	0.134
Neighborhood setting				
Disadvantage index	—	—	0.091	0.121
Inefficacy index	—	—	0.001	0.019
Scarcity of males	—	—	–0.127	0.180
Had neighborhood mentor	—	—	0.140	0.237
School setting				
Disadvantage index	—	—	0.021**	0.007
Inefficacy index	—	—	0.006	0.010
Disorder index	—	—	–0.013	0.022
Had school mentor	—	—	–0.232	0.154
Religious setting				
Religiosity scale	—	—	0.006	0.016
Involvement index	—	—	–0.009	0.018
Had religious mentor	—	—	0.403	0.366
Peer setting				
Violence index	—	—	0.043	0.027
Friend attempted suicide	—	—	0.232	0.216
Had peer mentor	—	—	0.134	0.162
Multiple disadvantages				
Log of interactive index	—	—	0.024	0.024
Intercept	–0.797***	0.119	1.238	1.219
N	4,034		3,167	
F-test	1.51		3.90***	

Source: Authors' calculations based on data set described in Harris and Udry (2008).
$+p < .10$; $*p < .05$; $**p < .01$; $***p < .001$

observe a reverse class gradient among black women in which the lower class are less likely to engage in unprotected sex than the higher classes.

In addition to the ascribed characteristics of age and foreign origins, the model takes into account age of first intercourse as a mediating factor. Not surprisingly, the older the age at first intercourse the more likely a woman is to use contraception. Thus, the various ecological factors that push black women toward sex at younger ages—exposure to a step- or single-parent household, a permissive rather than stern emotional style in the family, low collective efficacy at school, high interpersonal violence among peers, and skewed sex ratios in neighborhoods—indirectly increase the odds that the sexual debut will be unprotected. In addition to its indirect effect through age at first intercourse, the sternness of the family also functions directly to influence the odds of unprotected sex. Each unit increase in sternness reduced the odds of unprotected sex by around 0.7 percent, for a total potential effect of 70 percent. The only other strong effect is the material deprivation of the school. With each unit increase in school disadvantage, the likelihood of unprotected sex rises by around 2 percent. Growing up without a biological parent and with full health insurance coverage reduces the likelihood of unprotected sex, but the effects are marginal ($p < .10$).

In sum, the foregoing analyses reveal relatively minor differences by race and class in the odds of unprotected sex during first intercourse both before and after the introduction of ecological controls. In the absence of such controls, whites displayed a modest class gradient, the odds of unprotected sex falling as class rose. Lower-middle-class Hispanics were outliers, displaying an elevated likelihood of not using contraception. These differences, however, disappeared once ecological circumstances, ascribed characteristics, and predetermined conditions were controlled. What is perhaps most remarkable is the appearance of strong negative effects for African Americans once controls are applied. The implication is that if young African American women were to experience the same ecological circumstances as privileged groups in U.S. society, they would exhibit a significantly lower likelihood of engaging in unprotected sex than other groups. In addition, they would follow a reverse class gradient, whereby the lowest classes are least likely to eschew contraception, though all classes would remain more likely to use contraception during initial sex than upper-class whites.

The most important single predictor of the use of contraception during first intercourse was the age at which it occurred—the older young people were at the time of their sexual debut, the more likely they were to use contraception. Ecological circumstances that push young people toward early intercourse thus also raise the odds that the sexual encounter will be unprotected. Beyond age of sexual debut, family circumstances seem to matter most. Full access to health insurance coverage and family sternness together reduced the odds of unprotected sex among both men and women. In addition, material disadvantage at school increased the likelihood of unprotected sex among women, whereas among men it was exposure to peer violence that did so.

PAIRING UP

In the past, sexual activity was strongly connected to marriage and part of a socially sanctioned compact in which men acquired access to sex and women acquired a publicly recognized partner who would assume responsibility for any children that arose from the sexual union (McLanahan 2004). Effective contraception and the concomitant sexual revolution dramatically changed these circumstances, allowing women to engage in sex with multiple partners if they so choose without risk of pregnancy and with no particular incentive to marry. Since the 1960s, sex among American women has increasingly occurred outside marriage through informal pairings of varying stability and duration (Michael et al. 1994).

When sexual partners take up residence and live together, the arrangement is generally known as cohabitation and such informal living arrangements have become increasingly common throughout the developed world (Jayakody, Thornton, and Axinn 2007; Thornton, Axinn, and Xie 2007). Among American women age fifteen to forty-four, for example, about 50 percent have cohabited at some point in their lives, either before, after, or instead of marriage, whereas just 23 percent had married but never cohabited and 27 percent had neither married nor cohabited (Goodwin, Mosher, and Chandra 2010).

Figure 4.4 shows the share of Add Health respondents who had ever cohabited by Wave 3 of the survey classified by race and class. Asians again stand out from the other racial groups for their low likelihood of cohabitation, which ranges from 18 percent to 25 percent, with no particular class pattern. The frequency in other groups is much greater and generally displays a declining pattern with respect to social class. Among whites, for example, the frequency of cohabitation was 55 percent in the lower class, 47 percent in the lower middle class, 38 percent in the upper middle class, and 33 percent in the upper class. Likewise, the relative frequency of cohabitation among Hispanics was just under 40 percent in the lower and lower middle classes, 35 percent in the upper middle class, and 29 percent in the upper class. Among African Americans, the share is around 47 percent in the lower and

Figure 4.4   Ever Cohabiting

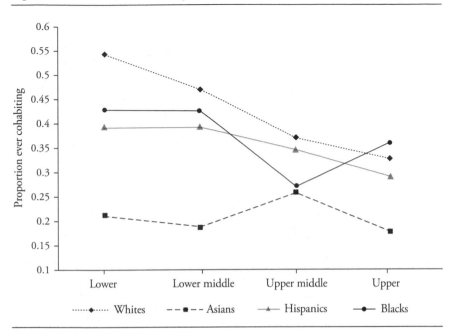

Source: Authors' compilation based on Harris and Udry (2008).

lower middle classes versus 26 percent in the upper middle class and 36 percent in the upper class.

Figure 4.5 presents a comparable graph showing the percentage of respondents who had ever married by Wave 3. As one might expect given the greater commitment involved in marriage, the frequencies are much lower than in the prior figure. Whereas rates of cohabitation ranged from 20 percent to 55 percent depending on race and class, rates of marriage ranged from only 5 percent to 27 percent. In this figure, however, Asians do not stand out for their low percentages, but the class pattern is quite different from other groups. After declining from 17 percent to 9 percent from the lower to lower middle class, the percentage ever married rises thereafter, reaching 13 percent in the upper middle class and 15 percent in the upper class, thus producing a U-shaped curve.

In contrast, the percentage ever married declines monotonically with class among other groups, though African Americans stand out for their very low likelihood of marriage across all classes. In the lower, lower middle, and upper

Figure 4.5   Ever Married

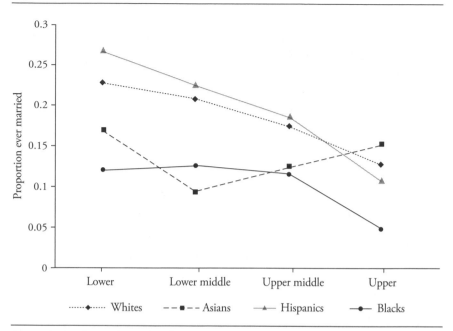

Source: Authors' compilation based on Harris and Udry (2008).

middle classes, for example, the percentage of black women who had ever married ranges narrowly between 12 percent and 13 percent before falling to 5 percent in the upper class. In contrast, among Hispanics the share ever married stood at 27 percent among those in the lower class, falling to 23 percent in the lower middle class, 18 percent in the upper middle class, and 11 percent in the upper class. Among whites the percentage married fell from 23 percent in the lower class to figures of 21 percent, 18 percent, and 13 percent in the lower middle, upper middle, and upper classes, respectively.

Asians are thus characterized by low rates of cohabitation and by not displaying a declining pattern of either marriage or cohabitation with rising social class, whereas blacks are characterized by very low rates of marriage. Having married or cohabited by Wave 3 are not mutually exclusive states, of course, and cohabitation often leads to marriage. Table 4.4 therefore uses a bivariate probit model to estimate the likelihood that young women in the Adolescent Health Survey had ever married or ever cohabited by Wave 3, treating the two states as separate but interrelated outcomes. This table esti-

Table 4.4   Likelihood of Female Cohabitation and Marriage

Independent Variables	Marriage		Cohabitation	
	B	SE	B	SE
Race-class group				
White lower	0.498***	0.125	0.584***	0.083
White lower middle	0.403***	0.097	0.353***	0.080
White upper middle	0.224**	0.083	0.108	0.074
White upper	—	—	—	—
Asian lower	0.316	0.386	−0.294	0.406
Asian lower middle	0.032	0.234	−0.471	0.289
Asian upper middle	0.147	0.307	−0.253	0.218
Asian upper	0.132	0.214	−0.600**	0.202
Hispanic lower	0.506**	0.169	0.081	0.185
Hispanic lower middle	0.382**	0.139	0.053	0.187
Hispanic upper middle	0.192	0.206	0.067	0.180
Hispanic upper	−0.216	0.233	0.066	0.220
Black lower	−0.141	0.130	0.216*	0.103
Black lower middle	−0.029	0.148	0.154	0.129
Black upper middle	−0.149	0.211	−0.318*	0.133
Black upper	−0.560**	0.205	−0.122	0.165
Intercept	−1.001***	0.073	−0.335***	0.062
Rho	0.160***	0.037		
N	4,755			
F-test	6.32***			

Source: Authors' calculations based on data set described in Harris and Udry (2008).
+$p < .10$; *$p < .05$; **$p < .01$; ***$p < .001$

mates a baseline model containing only dummy variables for race and class. The equations for marriage and cohabitation are estimated simultaneously, the reference category being never married or cohabited. Because cohabitation and marriage are not independent, the model estimates a rho coefficient to measure the degree to which entry into the two kinds of unions are associated with one another on a 0 to 1.0 scale. The estimated coefficient of 0.16 indicates a mild positive association between cohabitation and marriage among young women. At young ages, cohabitation thus appears to be more of an alternative than a precursor to marriage.

As indicated by the coefficients, white women display a clear class gradient in the proclivity to marry and cohabit, with the tendency toward partnering being greatest for women in the lower class, and declining progressively through the lower middle, upper middle, and upper classes. Compared with upper-class white women, the odds of marrying are 65 percent greater in the lower class, 50 percent greater in the lower middle class, and 25 percent greater in the upper middle class. Similarly, the odds of cohabitation are 79 percent greater for lower class white women compared with those in the upper class, 42 percent greater for lower-middle-class white women, and 11 percent greater for upper middle class women (though the last effect is not statistically significant).

Hispanic women display a similar class gradient with respect to marriage, but are relatively unlikely to cohabit in any class. Whereas lower-class Hispanic women are 66 percent more likely to marry than upper-class white women, their lower-middle-class counterparts are 47 percent more likely, and upper-middle-class Hispanic women 21 percent more likely. Hispanic women in all classes, however, display the same likelihood of cohabitation as upper-class white women. In contrast, Asian women are unlikely either to marry or cohabit irrespective of social class. In all cases save one, Asian women display the same odds of marriage and cohabitation as upper-class white women. Only upper-class Asian women are different, being 55 percent less likely to cohabit than their white counterparts.

Young black women are likewise unlikely to marry in any class, but especially in the upper middle and upper classes, where the demographic shortage of males is amplified by a remarkable social scarcity of men who have made it through college to join the ranks of the educated classes (Massey and Probosco 2010). Whereas black lower-class, lower-middle-class, and upper-middle-class black women have the same low likelihood of marriage as upper-class white women, the odds are actually 42 percent lower for upper-class black women. In terms of cohabitation, lower-class black women are 24 percent more likely to cohabit than upper-class white women, a figure well below that of lower-class white women. Other classes are either as or less likely to cohabit as upper-class white women.

In general, then, marriage and cohabitation are relatively common among white women, the likelihood varying by class and falling from lower to upper. Marriage is also common among Hispanic women, and indicates the same class pattern as among white women, but Hispanic females are very unlikely to cohabit. Asian women are unlikely either to marry or cohabit. Black women, especially those in the upper class, are unlikely to marry and, except for those in the lower class, are also relatively unlikely to cohabit.

Table 4.5 adds in controls for the ascribed characteristics of age and foreign origins as well as ecological circumstances in the family, neighborhood, school, religious, and peer environments and also takes as predetermined whether or not the respondent had begun having sex. Age at first intercourse cannot be included in the model because of excessive colinearity. As the table makes clear, the addition of controls eliminates the class differentials initially observed among white women, implying that if all whites experienced the same ecological circumstances, their behavior as upper-class whites with respect to marriage and cohabitation would be the same. Adding controls does not affect the relative propensity of Asian women to marry, but does cause the negative coefficients for cohabitation among the lower and lower middle classes to increase and become significant at the 10 percent level. Other things equal, therefore, young Asian women of all classes display the same likelihood of marriage as upper-class white women but have a stronger aversion to cohabitation.

The addition of controls also highlights the unique position of African American women in the partnering process. Of the eight coefficients shown, all are negative and seven are significant at least at the 10 percent level. In other words, other things equal, black women are very unlikely to marry irrespective of social class and are also quite unlikely even to cohabit. For black women, entering into a stable romantic union of any kind is a remote possibility. Given that black women are more likely to have sex, and to do so at younger ages than other groups, this result implies that most of the sex they experience occurs outside a stable relationship. In terms of exposure to the risk of unwed or teenage childbearing, this situation puts them at a clear disadvantage compared with other groups, despite their greater proclivity to use contraception during intercourse.

As one would logically expect, the likelihood of marriage and cohabitation increase with age and are markedly greater for those who have begun having sex. Very few young people in today's world are virgins when they marry. Each year of age increases the odds of marriage by 26 percent and the odds of cohabiting by 12 percent. Prior sexual experience increases the odds of both marriage and cohabitation by a factor of more than four. Foreign origins, however, has no effect on either marriage or cohabitation.

Table 4.5   Likelihood of Female Cohabitation and Marriage

Independent Variables	Marriage		Cohabitation	
	B	SE	B	SE
Race-class group				
White lower	−0.399	0.315	−0.257	0.313
White lower middle	−0.181	0.215	−0.137	0.223
White upper middle	−0.079	0.158	−0.154	0.165
White upper	—	—	—	—
Asian lower	−0.619	0.474	−1.056+	0.584
Asian lower middle	−0.587	0.423	−0.631+	0.349
Asian upper middle	0.108	0.398	−0.330	0.286
Asian upper	0.310	0.401	−0.700*	0.334
Hispanic lower	−0.558	0.366	−0.630	0.416
Hispanic lower middle	−0.269	0.291	−0.507	0.314
Hispanic upper middle	−0.345	0.289	−0.417	0.308
Hispanic upper	−0.367	0.347	−0.304	0.256
Black lower	−1.554***	0.374	−0.636+	0.383
Black lower middle	−1.007***	0.310	−0.493+	0.284
Black upper middle	−0.985***	0.252	−0.599**	0.238
Black upper	−1.274***	0.256	−0.212	0.234
Ascribed characteristics				
Age at wave 3	0.234***	0.023	0.114***	0.022
Parent foreign born	0.055	0.172	−0.089	0.121
Mediating conditions				
Had first intercourse	1.419***	0.210	1.413***	0.129
Ecological background				
Family configuration				
Two biological parents	—	—	—	—
Biological and stepparent	0.075	0.130	0.251*	0.106
One biological parent	−0.200*	0.089	0.182*	0.090
No biological parent	−0.243	0.310	0.217	0.300
Family material resources				
Household income	−0.011*	0.005	−0.006	0.005
Access to health insurance				
No coverage	—	—	—	—
Coverage less than a year	0.041	0.114	0.115	0.118
Coverage full year	−0.002	0.103	−0.213*	0.088
Family symbolic resources				
Parental prestige	−0.002	0.002	−0.001	0.002
Parent went to college	0.007	0.128	−0.178+	0.099
Family emotional resources				
Experienced a death	0.031	0.157	0.049	0.138

Table 4.5   (continued)

Independent Variables	Marriage		Cohabitation	
	B	SE	B	SE
Family sternness	−0.002	0.002	−0.005*	0.001
Father incarcerated	0.079	0.088	0.279***	0.073
Had family mentor	0.080	0.088	−0.139+	0.084
Neighborhood setting				
Disadvantage index	0.158*	0.079	−0.097	0.073
Inefficacy index	0.002	0.014	−0.015	0.012
Scarcity of males	−0.051	0.153	−0.026	0.083
Had family mentor	0.170	0.165	−0.008	0.146
School setting				
Disadvantage index	−0.007	0.007	0.003	0.005
Inefficacy index	0.005	0.008	0.013*	0.006
Disorder index	0.013	0.016	0.003	0.014
Had school mentor	−0.272*	0.137	−0.122	0.094
Religious setting				
Religiosity scale	0.028***	0.009	−0.014+	0.008
Involvement index	0.014	0.013	−0.023*	0.011
Had religious mentor	0.432*	0.180	−0.398*	0.190
Peer setting				
Violence index	−0.010	0.019	0.068***	0.020
Friend attempted suicide	−0.181	0.134	0.086	0.116
Had peer mentor	0.118	0.115	0.061	0.107
Multiple disadvantages				
Log of interactive index	0.034+	0.019	0.018	0.016
Intercept	−7.829***	0.935	−3.344***	0.899
Rho	−0.004	0.043		
N	3,733			
F-test	29.64***			

Source: Authors' calculations based on data set described in Harris and Udry (2008).
+*p* < .10; **p* < .05; ***p* < .01; ****p* < .001

Among ecological settings, the family and religious spheres appear to carry the most weight in determining union formation among women. Consistent with the existing literature, women who grew up in single-parent or step-families were more likely to cohabit than those growing up with two biological parents, and those growing in single-parent families were less likely to marry. For women originating in a single-parent household, the odds of cohabitation were 20 percent lower and the odds of marriage were 18 percent higher, whereas those growing up with a stepparent displayed 29 percent greater odds of cohabiting. In terms of material resources, higher income reduced the likelihood of marriage, which fell by 1.1 percent for each additional $1,000 dollars. Access to full health insurance coverage likewise lowered the odds of cohabitation by 19 percent and having a college-educated parent reduced the odds of cohabitation by 16 percent ($p < .10$).

In general, however, the decision to cohabit was most strongly connected to emotional than material or symbolic resources in the family. Each unit increase on the family sternness scale decreased the odds of cohabitation by 0.5 percent ($p < .05$) and having a family mentor reduced them by 13 percent ($p < .0.10$). The biggest effect, however, was having a father in jail or prison. Those young women whose father had been incarcerated displayed 32 percent greater odds of cohabiting than other women. None of these emotional circumstances had any apparent influence on the likelihood of marriage, however.

As one might expect, religiosity dramatically increased the likelihood of marriage (by 2.8 percent per unit, $p < .001$), yielding a total effect of 50 percent over the range of the scale, and more modestly reduced the likelihood of cohabitation (1.4 percent per unit, $p < .10$). Having a religious mentor likewise increased the odds of marriage and decreased the odds of cohabitation, raising the former by 54 percent and decreasing the latter by 33 percent. Religious involvement, however, decreased the odds of cohabitation, lowering them by 2.3 percent per unit of involvement, but had no effect on the likelihood of marriage.

In the neighborhood sphere, material disadvantage increased the odds of marriage, raising them by 17 percent per unit, for a total potential effect of 48 percent, but had no effect on cohabitation. In the school setting, having a mentor lowered the odds of marriage by 24 percent, whereas a lack of social efficacy increased the odds of cohabitation, raising them by 1.3 percent per unit on the inefficacy scale, for a total potential effect of 52 percent over the range of the index. Exposure to violence in the peer setting strongly increased the odds of cohabitation, raising them by 7 percent per unit on the violence scale, yielding a large potential total effect of 140 percent. Finally, the experience of multiple disadvantages across social spheres had a marginal ($p < .10$) effect in raising the odds of marriage, thus heightening the positive effect of neighborhood disadvantage.

UNWED PARENTHOOD

The key event in biological reproduction is obviously childbirth. As discussed earlier, however, the social circumstances of birth have powerful implications for the future welfare of parents and children. Research indicates basically two kinds of risky childbearing: giving birth outside marriage and having a child at a young age. Figure 4.6 shows the percentage of Add Health respondents who had become unwed parents by Wave 3 to reveal a very clear racial ordering in this risky outcome. The highest proportions are observed among blacks, followed by Hispanics, whites, and finally at a significantly lower level, Asians. Although social class clearly influences the relative propensity toward unwed parenthood within racial groups, it does not affect the racial rank ordering. Although the four curves touch at two points, they never really cross.

As one would expect given their lower rate of sexual debut, later age of first intercourse, and low likelihood of unprotected sex, Asians are extremely un-

Figure 4.6   Unwed Parents

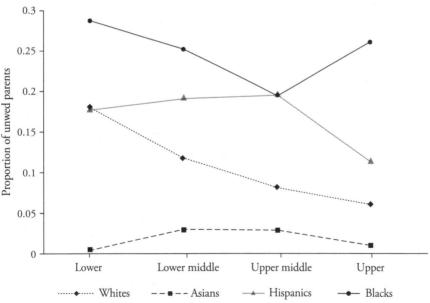

Source: Authors' compilation based on Harris and Udry (2008).

likely to become unwed parents. The share is essentially zero in the lower class, around 4 percent in the lower and upper middle classes, and 2 percent in the upper class. Thus Asians regardless of class tend to avoid the social risk of unwed parenthood. At the other extreme are African Americans. Again, consistent with their displaying the highest likelihood of sexual debut, the lowest age of first intercourse, and the lowest propensity to marry, the rate of unwed childbearing is quite high. By Wave 3 of the survey, 28 percent of lower-class black respondents reported having a child out of wedlock. Although the frequency declined to 25 percent and 20 percent in the lower middle and upper middle classes, respectively, in the upper class it rose back up to 26 percent. Thus unwed parenthood is by no means confined to the lower echelons of the black class distribution.

Although the frequency of unwed parenthood among Hispanics rose slightly, from around 18 percent in the lower class to 19 percent and 20 percent in the lower and upper middle classes, it dropped precipitously to just 12 percent in the upper class. For their part, whites displayed the clearest and most consistent class gradient, the share of unwed parents dropping from 18 percent in the lower class to 12 percent in the lower middle class and then 8 percent and 6 percent in the upper middle and upper classes, respectively. In terms of this form of risky reproduction, therefore, race clearly trumps class, even though class does play a modifying role among whites and, to a lesser extent, Hispanics.

We model the childbearing decision in table 4.6 using a multinomial logit model to predict whether young female respondents to Add Health gave birth to a child inside or outside marriage by Wave 3 (no children serving as the reference category). This table presents the baseline model using dummy variables to indicate the various race-class combinations and the left-hand columns very clearly confirm statistically what the prior figure showed visually: that nonmarital childbearing is much, much higher for African Americans than all other groups, especially in the lower classes. Compared with upper-class white women, for example, the odds of extramarital childbearing among blacks were 8.3 times greater for the lower class and 7.2 times greater for the lower middle class. The next highest effect is for lower-middle-class Hispanic women, whose odds of unwed childbearing were five times greater than upper-class white women. Although the likelihood of unwed mother-hood does not reach these heights for upper-middle-class and upper-class-

Table 4.6   Likelihood of Motherhood Within and Outside of Marriage

Independent Variables	Nonmarital Motherhood		Marital Motherhood	
	B	SE	B	SE
Race-class group				
White lower	1.562***	0.218	1.229***	0.277
White lower middle	0.846**	0.274	0.938***	0.254
White upper middle	0.570*	0.258	0.520	0.230
White upper	—	—	—	—
Asian lower	−2.534***	1.004	−0.103	0.965
Asian lower middle	−0.031	0.555	0.767	0.482
Asian upper middle	−0.926	0.807	−2.347**	0.919
Asian upper	−1.131	0.914	0.730	0.534
Hispanic lower	1.250***	0.371	1.227***	0.308
Hispanic lower middle	1.616***	0.401	1.381***	0.335
Hispanic upper middle	1.243**	0.392	0.766+	0.465
Hispanic upper	1.111*	0.508	−1.926**	0.773
Black lower	2.112***	0.271	0.614*	0.303
Black lower middle	1.974***	0.342	0.458	0.402
Black upper middle	1.314***	0.221	0.676	0.472
Black upper	1.379***	0.313	−0.325	0.573
Intercept	−2.471***	0.097	−2.517***	0.219
N	4,767			
F-test	8.62***			

Source: Authors' calculations based on data set described in Harris and Udry (2008).
+$p < .10$; *$p < .05$; **$p < .01$; ***$p < .001$

black women, they are nonetheless quite high, the odds being 3.7 and 4 times greater than upper-class white women, respectively.

The likelihood of nonmarital motherhood is also elevated among Hispanic women. In addition to being five times greater in the lower middle class, the odds of bearing a child out of wedlock are 3.5 times greater in the lower and upper middle classes and three times greater in the upper class, compared with upper-class white women. Among whites, these odds were only reached in the lower class, where they are 4.8 times greater but fall rapidly to 2.3 times greater in the lower middle class and 1.8 times greater in the upper middle class. The likelihood of unwed childbearing is clearly lowest among

Asian women. All four of the class coefficients are negative, though only that for the lower class is significant. Compared with upper-class white women, their odds of bearing a child out of marriage are 92 percent lower. Although the coefficients for upper-middle-class and upper-class Asian women are also quite large and negative, they do not achieve statistical significance because the standard errors are inflated by the combination of small cell sizes and the rarity of the event in question. As the best unbiased estimates, they nonetheless imply reductions of 60 percent and 68 percent in the odds compared with upper-class white women. Thus, regardless of class, Asian women never exceed the low likelihood of unwed childbearing displayed by upper-class white women, and sometimes the odds are much lower than that.

Among whites, the patterns of marital and nonmarital childbearing are quite similar and decline monotonically with rising class status. Whereas the odds of unwed motherhood were 4.8 times, 2.3 times, and 1.8 times greater in the lower, lower middle, and upper middle classes than in the upper class, respectively, the odds of marital childbearing were 3.4 times, 2.6 times, and 1.7 times greater. Although the likelihood of marital and nonmarital childbearing begins at roughly the same point in the lower class among Hispanics, the likelihood of marital childbearing falls more sharply with rising class status. Outside marriage, the relative odds of childbearing among Hispanic women are 3.5, 5, 3.4, and 3 times greater than upper-class white women moving from lower to upper class. In contrast, the respective odds of bearing a child within the confines of marriage are 3.4, 4, 2.2, and 0.14 times those of upper-class white women, moving from lower to upper class. Upper-middle-class and upper-class Hispanic women are apparently more likely to bear children outside than within marriage.

In statistical terms, all Asian women experience marital childbirth to the same extent as upper-class white women, with one exception. Among upper-middle-class Asian women, the odds of marital fertility are extremely low, 90 percent lower than upper-class white women. Indeed, upper-middle-class Asian women are unlikely to bear any children, either inside or outside marriage. Among black women, the odds of marital childbearing are very low, indeed much, much lower than the odds of nonmarital childbearing. Statistically, the probability of marital childbearing for lower-middle, upper-middle, and upper-class black women is the same as that among upper-class white women. The odds of bearing a child inside marriage, in contrast, are 85 percent greater for lower-class black women, but this is small compared with their odds of bearing a child outside of marriage, which are 8.3 times those of white women.

Table 4.7 repeats the foregoing analysis after adding controls. This addition reveals that the patterns of nonmarital childbearing just described are by no means accounted for by differing ecological circumstances. Among African American women, the addition of controls hardly changes the size of the point estimates for the four class categories in the equation predicting unwed fertility. All remain large, positive, and statistically significant. Among Hispanic women, the coefficients for lower-, lower-middle, and upper-middle-class women actually increase slightly in size. Only the coefficient for upper-class Hispanic women drops significantly, but the data in appendix C suggest this shift is likely an artifact of sample attrition rather than a substantive shift (https://www.russellsage.org/publications/sphere-influence). The coefficients for white women increase slightly in size when controls are introduced while preserving the class gradient. The values and significance of the Asian coefficients change somewhat, but the shifts are difficult to interpret given the small cell sizes and large standard errors, and could well be artifacts of sample attrition.

For white and Hispanic women, the class-specific coefficients for marital childbearing also change very little with the addition of controls. Once again, the shifts in the Asian coefficients are difficult to interpret and likely to reflect small numbers and sample attrition. Among black women, the higher level of marital fertility observed in the lower class is reduced and rendered insignificant, a shift that cannot be attributed to sample attrition. The large swing in the size of the negative coefficient for upper-class black women is not substantive, however, and is very likely due to the loss of cases in estimating the full model.

The effects of ascribed characteristics and mediating conditions are generally what one would expect. The likelihood of motherhood increases steadily with age, especially for childbearing within marriage and the odds of unwed childbearing are sharply reduced (by 64 percent) by having immigrant parents, which is perhaps not surprising given that most immigrants come from traditional cultures that regulate female sexuality more than is typical in the United States. Logically enough, those women who have begun sexual activity are much more likely to become mothers, but the connection to intercourse is much stronger for nonmarital than marital childbearing. Thus, having been initiated into sex increases the odds of marital fertility by a factor of

Table 4.7   Likelihood of Marital and Nonmarital Motherhood

Independent Variables	Nonmarital Motherhood		Marital Motherhood	
	B	SE	B	SE
Race-class group				
White lower	1.848**	0.636	1.222	0.865
White lower middle	0.972*	0.495	1.083+	0.599
White upper middle	0.812*	0.378	0.644	0.401
White upper	—	—	—	—
Asian lower	−1.637	1.174	0.464	1.381
Asian lower middle	1.422+	0.802	1.504	1.045
Asian upper middle	0.178	0.965	−1.942+	1.125
Asian upper	−1.469*	0.604	1.574+	0.833
Hispanic lower	2.302**	0.834	1.195	0.963
Hispanic lower middle	2.209***	0.548	1.618*	0.744
Hispanic upper middle	1.475**	0.547	0.349	0.718
Hispanic upper	0.430	0.621	−3.192***	0.994
Black lower	2.157**	0.702	0.114	0.871
Black lower middle	2.149***	0.585	0.152	0.764
Black upper middle	0.967*	0.460	−0.281	0.543
Black upper	1.465**	0.521	−1.955**	0.710
Ascribed characteristics				
Age at wave 3	0.161***	0.051	0.402***	0.054
Parent foreign born	−1.023***	0.312	−0.435	0.367
Mediating conditions				
Had first intercourse	4.679***	0.955	2.339***	0.565
Used no contraception	1.017***	0.138	0.778***	0.139
Ecological background				
Composition of origin family				
Two biological parents	—	—	—	—
Biological and stepparent	0.137	0.273	0.008	0.273
One biological parent	−0.177	0.179	−0.554***	0.172
No biological parent	−0.768	0.801	−0.807	0.840
Family material resources				
Household income	0.027**	0.010	0.019	0.015
Access to health insurance				
No coverage	—	—	—	—
Coverage less than a year	0.361	0.227	0.422	0.262
Coverage full year	0.155	0.227	0.342	0.242
Family symbolic resources				
Parental prestige	−0.003	0.004	0.007	0.005
Parent went to college	0.467+	0.273	0.863**	0.277

Table 4.7   (continued)

Independent Variables	Nonmarital Motherhood		Marital Motherhood	
	B	SE	B	SE
Family emotional resources				
Experienced a death	−1.486***	0.262	−1.269***	0.382
Family sternness	−0.011*	0.004	−0.014***	0.004
Father incarcerated	0.155	0.172	0.230	0.226
Had family mentor	−0.194	0.171	0.107	0.207
Neighborhood setting				
Disadvantage index	0.022	0.168	0.274*	0.134
Inefficacy index	−0.085**	0.030	−0.083***	0.025
Scarcity of males	−0.523+	0.312	−1.467***	0.401
Had neighborhood mentor	−0.418	0.277	−0.088	0.359
School setting				
Disadvantage index	−0.010	0.009	−0.011	0.011
Inefficacy index	−0.031**	.012	−0.018	0.014
Disorder index	0.017	0.036	0.030	0.030
Had school mentor	−0.557*	0.223	−0.495+	0.279
Religious setting				
Religiosity scale	0.005	0.020	0.047**	0.016
Involvement index	0.000	0.028	−0.019	0.024
Had religious mentor	−0.909+	0.511	0.489	0.452
Peer setting				
Violence index	−0.016	0.031	−0.034	0.046
Friend attempted suicide	−0.378	0.244	−0.434	0.327
Had peer mentor	−0.177	0.204	0.054	0.238
Multiple disadvantages				
Log of interactive index	0.235***	0.036	0.248***	0.040
Intercept	−17.880***	2.199	−21.285***	2.378
N	3,680			
F-test	27.08***			

Source: Authors' calculations based on data set described in Harris and Udry (2008).

$+p < .10$; $*p < .05$; $**p < .01$; $***p < .001$

10.3, but it raises nonmarital fertility by a factor of 108. The odds of becoming a mother were also greater if first intercourse was unprotected, suggesting that those who failed to use contraception the first time were likely to do so also on subsequent encounters, or possibly became pregnant as a result of first intercourse. Having first unprotected intercourse increased the odds of marital fertility by a factor of 2.2 and those of nonmarital fertility by 2.8.

Even though the main effects of race and class generally remain after the introduction of ecological controls, the likelihood of unwed childbearing is nonetheless exacerbated by those conditions that increase the likelihood of a sexual debut and raise the likelihood of unprotected sex on that occasion. In the former instance, those conditions are coming from a stepparent household, exposure to peer violence, a lack of collective efficacy at school, a low level of family sternness, the lack of mentors at school and among peers, and, especially, a low level of personal religiosity. In the latter instance, the conditions are lack of health insurance coverage, a low level of family sternness, and enrollment at a disadvantaged school.

Within the family setting, coming from a single-parent household sharply reduces the likelihood of fertility within marriage, lowering the odds by 42 percent compared with women from a two-parent family. Having a college-educated parent increases the odds of marital fertility by a factor of 2.4. Having such a parent also raises the likelihood of nonmarital childbearing, but the effect is more modest, raising the odds by around 60 percent ($p < .10$). Income somewhat surprisingly raises the odds of unwed childbearing (by 2.7 percent for every \$1,000) but has no effect on marital childbearing. The emotional stress of experiencing a death in the family is associated with sharply reduced levels of both marital and nonmarital fertility, however, lowering the former by 72 percent and the latter by 77 percent. In addition, the greater the sternness of a family's emotional tone, the less likely women are to become mothers, the odds dropping by 1.1 percent per unit outside marriage and 1.4 percent per unit inside it.

Three of the four neighborhood indicators have significant effects on childbearing within marriage. Although the degree of material hardship in the neighborhood has no effect on unwed childbearing, it increases the odds of marital fertility by around 32 percent per unit. Thus neighborhood disadvantage both increases the odds of marriage and the likelihood of childbearing within marriage. Not surprisingly, a demographic scarcity of young males reduces the odds of both marital and nonmarital childbearing, but the effect is much greater for the former. Each point shift in the ratio of women to men decreases not only the odds of unwed motherhood by 41 percent, but also those of married childbearing by 77 percent. The likelihood of childbearing is also strongly reduced by a lack of collective efficacy within neighborhoods, the odds of motherhood falling by around 8 percent per unit of inefficacy both inside and outside marriage. The likelihood of childbearing is similarly reduced by inefficacy at school, though the effect is only significant for child-bearing outside marriage, the odds dropping by around 3.1 percent per unit of school inefficacy. Having a school-based mentor also reduces the odds of motherhood, by around 43 percent outside marriage and 39 percent inside marriage.

Religiosity has no direct effect on nonmarital childbearing, (though as noted it has a strong indirect effect through its effect on entry into sexual in-tercourse. However, it does have a powerful effect on childbearing within marriage, raising it by around 4.8 percent per unit, or by 86 percent over the observed range of religiosity. The cumulative effect of disadvantage across spheres of social influence is to raise the odds of both marital and nonmarital childbearing, by 28 percent per unit in the former case and 26 percent per unit in the latter. In terms of social ecology, therefore, motherhood generally appears to be inhibited by a lack of warmth in the family of origin, a lack of social trust in schools and neighborhoods, a scarcity of males, and the pres-ence of a school-based mentor. In contrast, motherhood is encouraged by having a college-educated parent, and experiencing multiple disadvantages across social spheres. Beyond these common effects, childbearing outside marriage is promoted by high income in the family of origin and the lack of a religious mentor, whereas childbearing within marriage is promoted by in-dividual religiosity and coming from a disadvantaged neighborhood.

TEENAGE PARENTHOOD

The second category of risky reproduction is parenthood at an early age. Fig-ure 4.7 thus shows the proportion of Add Health respondents who had be-come parents before the age of eighteen by race and class, yielding a picture of risky reproduction that largely mirrors that presented in the plot of unwed parenthood. Once again, blacks are most prone to teenage parenthood, Asians are the least, and Hispanics and whites are in between. The share of teenage parents varies from around 9 percent to 13 percent for blacks and from 0 percent to 1.5 percent among Asians, both showing little systematic pattern by social class. In contrast, the frequency of teen parenthood falls steadily with rising class status among whites and Hispanics, dropping from 8.5 percent to just under 4 percent in the former and from 9 percent to 5 percent in the latter.

Figure 4.7   Parents Before Age Eighteen

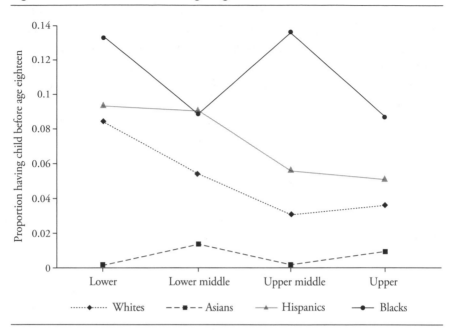

Source: Authors' compilation based on Harris and Udry (2008).

Table 4.8 analyzes these patterns statistically for females. The coefficients in the left-hand columns generally confirm the patterns revealed by inspecting figure 4.7. The odds of bearing a child before the age of eighteen were consistently greater for black women and consistently lower for Asian women regardless of class, whereas white and Asian women display a declining likelihood of teenage childbearing with rising social class. Compared with those of upper-class white women, the odds of early motherhood among Asians are three times greater in the lower class, 2.1 times greater in the lower middle class, and not significantly different in the upper middle class. In contrast, the relative odds are 4.1 times greater for lower-class blacks, 3.1 times greater for lower-middle-class blacks, 3.9 times for upper-middle-class blacks, and 3.2 times greater for upper-class blacks. Hispanic women generally exhibited elevated odds of teenage motherhood in the lower class, lower middle class, and upper class, the relative odds being increased by 2.7 times, 3.8 times, and 2.5 times, respectively.

Table 4.8   Likelihood of Motherhood Before Age Eighteen

Independent Variables	Group Effects		Full Model	
	B	SE	B	SE
Race-class group				
White lower	1.102***	0.299	1.129	0.911
White lower middle	0.745*	0.381	0.593	0.730
White upper middle	0.049	0.354	−0.188	0.540
White upper	—	—	—	—
Asian lower	−3.208**	1.110	−2.937+	1.589
Asian lower middle	−0.545	0.922	−0.018	1.049
Asian upper middle	−2.291***	0.592	−2.652*	1.058
Asian upper	−3.023***	0.728	−2.527***	0.718
Hispanic lower	1.009*	0.436	1.217	0.951
Hispanic lower middle	1.377*	0.542	1.357+	0.776
Hispanic upper middle	0.638	0.508	−0.022	0.834
Hispanic upper	0.897+	0.536	−0.434	0.934
Black lower	1.404***	0.179	1.735+	0.910
Black lower middle	1.129**	0.382	1.326*	0.653
Black upper middle	1.364**	0.428	1.233*	0.599
Black upper	1.171*	0.572	1.050	0.697
Ascribed characteristics				
Age at wave 3	—	—	−0.129*	0.065
Parent foreign born	—	—	−0.081	0.389
Mediating conditions				
Had first intercourse	—	—	6.351***	1.022
Used no contraception	—	—	1.006***	0.161
Ecological background				
Composition of origin family				
Two biological parents	—	—	—	—
Biological and stepparent	—	—	−0.200	0.404
One biological parent	—	—	−0.180	0.249
No biological parent	—	—	−2.434***	0.737
Family material resources				
Household income	—	—	0.021	0.015
Access to health insurance				
No coverage	—	—	—	—
Coverage less than a year	—	—	−0.040	0.307
Coverage a full year	—	—	0.008	0.289
Family symbolic resources				
Parental prestige	—	—	0.000	0.005
Parent went to college	—	—	0.507	0.321

Table 4.8   (continued)

Independent Variables	Group Effects		Full Model	
	B	SE	B	SE
Family emotional resources				
Experienced a death	—	—	−0.835*	0.387
Family sternness	—	—	−0.010+	0.005
Father incarcerated	—	—	−0.021	0.254
Had family mentor	—	—	−0.464*	0.233
Neighborhood setting				
Disadvantage index	—	—	−0.041	0.161
Inefficacy index	—	—	−0.053*	0.027
Scarcity of males	—	—	−0.622	0.461
Had neighborhood mentor	—	—	−0.161	0.366
School setting				
Disadvantage index	—	—	−0.001	0.013
Inefficacy index	—	—	−0.018	0.016
Disorder index	—	—	−0.022	0.035
Had school mentor	—	—	−0.161	0.253
Religious setting				
Religiosity scale	—	—	−0.015	0.022
Involvement index	—	—	0.005	0.030
Had religious mentor	—	—	−2.857**	0.932
Peer setting				
Violence index	—	—	0.072+	0.041
Friend attempted suicide	—	—	−0.145	0.306
Had peer mentor	—	—	−0.109	0.214
Multiple disadvantages				
Log of interactive index	—	—	0.139***	0.042
Intercept	−3.022***	0.289	−10.324***	2.685
N	4,763		3,678	
F-test	8.76***		8.46***	

Source: Authors' calculations based on data set described in Harris and Udry (2008).
+$p < .10$; *$p < .05$; **$p < .01$; ***$p < .001$

These race-class differentials are not really changed by the addition of background characteristics as controls. The coefficients for blacks remain universally high and those for Asians strongly negative with no significant changes in the size of coefficients. Although class effects for whites no longer attain statistical significance at conventional levels, the point estimates are largely unchanged by the addition of controls. The only significant shift is observed among Hispanic women, the elevated likelihood of a teen birth among upper-class women disappearing when background differences are held constant.

As we observed with respect to unwed motherhood, the odds of teen motherhood are significantly and very powerfully raised by a woman's sexual debut (by 573 times) and by not using contraception during first intercourse (by a factor of 2.7). Thus those ecological conditions that push young women toward an early sexual debut greatly and quite logically raise the risk of teenage childbearing. However, the very few women who came of age in a home without either biological parent displayed a much lower likelihood of having a child before the age of eighteen, the odds being lower by 91 percent. The only other family circumstances that influenced the odds of early childbearing were in the emotional sphere. The trauma of a family death reduced the odds of teenage motherhood by 57 percent; having a family mentor reduced them by 37 percent; and a stern emotional tone reduced them by about 1 percent. The odds of a teen birth are also lowered by exposure to social inefficacy in the neighborhood and the presence of a religious mentor. As with the other fertility outcomes, the odds of a teenage birth increase with the accumulation of disadvantage across spheres of influence.

THE ECOLOGY OF RISKY REPRODUCTION

In this chapter, we investigated the pathways to biological reproduction taken by young men and women in the United States at the end of the millennium, analyzing in some detail the rate and age at which they initiate sexual intercourse, the process by which they pair up through cohabitation or marriage, and the circumstances under which they ultimately reproduce by giving birth. In the United States, the postponement of childbearing beyond adolescence and early adulthood has become increasingly important in determining one's status and well-being in society. Postponement of fertility enables young people to complete more education, acquire additional skills, accumulate work experience, and generally establish a career before becoming enmeshed in the time-consuming and emotionally demanding tasks of child rearing.

Prior work has documented sharp differences in the likelihood of unwed and teenage childbearing between racial groups and across social classes and linked them to differentials in health, education, delinquency, and employment. Here we found a clear ordering in the likelihood of risky reproduction among major racial groups, African Americans displaying by far the greatest likelihood of early and unwed childbearing, followed by Hispanics, then whites, and at some distance Asians. We likewise documented social class gradients indicating that the likelihood of unwed and teenage childbearing generally falls with rising social class, at least in some groups.

Few prior studies have considered the effects of race and class simultaneously, however, and our contribution here is to show that race-class interactions in the process of human reproduction are anything but straightforward. Although whites and Hispanics display the typical class pattern of declining unwed and teenage childbearing with rising socioeconomic status, the same was not true of blacks or Asians. The former exhibited a uniquely high probability and the latter a distinctively low probability of these birth outcomes regardless of social class, though Asian patterns were somewhat obscured by the instability of estimates owing to sampling variability.

Having identified these interactions, we sought to understand the reasons for them by contextualizing women's reproductive behavior within the social ecologies they experience, which in chapters 2 and 3 we showed often differ quite dramatically by race and class. The many equations estimated and coefficients interpreted may seem to yield a complex welter of information but when one stands back and considers the overall pattern of results, a relatively straightforward picture does emerge. Table 4.9 summarizes the results of various social ecological analyses we undertook in this chapter.

In this display, the columns refer to the various reproductive outcomes modeled and rows refer to specific elements within the various social spheres considered. The resulting cells contain information about the estimated direction of effects (signaled by plus or minus signs) and their statistical significance (indicated by the number of signs shown, with four indicating $p < .001$, three indicating $p < .01$; two indicating $p < .05$; and one $p < .10$). A blank cell indicates no significant effect in any direction. Looking across the rows reveals whether and how a particular ecological factor determines a particular reproductive outcome. Looking down the columns indicates whether and how a specific outcome is determined by factors in the various social spheres.

The first column shows, for example, that the likelihood of a young woman's sexual debut is positively influenced by originating in a stepparent household, exposure to greater inefficacy at school, and greater violence within the peer network, but negatively predicted by family sternness, school disorder, individual religiosity, and having access to either a school or peer mentor. Of these effects, religiosity is the most significant (indicated by four negative signs), followed by school inefficacy and disorder (with two signs each), with the remaining effects are small (one sign each). The first row shows that originating in a stepparent household plays a significant role in determining the odds of a sexual debut, the age of first intercourse, and the likelihood of cohabitation but has no effect on the use of contraception, marriage, or fertility, the size of the significant effects being greatest for age at first intercourse, followed by cohabitation and then sexual debut.

A careful interpretation of the table allows us to see how young women progress through the stages of reproduction from sexual debut to childbirth. The effects captured in the first two columns yield a profile of the sort of woman prone to early sexual experience, namely one who originated in a stepparent or single-parent household characterized by a relative lack of sternness that imparted little religiosity or religious involvement. She also came from a neighborhood with a relatively favorable ratio of young single men to young single women but attended a school characterized by a lack of mutual trust and faced a peer environment with a high rate of interpersonal violence. She did not have access to mentors in her school or peer group, and her tendency toward early sexual involvement was greatly exacerbated if she experienced multiple disadvantages across social spheres. In addition, judging from the third column, if she succumbed to these social forces and made her sexual debut while attending a materially disadvantaged school, she was unlikely to use contraception, thus raising the odds of early pregnancy.

The social auspices of birth are governed primarily by the process of union formation. Marriage was a relatively likely outcome for a young woman from a religious, two-parent, low-income household living in a disadvantaged neighborhood and subject to the influence of a religious mentor. Cohabitation was likely for a woman from a stepparent or single-parent family without health insurance characterized by a lack of sternness and religiosity as well as the absence of a family mentor and an incarcerated father. A woman likely to cohabit also attended a school characterized by a high degree of social inefficacy and experienced a violent peer environment while facing multiple disadvantages across social spheres, which also acted to depress the odds of marriage.

In general, young women who were most likely to become mothers were those who did not experience the death of a family member, which is strongly disruptive of fertility. She also had a college-educated parent, her family did

Table 4.9 Predicting Female Reproductive Outcomes

	Sexual Debut	Age at Debut	No Contraception	Marriage	Cohabitation	Nonmarital Fertility	Marital Fertility	Teenage Fertility
Family composition								
Biological and stepparent	+	---			++			
One biological parent		-		-	++		---	
No biological parent		++	-					---
Family material resources								
Household income				-		+++		
Health insurance less than a year								
Health insurance a year or more			-		-			
Family symbolic resources								
Parental prestige		-						
Parent college graduate					-	+	+++	
Family emotional resources								
Family mortality						--	--	--
Family sternness	-	++++	--		-	--	---	-
Father incarcerated		-			++++			
Family mentor					-			-

Setting / Variable								
Neighborhood setting								
Disadvantage index				++			++	
Inefficacy index		+				--	—	-
Scarcity of males		++				-	—	
Neighborhood mentor								
School setting								
Disadvantage index	++	-	+++					
Inefficacy index					++	++		
Disorder index	--							
School mentor	-			-		-	-	
Religious setting								
Religiosity scale	---	+		++++	-			
Involvement index	++++	++++			--		+++	
Had religious mentor				++		-		--
Peer setting								
Violence index	+	---			++++			
Friend attempted suicide					++++			+
Peer mentor	-							
Multiple disadvantages								
Interactive index	-				++++	++++	++++	++++

Source: Authors' calculations based on data set described in Harris and Udry (2008).

not have a stern emotional character, she lived in a neighborhood characterized by social efficacy and a relative abundance of young, single men, and she
attended a school in which she found no mentor. This characterization applied to both married and unmarried childbearing. If in addition, the woman
came from a high-income family, attended a school with a high degree of
social inefficacy, did not have a religious mentor, and experienced multiple
disadvantages across spheres, she was likely to give birth outside marriage,
but if she originated in a single-parent family, grew up in a disadvantaged
neighborhood, but was herself very religious, the birth was likely to occur
inside marriage. Teenage motherhood was likewise predicted for women who
lacked access to a religious mentor, experienced violence in their peer networks and, most important, was exposed to disadvantages in multiple social
spheres.

Ultimately, then, the factors that push young women toward early sexual
experience, away from marriage, and toward nonmarital fertility are growing
up with a step- or single parent, a lack of emotional sternness in the family
sphere, inefficacy in the school sphere, a lack of faith and involvement in the
religious sphere, exposure to violence among peers, and the accumulation of
disadvantages across spheres. Table 4.10 summarizes what happens to race-
class differences once such ecological conditions are held constant. As can be
seen, whites, Asians, and Hispanics generally display few significant race-class
differences in the age of first intercourse or the likelihood of sexual debut, use
of contraception, marriage, cohabitation, marital childbearing, and teen
motherhood once ecological circumstances are controlled. Although a few
significant differences in teenage motherhood remain among Asian women,
those that do indicate a lower rather than a higher likelihood of risky
reproduction.

Race-class effects for teenage childbearing are also mostly eliminated by
controls among whites and Hispanics, but strong effects remain with respect
to unwed childbearing. In particular, lower-, lower-middle-, and upper-
middle-class white and Hispanic women display a higher likelihood of unwed
childbearing than the upper class of either group, a pattern of risky reproduction that is mitigated but not explained by differing ecological circumstances.
No group, however, displays the consistently high likelihood of unwed and
teenage childbearing characteristic of African American women regardless of
class. In addition, they differ markedly from other groups in their extremely
low probability of marriage, which increases the risk of teenage and unwed

Table 4.10   Female Reproductive Outcomes

	Sexual Debut	Age at Debut	No Contraception	Marriage	Cohabitation	Nonmarital Fertility	Marital Fertility	Teenage Fertility
WLO						+++		
WLM						++	+	
WUM						++		
ALO					-			-
ALM		++			-	-		
AUM							-	--
AUP					-	--	-	---
HLO						+++		
HLM						++++	+	+
HUM						+++		
HUP	++					----		
BLO			---	----	-	+++		+
BLM			---	----	-	+++		++
BUM			-	----	---	++		++
BUP				----		+++	---	

Source: Authors' calculations based on data set described in Harris and Udry (2008).

childbearing given their early initiation into sexual activity. Even though their sexual behavior is largely explained by ecological circumstances, high likelihoods and early ages of sexual intercourse nonetheless are behavioral realities given the universally low likelihood of marriage, and naturally yield a high level of risky childbearing. What appears to set African Americans apart from other groups in the United States is the virtual absence of marriage and even cohabitation as social institutions in the black community. As Ronald Haskins (2009) succinctly put it, in the end perhaps "Moynihan was right."

Table 4.9 is notable as much for what it does not show and for what it reveals. In particular, family socioeconomic status seems to matter relatively little in conditioning the process of reproduction. Out of eight possible cells, for example, household income was significant in only two, occupational prestige in one, health insurance in two, and parental education in three. In other spheres of influence, material circumstances also seemed to matter less.

School disadvantage was significant in just one cell and neighborhood disadvantage in two.

In general, the behaviors involved sexuality and childbearing among young American women are more tightly connected to emotional resources. Family sternness is significant in seven of eight cases, for example. Women who grew up in an emotionally distant, cold, and stern family environment were less likely to initiate sex and tended to debut at a later age and use contraception when they finally did have sex. They were less also likely to marry or cohabit, or to have children under any social auspices, either inside or outside marriage or before the age of eighteen.

Whether an emotionally distant, remote, and uncommunicative emotional style is good or bad depends of course on one's point of view. Although it lowers the odds of risky reproduction, among women it may also lower the likelihood of forming social attachments generally, a sexual union being among the most intimate bonds that humans can form. Other important emotional effects stem from experiencing a death in the family sphere, a traumatic and taxing event that significantly lowers the odds of childbearing for men and women alike. Coming from an inefficacious neighborhood characterized by a low level of trust and mutual support also acts strongly to increase the age of first intercourse and depress fertility among women. Social inefficacy in the school setting likewise lowers the odds of unwed fertility, though it also increases the likelihood of cohabitation and sexual debut. In general, however, coming of age in an emotionally austere family, coupled with anomic neighborhoods and schools, discourages the formation of sexual unions, entering into formal and informal romantic partnerships, and childbearing.

CHAPTER 5

Ecology Under the Skin

Human productivity is determined by how well three basic factors—land, labor, and capital—are combined to generate wealth and enhance material well-being. Land is used to produce food (through foraging, herding, or agriculture), extract natural resources (such as energy, minerals, or commodities), or simply as space (for living, working, and recreation). Labor refers to physical and mental activities carried out by human beings to produce goods and services using land and capital at their disposal. Of the three fundamental factors of production, capital is the most variegated, with at least five forms being identified by social scientists. *Social capital* is extracted from interpersonal ties or social structures when they are used instrumentally to achieve productive ends. *Cultural capital* refers to informal knowledge that, though not necessarily directly productive, helps people socially navigate a particular productive setting (Bourdieu 1986). *Physical capital* refers to plants, equipment, and other tools used to produce goods and services. *Financial capital* refers to the monetary instruments used to initiate, maintain, or expand economic production (Smith 1904).

Although the functions of physical and financial capital have long been appreciated within economics, economists in the 1960s identified another form of capital, *human capital*, as particularly critical to economic growth and productivity (Schultz 1963; Becker 1994). Human capital refers to the education, skills, and other inner resources that people acquire through growth, learning, and experience to increase their productivity as economic agents. Human capital can be broken down into two fundamental components—physical well-being and education—and investments in health and cognitive skills are now widely recognized as key inputs for economic growth and development for nations as well as individuals (Schultz 2003; Todaro and Smith 2008). Health is the foundation of human capital formation, for without health people are unable effectively to learn or apply skills. In this chapter, we set aside education as a matter to be taken up in the next chapter and concentrate instead on the ecological production of health—how the conditions that people experience in families, neighborhoods, schools, and peer networks get "under the skin" to influence health and human development (Taylor, Repetti, and Seeman 1997; Hertzman and Boyce 2010).

HEALTH DISPARITIES BY RACE AND CLASS

Although scholars and the public have long realized that poor people get sick, become disabled, and die at higher rates than the rich (see Antonovsky 1967), the modern era of research on class differentials in mortality and morbidity dates only to 1970s, with the seminal work of Evelyn Kitagawa and Phillip Hauser (1973) in the United States and Sir Michael Marmot in Britain (Marmot et al. 1978). Although British investigators initially expected to find that disparities in health would diminish in the wake of socialized medicine and the advent of universal health care (see Adler and Rehkopf 2008), they were taken aback to discover that socioeconomic gaps in health and mortality instead widened over time (Black et al. 1980; Gray 1982; Marmot, Shipley, and Rose 1984; Marmot et al. 1978). Since then, numerous studies have documented a strong and persistent inverse relationship between socioeconomic status and physical and mental health across a wide variety of indicators and settings (Robert and House 2000; Marmot 2004; Elo 2009).

Although the existence of socioeconomic differentials in mortality and morbidity are well documented and universally accepted, the reasons for these health disparities continue to be debated (Schnittker and McLeod 2005; Adler and Rehkopf 2008; Elo 2009; Hertzman and Boyce 2010). Numerous explanations and mechanisms have been advanced, perhaps the most obvious being that poor people do not have the money to purchase inputs to maintain health and treat disease, such as physician care, prescription drugs, hospital visits, clinical treatments, and surgical interventions, not to mention healthy food, secure housing, and a safe neighborhood (Marmot, Kogevinas, and Elston 1987; Wagstaff and van Doorslaer 2000). In the United States, moreover, poor families have also been less likely to be covered by health insurance and more likely to be underinsured or not insured (Monheit 1994). Holding such material constraints constant, education also appears to play an independent role in producing health, more education being associated with healthier lifestyles and greater fidelity to physician instructions and health-care directives (Pampel, Krueger, and Tenney 2010).

Researchers have also postulated a variety of class-related geographic influences on health. In general, affluent and poor households occupy very different residential environments (Massey and Fischer 2003; Fischer et al. 2004; Massey, Rothwell, and Domina 2009). As socioeconomic status falls, exposure to hazardous physical environments and toxic substances rises, access to health care diminishes, and the risk of experiencing disorder and violence increases (Yen and Syme 1999; Earls and Carlson 2001; Macmillan 2001; Bradley and Corwyn 2002; Evans and Kantrowitz 2002; Evans 2006). Health problems also tend to spread through social networks typically characterized by a high degree of homogeneity with respect to class, and not just infectious diseases such as influenza or AIDS, but also socially transmitted conditions such as obesity and depression as well as risky health behaviors such as smoking, drinking, and drug use (Smith and Christakis 2008).

Health researchers have long noted that exposure to stress is associated with poorer mental and physical health across a variety of dimensions (Taylor, Repetti, and Seeman 1997; Hammen 2005; McDade 2005; Kaestner et al. 2009). Stress is postulated to influence health through the intervening mechanism of allostatic load. *Allostasis* is the tendency for all organisms to maintain physiological stability through bodily changes in response to shifting environmental conditions and, in particular, to the appearance of threats (Sterling and Eyer 1988; McEwan and Lasley 2002). Whenever a person perceives an external threat, the brain's hypothalamus triggers an *allostatic response*, a complex interaction between the brain, the endocrine system, and the immune system.

On perceiving the threat, the hypothalamus signals the adrenal glands to release adrenaline (McEwan and Lasley 2002), which flows into the bloodstream to accelerate heartbeat, constrict blood vessels in the skin, increase blood flow to internal organs, dilate the bronchial tubes, trigger the release of fibrogen into the circulatory system (thus promoting clotting), release glucose and fatty acids into the bloodstream from stored fats (thus providing a ready source of energy), and signal the brain to produce endorphins (to mitigate any potential pain). At the same time, the hypothalamus also signals the pituitary gland to release adrenocorticotropic hormone, which causes the adrenal glands to secrete cortisol into the blood (McEwan and Lasley 2002). Cortisol acts to replace the energy stores depleted by adrenaline, converting them into glycogen and fat. It also promotes the conversion of muscle protein to fat, blocks insulin from taking up glucose, subtracts minerals from bones, and changes the external texture of white blood cells to make them more adhesive ("stickier").

These physiological responses generally work to maximize an organism's resources to meet an immediate, short-term threat. Long-term functions such as the building of muscle, bone, and brain cells are temporarily sacrificed to put more energy into the bloodstream for evasive or aggressive action (McEwan and Lasley 2002). The hypothalamic-pituitary-adrenal (HPA) axis is common to all mammals and evolved over time for infrequent and sporadic use. Repeated triggering of the allostatic response through chronic exposure to stressful events yields a condition known as *allostatic load*: as this load increases and persists over time, it has powerful negative effects on a variety of bodily systems (McEwan and Lasley 2002).

One important set of effects is cardiovascular. Chronically elevated levels of adrenaline increase blood pressure and raise the risk of hypertension. Elevated fibrogen levels increase the likelihood of blood clots and thrombosis. The build-up of "sticky" white blood cells causes the formation of arterial plaques that contribute to atherosclerosis. Elevated cortisol levels, meanwhile, cause the production of excess glycogen and fat, raising the risk of obesity, while the suppression of insulin leads to excessive blood sugar and a greater risk of Type II diabetes (McEwan and Lasley 2002).

Chronically elevated levels of adrenaline also disrupt the functioning of the vagal nervous system, which is responsible for slowing down the heart rate and reducing bodily tension, thus applying a physiological brake to the ACH axis. Disruption of the vagal system contributes to the expression of a Type A personality, which is associated with aggressiveness, impulsiveness, frustration, and a low threshold for anger. People with Type A personalities often try to reduce tension by self-medicating with drugs, alcohol, and tobacco and through these poor coping choices end up exacerbating allostatic load and causing secondary damage to vital organs such as the liver, lungs, and heart (McEwan and Lasley 2002).

Allostatic load also compromises the human immune system. Long-term exposure to elevated cortisol usually lowers the immune response to increase susceptibility to illness and infection (Schulz et al. 1998). In some circumstances, however, excess cortisol appears to overstimulate the immune system and mistakenly prompt it to attack targets within the body that do not normally pose any threat, leading to the expression of inflammatory diseases such as asthma and autoimmune diseases such as multiple sclerosis, arthritis, and Type I diabetes (McEwan and Lasley 2002).

Given that poor households generally experience higher levels of stress than affluent households, investigators have postulated elevated allostatic load as an important channel by which stressful ecological conditions get under the skin to affect physical and mental health (Aber et al. 1997; Seeman et al. 1997; McEwen 1998; McDade 2005; Adler and Rehkopf 2008; Berkman 2009; Miller et al. 2009; Chen, Cohen, and Miller 2010). Arlene Geronimus (2001) has argued that prolonged exposure to stress and the physiological changes that accompany it lead to a kind of human weathering in which people age prematurely and experience higher rates of morbidity and mortality given the accumulation of stress and other disadvantages over the life course (DiPrete and Eirich 2006; Geronimus et al. 2006; Walsemann, Geronimus, and Gee 2008). This process of weathering appears to be expressed at the microbiological level through the shortening of telomeres (Epel et al. 2004; Sapolsky 2004), which are special, looped assemblages of DNA at the end of chromosomes that prevent their binding with other chromosomal ends and thus hinder cell degeneration and senescence (Blackburn 2006). The shortening of telomeres is a physiological marker of aging and loss of vitality through stress.

Given that minority groups such as African Americans and Hispanics generally have lower socioeconomic status than whites and experience much higher rates of poverty and material disadvantage, all of the foregoing mechanisms may be expected to apply differentially to them and thus help explain racial differences in mortality and morbidity (Massey 2004; Geronimus et al. 2006). Although controlling for individual socioeconomic differences reduces intergroup differentials in health outcomes, however, significant gaps nonetheless persist even after extensive controls have been applied, suggesting other unique, racially specific causes for intergroup health disparities, especially black-white disparities (Lillie-Blanton et al. 1996; Dressler, Ochs, and Gravlee 2005).

Whatever stresses poor African Americans may share with poor whites by virtue of a low socioeconomic status, black adolescents experience additional burdens and stresses through exposure to racial prejudice, discrimination, and exclusion, thus potentially heightening their allostatic load and exacerbating the weathering effect compared with others having the same socioeconomic characteristics (Walsemann, Gee, and Geronimus 2009). Processes of racial exclusion and discrimination also influence the health of African Americans indirectly to the extent they lead to racial segregation in society, which concentrates socioeconomic disadvantage and the ills associated with it to create unusually dangerous and threatening environments within neighborhoods, schools, and peer networks (Massey and Denton 1993; Polednak 1997; Collins and Williams 1999; Williams and Collins 2001).

Research has demonstrated that African Americans and to a lesser extent Hispanics are exposed to school, neighborhood, and peer environments that are far more disadvantaged compared with those experienced by whites and Asians of similar class standing (Massey and Denton 1993; Jargowsky 1997; Sampson 2008; Peterson and Krivo 2010) and that it is very difficult for African Americans especially to break out of the cycle of segregation and spatial disadvantage through residential mobility (Massey, Gross, and Shibuya 1994; Quillian 2002; South, Crowder, and Chavez 2005; South, Crowder, and Pais 2008; Sampson and Sharkey 2008). As a result, African Americans encounter far worse health outcomes than their socioeconomic traits would predict.

RISKY HEALTH BEHAVIORS

The effects of allostatic load—weathering, telomere shortening, and premature aging—take time to be expressed, of course, and given the young ages of respondents to the Adolescent Health Survey we are not likely yet to observe many chronic health problems by the time of the third wave, when the oldest respondents are only in their mid-twenties. In general, ages eighteen to twenty-fix are characterized by low rates of mortality and morbidity. What we can observe are behavioral tendencies, physical conditions, and self-assessments that are known to predict poor health and higher mortality later in life.

Our approach here is to focus first on the ecological determinants of young people's propensity to engage in risky health behaviors, such as smoking cigarettes, abusing alcohol, using hard drugs, eating fast food, and having sex with risky partners. Holding these behaviors constant, we then link ecological circumstances to specific physical outcomes: limitations on physical activity, body mass, obesity, and whether a respondent was ever diagnosed with a sexually transmitted disease (STD), an infection to which people in

Figure 5.1   Proportion Smoking Regularly by Race and Class

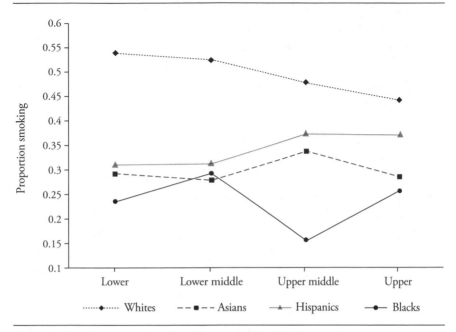

Source: Authors' compilation based on Harris and Udry (2008).

their teens and twenties are particularly prone. Finally, taking both sets of variables into account, we measure the effect of ecological circumstances on self-assessed general health, mental health, and the perceived likelihood of an early death, perhaps the most telling of all our indicators.

One of the best documented behavioral risks to health in the medical literature is cigarette smoking, which has been conclusively linked to numerous cardiovascular diseases and cancers (Surgeon General's Advisory Committee on Smoking and Health 1964; Preston 1970). Figure 5.1 shows how this risky behavior varies by race and class among young people in the United States by plotting the proportion of Add Health respondents who said they smoked regularly, defined as having at least one cigarette per day for thirty days. As the plot shows, white Americans very clearly display the highest rates of cigarette smoking. Although the likelihood of smoking declines with rising socioeconomic status, at each class level the frequency is much higher among whites than in any other group, incidence declining from 54 percent in the lower class, to 53 percent and 47 percent in the lower middle and upper middle class, respectively, to just below 45 percent in the upper class.

The next closest group is upper-class Hispanics with a relative frequency of 37 percent. For them, however, unlike whites, the likelihood of smoking rises with socioeconomic status, going from 31 percent and 32 percent in the lower class and lower middle class to around 37 percent in both the upper middle and upper classes. African Americans display the lowest rates of cigarette smoking, which never rise above 30 percent, and Asians are generally in the same range, though the incidence does rise to around 34 percent in the upper middle class. Once again, neither Asians nor African Americans display a consistent class gradient.

The baseline model shown in left-hand columns of table 5.1 confirm the significance of these intergroup differences. The likelihood of smoking is significantly greater for lower-class whites than for their upper-class counterparts and then steadily loses significance from the lower middle to the upper middle class. The coefficient for every other race-class combination carries a negative sign, eight of the twelve being statistically significant, and those for African Americans being most consistently negative and significant regardless of class.

The right-hand columns add in controls for ecological conditions in the five social spheres and ascribed characteristics, as in chapter 4. In addition, we control for the marital-parental status respondents had achieved by the third wave of the Adolescent Health Survey, which we take as predetermined (by social processes described in the prior chapter). We categorize current family situation by gender. Unmarried males without children are the reference category, to whom we compare married males without children, married fathers, and unmarried fathers. Among women, we compare the following categories to the same reference group: unmarried childless women, married childless women, married mothers, unmarried mothers who gave birth before age eighteen, and unmarried mothers who gave birth after eighteen.

Adding background controls and family circumstances to the model eliminates the class gradient among whites, and indeed switches the signs from positive to negative. However, the addition of controls does not eliminate the significant negative coefficients associated with the other race-class combinations, and if anything makes them stronger. Among Hispanics and blacks, all of the coefficient estimates are increased in size. Although many of these shifts are not themselves significant statistically, they nonetheless confirm that blacks and Hispanics are unlikely to take up smoking, which is notable given their generally disadvantaged ecological circumstances.

In terms of background factors, the odds of smoking are unrelated to age but are significantly reduced by immigrant origins and are generally greater among both males and females who have become parents—that is, those who had children before the age of twenty-six. Compared with an unmarried, nonparent male, the odds of smoking were 67 percent greater for married fathers and 59 percent greater for unmarried fathers. Among mothers, the figures were 55 percent if they were married and 25 percent if they were unmarried (though the latter was not significant statistically).

Turning to the family of origin, coming from a stepparent household was associated with a modest increase in the odds of smoking (29 percent) and all three peer group indicators positively predicted smoking. For each additional unit of exposure to peer violence the odds of being a regular smoker increased by 11 percent, for a total of 220 percent over the observed range of the violence index. The attempted suicide of a friend, meanwhile, was associated with a 55 percent increase in the odds of smoking; relying on a peer mentor increased those odds by 27 percent. Exposure to disorder and emotional turbulence in the peer network thus appears to be linked to a greater likelihood of smoking, possibly as a form of self-medication in response to stress.

In the family sphere, having access to full health insurance coverage substantially lowers the likelihood of smoking (by around 38 percent), whereas having an incarcerated father greatly increases them (by 43 percent). Family sternness, however, lowers the odds of smoking significantly (around 1.1 percent per unit). In contrast, exposure to social inefficacy at school was associated with an increase (1.9 percent per unit) and inefficacy within neighborhoods had an even stronger effect (5.2 percent per unit, a total of 83 percent over the scale's range). Finally, although religiosity per se has no influence on the likelihood of smoking, the odds of taking up cigarettes were sharply lower for those with a religious mentor (by 60 percent) and fell with greater religious involvement (2.9 percent per unit, or 35 percent over the observed range).

Thus the propensity for young people in the United States to smoke is connected most strongly to circumstances in the peer and religious environments, as well as to social inefficacy within neighborhoods and certain circumstances in the family sphere, such as access to health insurance, sternness of emotional style, and paternal incarceration. Another risky behavior common to young people in the United States is alcohol abuse, which we define

Table 5.1   Determinants of Regular Smoking

Independent Variables	Group Effects		Full Model	
	B	SE	B	SE
Race-class group				
White lower	0.387***	0.109	−0.595+	0.336
White lower middle	0.334***	0.100	−0.307	0.251
White upper middle	0.147	0.092	−0.125	0.154
White upper	—	—	—	—
Asian lower	−0.644	0.468	−0.981+	0.599
Asian lower middle	−0.709+	0.394	−0.486	0.462
Asian upper middle	−0.435	0.350	−0.064	0.397
Asian upper	−0.671***	0.241	−0.215	0.267
Hispanic lower	−0.562***	0.155	−1.425***	0.398
Hispanic lower middle	−0.546*	0.215	−0.990**	0.344
Hispanic upper middle	−0.281	0.233	−0.521	0.306
Hispanic upper	−0.290	0.293	−0.384	0.326
Black lower	−0.933***	0.170	−1.826***	0.401
Black lower middle	−0.644**	0.239	−1.296***	0.379
Black upper middle	−1.435***	0.221	−1.880***	0.287
Black upper	−0.816**	0.281	−1.056***	0.305
Ascribed characteristics				
Age	—	—	−0.029	0.024
Parent foreign born	—	—	−0.352**	0.126
Mediating conditions				
Family situation				
Unmarried male–not father	—	—	—	—
Married male–not father	—	—	−0.269	0.229
Married male–father	—	—	0.515**	0.175
Unmarried male–father	—	—	0.462*	0.205
Unmarried female–no birth	—	—	−0.005	0.088
Married female–no birth	—	—	−0.033	0.160
Married female–mother	—	—	0.195	0.141
Unmarried female–birth over eighteen	—	—	0.437**	0.163
Unmarried female–birth eighteen or younger	—	—	0.222	0.253
Ecological background				
Composition of origin family				
Two biological parents	—	—	—	—
Biological and stepparent	—	—	0.252*	0.126
One biological parent	—	—	0.027	0.110
No biological parent	—	—	0.178	0.373
Family material resources				
Household income	—	—	−0.006	0.006

Table 5.1   (continued)

Independent Variables	Group Effects		Full Model	
	B	SE	B	SE
Access to health insurance				
No coverage	—	—	—	—
Coverage less than a year	—	—	−0.030	0.116
Coverage full year	—	—	−0.482***	0.112
Family symbolic resources				
Parental prestige	—	—	0.001	0.002
Parent went to college	—	—	0.040	0.138
Family emotional resources				
Death in family	—	—	−0.095	0.154
Family sternness	—	—	−0.011***	0.003
Father incarcerated	—	—	0.360***	0.100
Had family mentor	—	—	0.131	0.114
Neighborhood setting				
Disadvantage index	—	—	−0.052	0.088
Inefficacy index	—	—	−0.054***	0.014
Scarcity of males	—	—	−0.078	0.126
Had neighborhood mentor	—	—	0.121	0.149
School setting				
Disadvantage index	—	—	−0.013*	0.006
Inefficacy index	—	—	0.019**	0.007
Disorder index	—	—	−0.001	0.017
Had school mentor	—	—	−0.087	0.105
Religious setting				
Religiosity scale	—	—	−0.011	0.008
Involvement index	—	—	−0.029**	0.011
Had religious mentor	—	—	−0.911***	0.011
Peer setting				
Violence index	—	—	0.107***	0.019
Friend attempted suicide	—	—	0.441**	0.150
Had peer mentor	—	—	0.239*	0.110
Multiple disadvantages				
Log of interactive index	—	—	0.029	0.021
Intercept	−0.230**	0.074	1.475	0.984
N	8,981		7,169	
F-test	11.42***		9.10***	

Source: Authors' calculations based on data set described in Harris and Udry (2008).
+*p* < .10; *p* < .05; **p* < .01; ***p* < .001

Figure 5.2   Proportion Abusing Alcohol by Race and Class

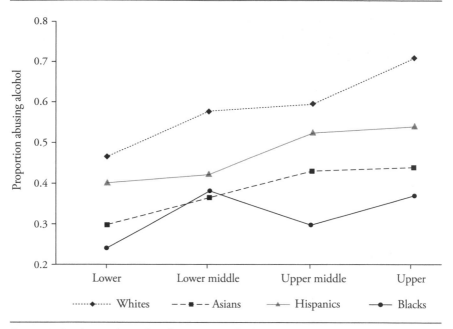

Source: Authors' compilation based on Harris and Udry (2008).

here as getting drunk more than once a month during the twelve months prior to the Wave 3 survey. The proportion doing so is shown by race and class in figure 5.2. Again, it is immediately apparent that whites display the riskiest behavior, but instead of exhibiting a negative gradient with respect to social class, as with smoking, the curve is positive, with alcohol abuse rising with socioeconomic status. Indeed, by far the greatest level of alcohol abuse is observed among upper-class whites, some 70 percent of whom fulfill the criteria for abuse, compared with 60 percent in the upper middle class, 58 percent in the lower middle class, and 47 percent in the lower class.

Although Hispanics and Asians also display a pattern of rising alcohol abuse as class standing increases, the frequencies are much lower. The Hispanic percentage increased from 40 percent to 55 percent moving from the lower to the upper class. Asians rise from 30 percent to 44 percent over the same range. As with smoking, blacks are least likely to engage in risky drinking behavior. Indeed, the lowest frequency of alcohol abuse of any race-class group, roughly 25 percent, is observed for lower-class African Americans. The incidence of alcohol abuse among blacks generally fluctuates between 20 percent and 40 percent across classes with no systematic downward or upward gradient.

The baseline model presented in the left-hand columns of table 5.2 generally confirms the statistical significance of these race-class differences. We observe large and highly significant negative coefficients for other race-class groups compared with upper-class whites. The most likely young people to engage in problem drinking are clearly upper-class whites. The only other groups that really come close are upper-middle-class and lower-middle-class whites. As indicated by the right-hand columns, however, these class differentials among whites disappear with the addition of background controls. Although the race-class coefficients for blacks are reduced, their statistical significance does not disappear, especially in the upper classes. Among Asians, likewise, the coefficients are reduced yet in three of the four cases remain at least marginally significant. In contrast, among Hispanics, all of the effect sizes are reduced and only one coefficient remains even marginally significant.

Thus differences in background characteristics explain some but not all of the race-class variation among blacks and Asians but most of the differences between whites and Hispanics. As one might expect, the likelihood of alcohol abuse rises with age and it is greatest for unmarried males who are not fathers—those without serious social obligations. Marriage and fatherhood generally reduce the likelihood of alcohol abuse among young men, but less so for those who were not married when they became fathers. Although the likelihood of alcohol abuse for unmarried females is 19 percent less than among unmarried males, marriage and childbirth lower the odds of drinking much further for woman. A female who has married but not given birth is 73 percent less likely to abuse alcohol than an unattached man, whereas a married woman who has become a mother is 80 percent less likely. An unmarried mother is 63 percent less likely to report alcohol abuse if she gave birth after eighteen and 54 percent less likely if she gave birth before eighteen. Thus the propensity to abuse alcohol varies systematically by gender, and the proclivity of both males and females toward problem drinking is conditioned by the social ties of marriage and parenthood, especially for women.

Holding constant a respondent's current family situation, the composition of his or her family of origin has no effect, nor do its material or symbolic resources. The abuse of alcohol by young people is more strongly influenced

Table 5.2   Determinants of Alcohol Abuse

Independent Variables	Group Effects		Full Model	
	B	SE	B	SE
Race-class group				
White lower	−1.024***	0.122	−0.286	0.406
White lower middle	−0.578***	0.105	−0.065	0.297
White upper middle	−0.509***	0.111	−0.160	0.208
White upper	—	—	—	—
Asian lower	−1.746***	0.476	−1.076+	0.644
Asian lower middle	−1.441***	0.296	−0.239	0.463
Asian upper middle	−1.167***	0.289	−0.752+	0.421
Asian upper	−1.131***	0.227	−1.018***	0.254
Hispanic lower	−1.294***	0.141	−0.103	0.476
Hispanic lower middle	−1.199***	0.151	−0.416	0.378
Hispanic upper middle	−0.790***	0.188	−0.367	0.268
Hispanic upper	−0.727**	0.232	−0.455+	0.252
Black lower	−2.034***	0.165	−0.769+	0.437
Black lower middle	−1.376***	0.152	−0.570+	0.341
Black upper middle	−1.749***	0.187	−1.041***	0.260
Black upper	−1.418***	0.175	−1.167***	0.248
Ascribed characteristics				
Age	—	—	0.050*	0.022
Parent foreign born	—	—	−0.013	0.143
Mediating conditions				
Family situation				
Unmarried male–not father	—	—	—	—
Married male–not father	—	—	−0.934***	0.238
Married male–father	—	—	−0.628**	0.214
Unmarried male–father	—	—	−0.379*	0.192
Unmarried female–no birth	—	—	−0.212**	0.083
Married female–no birth	—	—	−1.294***	0.164
Married female–mother	—	—	−1.601***	0.159
Unmarried female–birth over eighteen	—	—	−0.988***	0.150
Unmarried female–birth eighteen or younger	—	—	−0.769*	0.312
Ecological background				
Composition of origin family				
Two biological parents	—	—	—	—
Biological and stepparent	—	—	0.026	0.131
One biological parent	—	—	0.018	0.096
No biological parent	—	—	−0.024	0.293
Family material resources				
Household income	—	—	0.010	0.007

Table 5.2   (continued)

Independent Variables	Group Effects		Full Model	
	B	SE	B	SE
Access to health insurance				
No coverage	—	—	—	—
Coverage less than a year	—	—	0.191	0.132
Coverage full year	—	—	0.171	0.119
Family symbolic resources				
Parental prestige	—	—	0.002	0.002
Parent went to college	—	—	0.106	0.110
Family emotional resources				
Death in family	—	—	−0.039	0.175
Family sternness	—	—	−0.011***	0.003
Father incarcerated	—	—	0.360***	0.118
Had family mentor	—	—	0.507***	0.105
Neighborhood setting				
Disadvantage index	—	—	−0.265***	0.080
Inefficacy index	—	—	−0.014	0.013
Scarcity of males	—	—	0.322+	0.185
Had neighborhood mentor	—	—	0.118	0.144
School setting				
Disadvantage index	—	—	−0.017*	0.007
Inefficacy index	—	—	0.011	0.008
Disorder index	—	—	−0.029	0.021
Had school mentor	—	—	0.680***	0.125
Religious setting				
Religiosity scale	—	—	0.000	0.009
Involvement index	—	—	−0.040***	0.013
Had religious mentor	—	—	−0.709***	0.224
Peer setting				
Violence index	—	—	0.018	0.017
Friend attempted suicide	—	—	0.518***	0.157
Had peer mentor	—	—	0.318**	0.119
Multiple disadvantage				
Log of interactive index	—	—	−0.004	0.020
Intercept	0.894***	0.087	0.218	1.050
N	8,949		7,147	
F-test	16.00***		18.82***	

Source: Authors' calculations based on data set described in Harris and Udry (2008).

Note: Abuse is defined as being drunk more than once a month for the past twelve months.

+$p < .10$; *$p < .05$; **$p < .01$; ***$p < .001$

by emotional and social conditions in the family, school, peer, and religious spheres, as well as by material disadvantages in the neighborhood and school spheres. Coming from an emotionally remote, stern family lowers the odds of alcohol abuse by 1.1 percent per unit, whereas having a father in prison or jail raises them by 43 percent, as does reliance on a family, school, or peer-based mentor, by 66 percent, 97 percent, and 37 percent respectively. The attempted suicide of a friend is also associated with an increase, by around 68 percent.

In addition to being reduced by emotional sternness within the family, the likelihood of alcohol abuse is also lowered by associations in the religious sphere, each unit of religious involvement reducing the odds of abuse by around 4 percent and having a religious mentor reducing them by 51 percent. It might be surprising to some that material disadvantage in schools and social inefficacy in neighborhoods are associated with a lower likelihood of alcohol abuse, but other studies have found the same thing (Snedker, Herting, and Walton 2009). It is not minorities living in distressed neighborhoods and attending materially deprived schools who are most prone to alcohol abuse, but upper-class whites coming from advantaged school and neighborhood environments.

In general, alcohol abuse seems to be more of a social than an economic phenomenon. As the model shows, other things equal, the likelihood of problem drinking is not affected by family income, parental education, occupational status, or access to health insurance. Instead, problem drinking is influenced mostly by social circumstances, being reduced by the acquisition of adult responsibilities (marriage and parenthood), a stern emotional style in the family sphere, and greater involvement in the religious sphere, but increased by exposure to emotional shocks such as paternal imprisonment and the attempted suicide of a friend.

Although the frequencies are generally much lower, the abuse of hard drugs follows a similar pattern by race and class, whites leading the way, followed by Hispanics, Asians, and finally blacks. As before, we generally observe a positive class gradient for the first three groups but not the last. Figure 5.3 shows the proportion of respondents who reported ever using cocaine, crystal meth, or some other hard drug (not including marijuana) by race and class. As can be seen, drug use rises from around 21 percent among lower-class whites to 28 percent among their upper-class counterparts. Among Hispanics the corresponding progression is from 18 percent to 25 percent, whereas among Asians the increase is from 12 percent in the lower class to 20 percent in the upper middle class, before dropping to 15 percent in the upper

Figure 5.3   Proportion Using Hard Drugs by Race and Class

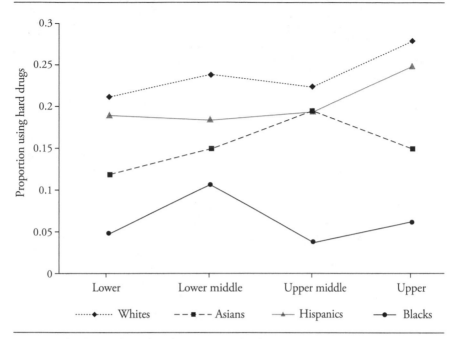

Source: Authors' compilation based on Harris and Udry (2008).

class. In contrast, black usage rates fluctuate between 4 percent and 11 percent with no particular pattern by social class. At no point in the class distribution do black frequencies overlap with the usage rates reported by other groups.

The statistical estimates in table 5.3 confirm that these race-class differences are highly significant statistically and that the frequency of drug use by African Americans, in particular, is remarkably low. Compared with upper-class whites, the odds of hard drug use are consistently lower across all other race-class groups, as indicated by the plethora of negative coefficients, thirteen of fifteen of which are significant. As with the models predicting alcohol abuse, the addition of controls generally eliminates class gradients for whites and Hispanics, but has less of an effect on African Americans, who continue to display an aversion to drug use across all class categories. Among Asians, the coefficients for the two middle classes decline, but the point estimates for upper and lower classes do not shift very much, though interpretation is difficult because of small cell sizes and low frequencies of drug use, which yield unreliability in estimated effects.

Table 5.3 Determinants of Hard Drug Use

Independent Variables	Group Effects B	Group Effects SE	Full Model B	Full Model SE
Race-class group				
White lower	−0.375***	0.136	−0.292	0.488
White lower middle	−0.218+	0.129	−0.197	0.317
White upper middle	−0.298*	0.126	−0.176	0.213
White upper	—	—	—	—
Asian lower	−1.068*	0.540	−0.921	0.846
Asian lower middle	−0.796+	0.484	−0.086	0.663
Asian upper middle	−0.474	0.373	−0.086	0.502
Asian upper	−0.795*	0.348	−0.779+	0.440
Hispanic lower	−0.507**	0.174	0.018	0.517
Hispanic lower middle	−0.546*	0.227	−0.168	0.460
Hispanic upper middle	−0.479+	0.246	−0.439	0.347
Hispanic upper	−0.162	0.301	−0.069	0.363
Black lower	−2.049***	0.259	−1.464***	0.459
Black lower middle	−1.174***	0.268	−0.794+	0.431
Black upper middle	−2.288***	0.479	−2.071***	0.588
Black upper	−1.770***	0.339	−1.322***	0.379
Ascribed characteristics				
Age	—	—	−0.088**	0.032
Parent foreign born	—	—	−0.079	0.173
Mediating conditions				
Family situation				
Unmarried male–not father	—	—	—	—
Married male–not father	—	—	−0.764**	0.278
Married male–father	—	—	−0.306	0.226
Unmarried male–father	—	—	−0.372	0.245
Unmarried female–no birth	—	—	−0.193+	0.106
Married female–no birth	—	—	−0.903***	0.234
Married female–mother	—	—	−1.117***	0.217
Unmarried female–birth over eighteen	—	—	−0.480*	0.235
Unmarried female–birth eighteen or younger	—	—	−0.771*	0.328
Ecological background				
Composition of origin family				
Two biological parents	—	—	—	—
Biological and stepparent	—	—	0.063	0.185
One biological parent	—	—	0.240*	0.117
No biological parent	—	—	0.249	0.426
Family material resources				
Household income	—	—	0.002	0.007

Table 5.3   (continued)

Independent Variables	Group Effects		Full Model	
	B	SE	B	SE
Access to health insurance				
No coverage	—	—	—	—
Coverage less than a year	—	—	0.005	0.168
Coverage full year	—	—	−0.439***	0.128
Family symbolic resources				
Parental prestige	—	—	0.009***	0.003
Parent went to college	—	—	0.172	0.135
Family emotional resources				
Death in family	—	—	0.068	0.187
Family sternness	—	—	−0.019***	0.003
Father incarcerated	—	—	0.393***	0.128
Had family mentor	—	—	0.005	0.127
Neighborhood setting				
Disadvantage index	—	—	−0.377***	0.116
Inefficacy index	—	—	−0.001	0.016
Scarcity of males	—	—	0.213	0.162
Had neighborhood mentor	—	—	−0.276	0.185
School setting				
Disadvantage index	—	—	−0.009	0.008
Inefficacy index	—	—	0.012+	0.007
Disorder index	—	—	−0.007	0.017
Had school mentor	—	—	0.121	0.136
Religious setting				
Religiosity scale	—	—	−0.160	0.011
Involvement index	—	—	−0.014	0.016
Had religious mentor	—	—	−0.201	0.259
Peer setting				
Violence index	—	—	0.123***	0.019
Friend attempted suicide	—	—	0.324***	0.135
Had peer mentor	—	—	−0.160	0.129
Multiple disadvantages				
Log of interactive index	—	—	−0.003	0.021
Intercept	0.941***	0.088	2.320+	1.359
N	8,997		7,174	
F-test	7.37***		12.67***	

Source: Authors' calculations based on data set described in Harris and Udry (2008).

Note: Hard drugs include cocaine, crystal meth, and other illegal drugs but do not include marijuana.

+$p < .10$; *$p < .05$; **$p < .01$; ***$p < .001$

Unlike alcohol abuse, the odds of hard drug use decline sharply with age, falling by around 8.4 percent per year. Once again, though, the acquisition of responsibilities through marriage and childbirth dramatically reduces the odds of drug use, especially among women. As before, family sternness reduces the relative likelihood of drug abuse (by 1.9 percent per unit) and having an incarcerated father raises it (by 48 percent). In the case of drugs, however, the composition of the family of origin and its material and symbolic resources also make a significant difference. Those coming from a single-parent household are about 27 percent more likely to use hard drugs and the odds of drug use rise by 0.9 percent per unit of parental occupational status, though they are 48 percent lower in families covered by health insurance. Exposure to violence among peers is strongly predictive of drug use, odds rising 13 percent per unit of exposure (for a total potential effect of 260 percent). As with alcohol abuse, the attempted suicide of a friend increases the odds of drug abuse, this time by 38 percent. Unlike alcohol consumption, however, drug use is unrelated to religiosity, religious involvement, or having a religious mentor.

Contrary to popular stereotypes, the likelihood of using drugs tends to be significantly lower in high-poverty neighborhoods. Each unit on the disadvantage scale reduces the odds of drug use by a robust 31 percent, or by 124 percent moving from lowest to highest disadvantage. Once again, it is not poor blacks with poor parents living in poor neighborhoods who are most prone to substance abuse, but upper-class whites in good neighborhoods with high-prestige parents. The tragic irony, of course, is that though the demand for drugs may be concentrated in upper-class white communities, the costs of the war on drugs are incurred predominantly by poor minority communities (Alexander 2010), yielding high rates of paternal incarceration that end up increasing rather than decreasing the likelihood of substance abuse among minority group members who are otherwise not disposed to drug abuse. The latter effect is well documented by Amanda Geller and colleagues (2009) and is indicated here by the significant positive effect of paternal incarceration in the models predicting smoking, drinking, and drug use.

Another major threat to public health in the United States is the rising tide of obesity, which is forecast to raise future rates of cardiovascular disease, diabetes, cancer, and disability (Visscher and Seidell 2001). According to the National Center for Health Statistics (2008), the frequency of age-standardized adult obesity rose from just 13 percent in the early 1960s to around 35 percent

Figure 5.4   Proportion Eating Fast Food During Prior Week by Race and Class

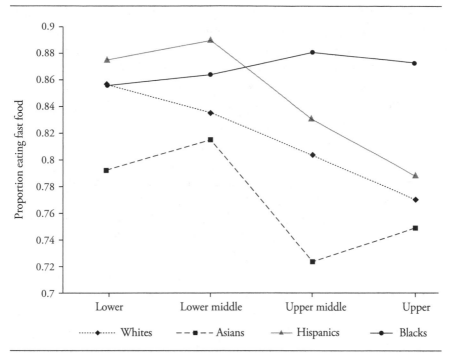

Source: Authors' compilation based on Harris and Udry (2008).

in the 2005–2006 school year; and among adolescents age twelve to nineteen the rate almost tripled, from 5 percent to 14 percent. In addition to a lack of exercise, excessive TV viewing, and too many hours spent surfing the Internet, a key factor implicated in the rise of adolescent obesity is the ubiquity of high-calorie "junk food" and its relentless marketing to children and teenagers (Nestle 2002). Accordingly, the Adolescent Health Survey sought to ascertain whether, over the prior seven days, respondents had eaten "food from a fast food place such as McDonalds, Kentucky Fried Chicken, Pizza Hut, Taco Bell, or some other local fast food restaurant." The share answering affirmatively is plotted by race and class in figure 5.4.

In the case of this risky health behavior, Asians are the outlier on the low side and African Americans on the high side. Moreover, whereas whites, Hispanics, and Asians display a declining gradient of fast-food consumption with rising social class, among blacks there is little variation but to that extent we observe a mildly positive gradient. The race-class differences are generally small in absolute terms, however, most combinations lying in the narrow range between 72 percent and 90 percent, thus confirming what the critics have alleged—that fast-food consumption among young people is high and widespread. Among Asians, the frequency of fast-food consumption falls from around 80 percent among those in the lower class and lower middle class to around 75 percent in the upper class. White consumption of fast food falls from around 86 percent in the lower class to 77 percent in the upper class, whereas black consumption starts at the some point and rises to 88 percent in the upper middle class and 87 percent in the upper class. Hispanic fast-food consumption generally falls from 88 percent to 89 percent in the two lowest class categories to around 79 percent in the highest.

The baseline model shown in table 5.4 reveals the significance of the negative class gradient among whites and Hispanics, and the generally rising curve among blacks, but none of the Asian categories is significantly different from upper-class whites. The lowest odds of junk food consumption are thus among upper-class and upper-middle-class whites and Asians regardless of class. Relative to these groups, lower-class whites are 79 percent more likely to consume fast food and lower-middle-class whites 50 percent more likely. The respective figures for lower-class and lower-middle-class Hispanics are 108 percent and 140 percent. In contrast, the odds of eating fast food among blacks increased from 76 percent and 89 percent in the lower class and lower middle classes, to 120 percent and 104 percent among upper-middle-class and upper-class blacks.

Although significance levels for the race-class coefficients drop when controls are added, owing to the inflation of standard errors, the point estimates don't change very much, suggesting that race-class differences are stable and not readily attributable to different ecological circumstances. The full model indicates that fast-food consumption is most likely among married males who have not yet become fathers and least likely among married and unmarried women who have not yet become mothers. Among ecological factors, few indicators are significant. The odds of consuming fast food are significantly greater when the father is incarcerated and when respondents turn to family members as mentors. A relative scarcity of young single males in the neighborhood lowered the odds of eating fast food, and social inefficacy in the neighborhood had a marginal effect in reducing its consumption. The relative likelihood of consuming fast food was also raised by exposure to multiple disadvantages across the various ecological spheres.

Table 5.4   Determinants of Eating Fast Food

Independent Variables	Group Effects B	Group Effects SE	Full Model B	Full Model SE
Race-class group				
White lower	0.581***	0.144	0.609	0.391
White lower middle	0.408***	0.112	0.493+	0.295
White upper middle	0.197	0.121	0.152	0.215
White upper	—	—	—	—
Asian lower	0.129	0.418	−0.211	0.662
Asian lower middle	0.272	0.390	0.574	0.551
Asian upper middle	−0.245	0.360	−0.351	0.439
Asian upper	−0.117	0.266	−0.432	0.346
Hispanic lower	0.734***	0.221	0.624	0.520
Hispanic lower middle	0.876***	0.217	0.675+	0.385
Hispanic upper middle	0.383	0.276	0.056	0.375
Hispanic upper	0.103	0.295	−0.048	0.303
Black lower	0.568***	0.164	0.615	0.484
Black lower middle	0.636**	0.210	0.742+	0.372
Black upper middle	0.790**	0.260	0.721*	0.348
Black upper	0.711+	0.416	0.535	0.434
Ascribed characteristics				
Age	—	—	−0.088**	0.032
Parent foreign born	—	—	0.123	0.153
Mediating conditions				
Family situation				
Unmarried male–not father	—	—	—	—
Married male–not father	—	—	−0.250	0.255
Married male–father	—	—	0.703**	0.278
Unmarried male–father	—	—	0.356	0.304
Unmarried female–no birth	—	—	−0.302***	0.088
Married female–no birth	—	—	−0.395+	0.226
Married female–mother	—	—	−0.153	0.232
Unmarried female–birth over eighteen	—	—	−0.291	0.284
Unmarried female–birth eighteen or younger	—	—	−0.303	0.256
Ecological background				
Composition of origin family				
Two biological parents	—	—	—	—
Biological and stepparent	—	—	−0.096	0.155
One biological parent	—	—	−0.127	0.121
No biological parent	—	—	−0.382	0.418
Family material resources				
Household income	—	—	0.008	0.007

Table 5.4   (continued)

Independent Variables	Group Effects		Full Model	
	B	SE	B	SE
Access to health insurance				
No coverage	—	—	—	—
Coverage less than a year	—	—	0.011	0.146
Coverage full year	—	—	−0.135	0.122
Family symbolic resources				
Parental prestige	—	—	0.002	0.003
Parent went to college	—	—	−0.089	0.136
Family emotional resources				
Death in family	—	—	−0.226	0.194
Family sternness	—	—	0.001	0.003
Father incarcerated	—	—	0.305*	0.145
Had family mentor	—	—	0.247*	0.120
Neighborhood setting				
Disadvantage index	—	—	0.146	0.140
Inefficacy index	—	—	−0.029+	0.017
Scarcity of males	—	—	−0.421**	0.142
Had neighborhood mentor	—	—	−0.051	0.177
School setting				
Disadvantage index	—	—	0.011	0.011
Inefficacy index	—	—	−0.003	0.008
Disorder index	—	—	0.022	0.022
Had school mentor	—	—	0.091	0.126
Religious setting				
Religiosity scale	—	—	0.004	0.012
Involvement index	—	—	0.014	0.016
Had religious mentor	—	—	0.041	0.220
Peer setting				
Violence index	—	—	−0.015	0.024
Suicide of friend	—	—	0.007	0.135
Had peer mentor	—	—	0.212	0.151
Multiple disadvantages				
Log of interactive index	—	—	0.048*	0.023
Intercept	1.208**	0.088	1.144	1.195
N	8,994		7,173	
F-test	3.61***		4.25***	

Source: Authors' calculations based on data set described in Harris and Udry (2008).

$+p < .10$; $*p < .05$; $**p < .01$; $***p < .001$

Figure 5.5   Proportion Having Risky Sex by Race and Class

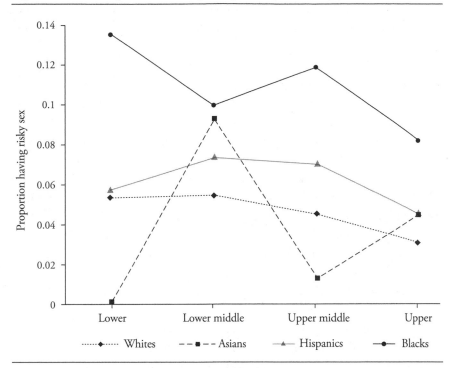

Source: Authors' compilation based on Harris and Udry (2008).

The last risky behavior we consider involves sex. We define risky sex as engaging in paid intercourse or having sex with a known drug user, acts that generally expose people to an elevated risk of contracting sexually transmitted diseases, including AIDS. As can be seen from figure 5.5, the cell sizes and outcome frequencies are too small to yield much in the way of interpretable results for Asians, the estimates fluctuating quite widely and without a systematic pattern across class categories. Setting Asians aside, whites display the lowest likelihood of engaging in risky sex and a declining class gradient, the share having paid sex or intercourse with a drug user decreasing from around 5 percent in the lower class and lower middle class to about 3 percent in the upper class. Close behind are Hispanics, who begin at around 6 percent in the lower class, rise to 7 percent or so in the lower and upper middle class, and then drop to under 5 percent in the upper class. Although blacks also display a declining pattern of risky sex with rising social class (albeit somewhat irregular), the proportion is greatest for them at all points in the plot, the figure decreasing from 14 percent in the lower class to 8 percent in the upper.

The coefficients estimated in the baseline model of table 5.5 are consistent with these patterns. Asian patterns remain difficult to interpret owing to sampling variability, but both whites and Hispanics display a declining, slightly convex pattern of risky behavior as social class rises. In contrast, blacks are much higher at all class levels, though generally showing a decline with socioeconomic status. Controlling for background characteristics generally eliminates class variation among Hispanics and reduces it somewhat among whites, but has relatively little effect on the coefficients estimated for African Americans, except perhaps in the upper class, where the coefficient falls once controls are introduced, though the shift is not significant statistically.

With respect to background characteristics, the propensity for risky sex generally rises with age, with the odds increasing by around 12 percent per year, and the odds are significantly greater (by 78 percent) among young people with foreign-born parents. The likelihood of risky sex is lower for women than men, and the male propensity for risky sex does not vary significantly by marital or parental status. Among women, however, all of the family status coefficients save one are negative and three are significant. According to the model, the odds of risky sex are lowest for unmarried women without children, followed by unmarried mothers who gave birth over age eighteen and unmarried women without children.

Few ecological indicators are significant in predicting the likelihood of engaging in risky sex. The two strongest predictors are disorder at school and violence in the peer network. For each unit on the disorder index, the odds of risky sex fall by 10 percent (190 percent over the range of the index), whereas for each unit of exposure to peer violence, the odds increase by around 13 percent (260 percent overall). Risky sex is also positively predicted by having a suicidal friend, which raises the odds by 58 percent, as well as by the sternness of the family emotional environment, which reduces the odds by 1.1 percent per unit. Coming from a single-parent family of origin has a marginally significant effect in raising the odds by an estimated 52 percent, but none of the material or symbolic resources associated with class are significant. Again, social and emotional circumstances are most important in predicting respondent behavior.

Table 5.5   Determinants of Having Risky Sex

Independent Variables	Group Effects B	Group Effects SE	Full Model B	Full Model SE
Race-class group				
White lower	0.577***	0.255	0.445	0.791
White lower middle	0.608**	0.236	0.585	0.535
White upper middle	0.399	0.112	0.546	0.418
White upper	—	—	—	—
Asian lower	−3.228***	0.985	−2.913*	1.257
Asian lower middle	1.183*	0.584	1.267	0.917
Asian upper middle	−0.953	0.937	−1.278	1.019
Asian upper	0.388	0.524	0.320	0.615
Hispanic lower	0.659+	0.363	0.177	0.803
Hispanic lower middle	0.930**	0.339	0.579	0.544
Hispanic upper middle	0.876*	0.418	0.293	0.476
Hispanic upper	0.415	0.499	0.044	0.483
Black lower	1.608***	0.219	1.419+	0.799
Black lower middle	1.265***	0.350	1.302+	0.679
Black upper middle	1.463***	0.284	1.181*	0.472
Black upper	1.043*	0.410	0.698	0.498
Ascribed characteristics				
Age	—	—	0.116**	0.043
Parent foreign born	—	—	0.579*	0.276
Mediating conditions				
Family situation				
Unmarried male–not father	—	—	—	—
Married male–not father	—	—	−0.239	0.542
Married male–father	—	—	0.118	0.324
Unmarried male–father	—	—	0.090	0.281
Unmarried female–no birth	—	—	−0.376*	0.193
Married female–no birth	—	—	−1.276*	0.597
Married female–mother	—	—	−0.293	0.314
Unmarried female–birth over eighteen	—	—	−0.621+	0.337
Unmarried female–birth eighteen or younger	—	—	0.334	0.295
Ecological background				
Composition of origin family				
Two biological parents	—	—	—	—
Biological and stepparent	—	—	0.121	0.234
One biological parent	—	—	0.419+	0.216
No biological parent	—	—	0.197	0.592
Family material resources				
Household income	—	—	0.012	0.012

Table 5.5   (continued)

Independent Variables	Group Effects		Full Model	
	B	SE	B	SE
Access to health insurance				
No coverage	—	—	—	—
Coverage less than a year	—	—	−0.104	0.237
Coverage full year	—	—	−0.303	0.239
Family symbolic resources				
Parental prestige	—	—	0.003	0.004
Parent went to college	—	—	−0.051	0.254
Family emotional resources				
Death in family	—	—	−0.386	0.313
Family sternness	—	—	−0.011*	0.005
Father incarcerated	—	—	−0.152	0.193
Had family mentor	—	—	−0.140	0.223
Neighborhood setting				
Disadvantage index	—	—	0.128	0.135
Inefficacy index	—	—	0.016	0.026
Scarcity of males	—	—	−0.261	0.355
Had neighborhood mentor	—	—	0.293	0.270
School setting				
Disadvantage index	—	—	−0.005	0.012
Inefficacy index	—	—	0.015	0.014
Disorder index	—	—	−0.107***	0.032
Had school mentor	—	—	−0.347	0.289
Religious setting				
Religiosity scale	—	—	−0.009	0.018
Involvement index	—	—	−0.025	0.029
Had religious mentor	—	—	−0.073	0.584
Peer setting				
Violence index	—	—	0.120***	0.022
Friend attempted suicide	—	—	0.458*	0.231
Had peer mentor	—	—	0.026	0.223
Multiple disadvantages				
Log of interactive index	—	—	0.032	0.037
Intercept	−3.465***	0.186	−5.492***	1.487
N	8,969		7,164	
F-test	9.51***		6.58***	

Source: Authors' calculations based on data set described in Harris and Udry (2008).

Note: Risky sex includes both paid intercourse and sex with a drug user.

$+p < .10$; $*p < .05$; $**p < .01$; $***p < .001$

ECOLOGY UNDER THE SKIN

The foregoing results yield a mixed picture with respect to risky health behaviors. In terms of cigarette smoking, alcohol abuse, and hard drug consumption, whites clearly display the highest rates, followed in descending order by Hispanics, Asians, and African Americans. In general, smoking displays a negative class gradient and the likelihood of alcohol abuse and drug consumption rises with social class, except among blacks where the odds of smoking, drinking, and drug-taking are consistently low regardless of class. Moreover, although the addition of background controls seems to explain class variations among whites, Hispanics, and to some extent Asians, it does not eliminate the large gap between blacks and others. Smoking is thus concentrated among lower-class whites and drinking and drug use among upper-class whites. African Americans are unlikely to engage in any of these behaviors.

Fast-food consumption was frequent across all race-class categories, though more likely among African Americans, followed by Hispanics, whites, and Asians. In addition, whereas fast-food consumption fell with rising social class among the latter three groups, it rose slightly among blacks. The propensity to engage in risky sex—with a sex worker or known drug user—was relatively low in all racial groups but was greatest for African Americans. The higher likelihood of consuming fast food and engaging in risky sex among young African Americans was also not eliminated by controlling for ecological and other background differences.

At this point, we move on to assess whether the foregoing health behaviors have any effect on the actual physical condition of respondents, focusing on reported limitations of physical activity, body mass, and diagnoses of sexually transmitted diseases. The third wave of Add Health asked respondents whether they had any limitations on the physical activities they could perform. Figure 5.6 shows the proportion who reported any such limitation by race and class. In general, we observe a negative class gradient, the highest degree of physical limitation being in the lower class and the lowest in the upper middle or upper class. For whites, the decline is monotonic, the limitation curve going from 32 percent in the lower class, to 27 percent and 26 percent in the lower middle and upper middle classes, and reaching 23 percent in the upper class.

Among African Americans, the rate of disability is generally lower, only 25

Figure 5.6   Proportion Reporting Limitation on Physical Activity by Race and Class

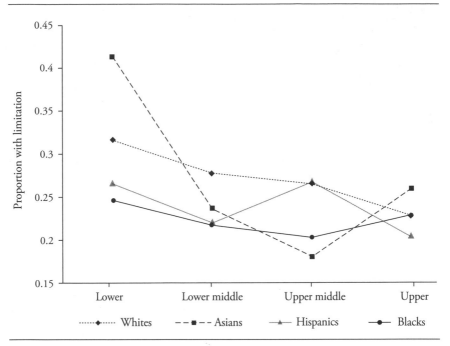

Source: Authors' compilation based on Harris and Udry (2008).

percent of those in the lower class reporting a physical limitation on movement, 22 percent in the lower middle class, 20 percent in the upper middle class, and 23 percent in the upper class. Hispanics generally lie between blacks and whites, in some classes closer to the former and in others to the latter. Moving from lower to upper class, those reporting a physical limitation are 26 percent, 25 percent, 27 percent, and 20 percent, respectively. The highest rate of physical disability occurs among lower-class Asians, 41 percent of whom report some limitation of activity. This high figure, however, drops sharply to 24 percent in the lower middle class and reaches 18 percent (the lowest observed rate) in the upper middle class, before rising to 26 percent in the upper class.

The left-hand columns of table 5.6 show a baseline logistic regression model that uses race-class dummies to predict whether respondents reported a physical limitation. In statistical terms, the likelihood of physical disability among Hispanics and blacks is no greater than among upper-class whites, irrespective of class standing; among Asians, the likelihood is only significantly greater in the lower class. Whites are the only group in which we observe a clear class gradient in statistical terms, the odds of physical limitation being 56 percent greater in the lower class, 25 percent greater in the lower middle class, and 21 percent greater in the upper middle class, compared with upper-class whites. Lower-class Asians, for their part, are 2.4 times more likely to display a physical limitation. All the remaining categories of Asians, and all classes of Hispanics and blacks, evince the same low odds of physical disability as upper-class whites.

As the right-hand columns show, controlling for background characteristics eliminates class differences among whites, but does not make the significant coefficient for lower-class Asians disappear, and that for upper-class Asians actually increases in size and becomes significantly positive, yielding a U-shaped class pattern with respect to the risk of disability. Coefficients for the other groups do not change significantly. Other things equal, therefore, lower- and upper-class Asians stand out for having high a high likelihood of physical disability, one that is not attributable to ecological circumstances. In contrast, whites display a class gradient that is fully accounted for by class differences in ecological conditions.

The likelihood of having a physical limitation falls with age and is greater for women than men. With each additional year of age, the odds of reporting a physical limitation drop by around 6 percent and they are at least 58 percent greater for women, and could be higher depending on marriage and parental status. The greatest odds of reporting a physical limitation (89 percent) are for married mothers. Men have the same likelihood of disability whether or not they are married and whether or not they have children. Holding gender and age constant, two risky behaviors significantly predict whether respondents reported a limitation of physical activity. Smoking increased the odds of a physical limitation by a factor of 2.1 and engaging in risky sex increased them by 43 percent. We also considered engaging in first intercourse without contraception (from the last chapter) as a risk factor, but it had no significant effect. The effects of drinking, drug taking, and consuming fast food were insignificant and generally close to zero.

In the family sphere, the likelihood of having a physical limitation is apparently not affected by the composition of the origin household or by symbolic resources such as parental prestige and college attainment. The only

Table 5.6   Determinants of Limitation on Physical Activity

Independent Variables	Group Effects B	Group Effects SE	Full Model B	Full Model SE
Race-class group				
White lower	0.447***	0.101	−0.014	0.380
White lower middle	0.226*	0.123	0.001	0.280
White upper middle	0.193+	0.107	0.021	0.193
White upper	—	—	—	—
Asian lower	0.869*	0.366	1.084+	0.605
Asian lower middle	0.046	0.315	0.429	0.492
Asian upper middle	−0.296	0.252	−0.345	0.362
Asian upper	0.169	0.207	0.635*	0.319
Hispanic lower	0.200	0.165	0.185	0.476
Hispanic lower middle	−0.043	0.195	−0.102	0.360
Hispanic upper middle	0.214	0.263	−0.023	0.352
Hispanic upper	−0.148	0.369	−0.271	0.364
Black lower	0.101	0.168	−0.338	0.446
Black lower middle	−0.064	0.207	−0.349	0.410
Black upper middle	−0.152	0.225	−0.545	0.312
Black upper	−0.002	0.249	−0.104	0.272
Ascribed characteristics				
Age	—	—	−0.059*	0.030
Parent foreign born	—	—	−0.232	0.177
Mediating conditions				
Risky behaviors				
Smoked regularly	—	—	0.739*	0.302
Abused alcohol	—	—	−0.055	0.092
Used hard drugs	—	—	−0.056	0.099
Ate fast food	—	—	0.055	0.095
Sex without birth control	—	—	0.043	0.146
Sex with risky partner	—	—	0.355*	0.146
Family situation				
Unmarried male–not father	—	—	—	—
Married male–not father	—	—	0.089	0.264
Married male–father	—	—	0.333	0.237
Unmarried male–father	—	—	−0.056	0.191
Unmarried female–no birth	—	—	0.459***	0.107
Married female–no birth	—	—	0.515**	0.186
Married female–mother	—	—	0.637***	0.177
Unmarried female–birth over eighteen	—	—	0.538***	0.170
Unmarried female–birth eighteen or younger	—	—	0.576*	0.235
Composition of origin family				
Two biological parents	—	—	—	—
Biological and stepparent	—	—	0.016	0.153

Table 5.6   (continued)

Independent Variables	Group Effects		Full Model	
	B	SE	B	SE
One biological parent	—	—	0.007	0.115
No biological parent	—	—	0.017	0.389
Family material resources				
Household income	—	—	−0.003	0.007
Access to health insurance				
No coverage	—	—	—	—
Coverage less than a year	—	—	0.057	0.113
Coverage full year	—	—	−0.292**	0.096
Family symbolic resources				
Parental prestige	—	—	0.000	0.002
Parent went to college	—	—	0.096	0.114
Family emotional resources				
Experienced a death	—	—	−0.014	0.183
Family sternness	—	—	−0.006*	0.003
Father incarcerated	—	—	0.189	0.138
Had family mentor	—	—	0.375***	0.121
Neighborhood setting				
Disadvantage index	—	—	0.032	0.087
Inefficacy index	—	—	0.023+	0.014
Scarcity of males	—	—	−0.153	0.135
Had neighborhood mentor	—	—	0.220	0.157
School setting				
Disadvantage index	—	—	0.002	0.006
Inefficacy index	—	—	0.011	0.007
Disorder index	—	—	−0.014	0.016
Had school mentor	—	—	0.198	0.146
Religious setting				
Religiosity scale	—	—	0.011	0.010
Involvement index	—	—	−0.006	0.015
Had religious mentor	—	—	0.452+	0.250
Peer setting				
Violence index	—	—	0.013	0.016
Friend attempted suicide	—	—	0.475***	0.131
Had peer mentor	—	—	0.240*	0.117
Multiple disadvantages				
Log of interactive index	—	—	−0.002	0.019
Intercept	−1.215***	0.082	0.179	1.134
N	8,831		6,844	
F-test	1.74*		5.25***	

Source: Authors' calculations based on data set described in Harris and Udry (2008).
+*p* < .10; **p* < .05; ***p* < .01; ****p* < .001

material resource that matters is full access to health insurance, which lowers the odds by around 25 percent; household income has no effect. The key ecological predictors are once again family emotional resources and social-emotional conditions in the peer environment. As before, emotional sternness plays a significant role, reducing the odds of disability by 0.6 percent per unit. Reliance on a family mentor is associated with 45 percent greater odds of reporting a physical limitation, and having a peer mentor increases them by 27 percent. The attempted suicide of a friend, meanwhile, is associated with 61 percent greater odds. Beyond these family and peer effects, only two other factors are significant, and then at a marginal level. Social inefficacy in the neighborhood increases the odds by 2.3 percent per unit, and having a religious mentor by 57 percent.

An important risk factor predicting impaired health later in life is excessive weight in youth. Figure 5.7 shows the body mass index (BMI), or the ratio in metric units between weight and height squared. People with a BMI from 25 to 30 are generally considered to be overweight whereas values of 30 or more indicate obesity. Figure 5.7 plots average BMI by race and class for Add Health respondents. In general, blacks and Hispanics have the highest BMIs and Asians are lowest, with whites falling in between. Average BMIs for Hispanics and African Americans generally fluctuate around values of 27 and 28 and show little class gradient. In contrast, the white BMI starts at around 27 in the lower and lower middle classes and then drops to 26 or even lower in the upper middle and upper classes. Asians have values around 24 in the lower and upper classes and around 26 in the lower middle and upper middle class. By conventional standards, therefore, respondents in all of the race-class groups are, on average, overweight, with the exception of lower- and upper-middle-class Asians.

The baseline model shown in the left-hand columns of table 5.7 indicate that the class gradient observed among whites is indeed statistically significant. Compared with upper-class whites, the BMI of lower-class whites is 1.25 points higher and that of lower-middle-class whites 1.15 points higher, whereas upper-middle-class whites are just 0.1 points higher (not significant). The remarkably lower BMI averages observed among lower- and upper-class Asians are highly significant, being 1.97 and 1.69 points below that of upper-class whites. In contrast, the BMI values for blacks and Hispanics are universally greater. In six of eight cases, the coefficients are statistically significant, with the increase in BMI relative to upper-class whites ranging from 0.81

Figure 5.7   Body Mass Index by Race and Class

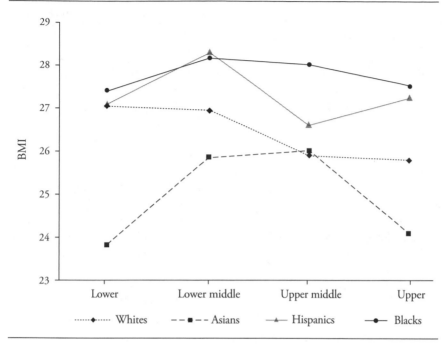

Source: Authors' compilation based on Harris and Udry (2008).

points to 2.49 points among Hispanics, and from 1.62 points to 2.36 points among blacks.

In general, class differences among whites are eliminated and the higher values observed for blacks disappear or are substantially reduced when background controls are added. The strong effects observed for upper- and lower-class Asians are not eliminated, however. The positive effects of lower-middle-class and upper-class status generally persist among Hispanics, though the effect for among the Hispanic lower class is reduced to insignificance. Seemingly, there is something about lower-middle and upper-class status among Hispanics that elevates body weight and something about upper- and lower-class status among Asians that lowers it. All remaining race-class differences in BMI can generally be attributed to background characteristics.

Foreign origins is associated with a significantly lower (by 1.04 points) body mass index, in keeping with other studies showing that one of the things that immigrants assimilate into within the United States is excessive

Table 5.7   Determinants of Body Mass Index

Independent Variables	Group Effects		Full Model	
	B	SE	B	SE
Race-class group				
White lower	1.246**	0.397	−0.094	1.037
White lower middle	1.146***	0.199	0.434	0.842
White upper middle	0.101	0.326	−0.375	0.465
White upper	—	—	—	—
Asian lower	−1.969*	0.937	−3.364*	1.350
Asian lower middle	0.076	0.883	0.507	1.272
Asian upper middle	0.211	1.019	0.465	1.029
Asian upper	−1.694*	0.649	−1.034	0.732
Hispanic lower	1.253**	0.424	0.432	1.070
Hispanic lower middle	2.493***	0.549	1.611+	0.977
Hispanic upper middle	0.810	0.567	0.640	0.770
Hispanic upper	1.446*	0.736	1.655+	0.594
Black lower	1.623***	0.443	−0.879	1.212
Black lower middle	2.362***	0.671	0.230	1.192
Black upper middle	2.212***	0.679	0.801	0.852
Black upper	1.712	1.137	0.777	1.045
Ascribed characteristics				
Age	—	—	0.316***	0.074
Parent foreign born	—	—	−1.039**	0.385
Mediating conditions				
Risky behaviors				
Smoked regularly	—	—	−0.001	0.891
Abused alcohol	—	—	−0.385	0.259
Used hard drugs	—	—	−0.889***	0.262
Ate fast food	—	—	0.127	0.230
Sex without birth control	—	—	0.241	0.229
Sex with risky partner	—	—	0.415	0.424
Family situation				
Unmarried male–not father	—	—	—	—
Married male–not father	—	—	−0.498	0.552
Married male–father	—	—	−0.498	0.557
Unmarried male–father	—	—	−1.582***	0.494
Unmarried female–no birth	—	—	−0.713**	0.246
Married female–no birth	—	—	0.118	0.604
Married female–mother	—	—	0.868+	0.458
Unmarried female–birth over eighteen	—	—	1.153+	0.599
Unmarried female–birth eighteen or younger	—	—	1.336	0.908

Table 5.7   (continued)

Independent Variables	Group Effects		Full Model	
	B	SE	B	SE
Ecological background				
Composition of origin family				
Two biological parents	—	—	—	—
Biological and stepparent	—	—	−0.734+	0.417
One biological parent	—	—	−0.444	0.284
No biological parent	—	—	−0.702	1.031
Family material resources				
Household income	—	—	−0.008	0.019
Access to health insurance				
No coverage	—	—	—	—
Coverage less than a year	—	—	0.023	0.375
Coverage full year	—	—	−0.271	0.348
Family symbolic resources				
Parental prestige	—	—	−0.008	0.006
Parent went to college	—	—	−0.451	0.425
Family emotional resources				
Experienced a death	—	—	0.173	0.502
Family sternness	—	—	0.002	0.007
Father incarcerated	—	—	0.874*	0.385
Had family mentor	—	—	0.314	0.300
Neighborhood setting				
Disadvantage index	—	—	0.693**	0.240
Inefficacy index	—	—	−0.008	0.041
Scarcity of males	—	—	0.225	0.384
Had neighborhood mentor	—	—	0.305	0.489
School setting				
Disadvantage index	—	—	−0.010	0.017
Inefficacy index	—	—	−0.004	0.019
Disorder index	—	—	0.117**	0.040
Had school mentor	—	—	0.945**	0.368
Religious setting				
Religiosity scale	—	—	0.004	0.026
Involvement index	—	—	0.109	0.039
Had religious mentor	—	—	0.102	0.590
Peer setting				
Violence index	—	—	0.030	0.049
Suicide of friend	—	—	0.768*	0.391
Had peer mentor	—	—	0.480	0.307

Table 5.7   *(continued)*

	Group Effects		Full Model	
Independent Variables	B	SE	B	SE
Multiple disadvantages				
Log of interactive index	—	—	–0.011	0.059
Intercept	25.789***	0.251	19.565***	2.839
N	8,575		7,226	
F-test	4.64***		5.50***	
R²	0.017		0.057	

Source: Authors' calculations based on data set described in Harris and Udry (2008).
+*p* < .10; *p* < .05; **p* < .01; ***p* < .001

body weight (Akresh 2007, 2008). Age is also significant, raising body mass by about 0.33 points per year. The only risky behavior related to body weight is the use of hard drugs, which lowers BMI by 0.89 points. Consumption of fast food has no discernable effect, possibly because so many respondents eat it. In terms of gender and parental-marital status, lower body weights characterize unmarried fathers (1.58 points lower) and unmarried females without children (0.71 points lower), whereas mothers generally have higher weights (0.86 points higher if married and 1.15 points if unmarried).

Relatively few ecological factors predict body weight. BMI is unrelated to any material or symbolic resource in the family sphere, but is positively predicted by neighborhood disadvantage and school disorder. For each unit in the disadvantage scale, BMI rises by 0.69 points (for a total of 2.76 points over the range of the index) and for each unit in the disorder scale it goes up by 0.12 points (for a total of 2.28 points). Given that the mean BMI is 26.6 and moving from the least to most disadvantaged neighborhood, or from the least to most disordered school, would push the average respondent roughly to the lower limit of the obese range. Body weight is also increased by the emotional traumas of paternal imprisonment and a friend's attempted suicide, by respective increments to BMI of 0.87 and 0.77 points. Having a school-based mentor is also associated with greater body mass, raising BMI by 0.95 points.

The last physical indicator we consider is the likelihood of having been diagnosed with a sexually transmitted disease (STD), and figure 5.8 plots the results by race and class. African Americans clearly stand out from other groups for their relatively high rate of STD infection, which is perhaps not surprising given their higher rates and earlier entry into sexual activity and

Figure 5.8   Proportion Ever Diagnosed with an STD by Race and Class

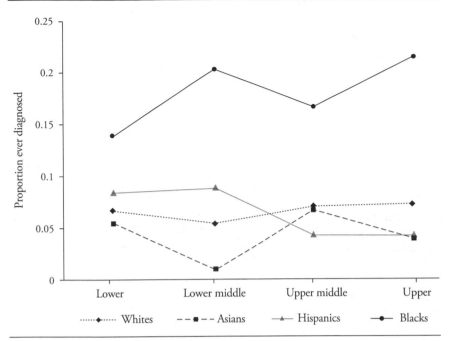

Source: Authors' compilation based on Harris and Udry (2008).

their tendency to engage in risky sex, as shown in earlier tables and figures. Whereas the share ever diagnosed with an STD never exceeds 9 percent for whites, Hispanics, and Asians and displays no strong class pattern, the class curve for blacks begins at 14 percent among those in the lower class, rises to 20 percent in the lower middle class, and then after slipping to around 16 percent in the upper middle class climbs back up to around 22 percent in the upper class. The risk of STD infection among African Americans thus generally rises with class.

The significance of these results is indicated by the baseline model presented in the left-hand columns of table 5.8. The coefficients for African Americans are universally positive and significant. The only other statistically significant race-class effect is negative, and that is for lower-middle-class Asians. Moreover, rather than eliminating the significant coefficients for blacks, the addition of controls sharpens the inverse class gradient. The odds of an STD diagnosis are lowest for lower-class blacks, intermediate for those in the middle classes, and highest among those in the upper class. Even after

Table 5.8   Determinants of STD Diagnosis

Independent Variables	Group Effects		Full Model	
	B	SE	B	SE
Race-class group				
White lower	−0.094	0.189	−0.452	0.680
White lower middle	−0.320	0.199	−0.688	0.523
White upper middle	−0.040	0.175	−0.279	0.318
White upper	—	—	—	—
Asian lower	−0.309	1.007	0.213	1.137
Asian lower middle	−2.031**	0.698	−1.601+	0.974
Asian upper middle	−0.089	0.544	0.482	0.696
Asian upper	−0.642	0.556	−0.227	0.638
Hispanic lower	0.147	0.245	0.125	0.822
Hispanic lower middle	0.206	0.276	0.023	0.629
Hispanic upper middle	−0.559	0.443	−0.443	0.611
Hispanic upper	−0.583	0.432	−0.997	0.633
Black lower	0.710***	0.191	0.286	0.763
Black lower middle	1.168***	0.229	0.881	0.548
Black upper middle	0.920***	0.240	0.846+	0.436
Black upper	1.237***	0.224	1.070***	0.307
Ascribed characteristics				
Age	—	—	0.034	0.039
Parent foreign born	—	—	−0.315	0.298
Mediating conditions				
Risky behaviors				
Smoked regularly	—	—	0.385	0.505
Abused alcohol	—	—	0.247	0.156
Used hard drugs	—	—	0.159	0.187
Ate fast food	—	—	0.016	0.152
Sex without birth control	—	—	0.432***	0.138
Sex with risky partner	—	—	0.985***	0.218
Family situation				
Unmarried male–not father	—	—	—	—
Married male–not father	—	—	−0.386	0.569
Married male–father	—	—	−0.033	0.600
Unmarried male–father	—	—	0.436	0.330
Unmarried female–no birth	—	—	1.532***	0.187
Married female–no birth	—	—	1.290***	0.349
Married female–mother	—	—	1.121**	0.430
Unmarried female–birth over eighteen	—	—	1.732***	0.289
Unmarried female–birth eighteen or younger	—	—	1.456***	0.340

Table 5.8   (continued)

Independent Variables	Group Effects		Full Model	
	B	SE	B	SE
Ecological background				
Composition of origin family				
Two biological parents	—	—	—	—
Biological and stepparent	—	—	0.018	0.236
One biological parent	—	—	0.189	0.170
No biological parent	—	—	0.224	0.495
Family material resources				
Household income	—	—	–0.003	0.011
Access to health insurance				
No coverage	—	—	—	—
Coverage less than a year	—	—	0.182	0.223
Coverage full year	—	—	0.298+	0.169
Family symbolic resources				
Parental prestige	—	—	0.002	0.004
Parent went to college	—	—	0.225	0.188
Family emotional resources				
Experienced a death	—	—	0.091	0.210
Family sternness	—	—	–0.007+	0.004
Father incarcerated	—	—	0.071	0.164
Had family mentor	—	—	0.153	0.194
Neighborhood setting				
Disadvantage index	—	—	0.256*	0.117
Inefficacy index	—	—	–0.025	0.025
Scarcity of males	—	—	–0.056	0.149
Had neighborhood mentor	—	—	0.431+	0.257
School setting				
Disadvantage index	—	—	–0.003	0.010
Inefficacy index	—	—	0.022+	0.012
Disorder index	—	—	0.019	0.022
Had school mentor	—	—	0.082	0.203
Religious setting				
Religiosity scale	—	—	–0.018	0.016
Involvement index	—	—	–0.015	0.020
Had religious mentor	—	—	–0.542	0.623
Peer setting				
Violence index	—	—	0.009	0.030
Friend attempted suicide	—	—	–0.074	0.239
Had peer mentor	—	—	0.061	0.218

Table 5.8   **(continued)**

Independent Variables	Group Effects		Full Model	
	B	SE	B	SE
Multiple disadvantages				
Log of interactive index	—	—	0.010	0.026
Intercept	−2.540***	0.129	−5.104***	1.475
N	8,947		6,954	
F-test	12.43***		7.89***	

Source: Authors' calculations based on data set described in Harris and Udry (2008).
+$p < .10$; *$p < .05$; **$p < .01$; ***$p < .001$

controlling for ecological and other factors, the odds of STD infection are almost three times greater for upper-class blacks than for their white counterparts.

Not surprisingly, the two mediating behaviors most significant in predicting STD infection are having initial sex without birth control (which raises the odds by 54 percent) and having sex with a risky partner (by a factor of 2.7). The likelihood of getting an STD is universally higher for women than men, the odds of STD infection ranging anywhere from three times to 5.7 times greater depending the woman's marital and maternal status. The likelihood of reporting an STD diagnosis is generally weakly connected to ecological circumstances, however. The only effect significant at the 5 percent level is neighborhood disadvantage. Each unit increase in the disadvantage index raises the odds of STD infection by 29 percent, or 116 percent over the range of the index, a rather large effect. The odds of having an STD are also marginally increased by school disorder (2.2 percent per unit), by having a mentor from the neighborhood (54 percent), and by health insurance coverage (35 percent) and is marginally decreased by family sternness (by 0.7 percent per unit). The effect of insurance may simply reflect better access to diagnostic services.

PREDICTING INDIVIDUAL WELL-BEING

To this point, we have examined race-class differences in the propensity to engage in various risky health behaviors and in the likelihood of exhibiting certain physical conditions. In preliminary work for this chapter, we consid-

Figure 5.9   Index of Poor Health by Race and Class

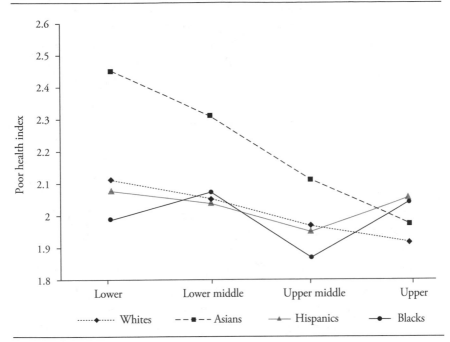

Source: Authors' compilation based on Harris and Udry (2008).

ered a variety of other health conditions assessed in the Add Health Survey, but, given that respondents are young and generally quite healthy, the frequencies were insufficient to sustain statistical analysis. To consider the ecological determinants of health, therefore, we turn to three general assessments of health the respondents provided. The first comes from a standard item on general health in which respondents are asked to rate their health as excellent, very good, good, fair, or poor, which we coded 1 to 5, larger numbers indicating poorer health. These ratings are plotted by race and class in figure 5.9.

Asians and whites display a clear social class gradient, health being worst in the lower class and steadily improving as class standing rises. The gradient is particularly steep for Asians. Lower-class Asians exhibit by far the worst health index at around 2.5, which falls to around 2.3 in the lower middle class, 2.1 in the upper middle class, and just under 2.0 in the upper class, which is only slightly above that of upper-class whites. The class gradient for whites is much less severe. The index of poor health begins in the lower class with an average value of just 2.1 and the falls to around 1.9 in the upper class, a shift of just 0.2 points. The Hispanic curve closely follows that of whites through the first three class categories but rises back up to 2.1 in the upper class. African Americans give themselves a fairly good health rating in all classes, the value fluctuating around 2.0 with no systematic gradient.

The baseline model shown in the left-hand columns of table 5.9 statistically confirms a class gradient among whites, Asians, and Hispanics but not among blacks. Among whites, compared with the upper class, the index of poor health is 0.19 points greater in the lower class, 0.13 points greater in the lower middle class, and 0.05 points greater in the upper middle class. Likewise, the progression of coefficients among Asians from lowest to highest class is 0.53, 0.39, 0.19, and 0.06. Among Hispanics it is 0.16. 0.12, 0.03, and 0.14, the last two values not being statistically significant. The only other significant effect was observed among lower-middle-class blacks, whose poor health rating was 0.15 points higher than upper-class whites.

The addition of control variables eliminates class differences among whites and Hispanics and gets rid of the significantly greater coefficient for lower-middle-class blacks but does not eliminate the class differential among Asians. Although the coefficient for immigrant origins is negative, consistent with a pattern of health-selective migration, it is not significant. Health improves significantly with age, however, the index of poor health dropping by 1.9 points per year. Among mediating conditions, poor health seems to be exacerbated by regular smoking, raising the index value by 0.25 points, though the p-value is significant only at the 10 percent level. Poor health is more strongly predicted by rising body mass (0.018 points per unit) and by limitation of physical activity (0.48 points). Compared with an unmarried man without children, health is better for married males without children (by 0.19 points) but worse for unmarried women without children (by 0.15 points).

As one might expect, health is significantly improved by access to health insurance, the poor health index dropping by 0.15 points for those with full coverage and by 0.12 points for partial coverage. Somewhat surprisingly, though, health is worse for respondents with a college-educated parent, though only by 0.09 points. Neither income nor occupational status has any significant effect. The only other factor in the family sphere to influence health is emotional sternness, which generally has a beneficial effect, reducing poor health by 0.005 points per unit, which, given the range observed for

Table 5.9   Determinants of Poor Health

Independent Variables	Group Effects		Full Model	
	B	SE	B	SE
Race-class group				
White lower	0.192***	0.043	−0.043	0.113
White lower middle	0.134**	0.048	−0.018	0.079
White upper middle	0.051	0.034	−0.031	0.048
White upper	—	—	—	—
Asian lower	0.532*	0.216	0.412+	0.226
Asian lower middle	0.393**	0.142	0.569***	0.165
Asian upper middle	0.194*	0.087	0.288**	0.104
Asian upper	0.058	0.087	0.105	0.092
Hispanic lower	0.158*	0.065	0.048	0.134
Hispanic lower middle	0.120+	0.067	0.037	0.108
Hispanic upper middle	0.032	0.088	−0.074	0.096
Hispanic upper	0.139	0.116	0.086	0.074
Black lower	0.068	0.060	−0.063	0.126
Black lower middle	0.154*	0.070	0.040	0.108
Black upper middle	−0.049	0.065	−0.012	0.097
Black upper	0.123	0.104	0.058	0.106
Ascribed characteristics				
Age	—	—	−0.019*	0.008
Parent foreign born	—	—	−0.086	0.056
Mediating conditions				
Risky behaviors				
Smoked regularly	—	—	0.251+	0.142
Abused alcohol	—	—	−0.050	0.031
Used hard drugs	—	—	0.016	0.034
Ate fast food	—	—	−0.030	0.036
Sex without birth control	—	—	0.021	0.029
Sex with risky partner	—	—	0.009	0.073
Reported health problems				
Ever had STD	—	—	0.054	0.049
Body mass index	—	—	0.018***	0.003
Limitation on activity	—	—	0.482***	0.027
Family situation				
Unmarried male–not father	—	—	—	—
Married male–not father	—	—	−0.186***	0.067
Married male–father	—	—	0.085	0.070
Unmarried male–father	—	—	0.056	0.071
Unmarried female–no birth	—	—	0.149***	0.032

Table 5.9   (continued)

Independent Variables	Group Effects		Full Model	
	B	SE	B	SE
Married female–no birth	—	—	0.113+	0.064
Married female–mother	—	—	–0.021	0.075
Unmarried female–birth over eighteen	—	—	0.060	0.057
Unmarried female–birth eighteen or younger	—	—	0.042	0.100
Ecological background				
Composition of origin family				
Two biological parents	—	—	—	—
Biological and stepparent	—	—	–0.043	0.058
One biological parent	—	—	–0.057	0.036
No biological parent	—	—	0.074	0.165
Family material resources				
Household income	—	—	0.000	0.002
Access to health insurance				
No coverage	—	—	—	—
Coverage less than a year	—	—	–0.124**	0.046
Coverage full year	—	—	–0.154***	0.037
Family symbolic resources				
Parental prestige	—	—	–0.001	0.001
Parent went to college	—	—	0.092*	0.043
Family emotional resources				
Experienced a death	—	—	–0.080	0.056
Family sternness	—	—	–0.005***	0.001
Father incarcerated	—	—	0.039	0.043
Had family mentor	—	—	0.071*	0.034
Neighborhood setting				
Disadvantage index	—	—	–0.005	0.030
Inefficacy index	—	—	0.008	0.005
Scarcity of males	—	—	0.059*	0.029
Had neighborhood mentor	—	—	0.052	0.055
School setting				
Disadvantage index	—	—	–0.002	0.002
Inefficacy index	—	—	0.011***	0.003
Disorder index	—	—	–0.009	0.005
Had school mentor	—	—	0.049	0.036
Religious setting				
Religiosity scale	—	—	–0.002	0.003

Table 5.9   (continued)

Independent Variables	Group Effects		Full Model	
	B	SE	B	SE
Involvement index	—	—	–0.008*	0.004
Had religious mentor	—	—	0.053	0.063
Peer setting				
Violence index	—	—	–0.014*	0.007
Friend attempted suicide	—	—	0.138**	0.046
Had peer mentor	—	—	0.058	0.040
Multiple disadvantages				
Log of interactive index	—	—	0.016*	0.006
Intercept	1.920***	0.029	1.675***	0.320
N	8,996		6,549	
F-test	3.55**		27.91***	
R²	0.009***		0.202	

Source: Authors' calculations based on data set described in Harris and Udry (2008).
$+p < .10$; $*p < .05$; $**p < .01$; $***p < .001$

this index, could potentially move a person all the way from poor to excellent health. In the neighborhood sphere, health is diminished by a relative scarcity of young unmarried males (0.059 points per unit), and within schools by greater levels of social inefficacy (0.011 points per unit). Health is significantly bolstered by religious involvement and, surprisingly, by exposure to peer violence. It is, though, undermined by a friend's suicide attempt as well as by the accumulation of multiple disadvantages across social spheres.

The survey also contained a battery of items asking how often respondents felt sad, blue, hopeless, listless, lonely, unwanted, and so on, which when combined yield a reliable scale of mental depression ($\alpha = .80$—see appendix B). Figure 5.10 shows average values on the depression scale by race and class. Whites are generally the least depressed, values falling from around 4.6 in the lower class to 4.4 and 4.3 in the lower middle and upper middle classes to 4.0 in the upper class. In contrast, African Americans display higher indices of depression that do not decline with class standing, values around 4.4 in the lower and lower middle classes, and 4.8 in the upper middle and upper classes. Asians display a U-shaped curve with quite high values in the lower (5.8) and upper (5.6) classes and more moderate values (around 4.6) in the lower and upper middle classes. The Hispanic pattern is irregular, falling

Figure 5.10   Index of Depression by Race and Class

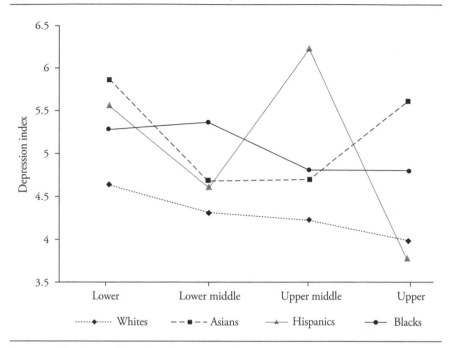

Source: Authors' compilation based on Harris and Udry (2008).

from 5.5 to 4.6 between the lower class and the lower middle class, and then climbing sharply to 6.3 (the highest value in the figure) in the upper middle class, and then plummeting to 3.8 in the upper class (the lowest value observed).

The left-hand columns in table 5.10 show estimated coefficients for the baseline model predicting depression from race and class dummy variables. Compared with upper-class whites, those in the lower class score 0.65 points higher on the depression scale and those in the lower middle and upper middle classes score 0.33 and 0.24 points higher, respectively (though the latter effects are not statistically significant). Although blacks also display a negative gradient moving from lower to upper class, they are significantly more depressed than whites in all class categories, the excess compared with upper-class whites being 1.3 to 1.4 points in the lower and lower middle classes and around 0.81 to 0.82 points in the upper middle and upper classes. Consistent with the plot in figure 5.10, Asians display significantly greater depression

Table 5.10   Determinants of Depression

Independent Variables	Group Effects		Full Model	
	B	SE	B	SE
Race-class group				
White lower	0.646**	0.227	0.326	0.604
White lower middle	0.329	0.221	0.175	0.459
White upper middle	0.240	0.208	0.192	0.330
White upper	—	—	—	—
Asian lower	1.861**	0.707	1.870+	0.992
Asian lower middle	0.698	0.562	0.784	0.779
Asian upper middle	0.707+	0.376	0.773	0.530
Asian upper	1.624**	0.555	1.113*	0.449
Hispanic lower	1.559***	0.332	0.738	0.820
Hispanic lower middle	0.621	0.387	0.197	0.574
Hispanic upper middle	2.234***	0.447	1.305+	0.713
Hispanic upper	−0.207	0.418	−0.516	0.448
Black lower	1.298***	0.307	0.914	0.720
Black lower middle	1.374***	0.377	0.764	0.610
Black upper middle	0.823+	0.427	0.595	0.529
Black upper	0.808*	0.372	0.736	0.384
Ascribed characteristics				
Age	—	—	−0.153***	0.040
Parent foreign born	—	—	0.126	0.227
Mediating conditions				
Risky behaviors				
Smoked regularly	—	—	−0.650	0.542
Abused alcohol	—	—	0.034	0.145
Used hard drugs	—	—	0.260+	0.156
Ate fast food	—	—	0.116	0.148
Sex without birth control	—	—	0.358*	0.163
Sex with risky partner	—	—	0.883**	0.333
Reported health problems				
Ever had STD	—	—	0.684*	0.289
Body mass index	—	—	−0.003	0.012
Limitation on activity	—	—	1.345***	0.172
Family situation				
Unmarried male–not father	—	—	—	—
Married male–not father	—	—	−0.231	0.337
Married male–father	—	—	−0.393	0.375
Unmarried male–father	—	—	1.195***	0.367
Unmarried female–no birth	—	—	0.712***	0.142

Table 5.10   (continued)

Independent Variables	Group Effects		Full Model	
	B	SE	B	SE
Married female–no birth	—	—	0.580+	0.311
Married female–mother	—	—	0.810**	0.295
Unmarried female–birth over eighteen	—	—	1.169***	0.314
Unmarried female–birth eighteen or younger	—	—	1.378**	0.493
Ecological background				
Composition of origin family				
Two biological parents	—	—	—	—
Biological and stepparent	—	—	−0.464+	0.259
One biological parent	—	—	−0.280	0.173
No biological parent	—	—	−0.492	0.502
Family material resources				
Household income	—	—	0.007	0.010
Access to health insurance				
No coverage	—	—	—	—
Coverage less than a year	—	—	−0.577**	0.207
Coverage full year	—	—	−0.540***	0.169
Family symbolic resources				
Parental prestige	—	—	−0.005	0.004
Parent went to college	—	—	0.206	0.226
Family emotional resources				
Experienced a death	—	—	−0.074	0.260
Family sternness	—	—	−0.028***	0.005
Father incarcerated	—	—	0.320	0.205
Had family mentor	—	—	0.048	0.182
Neighborhood setting				
Disadvantage index	—	—	−0.313*	0.156
Inefficacy index	—	—	0.077**	0.026
Scarcity of males	—	—	0.659*	0.266
Had neighborhood mentor	—	—	0.147	0.261
School setting				
Disadvantage index	—	—	0.004	0.011
Inefficacy index	—	—	0.016	0.011
Disorder index	—	—	−0.004	0.028
Had school mentor	—	—	0.232	0.194
Religious setting				
Religiosity scale	—	—	0.042*	0.019
Involvement index	—	—	−0.024	0.025
Had religious mentor	—	—	0.230	0.382

Table 5.10   (continued)

Independent Variables	Group Effects		Full Model	
	B	SE	B	SE
Peer setting				
Violence index	—	—	0.027	0.030
Friend attempted suicide	—	—	0.748***	0.235
Had peer mentor	—	—	0.214	0.193
Multiple disadvantages				
Log of interactive index	—	—	0.084*	0.035
Intercept	2.995***	0.142	4.489**	1.546
N	8,936		8,882	
F-test	4.41***		15.57***	
R^2	0.018		0.138	

Source: Authors' calculations based on data set described in Harris and Udry (2008).
$+p < .10$; $*p < .05$; $**p < .01$; $***p < .001$

scores in the lower and upper classes (with respective values 1.86 and 1.62 points higher compared with upper-class whites). In contrast, Hispanics are significantly more depressed in the lower and upper middle classes (with respective values 1.60 and 2.23 points higher relative to upper-class whites).

Adding controls reduces class effects for whites, Hispanics, and blacks and generally renders them insignificant, though one coefficient—for upper-middle-class Hispanics—remains marginally significant and the coefficients for blacks remain quite large in absolute terms. Nonetheless, the variables in the model do appear to account for much of the observed race-class variation, with the exception of the distinctive U-shaped Asian pattern. Thus the tendency toward depression among lower- and upper-class Asians does not reflect measured conditions in their social ecologies.

Mediating conditions associated with depression include the risky behaviors of drug abuse, having sex without contraception, and having sex with a risky partner (raising the depression score by 0.26, 0.36, and 0.88 points, respectively). Depression is also elevated by health issues such as having an STD or a limitation of activity. Compared with other males, those who are unmarried fathers are significantly more depressed (by 1.2 points). Among females, the tendency toward depression varies significantly by marital and motherhood status. Compared with a single male, married females experience the smallest increment to depression (0.58 points), and those who have given birth outside of marriage the highest (1.17 points if the birth after age eighteen and 1.38 before). Unmarried women with no births experienced 0.71 additional points on the depression scale. Married mothers experienced 0.81 additional points. Thus, for men, depression is not affected by marriage and is only increased by having children outside marriage, whereas women are always more depressed and experience more depression if they are unmarried with no children, more still if they are married with children, and most if they are unmarried and have children.

Within the family setting, depression is strongly reduced by access to health insurance (by 0.54 for incomplete and 0.58 for complete coverage) and by family sternness (by 0.028 points per unit). Material disadvantage within the neighborhood also surprisingly reduces depression (by 0.31 points per unit), but neighborhood social inefficacy and a scarcity of marriageable males increases it (by respective values of 0.077 and 0.659 points per unit). Depression is, not surprisingly, exacerbated by a friend's attempted suicide (yielding a 0.75 point increase) and by exposure to multiple disadvantages across social spheres (by 0.084 points per unit) and somewhat surprisingly by religiosity. The more religious a person is, the more likely he or she is to be depressed, by 0.042 points per unit or a possible 0.756 points moving from lowest to highest observed value. Whether religion makes people depressed or depressed people seek out religion is unclear, but the two conditions are clearly associated.

The Add Health Survey also contained two other questions relevant to individual well-being on the first and second waves. Respondents were asked to rate their chances of living to age thirty-five and the likelihood of being killed by age twenty-one using a four-point scale that ranged from almost certain to almost no chance, which we coded from 0 to 4 so that higher scores indicates a higher perceived likelihood of dying young. When the two items are combined across waves, they yield a sixteen-point scale with an acceptable reliability ($\alpha = 0.65$) and the resulting index is plotted by race and class in figure 5.11. As can be seen, the perceived likelihood of early death generally declines with rising social class among all groups but is higher for blacks and Hispanics than for whites and Asians. Whereas the white scale value declines from around 2.5 in the lower class to around 2.0 in the upper class, among African Americans the scale goes from 3.4 in the lower class to around 3.0 in the highest. Likewise, the Asian score drops from 2.6 to around

Figure 5.11   Subjective Likelihood of an Early Death by Race and Class

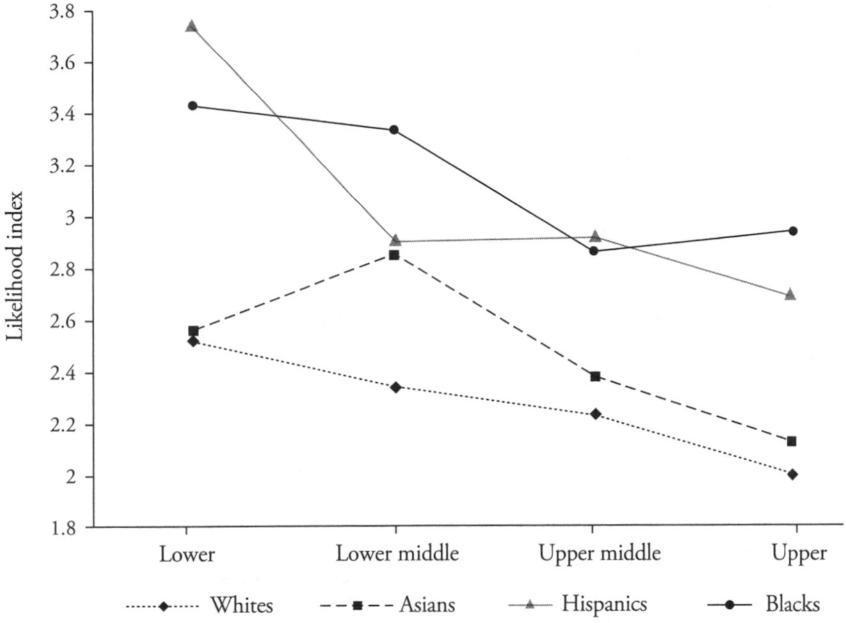

Source: Authors' compilation based on Harris and Udry (2008).

2.1 and the Hispanic from 3.7 and 2.7. Thus the poorest whites and Asians perceive a lower likelihood of early death than the most affluent blacks and Latinos, and lower-class members of the latter groups evince remarkably high scale values.

The left-hand columns of table 5.11 reveal that these race-class differences are highly significant. Compared with upper-class whites, those in the lower class display an early mortality expectation that is 0.51 points greater, those in the lower middle class one that is 0.34 points greater, and those in the upper-middle-class one 0.22 points greater. The coefficients for Asians, with the exception of its lower middle class, are quite similar. Among blacks and Hispanics, however, the coefficients are considerably greater, with the early mortality score for African Americans being 1.42 points, 1.32 points, 0.86 points, and 0.94 points higher than upper-class whites as one moves from lower to upper class, and Hispanics evincing respective increments of 1.73 points, 0.89 points, 0.91 points, and 0.68 points.

Table 5.11   Determinants of Likelihood of an Early Death

Independent Variables	Group Effects		Full Model	
	B	SE	B	SE
Race-class group				
White lower	0.512***	0.114	−0.738**	0.286
White lower middle	0.339**	0.117	−0.341+	0.200
White upper middle	0.222*	0.101	−0.146	0.130
White upper	—	—	—	—
Asian lower	0.560+	0.347	−0.714	0.469
Asian lower middle	0.850*	0.382	0.295	0.443
Asian upper middle	0.370	0.310	−0.146	0.271
Asian upper	0.124	0.262	−0.029	0.264
Hispanic lower	1.732***	0.230	0.383	0.348
Hispanic lower middle	0.895***	0.238	−0.058	0.324
Hispanic upper middle	0.912***	0.251	0.231	0.255
Hispanic upper	0.680*	0.279	0.584*	0.262
Black lower	1.422***	0.143	−0.194	0.319
Black lower middle	1.318***	0.184	−0.014	0.301
Black upper middle	0.855***	0.203	−0.034	0.226
Black upper	0.935***	0.236	0.249	0.304
Ascribed characteristics				
Age	—	—	0.130***	0.028
Parent foreign born	—	—	−0.052	0.133
Mediating conditions				
Risky behaviors				
Smoked regularly	—	—	−0.332	0.293
Abused alcohol	—	—	−0.162*	0.075
Used hard drugs	—	—	−0.003	0.096
Ate fast food	—	—	0.049	0.086
Sex without birth control	—	—	−0.083	0.081
Sex with risky partner	—	—	0.029	0.177
Reported health problems				
Ever had STD	—	—	0.034	0.153
Body mass index	—	—	−0.005	0.006
Limitation on activity	—	—	0.143*	0.071
Family situation				
Unmarried male–not father	—	—	—	—
Married male–not father	—	—	−0.070	0.213
Married male–father	—	—	0.497*	0.227
Unmarried male–father	—	—	0.286	0.212
Unmarried female–no birth	—	—	0.109	0.074

Table 5.11   (continued)

Independent Variables	Group Effects		Full Model	
	B	SE	B	SE
Married female–no birth	—	—	0.013	0.187
Married female–mother	—	—	0.064	0.147
Unmarried female–birth over eighteen	—	—	–0.291	0.171
Unmarried female–birth eighteen or younger	—	—	–0.292	0.233
Ecological background				
Composition of origin family				
Two biological parents	—	—	—	—
Biological and stepparent	—	—	–0.094	0.125
One biological parent	—	—	0.068	0.090
No biological parent	—	—	0.375	0.473
Family material resources				
Household income	—	—	–0.015*	0.005
Access to health insurance				
No coverage	—	—	—	—
Coverage less than a year	—	—	–0.294*	0.125
Coverage full year	—	—	–0.344***	0.106
Family symbolic resources				
Parental prestige	—	—	–0.007***	0.002
Parent went to college	—	—	–0.257*	0.116
Family emotional resources				
Experienced a death	—	—	0.157	0.177
Family sternness	—	—	–0.027***	0.003
Father incarcerated	—	—	–0.028	0.117
Had family mentor	—	—	–0.086	0.102
Neighborhood setting				
Disadvantage index	—	—	0.440***	0.092
Inefficacy index	—	—	0.052***	0.014
Scarcity of males	—	—	0.077	0.117
Had neighborhood mentor	—	—	–0.136	0.127
School setting				
Disadvantage index	—	—	0.002	0.006
Inefficacy index	—	—	0.031***	0.007
Disorder index	—	—	0.002	0.015
Had school mentor	—	—	–0.106	0.112
Religious setting				
Religiosity scale	—	—	0.007	0.009
Involvement index	—	—	–0.036**	0.013
Had religious mentor	—	—	–0.361+	0.205

Table 5.11 *(continued)*

Independent Variables	Group Effects		Full Model	
	B	SE	B	SE
Peer setting				
Violence index	—	—	0.136***	0.019
Friend attempted suicide	—	—	0.275+	0.144
Had peer mentor	—	—	0.003	0.112
Multiple disadvantages				
Log of interactive index	—	—	–0.046**	0.017
Intercept	2.005***	0.079	3.328**	1.060
N	8,996		6,550	
F-test	12.26***		19.17***	
R²	0.046		0.180***	

Source: Authors' calculations based on data set described in Harris and Udry (2008).
+$p < .10$; *$p < .05$; **$p < .01$; ***$p < .001$

In the full model, however, all of these race-class differences disappear or are reversed, with the exception of the coefficient for upper-class Hispanics. The perceived likelihood of an early death rises with age and is elevated among those reporting a limitation of physical activity and among married fathers and is slightly reduced among alcohol abusers. As one might expect, the expectation of an early death is reduced by resources associated with social class, declining by 0.015 points for every thousand dollars of income, being reduced by 0.34 points by full access to health insurance, falling by 0.007 points for each unit of occupational status, and being 0.26 points lower among those with college-educated parents. The perceived likelihood of early mortality also declines sharply with family sternness, falling by 0.027 points per unit on the sternness scale, or 2.7 points over the range of the scale.

In the other ecological spheres, the subjective likelihood of early death was generally increased by indicators of disadvantage and disorder, rising sharply with greater neighborhood disadvantage and inefficacy (by 0.44 points and 0.052 points per unit, respectively), with greater inefficacy at school (0.031 points per unit), with exposure to violence among peers (0.136 points per unit), and with a friend's attempted suicide (0.275 points). The expectation of early death is lowered, however, by religious involvement (0.036 points per unit) and by having a religious mentor (0.361 points), and—surprisingly—by exposure to multiple disadvantages across social spheres. In sum, minority youths from poor, low-status, uneducated families who live in disadvantaged, socially inefficacious neighborhoods, attend inefficacious schools, are exposed to high levels of peer violence, and lack the protective effects of religious involvement or a stern family tend to adopt a fatalistic outlook and perceive a relatively high likelihood that they will not survive into older adulthood.

THE SOCIAL ECOLOGY OF HEALTH

This chapter has documented the often sharp differences in health-related behaviors and outcomes by race and class. The likelihood of consuming and abusing controlled substances with well-known negative health effects—cigarettes, alcohol, and hard drugs—is greatest among whites and least among African Americans with Hispanics and Asians falling in between. Social class also conditions substance abuse, but acts in different ways in different racial groups. Among whites, the likelihood of smoking falls with class. Among Hispanics, it rises with class. Among blacks and Asians, it shows no particular pattern with respect to class. In contrast, the likelihood of abusing alcohol and drugs generally rises with class among whites, Asians, and Hispanics, but displays no consistent class pattern among blacks. Although blacks are least likely to abuse cigarettes, drugs, or alcohol, they are most likely to eat fast food and engage in risky sexual practices. Asians are generally least likely to eat poorly or have risky sex. Whites and Hispanics fall between blacks and Asians. Moreover, although fast-food consumption falls with class among whites, Asians, and Hispanics, it rises slightly among African Americans; and whereas risky sex becomes less likely as class rises among blacks, Hispanics, and whites, it has no class pattern among Asians.

These risky behaviors are associated with certain identifiable health outcomes. Regular smoking significantly increases the odds of having a limitation on physical activity and poorer self-assessed health, both directly and indirectly (by increasing the likelihood of physical disability). Although hard drug use reduces body weight, it increases the level of depression reported by respondents. Having sex with a risky partner increases the likelihood of having a physical limitation as well as obesity and getting a sexually transmitted disease. Not surprisingly, the failure to use contraception increases the likelihood of getting an STD. It is also associated with increased depression in respondents. The consumption of fast food has no significant effect on the health outcomes we considered, even body mass, and the only influence of alcohol was to reduce the perceived likelihood of an early death. Alcohol thus seems to promote a more benign outlook on life.

Although blacks were least likely to report a limitation on physical activity and generally rated their health as better than other groups, they were most likely to have a high BMI, to report ever having an STD, to be more depressed, and to anticipate an early death. Moreover, these risks varied less by class among blacks than among other groups. Among whites and Hispanics, the incidence of negative health conditions generally falls as class rises. Asians, however, often show a U-shaped pattern with extreme values in the lower and upper classes and moderate levels in the middle classes.

Table 5.12 summarizes the degree to which these health-related behaviors and outcomes are related to conditions in various ecological spheres. As in the last chapter, the direction of the effect is indicated by a plus or minus sign and the strength by the number of signs shown. Even a quick glance at the table reveals that the composition, material resources, and symbolic resources of the family of origin are not very strongly related to health behaviors and outcomes. The obvious exception is access to health insurance, which lowers the likelihood of smoking, reduces the likelihood of hard drug use, lowers the incidence of physical disability, and mitigates poor health, depression, and the perception of low life chances. Although growing up with a stepparent increases the likelihood of smoking, and coming of age with a single parent raises the likelihood of drug abuse, other health effects are either marginal (for risky sex, body mass, and depression) or nonexistent (everything else) and no effect is particularly strong. Parental occupational status actually increases the risk of drug abuse and parental college attainment increases the index of poor health but only marginally lowers the expectation of early death.

In contrast, both health behaviors and outcomes are strongly connected to emotional circumstances within the family. Although mortality within the immediate family surprisingly has no effect on any behavior or outcome, family sternness and paternal incarceration have ubiquitous and very strong effects. The more remote and stern the emotional style in the family of origin, the less likely respondents were to smoke, abuse alcohol, take hard drugs, engage in risky sex, report a physical limitation, get an STD, rate their health as poor, exhibit symptoms of depression, or perceive a high chance of early death. In contrast, the incarceration of a respondent's father increased the risk of smoking, alcohol abuse, drug use, and fast food consumption, while increasing body mass. People who relied on family mentors rather than no mentor were more likely to abuse alcohol, eat fast food, cite a physical limitation, and rate their health as poor.

A second key sphere of influence was the peer group. Exposure to peer violence greatly increased the odds of smoking, drug abuse, and risky sex and generally led to the perceived likelihood of an early death. The emotional blow of a friend's suicide attempt was associated with a greater likelihood of smoking, alcohol abuse, hard drug use, risky sex, physical disability, and greater body mass and to increase the tendency of respondents to report poor health, depressive symptoms, and perceptions of low life chances. Reliance on a peer mentor increased the risk of smoking, alcohol abuse, and physical disability.

Although not as consistently strong and significant as conditions in the family emotional ecology and peer settings, the neighborhood and school spheres also had a number of powerful effects. Material disadvantage within neighborhoods increased body mass and the tendency to expect an early death and to raise the odds of STD infection. Surprisingly, neighborhood disadvantage lowered the likelihood of alcohol and drug abuse and reduced the degree of depression. Material disadvantage within schools likewise lowered the likelihood of smoking and alcohol abuse. However, social inefficacy within neighborhoods raised the odds of physical disability, depression, and expectation of an early death. Inefficacy within schools raised the odds of smoking, drug use, and STD infection and increased perceptions of poor health and a likely early death.

In general, the religious sphere had only a modest effect on respondent health behaviors, the degree of religious involvement and having a religious mentor reducing the likelihood of cigarette smoking and alcohol abuse, and religious involvement improving perceived health and survival chances. As noted earlier, however, religiosity was associated with higher levels of depression. Finally, the accumulation of multiple disadvantages across spheres increased the likelihood of fast-food consumption, increased the perception of poor health, and raised the reporting of depressive symptoms. Surprisingly, however, it reduced the perceived likelihood of an early death.

All in all, then, respondent health seems to be driven primarily by family emotional circumstances and conditions in the peer environment, and to have strong effects also in the school and neighborhood settings, weaker ef-

Table 5.12 Significance of Ecological Conditions

	Risky Health Behaviors					Physical Outcomes			Self-Rated Health		
	Cigarettes	Alcohol Abuse	Hard Drug Use	Fast Food	Risky Sex	Physical Limitation	Body Mass Index	STD	Poor Health	Depression	Likely Early Death
Family composition											
Biological and stepparent	++						-			-	
One biological parent			++								
No biological parent					+						
Family material resources											
Household income	---		---								
Health insurance less than a year									--	--	-
Health insurance a year or more						--		+	---	---	---
Family symbolic resources											
Parental prestige			++++			--				---	---
Parent college graduate									++		-
Family emotional resources											
Family mortality	---	++++	---			--			---	---	---
Family sternness					-						
Father incarcerated	++++	++++	++++	++			++				
Family mentor		++++		++		++++			++		
Neighborhood setting											
Disadvantage index		---	---				+++	++		--	++++

Inefficacy index	---		-	+	++	+++	++++	
Scarcity of males	+		-		++	++		
Neighborhood mentor		+		+				
School setting								
Disadvantage index	-	-	-					
Inefficacy index	+++	+		+	++++		++++	
Disorder index			---	+++				
School mentor	++++	++++		+++				
Religious setting								
Religiosity scale					++			
Involvement index	--	---	-		-	-		
Had religious mentor	--	---	-	+	-		-	
Peer setting								
Violence index	++++	+++	++++	-	-	-	++++	
Friend attempted suicide	+++	++++	++	++++	+++	+++	++++	+
Peer mentor	++	+++	++	++	++			
Multiple disadvantages								
Interactive index	++		++		++	++	---	

Source: Authors' calculations based on data set described in Harris and Udry (2008).

Note: Significance in predicting health outcomes.

Table 5.13   Significance of Race-Class Effects

	Risky Health Behaviors					Physical Outcomes			Self-Rated Health		
	Cigarettes	Alcohol Abuse	Hard Drug Use	Fast Food	Risky Sex	Physical Limitation	Body Mass Index	STD	Poor Health	Depression	Likely Early Death
WLO	-										--
WLM											-
WUM				+							
ALO	-	-			-	+	-		+	+	
ALM									++++		
AUM		-							+++		
AUP		---	-			++				++	
HLO	---		---								
HLM	---		-	+			+				
HUM										+	
HUP		-				+	+				++
BLO	---	-	---		+						
BLM	---	-	-	+	+						
BUM	---	---	---	++	++			+			
BUP	---	---	---					++++			

Source: Authors' compilation.

Note: Significance in predicting health outcomes.

fects in the religious sphere, and—with the exception of access to health insurance—relatively weak effects with respect to family composition, material resources, and symbolic resources. Table 5.13 summarizes the race and class effects that remain after controlling for these ecological and mediating variables. As the bottom four rows indicate, the distinctive behavioral pattern of African Americans with respect to health is not explained by ecological circumstances. Indeed, as we have seen, taking account of the generally more disadvantaged circumstances of blacks tends to accentuate the distinctiveness of black behavioral patterns, both for good and for ill. Compared with other race-class groups, blacks are quite unlikely to take drugs, abuse alcohol, or smoke (and to begin later when they do smoke), but at the same time are more likely to consume fast food and to engage in risky sex. Nonetheless, once ecological conditions are taken into consideration, their physical condition and self-assessed mental and physical health are no different from other groups, with the sole exception of STD infection, which tends to be quite high in the upper middle and upper classes.

Among Hispanics, the application of controls eliminates most of the race-class variation. Taking into account the social ecology to which they are exposed, they still display lower likelihoods and later ages of smoking. Upper-class Hispanics also retain their bleak outlook on life and show a tendency to perceive a higher likelihood of premature death. Most of the other effects, however, are reduced to marginal significance or disappear entirely. Asians display no greater tendency toward risky health behaviors in the presence of ecological controls, and where significant effects do exist they are in the less risky direction. Nonetheless, upper- and lower-class Asians retain a greater likelihood of reporting physical disabilities and depression, and the lower and middle classes are more likely to rate their health as poor. Among whites, however, the various class gradients observed in basic tabulations generally disappear, fall to marginal significance, or reverse sign in the presence of ecological controls. In general, therefore, with a few notable exceptions, variation in health outcomes by race and class are largely accounted for by the different ecological circumstances to which adolescents are exposed, most notably the family emotional environment and the peer environment, but also social and material disadvantages in schools and neighborhoods. Having considered the health component of human capital formation, we now turn to cultivation of cognitive skills.

CHAPTER 6

Human Capital Formation

In no area of science has the nature-nurture debate played out more controversially than in the arena of human intelligence and scholastic achievement. During the late nineteenth century and early twentieth century, the prevailing view was that intelligence was largely under genetic control (Gould 1981). Genes for individual intelligence were thought to pass from parents to children and be duly expressed, subject possibly to minor influences from the environment, yielding a bell-shaped normal distribution of IQ scores that mainly reflected the influence of inherited factors (Guilford 1967). Inequality in the distribution of intelligence led, in turn, to inequality in the distribution of things that followed from it, such as income, education, and social status (Galton 1869). Differences in IQ by race and class are long standing and well documented (Jencks and Phillips 1998; Croizeta and Dutreacutevisa 2004), leading some observers to invoke genetics to justify obdurate racial and class inequalities in society (Rushton 1994; Herrnstein and Murray 1994).

The genetic determinist view of intelligence and inequality did not go unchallenged, of course, and periodically was subject to harsh scientific critiques (Boas 1940; Gould 1981; Fischer et al. 1996; Devlin et al. 1997). By the late twentieth century, however, the epigenetic revolution in biology and the accumulation of data in the social sciences began to shift the tide of scientific opinion against genetic determinism. As hard evidence of gene-environment interactions accumulated for a growing array of traits, it became harder to claim that human intelligence was somehow different from all other characteristics in being impervious to environmental influences. At the same time, a growing body of psychometric evidence indicated that cognitive ability was, in fact, quite malleable, with James Flynn (1987), in particular, demonstrating that IQ scores had increased substantially throughout the developed world in recent decades, a change so rapid and widespread that it could not reasonably be attributed to biological evolution (Flynn 2007).

The emerging consensus now is that cognitive skills, like other human traits, arise from complex gene-environment interactions that render human intelligence pliant and responsive to the ecological circumstances in which people find themselves (Nisbett 2009). Moreover, like other traits, intelligence builds on itself over time. Mounting empirical evidence links intelligence and scholastic achievement to environmental conditions experienced across the life cycle at key developmental stages (Cunha et al. 2006; Cunha and Heckman 2009). Environmental conditions are particularly important in early childhood because early learning provides a foundation for later intellectual growth and development (Heckman 2006, 2007).

The most important environment for human intellectual development, particularly early development, is obviously the family (Duncan and Brooks-Gunn 1997). However, studies have also linked neighborhood conditions to cognitive outcomes (Sampson, Sharkey, and Raudenbush 2008) and educational achievement (Garner and Raudenbush 1991; Foster and McLanahan 1996; Aaronson 1998; Harding 2003; Leventhal and Brooks-Gunn 2000). Conditions in school have also been shown to affect cognitive and educational achievement after controlling for individual and family circumstances (Chase-Lansdale et al. 1997; Duncan and Raudenbush 1999; Alexander, Entwisle, and Olson 2001, 2007; Crowder and South 2003; Pong and Hao 2007).

Most prior work has focused on just one or two ecological settings at a time, and within them just one kind of resource deprivation; to date, no study has considered how conditions in multiple ecological settings influence cognitive and educational outcomes across the full array of race-class combinations. Here we take advantage of rich data from the Adolescent Health Survey to undertake a systematic analysis of how conditions in five ecological spheres influence cognitive development and educational attainment among young people in the United States, and how differences in exposure to advantages and disadvantages across these spheres in adolescence may account for well-known racial and socioeconomic gaps in performance.

Although the Add Health data are rich, they have the obvious drawback of being gathered rather late in the developmental cycle. By adolescence, a lot of cognitive water has passed under the bridge, and recent work has pointed to the importance of differences in exposure to environmental resources in infancy and early childhood in accounting for differences in later intellectual performance. Nonetheless, the teenage years remain a critical stage in the development of many cognitive abilities, and the prefrontal cortex in particular does not fully mature until people are in their twenties. In addition, to the extent that ecological circumstances experienced in early life are correlated with those experienced in adolescence, our models will capture some early environmental effects. We should not expect the models estimated here to explain all of the race-class differences in intellectual performance, of course; but to the extent they reduce cognitive and educational differentials and reveal which ecological factors determine the acquisition of cognitive skills results should yield new insights into the ecology of human capital formation.

ATTENTION DEFICIT AND HYPERACTIVITY

Attention is a critical prerequisite to learning and skill formation. The inability to attend to explanations, pay attention to instructions, and mentally focus while learning a concept or performing a task clearly undermines a person's ability to gain proficiency in whatever cognitive skills are being transmitted by teacher or book. Over the years, psychologists and educators have come to understand that a collection of behaviors associated with inattention, hyperactivity, and impulsive behavior constitute a syndrome known as Attention Deficit and Hyperactivity Disorder, or ADHD (National Institute of Mental Health 2010). Symptoms of attention deficit in ADHD include being easily distracted, missing details, forgetting things, having difficulty focusing, becoming easily bored, frequent switching of tasks, recurrent daydreaming, not following instructions, slow processing of information, failing to listen, and not completing assigned tasks. Symptoms of hyperactivity in ADHD include fidgeting and squirming, nonstop talking, dashing about, trouble sitting still, being in constant motion, and difficulty performing quiet activities. The tendency toward impulsive behavior is indicated by impatience, spontaneous inappropriate comments, unrestrained displays of emotion, difficulty waiting, and frequent interrupting.

A set of eighteen items asking about the frequency of these traits was included in Wave 3 of the Add Health Survey to measure the degree to which

Figure 6.1 ADHD Score

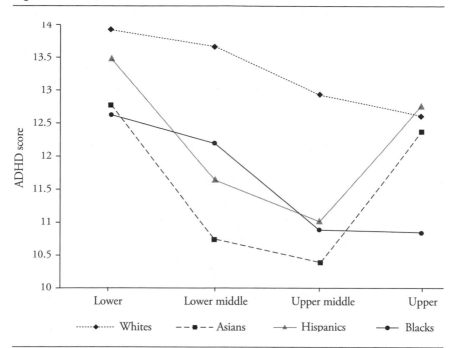

Source: Authors' compilation based on Harris and Udry (2008).

ADHD was exhibited by respondents. As shown in appendix B, respondents were asked about the frequency with which they displayed specific behavioral manifestations of inattention, hyperactivity, and impulsivity in terms of four adjectives—never or rarely, sometimes, often, or very often—which we coded from 0 to 3. Summing each person's score across the eighteen items yields a highly reliable ($\alpha = 0.90$) 54-point scale of ADHD (see appendix B). In figure 6.1, we plot the resulting ADHD scores by race and class.

In terms of race, whites generally exhibit the highest ADHD scores and Asians the lowest, blacks and Hispanics between them. Except for whites, however, overlap between groups is considerable. In addition, moving across class categories interpretation is complicated by two different class gradients. Among whites and blacks, the incidence of ADHD falls with rising social class, whereas among both Hispanics and Asians the class curve is U-shaped. The ADHD score for whites, for example, declines from 14 in the lower class to 13.6 and 13 in the lower middle and upper middle classes, to 12.6 in the upper class. Likewise, African Americans go from around 12.6 to 12.3 and 10.9 and 10.8, respectively, across the four class categories. In contrast, Hispanics drop from 13.5 to 11.6 to 11.0 moving from the lower to lower middle to upper middle classes, but then rebound to 12.7 in the upper class. Likewise, Asians fall from 12.6 to 10.8 to 10.4 in the lower, lower middle, and upper middle class, respectively, before rebounding to 12.4 in the upper class. Moreover, whereas levels of ADHD among whites are generally well in excess of those of Hispanics and Asians in the lower through upper middle classes, all three groups in the upper class display roughly the same ADHD score. Only African Americans remain below whites across all class categories.

The left-hand columns of table 6.1 present estimates for a baseline model that predicts a respondent's ADHD score using race-class dummy variables to confirm the statistical significance of the patterns just described. Among both blacks and whites, the ADHD score declines monotonically with rising class status and within each class category black scores are substantially below those of whites. In contrast, Asian and Hispanic scores fall from the lower to the upper middle class and then rise again in the upper class. Among upper-class respondents, the white, Asian, and Latino scores are not significantly different from one another, whereas that for blacks is significantly lower.

The right-hand columns show coefficients for a fully specified model, which includes controls for ascribed characteristics, mediating conditions, and ecological circumstances in addition to the dummy variables for race and class. Mediating conditions include current health and family status, which we assume are predetermined by ecological conditions (as modeled in chapters 4 and 5). The coefficients presented here thus capture the direct effects of ecological circumstances. Nonetheless, readers should also be attuned to potential indirect ecological effects through family composition and health status.

The race-class coefficients in the right-hand columns reveal that controlling statistically for background characteristics eliminates the class gradient among whites. Were all whites to experience the same ecological and mediating conditions regardless of class, they would display the same average ADHD score. The class gradient among blacks is also eliminated, but the lower levels of ADHD compared with whites persist. Indeed, the black-white gap uniformly increases and grows in significance, all of the coefficients being large and negative and three of the four being statistically significant. In other words, if blacks and whites experienced the same mediating and ecological conditions, African Americans would be even less likely to show symptoms of

Table 6.1   Determinants of ADHD

Independent Variables	Group Effects		Full Model	
	B	SE	B	SE
Race-class group				
White lower	2.031***	0.564	−0.069	1.716
White lower middle	1.383**	0.501	−0.209	1.089
White upper middle	0.278	0.527	−0.360	0.746
White upper	—	—	—	—
Asian lower	−0.342	1.108	−1.453	2.177
Asian lower middle	−1.929	1.207	−2.247	1.427
Asian upper middle	−2.274**	0.856	−2.568*	1.197
Asian upper	−0.582	0.839	−0.631	0.992
Hispanic lower	1.861*	0.959	−1.298	1.723
Hispanic lower middle	−0.832	0.811	−2.177+	1.239
Hispanic upper middle	−1.706*	0.799	−2.829**	1.033
Hispanic upper	1.416	1.707	−1.228	0.907
Black lower	0.762	0.969	−2.275	1.627
Black lower middle	0.029	0.946	−2.392+	1.265
Black upper middle	−1.439+	0.721	−3.297***	0.933
Black upper	−1.652*	0.721	−2.328**	0.932
Ascribed characteristics				
Age	—	—	−0.141	0.106
Parent foreign born	—	—	−0.556	0.559
Mediating conditions				
Health status				
Poor health index	—	—	0.808***	0.164
Depression scale	—	—	0.510***	0.043
Expectation of early death	—	—	0.152**	0.062
Current family situation				
Unmarried male–not father	—	—	—	—
Married male–not father	—	—	1.576	1.043
Married male–father	—	—	0.801	0.975
Unmarried male–father	—	—	−0.044	0.787
Unmarried female–no birth	—	—	−3.554***	0.325
Married female–no birth	—	—	−3.019***	0.585
Married female–mother	—	—	−2.875***	0.585
Unmarried female–birth over eighteen	—	—	−2.982***	0.672
Unmarried female–birth eighteen or younger	—	—	−3.727***	0.989
Ecological background				
Composition of origin family				
Two biological parents	—	—	—	—
Biological and stepparent	—	—	1.249*	0.615

Table 6.1   (continued)

Independent Variables	Group Effects		Full Model	
	B	SE	B	SE
One biological parent	—	—	0.172	0.504
No biological parent	—	—	1.448	1.120
Family material resources				
Household income	—	—	–0.016	0.026
Access to health insurance				
No coverage	—	—	—	—
Coverage less than a year	—	—	–0.771+	0.463
Coverage full year	—	—	–1.297**	0.427
Family symbolic resources				
Parental prestige	—	—	–0.002	0.009
Parent college graduate	—	—	0.452	0.556
Family emotional resources				
Experienced a death	—	—	–0.128	0.662
Family sternness	—	—	–0.022+	0.014
Father incarcerated	—	—	0.016	0.426
Family mentor	—	—	0.759+	0.404
Neighborhood setting				
Disadvantage index	—	—	–0.099	0.345
Inefficacy index	—	—	–0.048	0.060
Scarcity of males	—	—	–0.765	0.638
Neighborhood mentor			1.525*	0.620
School setting				
Disadvantage index	—	—	0.001	0.027
Inefficacy index	—	—	0.064*	0.030
Disorder index	—	—	–0.007	0.065
School mentor	—	—	0.124	0.515
Religious setting				
Religiosity scale	—	—	–0.043	0.041
Involvement index	—	—	0.037	0.049
Religious mentor	—	—	0.811	0.788
Peer setting				
Violence index	—	—	0.299***	0.077
Friend attempted suicide	—	—	1.727**	0.569
Peer mentor	—	—	1.277**	0.470
Multiple disadvantages				
Log of interactive index	—	—	–0.009	0.073
Intercept	13.918***	0.079	17.641***	3.687
N	8,996		7,138	
F-test	4.46***		16.78***	
R²	0.009		0.144	

Source: Authors' calculations based on data set described in Harris and Udry (2008).

$+p < .10$; $*p < .05$; $**p < .01$; $***p < .001$

ADHD than whites. Among Asians and Hispanics, the U-shape is not eliminated by the inclusion of controls, but as with blacks their lower proclivity
toward ADHD relative to whites is accentuated once background differences
are held constant.

Among ascribed characteristics, age and immigrant origins have no influence on the level of ADHD, but gender is highly significant. Females consistently score lower than males and differences by marital or childbearing status
are not significant. ADHD is quite strongly and significantly related to the
mediating health conditions we include in the model. Thus the ADHD score
rises by 0.81 points for each unit on the scale of poor health, by 0.51 units on
the depression scale, and by 0.15 units on the expectation of early death
scale, all very strong effects. Moving the three health variables from their
minimum to maximum observed values would raise the ADHD scale by
more than 18 points.

Among ecological factors, ADHD is most responsive to conditions in the
peer setting, with strong, significant, and positive effects estimated for peer
violence, a friend's attempted suicide, and having a peer mentor. Each unit
on the peer violence scale increases the ADHD score by around 0.30 points
(for a potential 6-point swing from minimum to maximum) whereas a
friend's suicide increased ADHD by 1.7 points and having a peer mentor by
1.3 points. In addition, ADHD is increased by experiencing greater social
inefficacy at school (by 0.06 points per unit), by having a family mentor (1.5
points), and by having a stepparent (1.2 points). In contrast, ADHD is reduced by access to health insurance, being 0.77 points lower for those with
partial access and 1.3 points lower for those with full access to health insurance. Given that access to health insurance also improves health, which also
itself improves ADHD, access to this important material resource carries
considerable potential to improve attention and lower hyperactivity among
young adults through both direct and indirect pathways.

COGNITIVE SKILLS

In addition to administering the module of questions on ADHD, Wave 3 of
the Add Health Survey also included items from the Peabody Picture Vocabulary Test (PVT) and the public data file contains age standardized scores
for all respondents. The PVT is a widely used measure of verbal intelligence.
Figure 6.2 plots average PVT scores by race and class. The figure clearly shows
that black and white scores both rise steadily moving from the lowest to the
highest class category. However, black scores fall well below those of whites

Figure 6.2   Picture Vocabulary Test Score

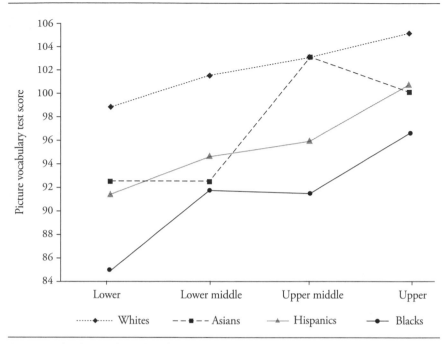

Source: Authors' compilation based on Harris and Udry (2008).

no matter which class category one considers and the racial gap shows no signs of diminishing as socioeconomic standing rises. Among whites, the average PVT score rises from around 99 in the lower class to 102 in the lower middle class and 103 in the upper middle class and 105 in the upper class. The respective four figures among blacks are 85, 92, 91, and 94. In other words, upper-class blacks have a lower PVT score than lower-class whites—a large gap by any standard.

The black and white curves form lower and upper bounds between which Hispanic and Asian scores generally vary. Asians and Hispanics begin at roughly the same point with a PVT score around 92 in the lower class. Moving into the lower middle class, however, the Hispanic score rises to around 95 but the Asian remains constant at 92. In the upper middle class, the Asian score increases markedly to equal whites at around 101, but the Hispanic score rises more modestly to reach 96. In the upper class, Hispanics continue to rise whereas Asians fall back, so that the two groups end up with roughly the same PVT score of 98 to 99, compared with 105 for upper-class whites and 94 for upper-class blacks.

As the baseline coefficients in the left-hand columns of table 6.2 reveal, the foregoing race-class differences are generally highly significant. Consider the class gradient among whites, for example. Compared with upper-class whites, those in the lower class have PVT scores 5.3 points lower, but those in lower middle class 3.6 points lower and those in the upper middle class 2.1 points lower. These class differences among whites pale in comparison to the observed racial differences between the various groups, however. With the exception of upper-middle-class Asians, PVT scores for all other race-class combinations lie at least 4.4 points below the average for upper-class whites, the absolute difference extending all the way up to a 20.2 point deficit.

The latter gap pertains to lower-class blacks. The gap with respect to upper-class whites drops to 13.5 points for both lower-middle- and upper-middle-class blacks, but remains 8.6 points among upper-class African Americans. Among Hispanics, the shortfall compared with upper-class whites is 13.8 points in the lower class and then falls to 10.6, 9.2, and 4.4 points, respectively, in the lower middle, upper middle, and upper classes. With the exception of the unusually high Asian PVT score in the upper middle class, the size of the deficit for this group is quite similar to Hispanics, dropping from 12.6 points in the lower and lower middle class, to 5.1 points in the upper class.

The right-hand columns show what happens to these race-class differences once background controls are introduced. As can be seen, the class gradient among whites disappears and the coefficients lose significance, suggesting that socioeconomic differences in verbal intelligence are largely attributable to differences in mediating and ecological conditions. Although other race-class differences are not eliminated entirely, they are substantially reduced. For example, the absolute value of the estimated coefficients for blacks drop from respective figures of 20.2, 13.5, 13.5, and 8.6 in the baseline model (going from lower to upper class) to respective values of 10.3, 4.6, 5.9, and 3.0 in the full model. In the upper class, the PVT score gap between whites and Hispanics and between Asians and whites disappears entirely with the addition of controls; in other class categories, the size of these differentials drops substantially and usually significantly.

Among ascribed characteristics, the PVT score rises by 0.52 points with each additional year of age, but having a foreign-born parent has no apparent

Table 6.2   Determinants of Score on Picture Vocabulary Test

Independent Variables	Group Effects		Full Model	
	B	SE	B	SE
Race-class group				
White lower	−5.337***	0.831	−2.065	1.831
White lower middle	−3.644***	0.696	−1.183	1.312
White upper middle	−2.109***	0.509	−0.348	0.819
White upper	—	—	—	—
Asian lower	−12.656***	2.621	−6.436*	3.217
Asian lower middle	−12.588**	4.103	−6.831+	3.863
Asian upper middle	−2.107	1.990	0.113	2.160
Asian upper	−5.090**	1.864	−2.625	1.670
Hispanic lower	−13.759***	1.335	−5.238**	2.238
Hispanic lower middle	−10.607***	1.329	−3.393+	1.768
Hispanic upper middle	−9.191***	1.846	−4.611**	1.500
Hispanic upper	−4.418**	1.508	−0.198	1.275
Black lower	−20.163***	1.712	−10.303***	2.100
Black lower middle	−13.493***	1.458	−4.648**	1.527
Black upper middle	−13.493***	1.458	−5.870***	1.518
Black upper	−8.645***	1.929	−2.965*	1.408
Ascribed characteristics				
Age	—	—	0.522***	0.168
Parent foreign born	—	—	−0.653	0.888
Mediating conditions				
Health status				
Poor health index	—	—	−0.085	0.257
Depression scale	—	—	−0.442***	0.079
Expectation of early death	—	—	−0.462***	0.108
Family situation				
Unmarried male–not father	—	—	—	—
Married male–not father	—	—	0.656	0.909
Married male–father	—	—	−0.083	0.990
Unmarried male–father	—	—	−2.033*	0.889
Unmarried female–no birth	—	—	−0.758	0.488
Married female–no birth	—	—	−1.551+	0.871
Married female–mother	—	—	−2.879**	0.923
Unmarried female–birth over eighteen	—	—	−2.671**	0.985
Unmarried female–birth eighteen or younger	—	—	−1.989	1.420
Ecological background				
Composition of origin family				
Two biological parents	—	—	—	—
Biological and stepparent	—	—	−0.308	0.775
One biological parent	—	—	1.170+	0.612
No biological parent	—	—	−0.842	2.370

Table 6.2   (continued)

Independent Variables	Group Effects		Full Model	
	B	SE	B	SE
Family material resources				
Household income	—	—	–0.034	0.029
Access to health insurance				
No coverage	—	—	—	—
Coverage less than a year	—	—	1.683*	0.761
Coverage full year	—	—	2.347***	0.610
Family symbolic resources				
Parental prestige	—	—	0.034**	0.013
Parent college graduate	—	—	1.610*	0.643
Family emotional resources				
Experienced a death	—	—	3.189***	0.721
Family sternness	—	—	–0.051***	0.015
Father incarcerated	—	—	–0.201	0.642
Family mentor	—	—	1.898**	0.404
Neighborhood setting				
Disadvantage index	—	—	–2.254***	0.604
Inefficacy index	—	—	0.427***	0.086
Scarcity of males	—	—	1.706*	0.769
Neighborhood mentor			2.353**	0.830
School setting				
Disadvantage index	—	—	–0.184***	0.055
Inefficacy index	—	—	0.090*	0.043
Disorder index	—	—	0.108	0.086
School mentor	—	—	6.074***	0.681
Religious setting				
Religiosity scale	—	—	–0.021	0.055
Involvement index	—	—	0.166*	0.073
Religious mentor	—	—	3.826***	1.127
Peer setting				
Violence index	—	—	0.088	0.086
Friend attempted suicide	—	—	1.112	0.757
Peer mentor	—	—	3.274***	0.661
Multiple disadvantages				
Log of interactive index	—	—	–0.378***	0.094
Intercept	105.199***	0.512	105.053***	4.742
N	8,669		6,897	
F-test	15.85***		31.45***	
R^2	0.152		0.273	

Source: Authors' calculations based on data set described in Harris and Udry (2008).
+$p < .10$; *$p < .05$; **$p < .01$; ***$p < .001$

effect on verbal intelligence. Gender has an effect, but it is conditioned by marital and childbearing status. In general, young women score lower than men on the PVT, though the effect is not significant for unmarried women without children. Becoming an unmarried mother after age eighteen, however, is associated with a deficit of 2.7 points, and the gap is even greater for married mothers at 2.9 points. Having an unmarried birth before age eighteen is associated with a 2-point gap, but the effect is not significant owing to the high standard error. Among males, being an unmarried father is associated with a 2-point deficit in verbal intelligence.

All of the mediating health measures included in the model have negative signs and two of the three coefficients are significant. A tendency toward depression and a pessimistic outlook on one's life chances are both associated with lower levels of verbal intelligence. For each unit increase in depression, the PVT score drops by 0.44 points and for each unit on the life expectation scale it drops by 0.46. Because the former has an observed range of 0 to 25 and the latter of 0 to 15, variation in depression and expectation of an early death potentially cause quite large swings of 11 points and 6.9 points, respectively. Although poor health also undermines verbal intelligence, the effect is small and not significant at just 0.085 points per unit, for a total of 0.34 points over the range of the health scale. Thus poor mental health has strong negative effects on the acquisition of cognitive skills, but poor physical health does not.

Holding current family status constant, the composition of the family of origin has little effect, though originating in a single-parent effect has a marginally significant effect in raising the PVT. Although income itself has no significant effect on verbal intelligence, other resources associated with class are quite important. Access to health insurance boosts PVT scores, raising it by 1.7 points if coverage is partial and by 2.3 points if it is complete. Likewise, the PVT score rises by 0.034 points for each unit of parental occupational prestige and is 1.6 points greater if the respondent has a college-educated parent.

In terms of emotional resources, experiencing a death in the family increases verbal intelligence by 3.2 points, whereas greater family sternness reduces it by 0.05 points. Apparently suffering the emotional trauma of a family death somehow boosts verbal intelligence both directly, as shown here, and indirectly by reducing the likelihood of nonmarital and teenage childbearing (see chapter 4), which, as the full model in table 6.2 shows, tends to depress performance on the PVT. In contrast, family sternness has mixed effects. Indirectly, coming from an emotionally stern, remote, and austere family background increases verbal intelligence by decreasing the likelihood of first intercourse and raising the age of sexual debut, by reducing the odds of unwed and teenage fertility, by lowering the likelihood of engaging in risky health behaviors, and by reducing depression and the expectation of an early death—all conditions associated with lower PVT scores (see chapters 4 and 5). At the same time, however, the direct effect of a stern emotional style inhibits the cultivation of verbal intelligence.

Having access to a trusted adult while growing appears to provide intellectual benefits irrespective of the social sphere in which the mentor is embedded. Perhaps not surprisingly, however, the greatest benefit is for having a mentor in the school setting (6.1 points on the PVT scale), but the benefits of having a mentor in the religious and peer settings are also significant at 3.8 and 3.3 points, respectively; having a neighborhood mentor boosts a respondent's PVT score by 2.4 points, whereas a family mentor increases it by 1.9 points. In addition to having a religious mentor, religious involvement also boosts the acquisition of cognitive skills, with each point on the involvement scale raising PVT performance by 0.17 points, or 2 points over the scale's observed 0 to 12 range. Combined with the effect of having a college-educated, high-status parent (essentially a young person's default mentor), mentorship and social support thus appear to be critical in promoting intellectual growth among adolescents.

Material disadvantages in neighborhoods and schools have rather strong negative effects on the acquisition of cognitive skills. Each point on the scale of neighborhood disadvantage reduces the PVT score by 2.25 points, for a total possible shift of around 9 points over the scale's range. Similarly, each additional point on the scale of school disadvantage lowers the PVT score by 0.18 points, for a potential swing of 7 points over the scale's observed range. In addition, the accumulation of disadvantages across social spheres has an effect in reducing intellectual growth, with each point on the index reducing the PVT score by 0.38 points, for a total of almost 14 points over the observed range.

In contrast, a lack of social efficacy within neighborhoods and schools has the opposite effect, as does a relative scarcity of young unmarried males. Each unit on the 0–16 neighborhood inefficacy index increases the PVT score by 0.43 points for a total potential shift of 6.9 points whereas each unit on the 0 to 40 school inefficacy index raises the PVT score by 0.18 points, or 7.2 points over the range of the scale. Growing up in a neighborhood where females outnumber males increased the odds of 1.7 points per unit, or almost 20 points over the range of the scale. In sum, when young people come of age in social environments that constrain the opportunities for rewarding social interactions—that is, anomic schools and neighborhoods with limited possibilities for dating and romance—intellectual growth appears to be encouraged.

Considering all of these effects, the profile of someone likely to thrive cognitively and display high verbal intelligence is someone who has access to an adult mentor of some sort; who is not depressed, does not perceive a low likelihood of survival into adulthood; and who manages to avoid early parenthood; who grew up in a family with health insurance headed by a high status, emotionally warm, college-educated parent; and who came of age in materially advantaged schools and neighborhoods that offered few competing social distractions. He or she was also religiously involved and did not experience cumulative disadvantage across social spheres. In contrast, someone likely to stagnate cognitively displays the opposite profile: someone who lacks access to an adult mentor; begins childbearing early; is depressed and perceives low survival chances; grew up without health insurance in a low-status family with a parent who never went to college and displayed a stern, distant emotional style; who inhabited materially disadvantaged schools and neighborhoods that provided abundant social distractions; and who was not involved religiously and faced multiple disadvantages across social spheres. Although the direction of causality may not always be certain, the pattern of association is clear.

HIGH SCHOOL ACADEMIC PERFORMANCE

By the third wave of the Adolescent Health Survey, the youngest of the respondents was eighteen and by conventional standards all should have completed high school. In this section, we examine the ecological determinants of high school academic performance controlling for ascribed characteristics, health status, cognitive skills, and family circumstances that are predetermined by prior ecological exposure. We focus on two easily measured but widely used outcomes: grade point average (GPA) and the proportion of courses failed (PCF). Figure 6.3 begins the analysis by plotting high school GPA by race and class.

Figure 6.3   High School Grade Point Average

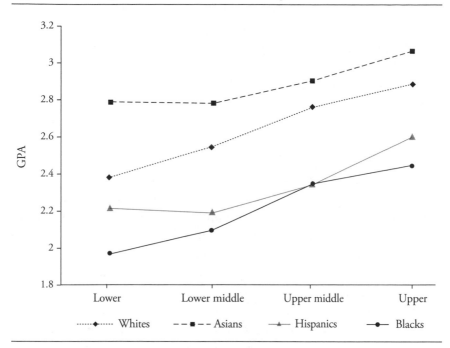

Source: Authors' compilation based on Harris and Udry (2008).

All racial groups display a pattern of rising grade achievement as class standing increases, though the trajectory is steeper for some racial groups than others. The class gradient observed within racial groups is generally dwarfed, however, by differentials in GPA between groups. Asians display the highest average GPA across all class categories, whereas blacks display the lowest average irrespective of class. Hispanics and whites fall between, the former being closer to blacks (indeed the curves touch in the upper middle class) and the latter being closer to Asians. Among Asians, GPA starts out at around 2.8 in the lower and lower middle classes, rises to around 2.9 in the upper middle class, and approaches 3.1 in the upper class. In contrast, whites begin at a much lower level, with a GPA of about 2.4 in the lower class, but performance rises more quickly to narrow the gap as class increases, reaching 2.5 in the lower middle class, nearly 2.8 in the upper middle class, and 2.9 in the upper class. At the other end of the academic spectrum, the black curve begins with a GPA under 2.0 in the lower class, rising to 2.1 in the lower middle class, 2.4 in the upper middle class, and moderates to reach almost 2.5 in the upper class. Hispanics begin with a GPA of 2.2 in the lower and lower middle classes and achieve roughly the same GPA as blacks in the upper middle class (2.4), but the trajectory then accelerates to reach 2.6 in the upper class.

The baseline model presented in the left-hand columns of table 6.3 formally tests the significance of these race-class differences with upper class whites as the reference category. As can be seen, in statistical terms Asians in the lower class, lower middle class, and upper middle class earn the same GPA as upper-class whites, and upper-class Asians earn a GPA that is 0.18 points higher. Thus Asians stand out from other groups irrespective of class, in contrast to whites, who exhibit a significant social class gradient in academic performance. Compared with upper-class whites, those in the lower class earn a GPA 0.50 points lower, those in the lower middle class earn one 0.34 points lower, and those in the upper middle class 0.12 points lower.

Although all these class effects are significant, they are nonetheless relatively small compared with those observed in other groups. Among African Americans, for example, lower-class blacks earn a GPA that is almost a full point lower (0.92) than upper-class whites. Similarly, among the lower middle and upper middle classes, the respective deficits are 0.80 and 0.54 points. Even in the upper class the gap remains sizeable at 0.44. In other words, the performance of the most economically advantaged African Americans is roughly on a par with lower-class whites and does not come close to equaling the superior performance of Asians in any class. Among Hispanics, the lags in academic performance are also large and significant. Relative to upper-class whites, the four classes of Hispanics earn GPAs that are 0.68. 0.70, 0.52, and 0.29 points lower, moving from lower to upper class, respectively.

The huge gaps in academic performance observed among Hispanics and blacks are mostly eliminated in the full model presented in the right-hand columns. All of the coefficients are significantly reduced in absolute value and only two retain values that are marginally significant (upper-middle-class Hispanics and upper-class blacks). Likewise, among whites, the class differentials disappear and the coefficients fall toward zero. However, the superior grade performance of Asians is not changed by the introduction of controls: if anything, it is somewhat enhanced. All of the coefficients increase in size, and that for lower-middle-class Asians rises from -0.109 to 0.245 to achieve significance at the 10 percent level. Although Asians outperform all other groups in terms of GPA in the real world, their advantage would be even greater if all groups experienced the same social ecology as upper-class whites.

Other things equal, grade performance is not associated with age or immigrant origins, but women who avoid childbearing earn significantly higher grades than men. Compared with an unmarried male without a child, GPA is 0.29 points greater for childless women who have not married and 0.32 points better for childless women who have married. Giving birth essentially eliminates this advantage. Among men, becoming a father is associated with a 0.17 point lower GPA within marriage and a 0.21 point lower one outside marriage, outcomes not significantly different from one another.

Among mediating conditions, the most important factors predicting GPA, perhaps unsurprisingly, are health, attention deficit disorder, and verbal intelligence. Each additional increment on the poor health index is associated with a 0.05 point reduction GPA and each additional unit on the ADHD index with 0.011 point reduction. Given that the observed range of the former is 1–5 and the latter 0–54, the potential effect on GPA is 0.2 points for health and 0.6 points for ADHD. Each unit on the Picture Vocabulary Test raises grade performance by around 0.014 points, or by 1.61 points over the observed 7–122 point range of the scale. Obviously these effects are quite large, meaning that ecological effects on health, ADHD, and PVT, described in the prior section, have strong indirect effects on grade performance.

In terms of direct effects, family emotional resources have no significant influence on grade performance, meaning that all the effects are indirect— through factors such as health, family status, and verbal ability. Likewise, material conditions in the various social spheres do not play much of a role in determining a student's GPA. Neither family income, neighborhood disadvantage, nor school disadvantage significantly influence GPA. Among material circumstances, only health insurance has a significant effect, raising GPA by 0.27 points with full coverage and by 0.13 points with partial coverage. These effects are in addition to the indirect effects of insurance through mental health, physical health, and cognitive skill.

Within the family sphere, the most important resources are symbolic. GPA rises by around 0.001 points per unit of parental occupational status, for example, and by 0.151 points if the respondent's parent was college educated. In neighborhood, school, and religious settings, the most important factors predicting GPA are generally social. For example, social inefficacy within neighborhoods and a relative scarcity of young unmarried males both

Table 6.3   Determinants of High School Grade Point Average

Independent Variables	Group Effects		Full Model	
	B	SE	B	SE
Race-class group				
White lower	−0.504***	0.056	−0.023	0.124
White lower middle	−0.341***	0.047	0.025	0.085
White upper middle	−0.124**	0.041	0.023	0.054
White upper	—	—	—	—
Asian lower	−0.099	0.203	0.409	0.267
Asian lower middle	−0.109	0.180	0.245+	0.142
Asian upper middle	0.015	0.110	0.095	0.107
Asian upper	0.180*	0.081	0.231*	0.093
Hispanic lower	−0.678***	0.097	0.010	0.154
Hispanic lower middle	−0.697***	0.088	−0.166	0.122
Hispanic upper middle	−0.524***	0.088	−0.202+	0.112
Hispanic upper	−0.287***	0.073	−0.089	0.085
Black lower	−0.922***	0.089	−0.101	0.149
Black lower middle	−0.795***	0.097	−0.176	0.119
Black upper middle	−0.536***	0.106	−0.095	0.100
Black upper	−0.437***	0.131	−0.188+	0.097
Ascribed characteristics				
Age	—	—	−0.013	0.010
Parent foreign born	—	—	0.059	0.045
Mediating conditions				
Cognitive skills				
ADHD index	—	—	−0.011***	0.002
Picture Vocabulary Score	—	—	0.014***	0.002
Health status				
Poor health index	—	—	−0.053***	0.015
Depression scale	—	—	0.000	0.003
Expectation of early death	—	—	0.002	0.006
Family situation				
Unmarried male–not father	—	—	—	—
Married male–not father	—	—	0.143+	0.076
Married male–father	—	—	−0.170*	0.082
Unmarried male–father	—	—	−0.208**	0.071
Unmarried female–no birth	—	—	0.290***	0.029
Married female–no birth	—	—	0.319***	0.060
Married female–mother	—	—	−0.095	0.068
Unmarried female–birth over eighteen	—	—	0.037	0.048
Unmarried female–birth eighteen or younger	—	—	−0.072	0.101

Table 6.3   (continued)

Independent Variables	Group Effects		Full Model	
	B	SE	B	SE
Ecological background				
Composition of origin family				
Two biological parents	—	—	—	—
Biological and stepparent	—	—	−0.042	0.045
One biological parent	—	—	−0.127***	0.129
No biological parent	—	—	−0.219	0.148
Family material resources				
Household income	—	—	0.001	0.002
Access to health insurance				
No coverage	—	—	—	—
Coverage less than a year	—	—	0.125**	0.045
Coverage full year	—	—	0.267***	0.036
Family symbolic resources				
Parental prestige	—	—	0.001*	0.0006
Parent college graduate	—	—	0.151***	0.047
Family emotional resources				
Experienced a death	—	—	0.002	0.057
Family sternness	—	—	−0.001	0.001
Father incarcerated	—	—	−0.005	0.042
Family mentor	—	—	0.048	0.035
Neighborhood setting				
Disadvantage index	—	—	−0.042	0.035
Inefficacy index	—	—	0.012*	0.005
Scarcity of males	—	—	0.068*	0.032
Neighborhood mentor			0.059	0.062
School setting				
Disadvantage index	—	—	−0.002	0.003
Inefficacy index	—	—	−0.009**	0.003
Disorder index	—	—	−0.001	0.006
School mentor	—	—	0.217***	0.037
Religious setting				
Religiosity scale	—	—	0.005	0.004
Involvement index	—	—	0.017***	0.005
Religious mentor	—	—	0.188***	0.056
Peer setting				
Violence index	—	—	−0.051***	0.006
Friend attempted suicide	—	—	0.021	0.036
Peer mentor	—	—	0.050	0.043

Table 6.3   (continued)

| | Group Effects | | Full Model | |
Independent Variables	B	SE	B	SE
Multiple disadvantages				
Log of interactive index	—	—	–0.013*	0.006
Intercept	2.888***	0.034	1.760***	0.409
N	7,277		5,653	
F-test	16.85***		35.57***	
R²	0.110		0.433	

Source: Authors' calculations based on data set described in Harris and Udry (2008).
+$p < .10$; *$p < .05$; **$p < .01$; ***$p < .001$

act to increase grade performance, with the former raising GPA by 0.012 points per unit and the latter by 0.068 points per unit, for total effects of 0.19 points and 0.78 points, respectively, over the range of these measures. As with verbal intelligence, a lack of opportunities for rewarding social interaction in the neighborhood seem to promote better grades. Likewise, greater involvement in the religious sphere and access to a religious mentor increase grade performance. Each increment on the 0–12 involvement index increases GPA by 0.017 points for a potential total increase of 0.20 over the scale's range, whereas having a religious mentor raises GPA by around 0.19 points. Having access to a trusted adult mentor at school also not surprisingly raises GPA, by around 0.22 points for those with access to such a mentor.

Inefficacy in the school setting, in contrast, reduces GPA, lowering it by 0.009 points per unit on the 40-point scale, for a total potential effect of 0.36 points. Likewise, exposure to violence in the peer environment has a strong negative effect, reducing GPA by 0.051 points per unit, potentially lowering GPA by a full point over the 0–20 scale. In addition, the accumulation of multiple disadvantages across social spheres has a significant negative effect on grade performance, reducing it by 0.013 points per unit, or 0.48 points over the observed range of the scale.

Another telling indicator of scholastic problems is the proportion of courses failed in the course of a high school career. A GPA of 3.0 means one thing if it was achieved by earning mostly Bs with a few As and some Cs, and quite another if it was achieved by earning As and Bs in tandem with a large quantity of Fs. Figure 6.4 thus shows the proportion of high school courses

Figure 6.4   High School Courses Failed

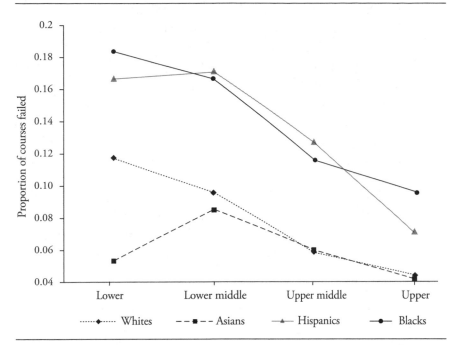

Source: Authors' compilation based on Harris and Udry (2008).

failed by race and class. All racial groups display a pattern of declining PCF with rising social class, but in terms of race the data fall into two basic categories. Blacks and Hispanics display relatively high rates of failure that are above those of Asians and whites at every level of social class. Thus the PCF is around 16 percent to 18 percent for lower-class blacks and Hispanics, falling to lows of 7 percent to 10 percent in the upper class, whereas the PCF among whites and Asians is 5 percent to 12 percent in the lower class and 4 percent in the upper class.

The baseline model shown in the left-hand columns of table 6.4 reveals the statistical significance of these race-class effects. Whites display a clear class gradient, the PCF being 0.071 greater in the lower class, 0.050 greater in the lower middle class, and 0.013 greater in the upper middle class, compared with upper-class whites. By contrast, Asians regardless of class display the same low PCF as upper-class whites. Upper-class blacks and Hispanics, on the other hand, fail a significantly larger share of courses than their upper-class white counterparts. Among blacks, the excess in the upper class is 0.051 and among Hispanics it is 0.026. As one moves down the class hierarchy, however, these figures rise sharply. Among African Americans, the PCF rises by 0.071 in the upper middle class, 0.121 in the lower middle class, and 0.137 in the lower class. Among Hispanics the respective figures are 0.081, 0.125, and 0.121.

In the full model, presented in the right-hand columns of the table, these sharp race-class differences in PCF virtually all disappear once background circumstances are held constant. All the coefficients fall toward zero and only one remains marginally significant. If all people experienced the same mediating and ecological conditions, in other words, they would achieve the same low rate of course failure as upper-class whites. Important mediating conditions are ADHD, verbal intelligence, poor health, and current marital-fertility status. Each additional unit on the ADHD scale increases the proportion of failed courses by 0.001, which yields a potential shift of 0.054 over the range of the scale. Likewise, each additional unit scored on the PVT reduces the proportion failed by 0.001, for a potential effect of 0.115 over the observed range. Poor health, meanwhile, raises the proportion by 0.006 for a potential effect of 0.024. To the extent that ecological conditions influence health, attention deficit disorder, and verbal intelligence, they have important indirect effects on course failure rate.

In general, women experience lower failure rates than men, but the level is contingent on marital and childbearing behavior. Compared with a childless, unmarried male, the PCF is 0.029 lower for an unmarried female without children and 0.033 lower for a married female without children, figures that are not significantly different from one another. The female advantage is nullified, however, by early entry into childbearing: those women who both marry and bear children early earn 37 cents less. Males experience a similar penalty for early marriage and parenthood, though the effect is not significant for them, whereas unmarried fathers experience a significant 0.05 penalty in the PCF. Among men, however, marriage by itself and in the absence of childbearing also lowers the PCF by 0.036.

Within the family sphere, growing up in a single-parent household is associated with a 0.022 increment in the PCF, whereas originating in a family covered by health insurance lowers it by 0.048 if the coverage is full and 0.034 if partial. The only other family characteristic to influence the course failure rate is parental education. Having a college-educated parent lowers the

Table 6.4   Determinants of Proportion of Courses Failed

Independent Variables	Group Effects		Full Model	
	B	SE	B	SE
Race-class group				
White lower	0.071***	0.011	0.018	0.026
White lower middle	0.050***	0.009	0.009	0.018
White upper middle	0.013*	0.006	−0.001	0.012
White upper	—	—	—	—
Asian lower	0.008	0.024	−0.042	0.051
Asian lower middle	0.040	0.040	−0.014	0.027
Asian upper middle	0.014	0.015	0.009	0.019
Asian upper	−0.003	0.013	−0.011	0.017
Hispanic lower	0.121***	0.021	0.032	0.032
Hispanic lower middle	0.125***	0.024	0.057+	0.029
Hispanic upper middle	0.081***	0.022	0.038	0.025
Hispanic upper	0.026*	0.013	−0.001	0.017
Black lower	0.137***	0.019	0.024	0.031
Black lower middle	0.121***	0.021	0.032	0.026
Black upper middle	0.071*	0.028	0.003	0.025
Black upper	0.051+	0.029	0.006	0.024
Ascribed characteristics				
Age	—	—	−0.001	0.002
Parent foreign born	—	—	−0.017	0.011
Mediating conditions				
Cognitive skills				
ADHD index	—	—	0.001**	0.0004
Picture Vocabulary Score	—	—	−0.001***	0.0003
Health status				
Poor health index	—	—	0.006+	0.003
Depression scale	—	—	0.000	0.001
Expectation of early death	—	—	0.001	0.001
Family situation				
Unmarried male–not father	—	—	—	—
Married male–not father	—	—	−0.036**	0.014
Married male–father	—	—	0.038	0.025
Unmarried male–father	—	—	0.050*	0.019
Unmarried female–no birth	—	—	0.029***	0.005
Married female–no birth	—	—	−0.033***	0.008
Married female–mother	—	—	0.037*	0.008
Unmarried female–birth over eighteen	—	—	−0.008	0.011
Unmarried female–birth eighteen or younger	—	—	0.028	0.038

Table 6.4   (continued)

Independent Variables	Group Effects		Full Model	
	B	SE	B	SE
Ecological background				
Composition of origin family				
Two biological parents	—	—	—	—
Biological and stepparent	—	—	0.005	0.010
One biological parent	—	—	0.022***	0.006
No biological parent	—	—	0.051	0.037
Family material resources				
Household income	—	—	0.000	0.000
Access to health insurance				
No coverage	—	—	—	—
Coverage less than a year	—	—	−0.034***	0.010
Coverage full year	—	—	−0.048***	0.008
Family symbolic resources				
Parental prestige	—	—	0.000	0.001
Parent college graduate	—	—	−0.030**	0.011
Family emotional resources				
Experienced a death	—	—	0.010	0.015
Family sternness	—	—	0.000	0.001
Father incarcerated	—	—	−0.004	0.010
Family mentor	—	—	−0.004	0.007
Neighborhood setting				
Disadvantage index	—	—	0.016*	0.008
Inefficacy index	—	—	−0.001	0.001
Scarcity of males	—	—	−0.003	0.007
Neighborhood mentor			−0.020+	0.011
School setting				
Disadvantage index	—	—	0.001*	0.0006
Inefficacy index	—	—	0.000	0.001
Disorder index	—	—	0.001	0.001
School mentor	—	—	−0.024**	0.007
Religious setting				
Religiosity scale	—	—	−0.001*	0.0006
Involvement index	—	—	−0.002**	0.001
Religious mentor	—	—	−0.019*	0.009
Peer setting				
Violence index	—	—	0.010***	0.002
Friend attempted suicide	—	—	−0.007	0.007
Peer mentor	—	—	−0.008	0.008

Table 6.4   (continued)

Independent Variables	Group Effects		Full Model	
	B	SE	B	SE
Multiple disadvantages				
Log of interactive index	—	—	0.000	0.002
Intercept	0.046***	0.005	0.235*	0.097
N	7,277		5,653	
F-test	8.87***		9.43***	
R²	0.069***		0.254***	

Source: Authors' calculations based on data set described in Harris and Udry (2008).
+$p < .10$; *$p < .05$; **$p < .01$; ***$p < .001$

PCF by 0.03 points. Course failure is unrelated to family emotional re-sources, household income, or parental occupational status. Experiencing material disadvantages in the neighborhood and school settings, however, in-creases the PCF significantly. For each unit on the neighborhood disadvan-tage scale, the PCF rises by 0.016, or a total of 0.064 over the range of the index. Likewise each unit of school disadvantage raises the proportion of failed courses by 0.001, yielding a 0.029 shift over the observed range of the index. The prevalence of course failure is also strongly boosted by exposure to violence in the peer environment. Each unit increase in the scale of peer vio-lence raises the proportion of courses failed by 0.01, yielding a substantial 0.20 increase over the scale's observed range.

These adverse effects are mitigated somewhat if a young person is able to establish a relationship with an adult mentor. Having a neighborhood men-tor lowers the PCF by 0.02, having a school mentor reduces it by 0.024, and having a religious mentor by 0.019. The PCF is also reduced by greater reli-giosity and greater religious involvement. For each unit increase in the religi-osity index, the PCF drops by 0.001. For each increment in the involvement scale, it falls by 0.002. Total potential effects are 0.018 and 0.024 over the range of these scales. In sum, the profile of someone least likely to experience course failure is a person who is religious and religiously involved; who has found a mentor in some social sphere; who attends a materially advantaged school, lives in an affluent neighborhood, and originated in a two-parent household; and who has a college-educated parent with health insurance coverage.

HIGH SCHOOL GRADUATION

The ultimate indicator of a successful adolescence is perhaps a high school diploma. Without a high school degree, college education will remain out of reach along with the white-collar and professional careers that come with college training. The most likely scenario option for a high school dropout is circulation through a series of menial, unskilled jobs that pay minimum wage. Under current recruitment policies, even the military is not an option for high school dropouts.

Figure 6.5 shows the proportion of Add Health respondents who graduated from high school by the time of the third wave. Although all racial groups exhibit a pattern of rising graduation rates with increasing social class, the gradient for Asians is almost negligible. They display a high probability of high school graduation no matter their class status and the highest rate of school completion across classes. In the lower class, especially, the Asian rate of high school graduation is markedly above that of other groups. Whereas in the lower class, whites, Hispanics, and blacks have respective graduation rates of 73 percent, 62 percent, and 68 percent, Asians have one of 90 percent. The rate drops to 87 percent among lower-middle-class Asians, but rises to 92 percent and 95 percent in the upper middle and upper classes.

The increase in graduation probabilities with rising class standing is steeper in the other groups, and the gap with Asians is progressively closed, though never eliminated. Hispanics are the least likely to graduate across all class categories, from 62 percent in the lower class to 69 percent in the lower middle class, 79 percent in the upper middle class, and 82 percent in the upper class. The class progression in graduation rates for African Americans is from 73 percent to 75 percent to 84 percent to 88 percent. That for whites is from 68 percent to 76 percent to 85 percent to nearly 95 percent, from lowest to highest class category.

The baseline model presented in the left-hand columns of table 6.5 confirms the statistical significance of these differentials. As with other cognitive outcomes, Asians perform as well or better than upper-class whites regardless of class standing. Upper-class blacks also are not significantly different from their upper-class white counterparts. All other race-class groups, however, have significantly and often substantially lower odds of high school graduation. The odds of graduation for lower-class whites, for example, are 79 percent lower than for upper-class whites, but 67 percent and 44 percent lower

Figure 6.5   Proportion Graduating from High School by Race and Class

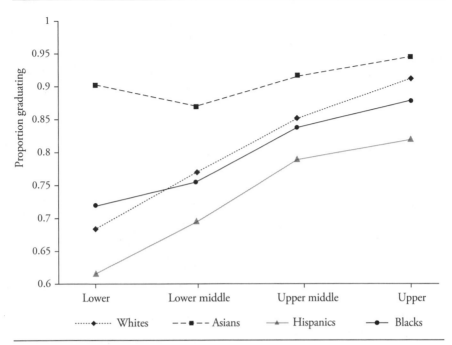

Source: Authors' compilation based on Harris and Udry (2008).

for those in the lower middle and upper middle classes. Among Hispanics, the reduction of odds goes from 84 percent in the lower class to 78 percent and 64 percent in the lower middle and upper middle class, and remains at 56 percent in the upper class. Among African Americans, the odds of graduation are 75 percent lower in the lower class, 70 percent lower in the lower middle class, and 50 percent lower in the upper middle class.

Controlling for background characteristics generally eliminates race-class differences for blacks and Hispanics (except for lower-class Hispanics, for whom the coefficient is reduced in absolute value but remains significant at the 10 percent level). Among whites, however, class differences, though reduced, nonetheless persist and remain significant at least at marginal levels. Something associated with lower class status among whites but not captured in our models appears to contribute to their high dropout rates. Neither age nor immigrant origins are related to the likelihood of high school graduation, nor are scores on the ADHD or PVT indices predictive of high school com-

Table 6.5   Determinants of High School Graduation

Independent Variables	Group Effects		Full Model	
	B	SE	B	SE
Race-class group				
White lower	−1.556***	0.167	−1.120*	0.564
White lower middle	−1.122***	0.158	−0.864+	0.463
White upper middle	−0.584***	0.165	−0.556+	0.311
White upper	—	—	—	—
Asian lower	−0.100	0.673	−0.668	0.923
Asian lower middle	−0.432	0.536	−1.170+	0.699
Asian upper middle	0.064	0.560	−0.524	0.801
Asian upper	0.500	0.494	0.141	0.629
Hispanic lower	−1.858***	0.188	−1.069+	0.641
Hispanic lower middle	−1.506***	0.202	−0.714	0.487
Hispanic upper middle	−1.009***	0.263	−0.124	0.522
Hispanic upper	−0.815*	0.376	0.322	0.645
Black lower	−1.380***	0.190	−0.383	0.672
Black lower middle	−1.206***	0.221	0.117	0.558
Black upper middle	−0.693**	0.264	−0.101	0.517
Black upper	−0.361	0.388	0.601	0.646
Ascribed characteristics				
Age	—	—	0.063	0.047
Parent foreign born	—	—	−0.248	0.270
Mediating conditions				
High school performance				
Grade point average	—	—	0.363	0.238
Proportion of courses failed	—	—	−8.152***	1.142
Cognitive skills				
ADHD index	—	—	−0.001	0.007
Picture Vocabulary Score	—	—	0.007	0.006
Health status				
Poor health index	—	—	0.150+	0.086
Depression scale	—	—	0.001	0.020
Expectation of early death	—	—	0.046	0.032
Family situation				
Unmarried male–not father	—	—	—	—
Married male–not father	—	—	−1.001**	0.437
Married male–father	—	—	−0.813*	0.411
Unmarried male–father	—	—	−0.904**	0.281
Unmarried female–no birth	—	—	−0.218	0.215
Married female–no birth	—	—	−1.144**	0.384

Table 6.5   (continued)

Independent Variables	Group Effects		Full Model	
	B	SE	B	SE
Married female–mother	—	—	−1.319***	0.300
Unmarried female–birth over eighteen	—	—	−0.563*	0.282
Unmarried female–birth eighteen or younger	—	—	−0.743	0.475
Ecological background				
Composition of origin family				
Two biological parents	—	—	—	—
Biological and stepparent	—	—	−0.189	0.279
One biological parent	—	—	0.415	0.255
No biological parent	—	—	−0.607	0.726
Family material resources				
Household income	—	—	−0.007	0.011
Access to health insurance				
No coverage	—	—	—	—
Coverage less than a year	—	—	0.593**	0.185
Coverage full year	—	—	0.665***	0.157
Family symbolic resources				
Parental prestige	—	—	0.003	0.004
Parent college graduate	—	—	−0.303	0.239
Family emotional resources				
Experienced a death	—	—	0.212	0.290
Family sternness	—	—	0.001	0.006
Father incarcerated	—	—	−0.266	0.201
Family mentor	—	—	−0.067	0.199
Neighborhood setting				
Disadvantage index	—	—	0.135	0.131
Inefficacy index	—	—	0.039	0.028
Scarcity of males	—	—	−0.084	0.130
Neighborhood mentor			−0.161	0.273
School setting				
Disadvantage index	—	—	0.018	0.011
Inefficacy index	—	—	0.021	0.015
Disorder index	—	—	−0.007	0.026
School mentor	—	—	0.491+	0.289
Religious setting				
Religiosity scale	—	—	0.028	0.024
Involvement index	—	—	−0.014	0.031
Religious mentor	—	—	−0.524	0.473

Table 6.5   (continued)

	Group Effects		Full Model	
Independent Variables	B	SE	B	SE
Peer setting				
Violence index	—	—	–0.072**	0.026
Friend attempted suicide	—	—	–0.100	0.269
Peer mentor	—	—	–0.206	0.204
Multiple disadvantages				
Log of interactive index	—	—	–0.055	0.041
Intercept	2.325***	0.143	2.021	2.325
N	8,990		5,652	
F-test	11.45***		9.96***	

Source: Authors' compilation based on data set described in Harris and Udry (2008).
$+p < .10$; $*p < .05$; $**p < .01$; $***p < .001$

pletion. Although the likelihood of high school graduation is not affected by GPA, it unsurprisingly rises very sharply as proportion of courses failed increases. Thus cognitive skills as measured by the ADHD and PVT indices do not affect graduation directly—only through their strong effect on the likelihood of course failure. High school graduation is more about persistence than performance.

Holding cognitive skills and academic performance constant, the odds of high school graduation are lower for those who entered early into marriage and childbearing. Among males, marriage lowers the odds of high school graduation by 63 percent and fatherhood lowers them in the range of 56 percent to 60 percent, depending on the social auspices of the birth. Among females, the odds of graduation drop by 68 percent with marriage but somewhat surprisingly the odds of school completion fall only in the range of 43 percent to 52 percent if a woman has a child out of wedlock.

Few ecological factors are directly related to high school graduation. Most of the ecological influences appear to be indirect, through their effect on the rate of course failure. Two effects stand out, however, for their combination of strong effects that are both direct and indirect. Access to health insurance improves the likelihood of high school graduation by lowering the share of courses failed, but also acts directly, increasing the odds by 94 percent if the coverage is full and by 81 percent if partial. Likewise, exposure to peer violence indirectly affects the likelihood of graduation through its strong positive effect on course failure. It also acts directly, reducing the odds by 6.9 percent for each additional unit on the peer violence index. Only one other ecological variable, having a school mentor, was significant in predicting graduation, and that was at a marginal level. As with insurance coverage and peer violence, having an adult mentor at school not only influences graduation rates indirectly through its effect on the relative number of courses failed, but also directly by increasing the odds of school completion by 63 percent.

THE ECOLOGICAL PRODUCTION OF HUMAN CAPITAL

The ecological production of human capital is summarized in table 6.6, which, as in earlier chapters, shows the relative significance and direction of effects for ecological variables on outcomes of interest. The expression of ADHD is most strongly connected to conditions in the peer environment—exposure to violence, suicide attempts, and peer mentors all being associated with higher scores on the ADHD scale. A person's ADHD level is also positively predicted by having mentors in the family and neighborhood spheres and by growing up with a stepparent. ADHD is sharply reduced by having full access to health insurance, however.

Verbal intelligence is strongly influenced by conditions in all spheres of social influence. In the family sphere, PVT scores are strongly boosted by access to health insurance, by access to the symbolic resources of college education and occupational prestige, and by the experience of a death in the family. A stern emotional style in the family, however, acts as a drag on the development of verbal intelligence. Exposure to material disadvantage within schools and neighborhoods and the accumulation of disadvantages across spheres also strongly lower scores on the PVT. Social inefficacy in schools and neighborhoods increases them, however, as does a scarcity of males in neighborhoods, suggesting that limited opportunities for socializing yield greater cognitive development. Having a mentor always improves verbal intelligence, whether in the family, neighborhood, school, peer, or religious setting. PVT scores also improve with religious involvement.

Grade performance is enhanced by having a parent who graduated from college, has a high occupational status, and heads an intact family with full health insurance coverage. GPA is unrelated to emotional conditions within

Table 6.6   Significance of Ecological Conditions

| | Cognitive Skills | | High School Achievement | | |
	ADHD	PVT	GPA	Courses Failed	Graduation
Family composition					
Biological and stepparent	++				
One biological parent		+	----	++++	
No biological parent					
Family material resources					
Household income					
Health insurance less than a year	-	++	+++	----	+++
Health insurance a year or more	---	++++	++++	----	++++
Family symbolic resources					
Parental prestige		+++	++		
Parent college graduate		++	++++	---	
Family emotional resources					
Family mortality		++++			
Family sternness	-	----			
Father incarcerated					
Family mentor	+	++++			
Neighborhood setting					
Disadvantage index		----		++	
Inefficacy index		++++	++		
Scarcity of males		++	++		
Neighborhood mentor	++	+++		-	
School setting					
Disadvantage index		----		++	
Inefficacy index	++	++	---		
Disorder index					
School mentor		++++	++++	---	+
Religious setting					
Religiosity scale				--	
Involvement index		++	++++	---	
Had religious mentor		++++	++++	--	
Peer setting					
Violence index	++++		----	++++	---
Friend attempted suicide	+++				
Peer mentor	+++	++++			
Multiple disadvantages					
Interactive index		----	--		

Source: Authors' calculations based on data set described in Harris and Udry (2008).
Note: Effects are on predicting cognitive and scholastic outcomes.

the family, however. Apart from the family, GPA is most strongly improved by having a school or religious mentor and by greater religious involvement. As with verbal intelligence, grades are enhanced by social inefficacy and a relative absence of young unattached males in the neighborhood. Unlike the PVT score, however, GPA is reduced by social inefficacy. Grade achievement is also sharply lowered by exposure to peer violence and by exposure to multiple disadvantages across spheres. The share of high school courses failed is mostly connected to the same family characteristics as GPA, being greater for respondents from single-parent families and less for those with a college-educated parent and access to health insurance. Course failure is also increased by exposure to disadvantage within schools and neighborhoods and to violence in the peer network, but is negatively predicted by access to school or religious mentors as well as by greater religiosity and involvement in the religious sphere. As noted earlier, the ecological effects on graduation are mostly indirect, through their effect on the share of courses failed, which very strongly predicts the odds of graduation. The strongest direct ecological effects on school completion are the positive effect of access to health insurance and the negative effect of exposure to peer violence.

Looking across the columns of table 6.6, access to health insurance stands out as a remarkably important determinant of cognitive skills and scholastic achievement, having strong and significant effects across all five outcomes, suggesting that the recent U.S. health insurance reform, which promises to expand coverage, may pay important dividends later by raising rates of human capital formation in the country. Access to a school-based mentor is also important in facilitating the formation of human capital, having significant effects on all outcomes save ADHD. Religious involvement and having a religious mentor, more than religiosity itself, also enhance human capital formation. Thus it is not spiritual capital but social capital from religious settings that contributes to the formation of human capital. By the same token, exposure to peer violence, which one might consider negative social capital, impedes the formation of human capital among adolescents simultaneously by increasing ADHD, reducing GPA, raising the rate of course failure, and reducing the odds of graduation.

As table 6.7 shows, holding constant the foregoing ecological conditions largely eliminates the performance gap displayed by African Americans with respect to indicators of high school achievement, but does not get rid of the consistently lower scores on the PVT and the ADHD indices. Much the

Table 6.7   Significance of Race-Class Effects

	Cognitive Skills		High School Achievement		
	ADHD	PVT	GPA	Courses Failed	Graduation
WLO					--
WLM					-
WUM					-
ALO		--			
ALM		-	+		-
AUM	--				
AUP			++		
HLO		---			-
HLM	-	-		+	
HUM	---	---	-		
HUP					
BLO		---			
BLM	-	----			
BUM	----	----			
BUP	---	--	-		

Source: Authors' calculations based on data set described in Harris and Udry (2008).
Note: Effects are on predicting cognitive and scholastic outcomes.

same pattern prevails for Hispanics. Taking into account ecological circumstances, we still observe lower ADHD and PVT scores and higher GPAs among Asians. Among whites, controlling for ecological and mediating circumstances eliminates class differences with respect to cognitive skill formation and scholastic achievement, except for high school graduation. Although the gradient in high school graduation among whites is reduced, it nonetheless remains marginally significant.

Results to this point have modeled fertility and family formation, the social production of health, and the formation of human capital through endogenous ecological processes unfolding across five social spheres. We have shown how exposure to advantages and disadvantages in family, school, neighborhood, peer, and religious environments produces often sharp differentials in well-being and performance by race and class. We suggest that equalizing access to resources across these social spheres would reduce and often eliminate many, though not all, race-class differentials observed with respect to unwed parenthood, health, cognition, and academic achievement, thus putting us into a good position to understand how adolescent achievements and their ecological precursors mediate the transition to adulthood. Before turning to that transition, however, we consider one final set of mediating adolescent outcomes, namely, involvement in crime and delinquency.

CHAPTER 7

Crime and Delinquency

Crime, violence, and delinquency are, unfortunately, common features of social life inherent to all human cultures. Within any society, however, the propensity to commit crimes and undertake delinquent acts is not spread evenly across the population, but concentrated in certain social and demographic groups. Within virtually all societies, rates of crime and delinquency are greatest among young, socially unattached males. In the United States, for example, about four-fifths of all crimes are committed by men and the overall crime rate for males is more than four times that of females (Steffensmeier and Allan 1996). In terms of age, patterns vary somewhat by type of offense, but in general rates of crime and delinquency begin to rise at around age twelve and then move rapidly upward to peak in the late teens before leveling off in the twenties and dropping precipitously in the thirties (Steffensmeier et al. 1989).

The tendency for young males to engage in crime and deviance stems primarily from the elevated presence in their bloodstreams of testosterone, a sex hormone that promotes physical strength and aggressive behavior and is found in much higher concentrations among men than women (Booth and Osgood 1993; Dabbs et al.1995). Women do have some testosterone in their systems, however, and those with higher levels of this hormone are indeed more prone to criminal behavior (Dabbs et al. 1988). The sharp rise in crime and delinquency during the teenage years thus reflects a sharp increase in testosterone that occurs among all males with the onset of puberty. The plateau during the twenties reflects the moderation of the hormonal surge but also the maturation of the prefrontal cortex, the part of the forebrain responsible for planning, control, and moderation of impulses (LeDoux 2002). The decline in crime and delinquency during the thirties reflects both a decline in testosterone and the steadily greater control imposed by the prefrontal cortex (Damasio 1994; Tiemeier et al. 2009). Delinquent behavior is also moderated by the accumulation of social ties over the life cycle, as responsibilities stemming from marriage, childbearing, work, and other social obligations act to moderate aggressive antisocial actions (Sampson and Laub 1993).

Given that crime and delinquency arise from a combination of social and biological influences, their expression is greatly influenced by interpersonal variation in temperament (Windle 1992) as well as location in the social structure (Sampson and Laub 1993). Some children are more subject to impulsive and aggressive behavior than others, and depending on how these behaviors are dealt with socially in family, school, neighborhood, and peer environments, delinquency and criminality may diminish or grow over the life cycle (Sampson and Laub 1993). The propensity to engage in criminal and delinquent acts has been linked empirically to variation in family composition (Franke 2000; Carlson and Corcoran 2001), school characteristics (Fergusson, Swain-Campbell, and Horwood 2004), neighborhood circumstances (Krivo and Peterson 1996, 2000; Sampson, Raudenbush, and Earls 1997; Morenoff, Sampson, and Raudenbush 2001; Peterson and Krivo 2010), religious participation (Johnson et al. 2000), and peer influences (Akers et al. 1979; Browning, Feinberg, and Dietz 2004; Carroll et al. 2008).

As in other chapters, here we consider the effects of ecological circumstances across all these social spheres simultaneously and measure their effects on crime and delinquency among respondents to the Adolescent Health Survey. As always, we focus on race-class variations in selected outcomes and seek to determine the extent to which such variation might be attributed to intergroup differences in social ecological circumstances, taking into account predetermined mediating effects of high school achievement, cognitive skill formation, health status, and family situation. In our analysis, we focus on three specific behavioral outcomes: degree of involvement in nonviolent crime, degree of involvement in violent crime, and extent of criminal justice involvement.

INVOLVEMENT IN NONVIOLENT CRIME

Wave 3 of the Add Health Survey included a series of questions about the frequency with which respondents committed various nonviolent offenses, such as damaging property, stealing, breaking into buildings, buying or holding stolen property, using someone else's bank or credit card without authorization, and selling marijuana or other drugs. The possible response categories were never, one to two times, three to four times, or five or more times, which we coded 0 to 3 and summed to create a reliable 21-point index of involvement in nonviolent crime ($\alpha = 0.69$, see appendix B). This index is plotted by race and class in figure 7.1. As evident from the low average values, the index is highly skewed, with many zeros, a few people reporting some criminal activity, and a few reporting considerable criminal involvement, a distribution that is consistent with research indicating a disproportionate share of all crimes are committed by a tiny percentage of individuals (Wolfgang, Figlio, and Sellin 1972). As indicated by the table in appendix A, however, the resulting index nonetheless yields scores that fall along the entire range of the index.

As figure 7.1 makes clear, class variation with respect to engagement in nonviolent crime and delinquency shows no consistent pattern. Among whites, degree of involvement in nonviolent crime generally rises with social class, the average index going from 0.38 in the lower class to around 0.55 in the lower middle and upper middle classes, and then climbing to 0.70 in the upper class. The lowest value of nonviolent crime index, just 0.15, is observed for lower-class Asians. The Asian index then rises to 0.22 in the lower middle class and reaches 0.50 in the upper middle class before dropping back to around 0.39 in the upper class. Blacks and Latinos display no systematic class pattern whatsoever. The black index of involvement in nonviolent crime jumps from 0.49 in the lower class to 0.80 in the lower middle class then falls to 0.55 in the upper middle class before climbing again to 0.72 in the upper class. The Hispanic index similarly zigzags, from 0.55 to 0.57 between the lower and lower middle class, rising to 0.61 in the lower upper middle class, and then down to 0.43 in the upper class.

Despite these variations, Asians generally tend to display the lowest values on the nonviolent crime index and blacks overall the highest, Hispanics and whites falling between the two. In some categories, however, the values are quite close together and the racial curves cross at several points in the class distribution. The one clear finding is that among young people of the upper class, the highest indices of involvement in nonviolent crime are observed for blacks and whites, among whom there is little difference, around 0.71 to 0.72, and the lowest values are for Hispanics and Asians, about 0.39 and 0.45, respectively.

Figure 7.1   Nonviolent Crime Index

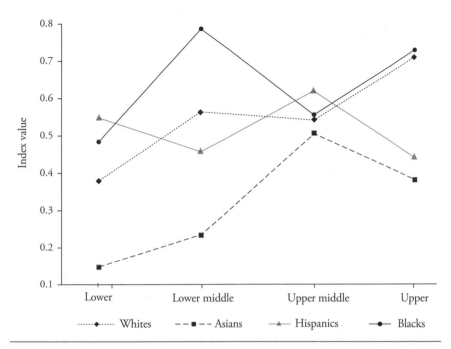

Source: Authors' compilation based on Harris and Udry (2008).

To determine what might account for the generally higher rates of nonviolent criminal involvement among black and white upper-class adolescents, we followed our usual procedure of estimating regression models to predict the degree of criminal involvement using dummy variables for race and class, and then again using dummy variables plus controls. Given the skewed distribution of the outcome variable, we explored several specifications of the model, including a log transformation, binomial regression, Poisson regression, and a 0–1 dichotomous coding of nonviolent involvement; but none of these alternative specifications provided results that were clearly preferable to those obtained using ordinary least squares, so in the interests of parsimony and simplicity we present OLS (ordinary least square) estimates in table 7.1. In any event, findings are also robust with respect to different model specifications.

The race-class coefficients shown in the left-hand columns indicate that nonviolent crime is largely the province of upper-class whites. Compared to that group, most other race-class categories carry a negative coefficient. In-

Table 7.1   Determinants of Involvement in Nonviolent Crime

Independent Variables	Group Effects		Full Model	
	B	SE	B	SE
Race-class group				
White lower	−0.333***	0.082	−0.039	0.265
White lower middle	−0.150	0.097	0.081	0.199
White upper middle	−0.170*	0.087	−0.030	0.137
White upper	—	—	—	—
Asian lower	−0.566***	0.104	−0.230	0.284
Asian lower middle	−0.477***	0.105	−0.150	0.242
Asian upper middle	−0.205	0.188	−0.102	0.205
Asian upper	−0.330**	0.106	−0.310*	0.139
Hispanic lower	−0.162	0.104	0.403	0.293
Hispanic lower middle	−0.253*	0.121	0.137	0.212
Hispanic upper middle	−0.092	0.164	−0.003	0.182
Hispanic upper	−0.258*	0.376	−0.291*	0.142
Black lower	−0.227*	0.097	0.297	0.314
Black lower middle	0.076	0.234	0.341	0.355
Black upper middle	−0.157	0.133	0.111	0.219
Black upper	0.020	0.165	−0.096	0.253
Ascribed characteristics				
Age	—	—	−0.106***	0.019
Parent foreign born	—	—	−0.056	0.098
Mediating conditions				
High school achievements				
High school graduate	—	—	0.051	0.091
Grade point average	—	—	−0.022	0.075
Proportion of courses failed	—	—	−0.167	0.286
Cognitive skills				
ADHD index	—	—	0.015***	0.005
Picture Vocabulary Score	—	—	0.002	0.002
Health status				
Poor health index	—	—	0.077*	0.036
Depression scale	—	—	0.009	0.008
Expectation of early death	—	—	−0.024+	0.013
Family situation				
Unmarried male–not father	—	—	—	—
Married male–not father	—	—	−0.568***	0.143
Married male–father	—	—	−0.526***	0.106
Unmarried male–father	—	—	−0.486***	0.117
Unmarried female–no birth	—	—	−0.579***	0.075
Married female–no birth	—	—	−0.692***	0.072

Table 7.1 (continued)

Independent Variables	Group Effects		Full Model	
	B	SE	B	SE
Married female–mother	—	—	–0.814***	0.064
Unmarried female–birth over eighteen	—	—	–0.725***	0.080
Unmarried female–birth eighteen or younger	—	—	–0.773***	0.135
Ecological background				
Composition of origin family				
Two biological parents	—	—	—	—
Biological and stepparent	—	—	–0.113	0.131
One biological parent	—	—	–0.060	0.077
No biological parent	—	—	0.289	0.285
Family material resources				
Household income	—	—	0.004	0.005
Access to health insurance				
No coverage	—	—	—	—
Coverage less than a year	—	—	0.127	0.121
Coverage full year	—	—	–0.093	0.109
Family symbolic resources				
Parental prestige	—	—	0.003+	0.002
Parent college graduate	—	—	0.152	0.111
Family emotional resources				
Experienced a death	—	—	0.181	0.133
Family sternness	—	—	–0.004*	0.002
Father incarcerated	—	—	0.288*	0.127
Family mentor	—	—	–0.133	0.097
Neighborhood setting				
Disadvantage index	—	—	0.032	0.077
Inefficacy index	—	—	–0.017	0.012
Scarcity of males	—	—	0.027	0.151
Neighborhood mentor			0.155	0.172
School setting				
Disadvantage index	—	—	0.000	0.005
Inefficacy index	—	—	0.014*	0.007
Disorder index	—	—	–0.004	0.014
School mentor	—	—	0.052	0.112
Religious setting				
Religiosity scale	—	—	–0.007	0.008
Involvement index	—	—	–0.004	0.011
Religious mentor	—	—	–0.096	0.153

Table 7.1   *(continued)*

	Group Effects		Full Model	
Independent Variables	B	SE	B	SE
Peer setting				
Violence index	—	—	0.063***	0.024
Friend attempted suicide	—	—	0.441**	0.162
Peer mentor	—	—	–0.118	0.101
Multiple disadvantages				
Log of interactive index	—	—	–0.006	0.018
Intercept	0.712***	0.072	2.759**	0.949
N	8,837		5,597	
F-test	3.79***		5.49***	
R^2	0.006		0.122	

Source: Authors' calculations based on data set described in Harris and Udry (2008).
$+p < .10$; $*p < .05$; $**p < .01$; $***p < .001$

deed, of the fifteen race-class coefficients shown, thirteen are negative and eight are significant. Among whites, we observe a clear class gradient with respect to nonviolent criminality, with degree of involvement rising as class increases; but there is no clear class gradient for the other racial groups. In statistical terms, upper-class whites share the same elevated rate of nonviolent criminal involvement as blacks in the lower middle class, upper middle class, and upper class, as well as lower- and upper-middle-class Hispanics, upper-middle-class Asians, and lower-middle-class whites.

As seen in the right-hand columns, these significant race-class effects are mostly eliminated by the addition of background controls, which leaves only upper-class Asians and upper-class Hispanics with statistically significant negative effects. Upper-class members of these two minority groups thus appear unusually loath to engage in nonviolent crime. The class gradient among whites, however, disappears in the full model. Given that respondents to the third wave of Add Health are all eighteen or older and have reached the peak of criminality, the coefficient for age is strongly and significantly negative, indicating a steady downturn in criminal engagement with rising age. Among mediating factors, nonviolent crime is positively predicted by the attention deficit and hyperactivity disorder (ADHD) score and the poor health index.

As expected, women display a lower likelihood of nonviolent criminal involvement than men no matter their marital or fertility status, though the acquisition of social ties through marriage and childbearing appear to reduce the odds even more. Compared with an unmarried childless male, the degree of nonviolent criminal involvement is 0.58 points lower for unmarried women without children, 0.69 points lower for a married childless woman, 0.81 points lower for a married mother, and 0.72 to 0.77 points lower for unmarried women with children, depending on age at birth. Consistent with prior research (Sampson and Laub 1993), marriage and parenthood also reduce criminal involvement among men. Compared with an unmarried, childless man, married men are 0.57 points lower on the scale of nonviolent criminality if they have no children and 0.53 points lower if they have children, whereas unmarried fathers are 0.49 points lower. The latter three effects are not significantly different from one another, but are from the reference category of unmarried childless males.

Among ecological effects, nonviolent criminal involvement is most strongly linked to conditions in the school and peer settings, although the family emotional environment also plays an important role. In contrast, involvement in nonviolent crime has little to do with material or symbolic resources within the family. Specifically, it is unrelated to income and education and only marginally related to occupational status. Within the peer environment, however, each additional unit of exposure to violence raises nonviolent criminal involvement by 0.063 points, for a potential increase of 1.26 points over the scale's observed range. Likewise social inefficacy within the educational sphere boosts nonviolent criminal involvement by 0.014 points per unit, yielding a potential 0.56 increase. The suicide attempt of a friend also increases nonviolent criminal involvement by 0.44 points. Paternal incarceration raises it by 0.29 points. Family sternness, however, generally acts as a brake on nonviolent criminality, reducing involvement by 0.004 points per unit for a potential effect of 0.40. According to our model, then, the person most prone to nonviolent crime is a younger, unmarried, childless male with a high level of ADHD and poor health who came from a family characterized by loose discipline, attended a socially inefficacious school, had a suicidal friend, and was exposed to high levels of violence within his peer network.

COMMITTING VIOLENT CRIMES

In addition to questions about nonviolent infractions, the third wave of the Adolescent Health Survey asked about the frequency of certain violent or

Figure 7.2   Violent Crime Index

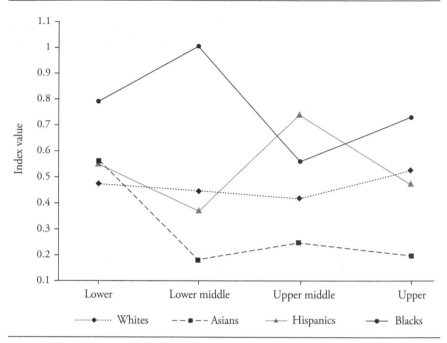

Source: Authors' compilation based on Harris and Udry (2008).

potentially violent criminal behaviors, such as using a weapon to steal something, using a weapon in a fight, carrying a handgun to school or work, owning multiple handguns, getting badly injured in a fight, hurting someone badly in a fight, and taking part in a fight between friends and another group. The frequency categories ranged from never to five or more, sometimes in four intervals and sometimes in five, which when coded into 0–3 or 0–4 scales and summed yielded a reliable 24-point scale of violent criminal involvement ($\alpha = 0.67$, see appendix B). The index is plotted by race and class in figure 7.2.

As in figure 7.1, Asians generally display the lowest values on the violent crime index and blacks the highest, Hispanics and whites falling between the two. Moreover, again the curves often cross and within some class categories the averages are quite close together. In this case, however, none of the racial groups displays a clear class gradient. Whites generally display a flat class curve, the index varying narrowly between 0.41 and 0.51. Blacks, for their part, display a seesaw pattern that goes from 0.80 in the lower class to 1.0 in the lower middle class and then falls to 0.56 in the upper middle class before rising again to 0.72 in the upper class. Hispanics also zigzag from 0.55 to 0.48 between the lower and lower middle classes and from 0.73 to 0.69 in the upper middle and upper classes. Asians begin at around 0.55 in the lower class and then drop to around 0.20, a value that is essentially maintained in the lower middle through upper classes.

In table 7.2, we show baseline and full regression models predicting the degree of violent criminal involvement among respondents. The uncontrolled race-class coefficients reveal no significant class effects among whites, meaning that all whites display the same proclivity to criminal violence as those in the upper class. Asians are generally less prone than whites, showing significant negative coefficients in all but the lowest class. Hispanics display much the same propensity as whites, with the possible exception of those in the lower middle class, whose criminal violence score is marginally lower. Upper-middle-class and upper-class blacks are not significantly different from upper-class whites in their propensity to display violent criminal tendencies, but blacks in the lower and lower middle classes display significantly higher levels of criminal involvement. Indeed, they display the very highest values on the violent crime index.

As seen in the right-hand columns, however, once ascribed, mediating, and ecological circumstances are held constant, all race-class differences all disappear. As with the nonviolent crime index, the degree of involvement in violent crime declines with age and increases with a rising ADHD score. Poor health has no significant effect, however. A higher grade point average (GPA) during high school has a strong effect in reducing violent criminal involvement. Each point increase in GPA lowers the violence scale by 0.19 points, each year of age lowers it by 0.05 points, and each unit in the ADHD scale raises it by 0.01 points, for potential total effects of 0.76 points, 0.3 points, and 0.54 points, respectively, over the range of these scales.

As expected, women universally display lower levels of violence than men, the degree of involvement being especially low for mothers, though all females display indices well below those of males regardless of marital and fertility status. Compared with a single, childless male, an unmarried, female without children scores 0.49 points lower on the violence scale whereas a married childless female scores 0.31 points lower. But those who are mothers score anywhere from 0.63 points to 0.74 points lower, depending on the so-

Table 7.2   Determinants of Involvement in Violent Crime

Independent Variables	Group Effects		Full Model	
	B	SE	B	SE
Race-class group				
White lower	−0.052	0.078	−0.052	0.214
White lower middle	−0.080	0.072	−0.090	0.164
White upper middle	−0.107	0.069	−0.070	0.100
White upper	—	—	—	—
Asian lower	0.034	0.480	0.389	0.588
Asian lower middle	−0.347**	0.111	−0.118	0.194
Asian upper middle	−0.277*	0.181	−0.090	0.205
Asian upper	−0.327***	0.084	−0.141	0.140
Hispanic lower	0.024	0.079	−0.126	0.246
Hispanic lower middle	−0.157+	0.092	−0.204	0.188
Hispanic upper middle	0.215	0.205	0.011	0.239
Hispanic upper	−0.032	0.163	−0.155	0.171
Black lower	0.263+	0.141	0.067	0.246
Black lower middle	0.481*	0.209	0.260	0.280
Black upper middle	0.035	0.129	−0.030	0.217
Black upper	0.202	0.203	−0.079	0.264
Ascribed characteristics				
Age	—	—	−0.047**	0.015
Parent foreign born	—	—	−0.085	0.083
Mediating conditions				
High school achievements				
High school graduate	—	—	0.062	0.114
Grade point average	—	—	−0.192***	0.048
Proportion of courses failed	—	—	0.082	0.334
Cognitive skills				
ADHD index	—	—	0.010**	0.004
Picture Vocabulary Score	—	—	−0.004	0.003
Health status				
Poor health index	—	—	−0.041	0.034
Depression scale	—	—	0.001	0.008
Expectation of early death	—	—	0.016	0.014
Family situation				
Unmarried male–not father	—	—	—	—
Married male–not father	—	—	0.034	0.165
Married male–father	—	—	−0.137	0.170
Unmarried male–father	—	—	−0.194	0.160
Unmarried female–no birth	—	—	−0.491***	0.056
Married female–no birth	—	—	−0.312***	0.088

Table 7.2 *(continued)*

Independent Variables	Group Effects		Full Model	
	B	SE	B	SE
Married female–mother	—	—	–0.630***	0.064
Unmarried female–birth over eighteen	—	—	–0.661***	0.085
Unmarried female–birth eighteen or younger	—	—	–0.742***	0.135
Ecological background				
Composition of origin family				
Two biological parents	—	—	—	—
Biological and stepparent	—	—	–0.136	0.109
One biological parent	—	—	–0.012	0.065
No biological parent	—	—	–0.079	0.145
Family material resources				
Household income	—	—	0.001	0.004
Access to health insurance				
No coverage	—	—	—	—
Coverage less than a year	—	—	0.263**	0.088
Coverage full year	—	—	0.119+	0.067
Family symbolic resources				
Parental prestige	—	—	0.000	0.002
Parent college graduate	—	—	–0.083	0.092
Family emotional resources				
Experienced a death	—	—	0.124	0.101
Family sternness	—	—	0.002	0.002
Father incarcerated	—	—	0.286**	0.108
Family mentor	—	—	–0.007	0.081
Neighborhood setting				
Disadvantage index	—	—	0.111+	0.068
Inefficacy index	—	—	–0.014	0.010
Scarcity of males	—	—	–0.168+	0.094
Neighborhood mentor			0.113	0.129
School setting				
Disadvantage index	—	—	0.001	0.003
Inefficacy index	—	—	0.005	0.005
Disorder index	—	—	–0.006	0.010
School mentor	—	—	–0.071	0.070
Religious setting				
Religiosity scale	—	—	–0.006	0.008
Involvement index	—	—	0.014	0.011
Religious mentor	—	—	–0.143	0.105

Table 7.2   *(continued)*

Independent Variables	Group Effects		Full Model	
	B	SE	B	SE
Peer setting				
Violence index	—	—	0.137***	0.024
Friend attempted suicide	—	—	0.414**	0.139
Peer mentor	—	—	0.033	0.074
Multiple disadvantages				
Log of interactive index	—	—	–0.026+	0.015
Intercept	0.526***	0.055	2.951***	0.810
N	8,767		5,578	
F-test	3.26***		4.63***	
R^2	0.011		0.172	

Source: Authors' calculations based on data set described in Harris and Udry (2008).
$+p < .10$; $*p < .05$; $**p < .01$; $***p < .001$

cial auspices of birth. Moreover, unlike nonviolent criminality, involvement in violent crime among men is not reduced by marriage or childbearing, either alone or in combination, at least in the presence of controls for other ecological, ascribed, and mediating variables.

Among ecological factors, involvement in violent crime is most strongly predicted by having partial as opposed to no or full insurance coverage in the family setting, by having an incarcerated father, by exposure to violence in the peer setting, and by having a suicidal friend. Smaller effects on the margins of significance are observed for having full insurance coverage and coming from a neighborhood characterized by material disadvantage and a scarcity of males. Interestingly, although neighborhood disadvantage positively predicts criminality, as the neighborhood effects literature would suggest, a relative scarcity of young single men within neighborhoods is negatively related to violent criminal involvement, such that the greater the scarcity of marriageable men, the lower the tendency toward violent crime. Perhaps in areas where men are scarce, the odds of forming relationships with women are greater and yield lower levels of criminal involvement for men, other things equal. In general, the profile of someone involved in violent crime is a young man from a partially insured family with an incarcerated father, a violent peer network, and a suicidal friend, who lives in a neighborhood that is poor but not characterized by a particular scarcity of males.

CRIMINAL JUSTICE INVOLVEMENT

Finally, the Add Health questionnaire also included a series of items assessing the degree of personal involvement with criminal justice authorities, including the frequency of stops by police, the number arrests before age eighteen, the number of convictions and guilty pleas, and the duration of time spent in detention or on probation. The frequency categories were 0, 1–2, 3–4, or 5+, which we coded 0–4. When combined with the dichotomous indicator of whether the respondent was ever in jail or prison, these items yield a 17-point scale (see appendix B) with a modest though serviceable reliability ($\alpha = 0.58$). The resulting index of criminal justice involvement is plotted by race and class in figure 7.3.

As can be seen, criminal justice involvement for blacks and whites fluctuates by class with no clear trend, white scores moving back and forth narrowly between 0.42 and 0.50 and black scores seesawing more widely be-

Figure 7.3   Criminal Justice Involvement

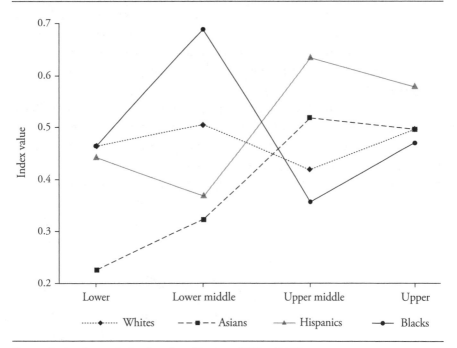

Source: Authors' compilation based on Harris and Udry (2008).

tween 0.35 and 0.70. In contrast, criminal justice involvement for Hispanics and Asians tends to rise as class standing increases. Among Hispanics, the respective index values were 0.44 and 0.38 in the lower and lower middle classes, but 0.62 and 0.58 in the upper middle and upper classes. Likewise, the Asian index rose from a low value of 0.22 in the lower class to 0.32 in the lower middle class and 0.51 in the upper middle class before declining slightly to around 0.50 in the upper class.

Table 7.3 presents baseline and controlled regression models predicting extent of contact with the criminal justice system. The left-hand columns confirm the lack of a strong pattern of variation by race and class. Only one coefficient—that for lower-class Asians—is statistically significant and its effect is negative. Although lower-class Asians may be less likely to come into contact with the criminal justice system than upper-class whites, therefore, all other race-class groups evince the same degree of criminal justice involvement. When controls are applied, however, we see that the lower classes of all racial groups display a significantly lower level of criminal justice involvement than upper-class whites. In other words, were it not for their disadvantaged position on other indicators in the model, the nonwhite poor would have markedly lower rates of criminal justice involvement. In addition, among Hispanics, this decreased contact extends to the lower middle and upper middle classes. If they shared the salubrious ecological circumstances of upper-class whites, their level of criminal justice involvement would also be markedly lower.

Among whites, we observe a clear class pattern once controls are applied, the lowest level being observed in the lower class, followed in ascending order by the lower middle, upper middle, and upper classes. Relative to other race-class groups, in other words, upper-class whites generally enjoy substantial protection from criminal justice involvement owing to their privileged ecological and favorable mediating circumstances. Although upper-class whites display much the same levels of violent criminal involvement and even higher rates of nonviolent criminal involvement as other groups, they are much less likely to end up with criminal justice entanglements.

As one would expect, the degree of involvement in the criminal justice system falls with age and is universally lower for women than men. No matter what their marital status, women are much less likely to have contact with criminal justice authorities than are men; but women with children are especially unlikely to be involved. Whereas the index of criminal justice involve-

Table 7.3   Determinants of Involvement in Criminal Justice System

Independent Variables	Group Effects		Full Model	
	B	SE	B	SE
Race-class group				
White lower	−0.034	0.064	−0.585*	0.234
White lower middle	0.007	0.065	−0.433*	0.177
White upper middle	−0.080	0.059	−0.285*	0.122
White upper	—	—	—	—
Asian lower	−0.270*	0.134	−0.742**	0.259
Asian lower middle	−0.173	0.146	−0.208	0.250
Asian upper middle	0.021	0.144	−0.001	0.223
Asian upper	−0.002	0.139	0.346	0.218
Hispanic lower	−0.055	0.100	−0.619*	0.268
Hispanic lower middle	−0.130	0.084	−0.366+	0.206
Hispanic upper middle	0.137	0.178	−0.345+	0.187
Hispanic upper	0.080	0.148	−0.131	0.140
Black lower	−0.032	0.086	−0.674*	0.277
Black lower middle	0.193	0.165	−0.270	0.230
Black upper middle	−0.142	0.094	−0.253	0.179
Black upper	−0.028	0.104	−0.038	0.128
Ascribed characteristics				
Age	—	—	−0.035*	0.017
Parent foreign born	—	—	−0.077	0.082
Predetermined conditions				
Criminal involvement				
Nonviolent crime	—	—	0.174***	0.029
Violent crime	—	—	0.119***	0.034
High school achievement				
High school graduate	—	—	−0.121	0.115
Grade point average	—	—	−0.057	0.046
Proportion of courses failed	—	—	−0.039	0.328
Cognitive skills				
ADHD index	—	—	0.003	0.003
Picture Vocabulary Score	—	—	0.003*	0.001
Health status				
Poor health index	—	—	0.018	0.030
Depression scale	—	—	0.006	0.008
Expectation of early death	—	—	0.027*	0.013
Family situation				
Unmarried male–not father	—	—	—	—
Married male–not father	—	—	−0.207	0.160
Married male–father	—	—	−0.063	0.174

Table 7.3   (continued)

Independent Variables	Group Effects		Full Model	
	B	SE	B	SE
Unmarried male–father	—	—	–0.023	0.155
Unmarried female–no birth	—	—	–0.277***	0.053
Married female–no birth	—	—	–0.199***	0.090
Married female–mother	—	—	–0.430***	0.069
Unmarried female–birth over eighteen	—	—	–0.387***	0.065
Unmarried female–birth eighteen or younger	—	—	–0.437***	0.082
Ecological background				
Composition of origin family				
Two biological parents	—	—	—	—
Biological and stepparent	—	—	–0.037	0.078
One biological parent	—	—	–0.051	0.066
No biological parent	—	—	0.909*	0.406
Family material resources				
Household income	—	—	–0.009*	0.004
Access to health insurance				
No coverage	—	—	—	—
Coverage less than a year	—	—	–0.138+	0.077
Coverage full year	—	—	–0.091	0.067
Family symbolic resources				
Parental prestige	—	—	0.001	0.001
Parent college graduate	—	—	0.150*	0.067
Family emotional resources				
Experienced a death	—	—	–0.003	0.101
Family sternness	—	—	–0.001	0.002
Father incarcerated	—	—	0.107	0.083
Family mentor	—	—	0.184**	0.057
Neighborhood setting				
Disadvantage index	—	—	–0.039	0.045
Inefficacy index	—	—	0.000	0.008
Scarcity of males	—	—	0.026	0.079
Neighborhood mentor			0.148	0.107
School setting				
Disadvantage index	—	—	0.003	0.004
Inefficacy index	—	—	–0.002	0.004
Disorder index	—	—	0.003	0.007
School mentor	—	—	0.139*	0.056

CRIME AND DELINQUENCY   261

Table 7.3   (continued)

Independent Variables	Group Effects		Full Model	
	B	SE	B	SE
Religious setting				
Religiosity scale	—	—	0.008	0.007
Involvement index	—	—	−0.021**	0.008
Religious mentor	—	—	0.104	0.094
Peer setting				
Violence index	—	—	0.069***	0.018
Friend attempted suicide	—	—	0.141	0.105
Peer mentor	—	—	0.120*	0.055
Multiple disadvantages				
Log of interactive index	—	—	0.003	0.012
Intercept	0.497***	0.042	1.341***	0.617
N	8,827		5,488	
F-test	0.76		12.09***	
R^2	0.003		0.221	

Source: Authors' calculations based on data set described in Harris and Udry (2008).
$+p < .10$; $*p < .05$; $**p < .01$; $***p < .001$

ment for women who are not mothers is 0.28 points lower if they are unmarried and 0.20 points lower if married, that for motherhood is associated with a drop of 0.39 to 0.44 points, depending on the auspices of birth. The family situation of males has no effect on criminal justice involvement, however. Other things equal, all males display the same level of involvement regardless of parental or marital status.

The higher level of male involvement stems mainly from the greater involvement of men in violent and nonviolent criminal actions. Not surprisingly, the degree of criminal justice involvement rises very sharply and significantly with that of violent and nonviolent criminal involvement. Each unit on the violent crime scale increases criminal justice involvement by 0.12 points and each on the nonviolent crime scale by 0.17 points for rather large total effects of 2.52 and 3.57 points, respectively, over the range of the scales. Greater criminal justice involvement is also predicted by the mediating factors of verbal intelligence and expectation of early death. Smart young people who do not expect to live very long are, perhaps not surprisingly, more likely to become entangled with the criminal justice system.

Among ecological conditions, criminal justice involvement is most strongly predicted by exposure to violence in the peer setting. Each unit of exposure on the peer violence scale increases criminal justice involvement by 0.069 points for a total of 1.38 points over the scale's range. The degree of involvement is also significantly increased by growing up without a biological parent (by 0.91 points) and somewhat surprisingly by having a family, school, or peer mentor (0.18, 0.14, and 0.12 points, respectively) and by having a college-educated parent (0.15 points). Criminal justice involvement is reduced, however, by rising income (by 0.009 points per thousand dollars) and greater religiosity (0.021 points per unit). In sum, the profile of someone likely to exhibit a high degree of involvement in the criminal justice system is a verbally intelligent young male who comes from a poor, irreligious family, frequently engages in both violent and nonviolent criminal behaviors, is exposed to a high degree of violence in the peer network, perceives survival chances as dim, and reports having a peer, family, or school mentor. The latter association, of course, could be a case of reverse causality in which mentors are assigned or gravitate toward troubled young men.

CRIME IN THE MAKING

Although for biological reasons young males are at greatest risk of exhibiting delinquent and criminal behaviors, not all succumb to the elevated risks associated with testosterone and an immature forebrain. The expression of crime and delinquency over their life cycles is substantially under social control. Table 7.4 summarizes the ecological influences on the expression of nonviolent and violent crime and criminal justice involvement we have documented during adolescence and young adulthood. As the table makes clear, the strongest and most consistent effects on criminality and criminal justice involvement lie in the peer setting. Exposure to violence in the peer network very sharply increases values on all three indices, having a suicidal friend increases the propensity to engage in criminal activities, and relying on a peer mentor increases the odds of contact with the criminal justice system.

The next most consistent effects occur with respect to emotional circumstances in the family sphere. Although family sternness is associated with lower involvement in nonviolent crime, it has no effect on violent crime or criminal justice involvement. A much stronger predictor of criminality is paternal incarceration. Having a father who has been imprisoned or jailed, not surprisingly, increases the degree to which both violent and nonviolent crimi-

Table 7.4   Significance of Ecological Conditions

	Nonviolent Crime	Violent Crime	Criminal Justice Involvement
Family composition			
Biological and stepparent			
One biological parent			
No biological parent			++
Family material resources			
Household income			--
Health insurance less than a year		+++	-
Health insurance a year or more		+	
Family symbolic resources			
Parental prestige	+		
Parent college graduate			++
Family emotional resources			
Family mortality			
Family sternness	--		
Father incarcerated	++	+++	
Family mentor			+++
Neighborhood setting			
Disadvantage index		+	
Inefficacy index			
Scarcity of males		-	
Neighborhood mentor			
School setting			
Disadvantage index			
Inefficacy index	++		
Disorder index			
School mentor			++
Religious setting			
Religiosity scale			
Involvement index			---
Had religious mentor			
Peer setting			
Violence index	++++	++++	++++
Friend attempted suicide	+++	+++	
Peer mentor			++
Multple disadvantages			
Interactive index		-	

Source: Authors' calculations based on data set described in Harris and Udry (2008).

nal behaviors are expressed. Reliance on a family mentor, though not affecting criminal behavior, is associated with a higher degree of involvement in the criminal justice system. In this way, criminality is perpetuated across the generations and within family networks. Rather than breaking the intergenerational cycle of crime, therefore, mass incarceration likely strengthens it by raising the odds of criminal involvement above what they would have been from family, neighborhood, school, and peer circumstances alone.

Apart from incarceration, other family circumstances have less consistent effects. Having partial rather than no health insurance is strongly associated with involvement in violent crime. Although greater household income has no effect on involvement in criminal or noncriminal activities, it does significantly reduce the likelihood of criminal justice involvement. Whatever their level of criminal involvement, the rich are less likely to end up in the criminal justice system. Surprisingly, however, having a college-educated parent increases criminal justice involvement, and having a high-prestige parent increases involvement in nonviolent crime (though the latter effect is only significant at $p < 0.10$).

We observe few strong or consistent effects in other social spheres other than the family or peer group. Social inefficacy in schools is generally associated with higher levels of nonviolent criminality; having a school-based mentor predicts higher levels of criminal justice involvement; and greater religious involvement lowers the degree of contact with the criminal justice system. Thus the expression of crime and delinquency among young people in the United States is most strongly connected to conditions in the peer and family spheres.

As table 7.5 shows, after taking these effects into account, we observe very few differences in the expression of either violent or nonviolent criminal behavior by race and class. All groups express the same proclivity toward crime and delinquency as upper-class whites, with the exception of upper-class Asians and Hispanics, whose involvement in nonviolent crimes is lower. The major effects of race and class occur with respect to criminal justice involvement. Absent any adjustment for ecological or mediating conditions, all race-class groups display the same level of criminal justice involvement as upper-class whites save lower-class Asians, whose involvement is significantly lower. Adjusting for these conditions statistically, however, lower-, lower-middle-, and upper-middle-class Hispanics, and lower-class blacks and Asians evince significantly lower levels of criminal justice involvement. If these groups had

Table 7.5   Significance of Race-Class Effects

	Level of Involvement in		
	Nonviolent Crime	Violent Crime	Criminal Justice
WLO			--
WLM			--
WUM			--
ALO			---
ALM			
AUM			
AUP	--		
HLO			--
HLM			-
HUM			-
HUP	--		
BLO			--
BLM			
BUM			
BUP			

Source: Authors' calculations based on data set described in Harris and Udry (2008).
Note: Effects are on crime and delinquency after controlling for ecological background.

the same advantaged circumstances as upper-class whites, they would have far fewer entanglements with the criminal justice system. Put another way, if upper-class whites did not enjoy so many ecological and other advantages, they would have far higher rates of criminal justice involvement. White skin and upper-class status continue to have their privileges in the United States.

CHAPTER 8

Transitions to Adulthood

When they were interviewed for the third wave of the survey, Add Health respondents were age nineteen to twenty-six and either poised for entry into adulthood or in the process of making that transition. Some already may have achieved it. We define a successful transition to adulthood as the attainment of economic independence, signaled by completing one's education, getting a job, and generally becoming self-sufficient. As the demands of a knowledge-based, postindustrial service economy have put an increasing premium on the acquisition of skills and education, the transition to adulthood has generally lengthened and extended well into the twenties (Arnett 2010). At the same time, given widespread access to birth control, growing social acceptance of premarital sex, and rising rates of cohabitation and other informal living arrangements, adulthood—economic independence—has increasingly become decoupled from marriage and parenthood. Indeed, in today's social world, early entry into parenthood and marriage is more likely to undermine the ability of a person to achieve economic self-sufficiency.

When we began work on this project, data from the fourth wave of the Adolescent Health Survey were still being processed and not yet publicly available. By the time we had worked through the sequential ecological analyses described in the preceding chapters, however, the first public use file of Wave 4 data had been released, enabling us to complete our study by considering the long-term effects of ecological background on the transition to adulthood. By the fourth wave, the Add Health respondents were twenty-four to thirty-two years old and most had made the transition to a self-sufficient life. Here we investigate this transition by considering attainments in higher education, employment, earnings, and receipt of government transfers.

COLLEGE ATTAINMENT

As the economy has globalized and shifted from the production of goods to the creation of knowledge and manipulation of information, human capital has become increasingly important to both individual and national well-being. The economic returns to additional years of schooling rose rapidly in the late twentieth century and higher education became increasingly critical to securing middle class status (Goldin and Katz 1999, 2008). To gauge the degree of variation in access to this critical individual resource, figure 8.1 plots the proportion of Add Health respondents who had graduated from college by the fourth wave of the survey. This plot clearly reveals that college attainment is very strongly conditioned by class. As can be seen, lower-class respondents cluster in a narrow band to the left of the figure, their completion rates ranging from around 14 percent to 20 percent with relatively little variation by race.

As one moves from left to right and proceeds up the class hierarchy, however, a sharp interaction between race and class becomes increasingly apparent. Among Asians, the share of college graduates rises very rapidly across the lower reaches of the class hierarchy, going from 20 percent in the lower class to 40 percent in the lower middle class and reaching 60 percent in the upper middle class. Thereafter the rapid increase stalls and upper-class Asians show the same 60 percent rate in college completion as those in the upper middle class. Despite the lack of any increase between the upper-middle- and upper-class categories, however, Asians always have the highest rate of college graduation in any class category. Indeed, the gap progressively widens as one moves from the lower class to the upper middle class.

Hispanics generally anchor the bottom of the educational distribution, though their rates of college completion are not that different from those of whites and blacks until the upper class. The share of Hispanics completing college, for example, declines from 18 percent to 12 percent between the lower and lower middle classes, then rises to 33 percent in the upper middle class before dropping back to around 27 percent in the upper class. As a result of this uneven performance, the gap between Hispanics and Asians continuously widens as class increases.

In contrast, the gap between Asians and both whites and blacks widens

Figure 8.1 College Graduation

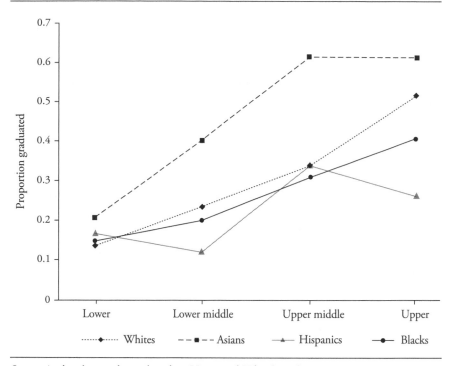

Source: Authors' compilation based on Harris and Udry (2008).

through the middle classes and then closes somewhat in the upper class, especially among whites, from around 14 percent in the lower class to 24 percent in the lower middle class, 34 percent in the upper middle class, and 52 percent in the upper class. Blacks roughly keep pace with whites moving from the lower class to upper middle class before lagging in the upper class. The share of black college graduates thus increases from 15 percent in the lower class to 20 percent in the lower middle class and 31 percent in the upper middle class before reaching 41 percent in the upper class. The black-white gap in college attainment is thus much greater in the upper class than in other class categories.

Thus Asians are clearly the standout group, having more than twice as many college graduates as Hispanics in the upper class, 50 percent more than blacks, and 17 percent more than whites. Table 8.1 shows a logistic regression model estimated to predict the attainment of a college degree by Wave 4, with the left-hand columns showing, as always, baseline race-class coefficients. The right-hand columns show what happens to the corresponding race-class effects when all ascribed, mediating, and ecological characteristics are included as controls in the prediction equation.

The baseline model confirms the significance of Asians' remarkable pattern of college attainment. Only lower-class Asians display a significantly lower likelihood of completing college, about 75 percent, compared with upper-class whites. In contrast, among whites, all other classes are less likely to graduate from college than those in the upper class: 85 percent in the lower class, 71 percent in the lower middle class, and 52 percent in the upper middle class.

The baseline model also confirms statistically our earlier observation that Hispanics have the least access to a college education, even compared with African Americans, historically the most disadvantaged group in the United States. Whereas upper-class African Americans are as statistically likely to complete college as their white counterparts, upper-class Hispanics are far less likely—67 percent—to do so. According to the model, the odds of college graduation are 81 percent lower for Hispanics in the lower class, 87 percent in the lower middle class, and 51 percent in the upper middle class. The odds of completing college are also quite low among African Americans in the lower classes. Lower-class black respondents, for example, are 84 percent less likely to graduate from college than upper-class whites, the lower middle class 76 percent less likely, and the upper middle class 58 percent.

As the right-hand columns of table 8.1 indicate, these sharp and significant differences in the likelihood of college graduation disappear entirely when background characteristics are held constant. Somewhat surprisingly, the odds of college graduation are not influenced by high school graduation, or by the number of failed high school courses. College attainment is predicted only by high school grade point average (GPA), each additional grade point raising the odds of completion by a factor of 7.4, a huge effect. As one would expect, the likelihood of completing college also rises with age, the odds increasing by 15 percent with each additional year. The likelihood of graduating from college is significantly reduced by poor health and by the expectation of an early death as well as by greater involvement in violent crime. Each point increase in the scale of poor health lowers the odds of college graduation by around 18 percent, in involvement in violent crime by 15 percent, and in the expectation of an early death by 6 percent.

Table 8.1   Determinants of Completing College Degree

Independent Variables	Group Effects B	Group Effects SE	Full Model B	Full Model SE
Race-class group				
White lower	−1.901***	0.178	−0.079	0.609
White lower middle	−1.235***	0.112	−0.269	0.413
White upper middle	−0.724***	0.114	−0.273	0.271
White upper	—	—	—	—
Asian lower	−1.394*	0.572	0.056	0.869
Asian lower middle	−0.453	0.344	−0.093	0.600
Asian upper middle	0.407	0.301	0.363	0.603
Asian upper	0.394	0.292	0.445	0.457
Hispanic lower	−1.648***	0.238	0.592	0.677
Hispanic lower middle	−2.019***	0.262	−0.130	0.484
Hispanic upper middle	−0.722**	0.229	0.649	0.414
Hispanic upper	−1.097***	0.259	−0.170	0.380
Black lower	−1.812***	0.247	0.633	0.600
Black lower middle	−1.432***	0.233	0.616	0.467
Black upper middle	−0.856***	0.243	0.236	0.408
Black upper	−0.432	0.311	0.512	0.360
Ascribed characteristics				
Age	—	—	0.136***	0.039
Parent foreign born	—	—	0.182	0.203
Mediating conditions				
Criminal involvement				
Nonviolent crime	—	—	0.049	0.036
Violent crime	—	—	−0.166***	0.050
Criminal justice	—	—	0.022	0.055
High school achievement				
High school graduate	—	—	0.207	0.285
Grade point average	—	—	1.996***	0.113
Proportion of courses failed	—	—	1.328	1.083
Health status				
Poor health index	—	—	−0.193**	0.067
Depression scale	—	—	−0.005	0.015
Expectation of early death	—	—	−0.057+	0.030
Family situation				
Unmarried male–not father	—	—	—	—
Married male–not father	—	—	−0.687+	0.366
Married male–father	—	—	−1.534***	0.427
Unmarried male–father	—	—	−0.846*	0.387

Table 8.1 (continued)

Independent Variables	Group Effects		Full Model	
	B	SE	B	SE
Unmarried female–no birth	—	—	0.145	0.118
Married female–no birth	—	—	–0.806*	0.327
Married female–mother	—	—	–1.513***	0.292
Unmarried female–birth over eighteen	—	—	–1.307***	0.280
Unmarried female–birth eighteen or younger	—	—	–0.922+	0.513
Ecological background				
Composition of origin family				
Two biological parents	—	—	—	—
Biological and stepparent	—	—	–0.007	0.236
One biological parent	—	—	0.133	0.166
No biological parent	—	—	–0.341	0.400
Family material resources				
Household income	—	—	0.008	0.009
Access to health insurance				
No coverage	—	—	—	—
Coverage less than a year	—	—	0.217	0.199
Coverage full year	—	—	0.844***	0.237
Family symbolic resources				
Parental prestige	—	—	0.010**	0.004
Parent college graduate	—	—	0.424*	0.181
Family emotional resources				
Experienced family death	—	—	–0.180	0.264
Family sternness	—	—	0.000	0.004
Father incarcerated	—	—	–0.390*	0.177
Had family mentor	—	—	0.271+	0.154
Neighborhood setting				
Disadvantage index	—	—	–0.021	0.160
Inefficacy index	—	—	0.061**	0.022
Scarcity of males	—	—	0.893	0.931
Had neighborhood mentor	—	—	0.224	0.234
School setting				
Disadvantage index	—	—	–0.017+	0.010
Inefficacy index	—	—	–0.008	0.010
Disorder index	—	—	0.051*	0.023
Had school mentor	—	—	0.397*	0.162
Religious setting				
Religiosity scale	—	—	0.052**	0.019

Table 8.1 *(continued)*

Independent Variables	Group Effects		Full Model	
	B	SE	B	SE
Involvement index	—	—	0.008	0.023
Had religious mentor	—	—	−0.062	0.310
Peer setting				
Violence index	—	—	0.056+	0.030
Friend attempted suicide	—	—	−0.029	0.182
Had peer mentor	—	—	0.058	0.164
Multiple disadvantages				
Log of interactive index	—	—	−0.044	0.031
Intercept	0.062	0.097	−10.919***	1.938
N	7,851		5,013	
F-test	17.78***		11.48***	

Source: Authors' calculations based on data set described in Harris and Udry (2008).

+p < .10; *p < .05; **p < .01; ***p < .001

Among men, both marriage and childbearing by themselves reduce the odds of graduating from college, by 50 percent and 57 percent respectively. Marriage and childbearing together reduce the odds even more, by a substantial 78 percent. Other things equal, a single female without children is just as likely to earn a college degree as a single male without children. Although the coefficient suggests that the odds of college completion are 16 percent greater for unmarried women without children, in keeping with statistics showing that females are now a majority of enrolled college students and college graduates (National Center for Education Statistics 2009), the effect is modest and not statistically significant. As with men, marriage and childbearing reduce the likelihood of college graduation among women. Just getting married reduces the odds of female graduation by 55 percent; getting married and having a child reduce them by 78 percent. Among unmarried women, the odds of college graduation are reduced by 73 percent if the birth occurs when the mother is over eighteen and by 60 percent if under eighteen. For both men and women, therefore, marriage and childbearing are significant deterrents to the timely completion of a college education.

Once current family status is taken into account, however, the composition of the family of origin has no effect on college attainment. Within the family setting, likelihood of college graduation is very sharply increased by access to the material resource of health insurance, as well as by the symbolic resources of parental prestige and college education and the emotional resource of having a family mentor. In numerical terms, having full access to health insurance in the family of origin increases the odds of college graduation by a substantial 133 percent. Likewise, having a college-educated parent raises them by 53 percent and each additional unit of parental occupational status raises by around 1 percent. Having a family mentor raises the odds by 31 percent, though this effect only lies on the margins of statistical significance. In contrast, coming from a family where the father was incarcerated was associated with a 32 percent reduction, offering more evidence that America's criminal justice complex retards socioeconomic achievement and helps perpetuate disadvantage (Western 2006).

Outside the family, ecological effects are relatively sparse. Within neighborhoods, social inefficacy paradoxically increases the odds of college graduation, by around 6.3 percent per unit. With the school environment, material disadvantage has a marginal effect in lowering the odds (by around 1.7 percent per unit), whereas access to a school-based mentor substantially raises them (by 49 percent). Somewhat surprisingly, the odds of college graduation are increased by school disorder, each point on the disorder scale raising the odds of graduation by 5.2 percent. Within the religious sphere, religiosity increases the odds by 5.3 percent per unit but religious involvement and having a religious mentor have no significant effect. Consistent with the positive effect of school disorder, exposure to peer violence has a marginally significant effect in raising the odds by around 5.8 percent per unit. Thus, it seems that coming from harsh neighborhood, school, and peer environments seem to provide motivation for achievement in college.

In sum, the adolescent most likely to grow up and complete a college degree is a single, childless male or female from a family that included a high-status, college-educated parent with full health insurance. The father was never imprisoned and the extended family provided access to a trusted mentor who offered guidance. The person most likely to graduate from college also achieved a strong GPA in high school, was in good health, expected to live well into adulthood, and was not involved in violent crime. He or she lived in a socially inefficacious neighborhood, however, and attended a relatively disordered school but was exposed to a relatively high degree of peer violence. Despite these disadvantages, the student nonetheless attended a materially advantaged school that provided access to a school-based mentor.

Holding constant differences in these ecological circumstances, race-class differences in the likelihood of college graduation mostly disappear.

GRADUATE EDUCATION

The economic returns to schooling do not stop with a bachelor's degree, of course, but extend upward to graduate education. As the skills premium has increased and the competition for human capital has grown, attending graduate or professional school has become essential for success in many fields, especially in the sciences, technology, medicine, law, business, and finance. Figure 8.2 thus shows the proportion of Add Health respondents who had earned a graduate degree by Wave 4 of the survey. The share holding a graduate degree is obviously much lower than that holding a simple bachelor's degree, from 2 percent to 14 percent depending on race and class (compared with a range of 14 percent to 61 percent for college degrees). The overall pattern of results is much the same, however. Asians achieve graduate degrees at the highest rates and Latinos at the lowest rates. As before, the share holding a graduate degree rises with class, and racial differentials generally widen as we move from the lower to the upper end of the class distribution.

In the lower class, for example, the range in graduate degree completion across racial groups goes from 2 percent to 5 percent, but in the upper class it is 5.5 percent to 13.5 percent. Asians once again display the sharpest class gradient, moving from 5 percent to 13 percent between the lower and lower middle class before dropping to around 9.5 percent in the upper middle class and then rising once again to 13.5 percent in the upper class. The share of blacks and whites with graduate degrees likewise rises with class standing, but the increases—unlike those of Asians—are concentrated in the upper reaches of the class distribution. From the lower to the lower middle class, blacks shift only from 2.5 percent to 3 percent and whites from 2 percent to 3.5 percent, thus widening the gap relative to Asians. The gap closes somewhat in the upper middle class as blacks and whites achieve graduate degree rates of around 6 percent and the Asian rate falls to 9.5 percent. In the upper class, whites continue to close the gap with Asians, reaching 12 percent to the Asian 13.5 percent. Although the share of blacks with graduate degrees also increases, the rise is generally parallel to that for Asians and the black-Asian gap remains constant.

In the left-hand columns of table 8.2, we again present results from a logistic regression equation estimated to predict the likelihood of attaining a

Figure 8.2   Graduate Degree

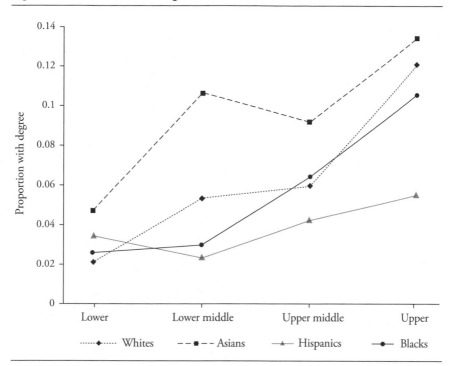

Source: Authors' compilation based on Harris and Udry (2008).

graduate degree from race-class dummy variables. The pattern of race-class effects in the baseline model is quite similar to the one we observed in the model predicting college attainment. Asians display the same likelihood of attaining a graduate degree as upper-class whites regardless of class standing; and as before, whites display a sharp class gradient. Compared with whites in the upper class, those in the lower class are 84 percent less likely to earn a graduate degree and those in the lower middle and upper middle classes 58 percent and 54 percent less likely, respectively.

Once again, Hispanics generally display the lowest degree of educational attainment. Compared with upper-class whites, the odds of earning a graduate degree are 75 percent lower among the lower class, 82 percent in the lower middle class, and 68 percent in the upper middle class. Although the coefficient for upper-class Hispanics is not statistically significant, it is rather larger and would imply a 58 percent reduction in the odds of attaining a

Table 8.2   Determinants of Completing Graduate Degree

Independent Variables	Group Effects		Full Model	
	B	SE	B	SE
Race-class group				
White lower	−1.827***	0.318	−0.553	0.893
White lower middle	−0.877***	0.168	−0.288	0.582
White upper middle	−0.772***	0.180	−0.413	0.393
White upper	—	—	—	—
Asian lower	−0.996	0.955	0.088	1.422
Asian lower middle	−0.135	0.387	−0.416	0.854
Asian upper middle	−0.294	0.422	−0.323	0.583
Asian upper	0.128	0.433	−0.334	0.580
Hispanic lower	−1.334***	0.390	−0.113	0.878
Hispanic lower middle	−1.729***	0.518	0.284	0.755
Hispanic upper middle	−1.127**	0.417	−0.323	0.588
Hispanic upper	−0.855	0.545	−0.041	0.622
Black lower	−1.627***	0.378	−0.229	0.834
Black lower middle	−1.473***	0.328	−0.386	0.695
Black upper middle	−0.683*	0.340	0.228	0.590
Black upper	−0.150	0.404	0.362	0.439
Ascribed characteristics				
Age	—	—	0.268***	0.049
Parent foreign born	—	—	0.009	0.242
Mediating conditions				
Criminal involvement				
Nonviolent crime	—	—	0.002	0.046
Violent crime	—	—	−0.433*	0.174
Criminal justice	—	—	0.171+	0.091
High school achievement				
High school graduate	—	—	0.325	0.423
Grade point average	—	—	1.712***	0.195
Proportion of courses failed	—	—	0.606	2.037
Health status				
Poor health index	—	—	−0.076	0.075
Depression scale	—	—	−0.027	0.026
Expectation of early death	—	—	−0.050	0.040
Family situation				
Unmarried male–not father	—	—	—	—
Married male–not father	—	—	0.635+	0.347
Married male–father	—	—	0.220	0.772
Unmarried male–father	—	—	0.289	0.854

Table 8.2   (continued)

Independent Variables	Group Effects		Full Model	
	B	SE	B	SE
Unmarried female–no birth	—	—	0.485*	0.215
Married female–no birth	—	—	0.106	0.368
Married female–mother	—	—	–0.396	0.649
Unmarried female–birth over eighteen	—	—	–0.730	0.523
Unmarried female–birth eighteen or younger	—	—	–1.100	0.988
Ecological background				
Composition of origin family				
Two biological parents	—	—	—	—
Biological and stepparent	—	—	0.542	0.326
One biological parent	—	—	0.243	0.213
No biological parent	—	—	0.789	0.549
Family material resources				
Household income	—	—	–0.005	0.013
Access to health insurance				
No coverage	—	—	—	—
Coverage less than a year	—	—	0.815*	0.318
Coverage full year	—	—	1.259***	0.330
Family symbolic resources				
Parental prestige	—	—	0.003	0.004
Parent college graduate	—	—	0.317	0.297
Family emotional resources				
Experienced family death	—	—	–0.075	0.345
Family sternness	—	—	–0.002	0.005
Father incarcerated	—	—	0.349	0.281
Had family mentor	—	—	–0.373	0.237
Neighborhood setting				
Disadvantage index	—	—	0.288+	0.165
Inefficacy index	—	—	0.070**	0.028
Scarcity of males	—	—	0.262+	0.150
Had neighborhood mentor	—	—	–0.795*	0.375
School setting				
Disadvantage index	—	—	–0.011	0.014
Inefficacy index	—	—	–0.004	0.017
Disorder index	—	—	0.041	0.028
Had school mentor	—	—	0.028	0.230
Religious setting				
Religiosity scale	—	—	0.026	0.022

Table 8.2   (continued)

Independent Variables	Group Effects		Full Model	
	B	SE	B	SE
Involvement index	—	—	0.008	0.023
Had religious mentor	—	—	0.024	0.026
Peer setting				
Violence index	—	—	0.047	0.052
Friend attempted suicide	—	—	−0.151	0.300
Had peer mentor	—	—	−0.632	0.245
Multiple disadvantages				
Log of interactive index	—	—	−0.069	0.047
Intercept	−1.992***	0.105	−13.613***	2.480
N	7,851		5,013	
F-test	5.92***		9.04***	

Source: Authors' calculations based on data set described in Harris and Udry (2008).
+$p < .10$; *$p < .05$; **$p < .01$; ***$p < .001$

graduate degree were it significant. The lack of statistical significance likely reflects, at least in part, the small number of upper-class Hispanics, which yields a rather large standard error. As with whites, African Americans display a sharp class gradient. Upper-class whites and blacks are equally likely to earn a graduate degree, but the odds are 80 percent lower for lower-class blacks, 77 percent lower for lower-middle-class blacks, and 49 percent lower for upper-middle-class blacks.

As seen in the right-hand columns, these pronounced race-class differences in graduate attainment once again disappear after background controls are introduced. As one would expect, the odds of earning a graduate degree rise with age, by a remarkable 31 percent per year. As in the prior model, graduate attainment is unaffected by high school graduation or the relative frequency of high school course failure, but is strongly predicted by high school GPA. Each additional grade point raises the odds of earning a graduate degree by a factor of 5.5. The only other mediating factors that influence graduate attainment come under the rubric of criminal involvement. Involvement in violent crime reduces the odds of earning a graduate degree by 35 percent per unit on the involvement scale, whereas criminal justice involvement raises them 19 percent, though the effect is only marginally significant. Unlike college attainment, graduate attainment is not very strongly predicted by a person's current family situation. Compared with an unmarried, childless male, a married male without children is around 89 percent more likely to earn a graduate degree and an unmarried childless female is about 62 percent more likely, but apart from these two effects family status, and particularly fertility status, does not appear to influence the odds of achievement at the graduate level.

Likewise, conditions in the family of origin are largely unrelated to graduate attainment. In the family sphere, only health insurance coverage has a significant effect on the odds of earning a graduate degree, raising them by a factor of 3.5 in the case of full coverage and 2.3 in the case of partial coverage. Parental prestige and parental education play no role in graduate achievement. Similarly, the odds of earning a graduate degree are not affected by composition or emotional resources within the origin family. Outside the family sphere, graduate attainment is not affected by conditions in the school, religious, or peer environments.

In terms of social ecology, only circumstances in the neighborhood setting seem to matter for graduate attainment. Greater exposure to neighborhood disadvantage and a lack of neighborhood efficacy once again appear to act as motivators, raising the odds of earning a graduate degree by 33 percent and 7 percent per unit, respectively. Coming from a neighborhood characterized by a scarcity of males also marginally increases the odds of completing a graduate degree (by around 30 percent per unit), but having a neighborhood mentor sharply lowers them, by a total of around 45 percent. Thus the person most likely to complete a graduate degree is an older married male or unmarried female who earned good grades in high school, stayed out of trouble, enjoyed health insurance coverage while growing up, but came from a relatively disadvantaged, socially inefficacious neighborhood characterized by a relative scarcity of males. Within this setting, it was important to avoid close personal contacts, for those who reported having a neighborhood mentor evinced sharply lower odds of completing a graduate degree, other things equal.

EMPLOYMENT

The final stage in completing the transition to adulthood is the achievement of self-sufficiency through gainful employment. Figure 8.3 shows the proportion of Add Health respondents who reported holding full-time jobs by the fourth wave of the survey broken down by race and class. Despite their edu-

Figure 8.3   Full-Time Work

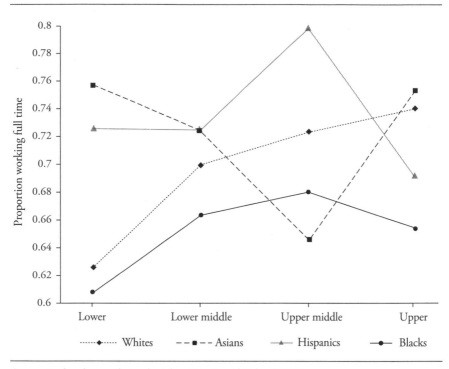

Source: Authors' compilation based on Harris and Udry (2008).

cational disadvantages, Hispanics generally display the highest likelihood of full-time employment and blacks the lowest, but once again variation by social class is considerable. Blacks display a curvilinear pattern with respect to class, the share working full time rising from around 61 percent in the lower class to 66 percent in the lower middle class and peaking at around 68 percent in the upper middle class before falling back to 65 percent in the upper class. In contrast, the employment rate for Hispanics stands at around 77 percent in both the lower and lower middle classes, rises to nearly 80 percent in the upper middle class, and then drops to around 69 percent in the upper class. The odds of full-time work for Asians fall steadily from the lower class to the upper middle class, going from 76 percent to 65 percent, but then rebound to 75 percent in the upper class. Whites are the only racial group to display a clear, consistent, and positive class gradient, the share employed rising from 63 percent in the lower class to 70 percent and 72 percent in the lower and upper middle classes to 74 percent in the upper class.

Employment patterns are complicated by the fact that some people age twenty-four to thirty-two may still be completing their studies and either not working or combining school with part-time work. Table 8.3 takes into account these possibilities by estimating a multinomial logistic regression model to predict two competing labor market outcomes: part-time work and full-time work versus a reference category of not working. The relatively few respondents who went into the military are grouped with full-time workers. In the interest of conserving space, standard errors are not reported, though statistical significance is indicated by the usual sets of asterisks. The coefficients in the left-hand columns confirm the positive class gradient observed earlier among whites for full-time work and extends it to part-time work. Compared with whites in the upper class, the odds of part-time employment are 43 percent lower among those in the lower class, 17 percent in the lower middle class, and 4 percent in the upper middle class, though the latter two effects are not statistically significant. Likewise, among whites, the odds of full-time employment are 55 percent less for the lower class, 30 percent less for the lower middle class, and 13 percent less for the upper middle class, the last effect being insignificant statistically.

We do not observe such clear class gradients in the likelihood of employment among members of the other three groups. Asians show a universally high likelihood of working, those in all class categories displaying the same odds of both full-time and part-time employment as upper-class whites. Among Hispanics, those in the lower classes display very low likelihoods of part-time employment, 70 percent lower in the lower class and 42 percent in the lower middle class. Hispanics of all classes display the same high likelihood of full-time employment as upper-class whites.

The baseline coefficient estimates also underscore blacks' unusual curvilinear pattern of employment with respect to class, which indicates remarkably low likelihoods of both part-time and full-time work in both the lower and upper classes. Compared with upper-class whites, for example, the odds of part-time employment for upper-class blacks are 56 percent lower but those of full-time employment are 53 percent lower. Likewise, among lower-class blacks, the odds of part-time employment are 42 percent lower and those of full-time employment are 58 percent lower. In contrast, the odds of both part-time and full-time employment for lower- and upper-middle-class blacks are at the same high level observed for upper-class whites.

The full multinomial model estimated in the right-hand columns of table 8.3 shows what happens to these race-class differences once ascribed, mediat-

Table 8.3   Determinants of Full-Time Versus Part-Time Employment

Independent Variables	Group Effects		Full Model	
	Part-Time	Full-Time	Part-Time	Full-Time
Race-class group				
White lower	−0.565***	−0.792***	0.572	−0.164
White lower middle	−0.184	−0.363*	0.591	0.086
White upper middle	−0.045	−0.143	0.333	0.061
White upper	—	—	—	—
Asian lower	−0.718	−0.301	0.672	0.084
Asian lower middle	0.097	−0.168	0.182	−0.708
Asian upper middle	0.394	−0.382	0.458	−1.380*
Asian upper	−0.177	−0.031	−0.141	−0.170
Hispanic lower	−1.189***	−0.439	0.067	−0.186
Hispanic lower middle	−0.550+	−0.370	0.746	−0.073
Hispanic upper middle	0.625	0.594	0.449	0.661
Hispanic upper	−0.472	−0.458	−0.503	0.250
Black lower	−0.548*	−0.875***	1.119	0.078
Black lower middle	−0.128	−0.476	1.464*	0.084
Black upper middle	−0.265	−0.499	0.896+	0.367
Black upper	−0.818**	−0.757**	−0.182	0.495
Ascribed characteristics				
Age	—	—	0.044	0.035
Parent foreign born	—	—	0.498	0.631
Mediating conditions				
Higher education				
Not college graduate	—	—	—	—
College graduate	—	—	−0.244	0.391*
Graduate degree	—	—	−0.246	0.314
Criminal involvement				
Nonviolent crime	—	—	0.043	−0.053
Violent crime	—	—	−0.068	0.001
Criminal justice	—	—	0.063	−0.020
High school achievement				
High school graduate	—	—	0.119	0.243
Grade point average	—	—	−0.046	−0.206
Proportion of courses failed	—	—	−1.327	−1.492*
Health status				
Poor health index	—	—	−0.221**	−0.139*
Depression scale	—	—	0.020	−0.029+
Expectation of early death	—	—	0.007	−0.018

Table 8.3   (continued)

Independent Variables	Group Effects		Full Model	
	Part-Time	Full-Time	Part-Time	Full-Time
Family situation				
Unmarried male–not father	—	—	—	—
Married male–not father	—	—	0.739	1.229*
Married male–father	—	—	0.502	1.059*
Unmarried male–father	—	—	0.053	0.241
Unmarried female–no birth	—	—	0.303	–0.541
Married female–no birth	—	—	–0.077	–1.816***
Married female–mother	—	—	–0.318	–1.470***
Unmarried female–birth over eighteen	—	—	0.275	–1.091***
Unmarried female–birth eighteen or younger	—	—	–0.046	–0.666
Ecological background				
Composition of origin family				
Two biological parents	—	—	—	—
Biological and stepparent	—	—	–0.088	–0.016
One biological parent	—	—	–0.229	–0.028
No biological parent	—	—	–0.400	–0.056
Family material resources				
Household income	—	—	0.014	0.004
Access to health insurance				
No coverage	—	—	—	—
Coverage less than a year	—	—	0.782**	0.425**
Coverage full year	—	—	0.518**	0.487*
Family symbolic resources				
Parental prestige	—	—	0.007	0.002
Parent college graduate	—	—	0.338	–0.204
Family emotional resources				
Experienced family death	—	—	–0.180	0.154
Family sternness	—	—	0.005	0.008
Father incarcerated	—	—	0.228	0.100
Had family mentor	—	—	–0.239	0.073
Neighborhood setting				
Disadvantage index	—	—	–0.362*	–0.233+
Inefficacy index	—	—	–0.006	–0.026
Scarcity of males	—	—	–0.237	–0.258
Had neighborhood mentor	—	—	–0.796*	0.130

Table 8.3   (continued)

Independent Variables	Group Effects		Full Model	
	Part-Time	Full-Time	Part-Time	Full-Time
School setting				
Disadvantage index	—	—	−0.002	0.009
Inefficacy index	—	—	−0.021	−0.004
Disorder index	—	—	0.034	0.035
Had school mentor	—	—	−0.712**	−0.128
Religious setting				
Religiosity scale	—	—	−0.021	−0.005
Involvement index	—	—	−0.006	−0.003
Had religious mentor	—	—	−1.319**	−0.377
Peer setting				
Violence index	—	—	−0.007	0.003
Friend attempted suicide	—	—	0.018	0.053
Had peer mentor	—	—	−0.206	0.127
Multiple disadvantages				
Log of interactive index	—	—	0.007	−0.030
Intercept	−0.191	1.784***	2.206	
N	7,821		5,005	
F-test	3.10***		11.39***	

Source: Authors' calculations based on data set described in Harris and Udry (2008).
$+p < .10$; $*p < .05$; $**p < .01$; $***p < .001$

ing, and ecological characteristics are held constant. As the table makes clear, addition of these controls generally eliminates significant race-class differences with respect to the likelihood of full-time and part-time employment. The only exceptions are the significantly lower odds of full-time employment observed among upper-middle-class Asians (75 percent lower than upper-class whites) and the greater odds of part-time employment among lower-middle- and upper-middle-class blacks (4.3 times greater and 2.4 times greater, respectively). In other words, once the influence of background factors is held constant, blacks in these class categories display a greater propensity than others toward part-time employment.

Only one mediating condition, poor health, significantly predicts part-time employment. The odds of working part time drop by 20 percent with each point increase in the poor health scale. Full-time employment, however, is more strongly connected to the mediating conditions included in the model. The odds of working full time, for example, are 48 percent greater for college graduates, and, though the likelihood of full-time employment is not influenced by high school graduation or high school GPA, the odds of working drop by 73 percent with each point increase in the percentage of high school courses failed. As with part-time employment, the odds of full-time work fall with poor health, dropping by 13 percent with each additional point on the index. The odds of working full time also decline by 2.8 percent with each increment on the depression scale. Mental and physical health thus strongly condition the likelihood of full-time employment.

A person's current family situation also has powerful effects on employment, but the effects are opposite for men and women. Among males, marriage and parenthood increase the likelihood of full-time employment, whereas among women they reduce it. Compared with an unmarried, childless male, the odds of full-time work are 3.4 times greater for a married childless male and 2.9 times greater for a married father. Unmarried fathers have the same likelihood of full-time work as unmarried, childless males. Among women, those who are childless and unmarried are as likely to work full time as unmarried, childless men, but those who are married with no children are 84 percent less likely, and those who are married with children are 77 percent less likely. Women who are unmarried with a child are 66 percent less likely to work full time if the child was born after the mother was eighteen and 49 percent lower if born before. The influence of marriage and childbearing on work is thus highly gendered.

Holding constant the effects of these mediating family circumstances, ecological conditions have a relatively modest influence on employment patterns. The strongest and most consistent effect is for originating in a family with health insurance coverage. Having full coverage raises the odds of part-time employment by 168 percent and those of full-time employment by 163 percent. Having partial coverage raises the odds of part-time work by 219 percent and those of full-time work by 153 percent. Aside from insurance coverage, no other circumstance in the family sphere really affects the likelihood of working—neither composition, nor material resources, nor symbolic resources, nor emotional resources.

Disadvantage within the neighborhood sphere, however, significantly lowers the odds of both part-time and full-time employment, each additional unit on the scale reducing the odds of the former by 30 percent and the latter by 21 percent. Having a mentor from the neighborhood also reduces the likelihood of part-time employment but has no effect on those of full-time employment, a pattern that also prevails for school mentors and religious mentors as well. Thus the odds of part-time employment are reduced by 55 percent by a neighborhood mentor, 51 percent by a school mentor, and 73 percent by a religious mentor. A peer mentor was similarly associated with a 19 percent reduction in the odds of part-time work and a family mentor with a 21 percent reduction, though these effects were not significant. In general, mentors appear to steer young people away from part-time employment irrespective of the setting from which they come. The person most likely to work full time is thus a married male college graduate who is in good health, failed few courses in high school, came from a family with full health insurance coverage, and lived in an economically advantaged neighborhood.

EARNINGS

Employment is clearly a crucial step in achieving adult self-sufficiency, but earnings also play a role. In general, the greater a person's income, the fewer the constraints on individual action and the larger the range of potential life options. Figure 8.4 therefore plots annual earnings by race and class at Wave 4 to reveal rather strong main effects in both cases. In general, earnings rise as class standing increases and are greatest for Asians and least for blacks. The class curves for Asians, whites, and blacks do not cross, those pertaining to Asians and blacks are almost parallel, and whites gain ground on Asians in the upper classes.

Thus black incomes rise from around $20,000 in the lower class to $25,000 to $26,000 in the lower middle and upper middle class, to around $30,000 in the upper class. Asians shift more markedly, from $30,000 in the lower class to around $38,000 in the lower middle and upper middle class, to $44,000 in the upper class. Whites, meanwhile, increase from $24,000 in the lower class to $29,000 and $34,000 in the lower and upper middle classes, to $39,000 in the upper class. Hispanic earnings generally lie between these two extremes, except that in moving from the upper middle to the upper class, Hispanic earnings stagnate and the white and Hispanic curves cross, leaving the former with annual earnings of $39,000 and the latter of around $36,000.

In table 8.4, we explore the roots of these earnings differentials by regressing the log of annual earnings on race-class dummy variables in the left-hand columns, and race-class dummies plus background controls in the right-hand

Figure 8.4   Annual Earnings

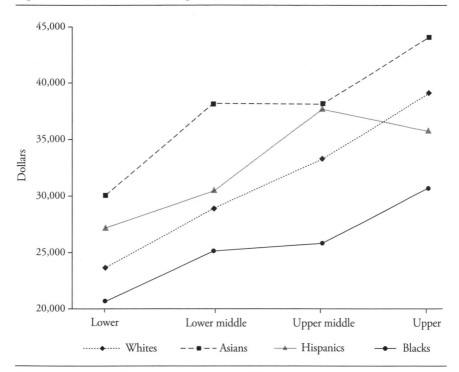

Source: Authors' compilation based on Harris and Udry (2008).

columns. Because the outcome is expressed in logarithmic form, the coefficients give the percentage change in earnings associated with one unit of the variable in question. The baseline estimates in the left column confirm the remarkable earning power displayed by Asians. In statistical terms, lower-class Asians earn the same as upper-class whites; the same is true for Asians in the lower middle class and upper middle class; and upper-class Asians actually enjoy a 22 percent earnings premium compared with upper-class whites.

All of the other three groups display a significant class gradient with respect to annual earnings. Among whites, for example, those in the lower class earn 43 percent less than those in the upper class, those in the lower middle class 27 percent less, and those in the upper middle class 15 percent less. The class differential is even sharper among African Americans. Black lower-class respondents earned 58 percent less than upper-class whites, and lower-middle-class and upper-middle-class blacks earned 42 percent and 34 percent

Table 8.4   Determinants of Natural Log of Annual Earnings

Independent Variables	Group Effects		Full Model	
	B	SE	B	SE
Race-class group				
White lower	−0.425***	0.079	−0.208	0.141
White lower middle	−0.268***	0.046	−0.163	0.101
White upper middle	−0.146**	0.045	−0.113+	0.064
White upper	—	—	—	—
Asian lower	−0.306	0.234	−0.235	0.302
Asian lower middle	0.080	0.127	0.039	0.158
Asian upper middle	−0.132	0.228	−0.183	0.132
Asian upper	0.223*	0.093	0.080	0.101
Hispanic lower	−0.213**	0.067	−0.267	0.175
Hispanic lower middle	−0.242*	0.117	−0.257+	0.138
Hispanic upper middle	−0.056	0.082	−0.019	0.120
Hispanic upper	−0.031	0.107	0.007	0.129
Black lower	−0.577***	0.081	−0.449*	0.200
Black lower middle	−0.424***	0.082	−0.184	0.134
Black upper middle	−0.341***	0.079	−0.152+	0.092
Black upper	−0.109	0.106	0.000	0.115
Ascribed characteristics				
Age	—	—	0.045***	0.011
Parent foreign born	—	—	0.125**	0.048
Mediating conditions				
Higher education				
Not college graduate	—	—	—	—
College graduate	—	—	0.224***	0.050
Graduate degree	—	—	0.158***	0.046
Criminal involvement				
Nonviolent crime	—	—	0.004	0.011
Violent crime	—	—	0.033*	0.014
Criminal justice	—	—	−0.035*	0.015
Secondary education				
High school graduate	—	—	−0.020	0.065
Grade point average	—	—	0.093**	0.035
Proportion of courses failed	—	—	−0.106	0.209
Health status				
Poor health index	—	—	−0.034+	0.021
Depression scale	—	—	−0.020***	0.005
Expectation of early death	—	—	−0.010	0.011

Table 8.4   *(continued)*

Independent Variables	Group Effects		Full Model	
	B	SE	B	SE
Family situation				
Unmarried male–not father	—	—	—	—
Married male–not father	—	—	0.200*	0.093
Married male–father	—	—	0.225***	0.066
Unmarried male–father	—	—	0.090	0.090
Unmarried female–no birth	—	—	–0.214***	0.045
Married female–no birth	—	—	–0.346***	0.097
Married female–mother	—	—	–0.553***	0.124
Unmarried female–birth over eighteen	—	—	–0.507***	0.075
Unmarried female–birth eighteen or younger	—	—	–0.258**	0.104
Ecological background				
Composition of origin family				
Two biological parents	—	—	—	—
Biological and stepparent	—	—	–0.026	0.062
One biological parent	—	—	0.053	0.045
No biological parent	—	—	–0.066	0.109
Family material resources				
Household income	—	—	–0.001	0.002
Access to health insurance				
No coverage	—	—	—	—
Coverage less than a year	—	—	0.068	0.050
Coverage full year	—	—	0.154**	0.052
Family symbolic resources				
Parental prestige	—	—	–0.001	0.001
Parent college graduate	—	—	–0.009	0.057
Family emotional resources				
Experienced family death	—	—	0.013	0.077
Family sternness	—	—	–0.001	0.001
Father incarcerated	—	—	–0.061	0.042
Had family mentor	—	—	0.034	0.063
Neighborhood setting				
Disadvantage index	—	—	–0.020	0.046
Inefficacy index	—	—	–0.013*	0.006
Scarcity of males	—	—	0.133	0.093
Had neighborhood mentor	—	—	0.188**	0.064
School setting				
Disadvantage index	—	—	0.003	0.003

Table 8.4 *(continued)*

Independent Variables	Group Effects		Full Model	
	B	SE	B	SE
Inefficacy index	—	—	0.003	0.003
Disorder index	—	—	−0.004	0.007
School mentor	—	—	0.089+	0.048
Religious setting				
Religiosity scale	—	—	0.004	0.004
Involvement index	—	—	−0.006	0.005
Had religious mentor	—	—	0.057	0.115
Peer setting				
Violence index	—	—	0.013+	0.008
Friend attempted suicide	—	—	−0.075	0.062
Peer mentor	—	—	0.066	0.053
Multiple disadvantages				
Log of interactive index	—	—	0.002	0.009
Intercept	10.459***	0.037	9.247***	0.451
N	6,093		4,020	
R²	0.038		0.175	
F-test	8.62**		17.81***	

Source: Authors' calculations based on data set described in Harris and Udry (2008).

$+p < .10$; $*p < .05$; $**p < .01$; $***p < .001$

less, respectively. Although the coefficient for upper-class blacks is negative, it is not significant, so statistically speaking they earn the same as upper-class whites. The class gradient is least sharp among Hispanics. Compared with upper-class whites, lower-class Hispanics earn 21 percent less and lower-middle-class Hispanics 24 percent less, but those in the upper middle and upper classes earn the same amount in statistical terms.

The full model reveals that these race-class differences in earnings mostly disappear once background controls are introduced. Only lower-class blacks stand out with an unambiguously significant negative effect, earning 45 percent less than upper-class whites, other things equal. Meanwhile, the coefficient for upper-middle-class blacks is cut in half and reduced to the margins of significance. The coefficient for upper-middle-class whites likewise remains marginally significant, though only slightly reduced from the baseline model. The significant negative coefficients for lower-class and lower-middle-class

Hispanics in the baseline model actually increase slightly in the full model, even though they drop in terms of significance. None of the other race-class coefficients is statistically significant.

Turning to the control variables, we see that earnings rise sharply with age, as is typical during the early stages of a worker's career, and they are 13 percent greater for people with immigrant parents. When it comes to higher education, holding a college degree raises earnings by 22 percent while holding a graduate degree as well raises them by 16 percent. Earnings are also increased by achieving a higher GPA in high school, earnings rising by 9.3 percent per grade point. However, neither high school graduation nor the relative frequency of course failure has any influence on earnings. Somewhat surprisingly, greater involvement in violent crime during adolescence is associated with greater earnings in adulthood, but only if such criminality does not lead to involvement in the criminal justice system. Thus, whereas violent criminal involvement raises earnings by 3.3 percent per unit, criminal justice involvement lowers them by 3.5 percent. As one would expect, health problems in adolescence generally reduce earnings in adulthood. Each additional unit on the depression scale reduces earnings by 2 percent and on the poor health index by 3.4 percent, though the latter is significant only at the 10 percent level.

An individual's current family situation has a strong influence on earnings. As in the employment model, the effects of marriage and childbearing differ dramatically by gender. Whereas acquiring the responsibilities of a spouse and children boost male earnings, they generally depress female earnings. Among men, for example, marriage raises earnings by around 20 percent compared with those who are unmarried and childless, and being a married father by 22 percent. Having a child outside marriage has no effect on male earnings, however. In contrast, females experience lower earnings than males no matter what their marital or childbearing status, and acquiring a spouse or children reduces them even further. Compared with an unmarried childless male, a female without a child or spouse earns 21 percent less; if she gets married, however, the earnings penalty increases to 35 percent and if she has a child to 55 percent. Likewise, the earnings penalty for having a child outside marriage is 50 percent if the mother is over eighteen and 26 percent if younger. Access to employment and income through work is thus a highly gendered process in which marriage and childbirth carry radically different implications for men and women.

Holding constant an individual's current family situation, the composition of the family of origin has no effect on adult earnings. Indeed, access to material, symbolic, and emotional resources within the family sphere play almost no direct role in determining earnings in adulthood. The only significant effect is observed for full access to health insurance while growing up, which is associated with a 15 percent earnings premium in young adulthood. Significant effects are also sparse in the other ecological spheres. Coming of age in a socially inefficacious neighborhood reduces adult earnings by 1.3 percent per unit, whereas having a neighborhood mentor yields a 19 percent premium. Having a school-based mentor is associated with a premium of 9 percent, though this effect is only marginally significant, as is the effect of violence in the peer setting, which increases earnings by 1.3 percent per unit on the violence scale.

In general, direct ecological effects on adult earnings are few, implying that social ecology generally affects earnings indirectly through mediating outcomes such as education, criminality, health, and marital and childbearing behavior. The highest earnings are thus predicted for older, married males of immigrant origin who earned good grades in high school, graduated from college, stayed clear of entanglements with the criminal justice system, enjoyed good health, evinced few symptoms of depression, and grew up with health insurance coverage in a socially efficacious neighborhood that offered access to a mentor.

DEPENDENCE

At the opposite end of the continuum of high earnings and financial independence is the lack of meaningful earned income and dependence on public transfers. Figure 8.5 shows the proportion of respondents who reported ever receiving a public transfer by the time of the fourth wave of the Add Health Survey, including AFDC, TANF, food stamps, and other means-tested entitlement programs. The figure once again reveals rather sharp differences by race and class. In terms of race, blacks clearly evince the highest rates of dependency and Asians the lowest. In terms of class, dependency generally falls with rising class standing in each racial group.

Despite displaying some class variation, the degree of black dependency is above that observed for all other groups within every class category. In contrast, the degree of Asian dependency is similarly below that observed for other racial groups. The percentage receiving a public transfer among African

Figure 8.5   Public Transfers

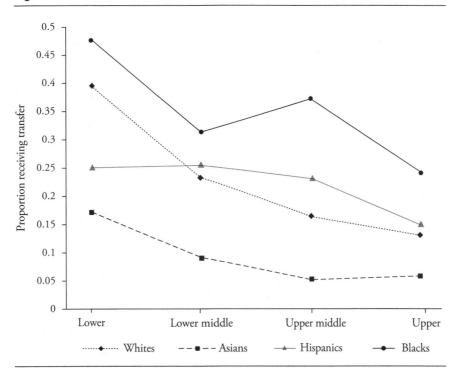

Source: Authors' compilation based on Harris and Udry (2008).

Americans is thus around 47 percent in the lower class, 31 percent in the lower middle class, 36 percent in the upper middle class, and 24 percent in the upper class. In contrast, lower-class Asians display a dependency rate of just 16 percent in the lower class (that is, below that observed for blacks in the upper class), falling to 9 percent in the lower middle class and reaching around 5 percent in the upper middle and upper classes. Whites and Hispanics generally display similar levels of dependency, except in the lower class, where the percentage ever receiving a transfer stood at 40 percent for whites but only 25 percent for Hispanics. In the lower middle class, however, dependency rates are quite similar, 25 percent for Hispanics and 24 percent for whites. Although the Hispanic-white gap increases somewhat in the upper middle class, 24 percent for Hispanics versus 16 percent for whites, it diminishes in the upper class, 15 percent for Hispanics versus 14 percent for whites.

The left-hand columns of table 8.5 show a baseline model predicting the odds of receiving public transfers from race-class dummy variables and reveals that the foregoing race-class differences are generally quite significant statistically. Compared with upper-class whites, African Americans display a significantly higher likelihood of receiving state transfers across all class categories, the odds being six times greater for the lower class, three times greater for the lower middle class, four times greater among the upper middle class, and more than two times greater for the upper class.

In contrast, the odds that lower-class and lower-middle-class Asians receive transfers are statistically the same as for upper-class whites, whereas the odds are around 60 percent lower among Asians in the upper middle class and upper class. Although upper-class Hispanics display the same likelihood of dependence as upper-class whites, the odds are 2.2 times greater among lower-class Hispanics, 2.3 times greater in the lower middle class, and 2.0 times greater in the upper middle class. Whites display a similar though sharper class differential, the odds of receiving transfers being 4.3 times greater for the lower class than for the upper class, and twice as great in the lower middle class but only 30 percent greater in the upper middle class.

The right-hand columns of table 8.5 reveal that controlling for differences in background characteristics eliminates most but not all of the statistical differences between race-class groups. Only lower-class and upper-middle-class blacks retain statistically significant coefficients after the addition of controls. However, in many cases—lower-, lower-middle-, and upper-middle-class Hispanics, lower-class whites, and upper-middle-class Asians—the point estimates do not change that much and the drop in significance comes as much from the increase in the size of the standard error than any shift in the actual size of the coefficient. Nonetheless, one finding clearly stands out: the higher odds of transfer receipt displayed by lower-class blacks irrespective of their standing on other variables in the model.

As one would expect, the likelihood of receiving public transfers is sharply reduced by full-time employment and college graduation (by 47 percent and 51 percent, respectively). The odds of transfer receipt are also significantly lower for those of immigrant origin (some 45 percent lower) and are progressively reduced by greater criminal justice involvement (by 7.5 percent per unit, $p < 0.10$). The latter two effects are not surprising, given that immigrants and felons are legally barred from receiving entitlements in many states. Holding constant achievements in higher education, those in high

Table 8.5   Determinants of Ever Receiving Public Transfer

Independent Variables	Group Effects		Full Model	
	B	SE	B	SE
Race-class group				
White lower	1.466***	0.150	0.909	0.574
White lower middle	0.700***	0.134	0.323	0.389
White upper middle	0.264+	0.142	0.059	0.271
White upper	—	—	—	—
Asian lower	0.324	0.783	−0.040	1.138
Asian lower middle	−0.390	0.726	0.372	0.845
Asian upper middle	−0.979+	0.535	−0.802	0.824
Asian upper	−0.886+	0.504	−0.457	0.739
Hispanic lower	0.800***	0.217	0.619	0.551
Hispanic lower middle	0.825***	0.239	0.697	0.495
Hispanic upper middle	0.696**	0.258	0.542	0.429
Hispanic upper	0.162	0.300	−0.321	0.383
Black lower	1.802***	0.170	1.226*	0.551
Black lower middle	1.111***	0.247	0.057	0.495
Black upper middle	1.371***	0.268	0.658+	0.358
Black upper	0.756**	0.277	−0.081	0.371
Ascribed characteristics				
Age	—	—	−0.014	0.034
Parent foreign born	—	—	−0.597*	0.255
Mediating conditions				
Labor force participation				
Not working	—	—	—	—
Working part-time	—	—	−0.168	0.158
Working full-time	—	—	−0.631***	0.128
Higher education				
Not college graduate	—	—	—	—
College graduate	—	—	−0.707***	0.174
Graduate degree	—	—	0.192	0.296
Criminal involvement				
Nonviolent crime	—	—	0.045	0.037
Violent crime	—	—	−0.008	0.031
Criminal justice	—	—	−0.078+	0.047
Secondary education				
High school graduate	—	—	−0.220	0.191
Grade point average	—	—	−0.083	0.134
Proportion of courses failed	—	—	0.039	0.564

Table 8.5   (continued)

Independent Variables	Group Effects		Full Model	
	B	SE	B	SE
Health status				
Poor health index	—	—	0.149*	0.062
Depression scale	—	—	0.027*	0.013
Expectation of early death	—	—	0.042+	0.023
Family situation				
Unmarried male–not father	—	—	—	—
Married male–not father	—	—	0.625+	0.364
Married male–father	—	—	0.450	0.348
Unmarried male–father	—	—	0.077	0.271
Unmarried female–no birth	—	—	0.205+	0.124
Married female–no birth	—	—	0.520*	0.234
Married female–mother	—	—	0.686***	0.196
Unmarried female–birth over eighteen	—	—	1.292***	0.179
Unmarried female–birth eighteen or younger	—	—	1.678***	0.314
Ecological background				
Composition of origin family				
Two biological parents	—	—	—	—
Biological and stepparent	—	—	–0.133	0.226
One biological parent	—	—	0.014	0.147
No biological parent	—	—	–0.953	0.584
Family material resources				
Household income	—	—	0.011	0.009
Access to health insurance				
No coverage	—	—	—	—
Coverage less than a year	—	—	–0.373*	0.179
Coverage full year	—	—	–0.649***	0.154
Family symbolic resources				
Parental prestige	—	—	0.001	0.003
Parent college graduate	—	—	–0.078	0.143
Family emotional resources				
Experienced family death	—	—	–0.349	0.220
Family sternness	—	—	0.000	0.004
Father incarcerated	—	—	0.219+	0.131
Had family mentor	—	—	–0.134	0.137
Neighborhood setting				
Disadvantage index	—	—	0.157	0.140
Inefficacy index	—	—	–0.009	0.020

Table 8.5   (continued)

Independent Variables	Group Effects		Full Model	
	B	SE	B	SE
Scarcity of males	—	—	0.324+	0.191
Had neighborhood mentor	—	—	0.024	0.225
School setting				
Disadvantage index	—	—	−0.003	0.008
Inefficacy index	—	—	0.003	0.010
Disorder index	—	—	−0.039+	0.023
School mentor	—	—	−0.142	0.166
Religious setting				
Religiosity scale	—	—	−0.033*	0.017
Involvement index	—	—	0.008	0.025
Had religious mentor	—	—	−0.020	0.308
Peer setting				
Violence index	—	—	−0.024	0.022
Friend attempted suicide	—	—	0.338+	0.176
Peer mentor	—	—	−0.193	0.158
Multiple disadvantages				
Log of interactive index	—	—	0.061**	0.023
Intercept	−1.894***	0.126	−2.653+	1.553
N	7,839		5,001	
F-test	22.67***		9.10***	

Source: Authors' calculations based on data set described in Harris and Udry (2008).
+$p < .10$; *$p < .05$; **$p < .01$; ***$p < .001$

school have no effect on dependency, but poor physical and mental health significantly raise the odds of transfer receipt, boosting them by 16 percent per unit on the poor health index and by 2.7 percent per unit on the depression scale. Perceiving a lower likelihood of survival into adulthood also increases the odds of dependency, raising them by around 4.3 percent per unit, though the effect is only marginally significant at the 10 percent level.

As one might expect, given that public welfare entitlements focus on women with children, the odds of transfer receipt are greater for women than men and are significantly raised by the presence of children. Compared with a single, childless man, a single woman without children is only slightly more likely to report receiving transfers, about 23 percent. Marriage increases the likelihood of transfer receipt, the odds rising to 68 percent, and if the woman goes on to have a child, the odds nearly double. It is unwed childbearing that really raises the odds of dependency, however, increasingly them 3.6 times if the mother is older than eighteen and by 5.4 if younger.

Once again, aside from current composition, the only strong and consistent ecological effect in the family sphere is access to health insurance. Having partial access while growing up lowers the odds of receiving transfers by 31 percent whereas full access reduces them by 48 percent. Having an incarcerated father increases the odds by around 20 percent, though the effect is significant only at the 10 percent level. Relatively few ecological effects originate outside the family. Religiosity significantly lowers the odds of receiving transfers, by 3.2 percent per unit, whereas exposure to multiple disadvantages across spheres increases them by 6.4 percent per unit on the interactive logarithmic scale. All remaining ecological effects are on the margins of significance, a scarcity of males raising the odds of transfer receipt by around 28 percent and the attempted suicide of a friend by 29 percent, and disorder in the school setting reducing them by around 3.2 percent per unit.

SUCCESSFUL TRANSITION TO ADULTHOOD

As in earlier chapters, we summarize ecological effects on achievements in higher education, labor force participation, and dependency in table 8.6. In the family sphere, these outcomes are not at all related to the composition of the family of origin or to the material resource of family income. Far more important is access to health insurance, which acts sharply to raise the odds of earning college and graduate degrees and the likelihood of being gainfully employed and to lower the odds of receiving transfer and increasing earnings. No other single ecological condition has such strong and consistent effects. In a very real way, therefore, our results suggest that societal investments in health are investments in human capital that offer strong returns later on in the form of employment and earnings and the taxes and other positive externalities.

Among other circumstances in the family sphere, the odds of graduating from college are strongly related to parental occupational attainment and education, as one would expect, though graduate attainment is not affected by these factors. Having a mentor within the extended family modestly increases the odds of college graduation. Experiencing the incarceration of one's father in adolescence is reduces the odds of college graduation and increases the likelihood of being dependent on transfers as an adult. Recall from chap-

Table 8.6 Significance of Ecological Conditions

	Higher Education		Labor Force Outcomes			Dependency
	College Graduate	Graduate Degree	Employed Part Time	Employed Full Time	Earnings	Receiving TANF
Family composition						
Biological and stepparent						
One biological parent						
No biological parent						
Family material resources						
Household income						
Health insurance less than a year		++	++	+++		–
Health insurance a year or more	++++	++++	+++	++	+++	– –
Family symbolic resources						
Parental prestige	+++					
Parent college graduate	++					
Family emotional resources						
Family mortality						
Family sternness						
Father incarcerated	–					+
Family mentor	+					
Neighborhood setting						
Disadvantage index		+	–	–		
Inefficacy index	+++	+++			–	
Scarcity of males		+				+

Table 8.6 (continued)

	Higher Education		Labor Force Outcomes			Dependency
	College Graduate	Graduate Degree	Employed Part Time	Employed Full Time	Earnings	Receiving TANF
Neighborhood mentor		-	-		+++	
School setting						
Disadvantage index	-					
Inefficacy index						
Disorder index	++			+		-
School mentor	++		---		+	
Religious setting						
Religiosity scale						--
Involvement index						
Had religious mentor			---			
Peer setting						
Violence index	-				+	
Friend attempted suicide						+
Peer mentor						
Multple disadvantages						
Interactive index						+++

Source: Authors' calculations based on data set described in Harris and Udry (2008).

Note: Effects are on predicting transition to adulthood.

ter 7 that having an incarcerated father increases a respondent's likelihood of engaging in both violent and nonviolent criminal actions and criminal justice involvement, and that these outcomes in turn lower the likelihood of graduate education and earnings. Whereas investments in health insurance are an investment in human capital formation that yields positive returns, investments in prisons undermine human capital formation and yield negative returns.

Having access to a neighborhood-based and especially a school-based mentor increases the odds of earning a college degree, and having a neighborhood mentor also sharply increases earnings and reduces the odds of part-time employment. Other things equal, coming from a disadvantaged neighborhood increases the odds of earning a graduate degree, as does originating in a neighborhood with a relative scarcity of males, though these conditions have no effect on undergraduate attainment, though neighborhood disadvantage generally reduces the odds of employment. In contrast, social inefficacy within neighborhoods raises the odds of earning both college and graduate degrees but has a negative effect on earnings. Although school disadvantage acts weakly to reduce the likelihood of earning a college degree, disorder in the school setting raises the odds of college completion and employment and reduces the odds of dependency. Not surprisingly, having a school-based mentor increases the likelihood of college completion, reduces the odds of part-time employment, and increases earnings. Having a religious mentor likewise reduces the odds of part-time employment, and religiosity reduces the odds of receiving public transfers. The likelihood of receiving a transfer is strongly predicted by growing up with multiple disadvantages.

Table 8.7 shows which race-class effects remain once ecological and other background conditions are controlled. As can be seen, most race-class differences disappear, with a few exceptions. Other things equal, upper-middle-class Asians appear unlikely be employed full time and upper-middle-class whites and Hispanics earn slightly lower earnings. The most salient effects occur among African Americans, however. Lower-class blacks stand out for their lower earnings and higher likelihood of receiving public transfers, whereas their lower-middle and upper-middle-class counterparts stand out for their high likelihood of part-time employment, the latter for their low earnings and higher odds of dependency as well.

In addition to the ecological effects just described, one of the strongest and most consistent influences on the transition to adult economic independence

Table 8.7   Significance of Race-Class Effects

	Higher Education		Labor Force Outcomes			Dependency
	Collge Graduate	Graduate Degree	Employed Part Time	Employed Full Time	Earnings	Receiving TANF
WLO						
WLM						
WUM					-	
ALO						
ALM						
AUM				--		
AUP						
HLO						
HLM					-	
HUM						
HUP						
BLO					--	++
BLM			++			
BUM			+		-	+
BUP						

Source: Authors' calculations based on data set described in Harris and Udry (2008).
Note: Effects are on transition to adulthood after controlling for ecological background.

was the mediating variable of family status. For both men and women, early entry into marriage and childbearing strongly reduce the likelihood of finishing college, whether the childbearing is inside or outside marriage. Whereas the effect of early marriage and childbearing is equally detrimental to the odds of college completion for both men and women, it carries radically different implications for employment, earnings, and dependency. Marriage and childbearing within marriage generally increase the likelihood of full-time employment and raise earnings for men, though unmarried childbearing has no effect on these outcomes. Among women, in contrast, marriage and childbearing inside or outside marriage have strong negative effects on the likelihood of full-time employment and earnings. Whereas early marriage and parenthood have no strong implications for male dependency, they do strongly increase the likelihood that women will end up receiving state transfers. The family status achieved by young adults thus emerges as a key nexus though which socioeconomic disadvantage is reproduced. Although the social ecology experienced by young people in adolescence has some direct influences on the transition to economic independence, many of the ecological effects can be expected to be indirect, through their effect on family status. It is to the cumulative direct and indirect effects of ecological circumstances that we turn to in the next chapter.

CHAPTER 9

What If? A Counterfactual Analysis

The transition to adulthood is a cumulative process whereby prior attainments provide the foundation for later attainments to generate life outcomes, which in turn carry implications for social and economic outcomes later on. The cumulative nature of development means that advantages and disadvantages tend to reinforce one another over the life cycle, creating self-reinforcing cycles of growth or stagnation. To develop fully, people must extract or be provided with sufficient material, symbolic, and emotional resources from the environments they inhabit, but for them, unlike other mammals, the critical environment for human development is social rather than physical. In contemporary postindustrial societies, social ecology carries more weight in conditioning developmental outcomes than the physical environment.

We have argued that human social ecology is defined by four fundamental social spheres that virtually all denizens of advanced society progressively experience as they grow up: families, neighborhoods, schools, and peers. Exposure to resource-rich versus resource-poor ecological spheres early in life can set otherwise equivalent individuals on markedly different paths, yielding future inequalities in social and economic well-being. To some extent, the social production of advantage and disadvantage may be reinforced or mitigated by resources in a fifth social sphere that some but by no means all people experience: a religious setting.

As summarized earlier, in figure 1.1, we have endeavored to use a uniquely rich longitudinal data set to measure conditions in these five spheres at one point in time (1994 through 1996 but in some cases 1994 through 2000) and then to assess their influence on human developmental outcomes at a second point (2001 to 2002) before finally measuring how these intermediate outcomes (with respect to reproduction, health, education, delinquency) work in combination with existing ecological circumstances to affect the transition to economic independence during adulthood (2007 to 2008).

Although the Adolescent Health Survey has the advantage of being longitudinal and unusually rich in social indicators, it is by no means perfect. For one thing, the survey picks up only respondents in adolescence, when they were roughly twelve to eighteen years old, by which time significant development has already occurred. Given that recent research underscores the importance of social influences and environmental circumstances in early childhood (Eliot 1999), relying on Add Health in some sense stacks the deck against finding strong ecological effects. Thus, the estimates presented here likely understate the true extent of social ecological effects on adolescent development and adult status attainment.

In addition, despite the richness of the data, the Add Health survey contains a limited and crude set of measures of emotional resources within the family, particularly in comparison with indicators of material well-being. As noted earlier, generations of studies have emphasized the importance of love, warmth, nurturing, caring, contact, and concern in human development, but Add Health, like most other social surveys, does a poor job of capturing such critical family inputs. As a result, our indicators of emotional resources within the family are rather impoverished and by no means capture the full richness of the familial emotional environment.

Another epistemological problem concerns causality. Because ecological circumstances are measured at a point in time before the intermediate developmental outcomes, we can generally assume causality works from social ecology forward to reproduction, health, cognition, and delinquency. However, Add Health data do not enable us easily to sort out the timing of these intermediate developmental outcomes relative to each other. As a result, we were forced to impose an a priori ordering of intermediate outcomes, beginning first with sexuality and reproduction then moving on to successively predict mental and physical health, cognition and education, and finally crime and delinquency, at each point controlling for predetermined outcomes.

Our model implicitly assumes that young people begin sexual relations first and that decisions made about sex, contraception, union formation, and fertility carry later implications for health, which in turn affect cognition and education and ultimately crime and delinquency. In reality, of course, these events are to a greater or lesser degree endogenous and depend on one another in ways we cannot fully capture here. Nonetheless, we believe that the general thrust of causality happens as assumed; in any event, our goal is not to model the precise causal interrelation of reproductive, health, educational, and criminal outcomes in adolescence and young adulthood, but to understand how social ecology determines outcomes in key developmental domains in ways that cumulate to produce qualitatively different transitions to adulthood. As documented in chapters 2 and 3, young people growing up in the United States today face dramatically different family, neighborhood, school, peer, and religious environment that offer notably different degrees of access to material, symbolic, and emotional resources, depending on the accident of birth into a specific race-class category. In determining access to developmental inputs, moreover, race and class often function interactively, not just as main effects.

Despite the complexities posed by race-class interactions, however, it is generally true that lower-class blacks experience the most consistently disadvantaged ecological circumstances in American society and upper-class whites the most consistently advantaged, and that these disadvantages and advantages produce markedly different socioeconomic outcomes for the two groups in adulthood. The models we have estimated to this point enable us to ask two important counterfactual questions: How would things turn out for poor black adolescents if they grew up experiencing the more advantaged ecological circumstances of upper-class whites? What the world look like for upper-class whites if they came of age under the ecological conditions experienced by lower-class blacks? The answers to these questions offer a way to understand the power of social ecology in determining life chances for young people making the transition to adulthood in the United States at the dawn of the twenty-first century.

WHAT IF LOWER-CLASS BLACKS EXPERIENCED THE SOCIAL ECOLOGY OF UPPER-CLASS WHITES?

We begin our analysis by summarizing the contrasting social ecologies experienced by lower-class blacks and upper-class whites according to data from the Adolescent Health Survey. Table 9.1 thus summarizes key indicators of ecological conditions in the family, neighborhood, school, religious, and peer settings inhabited by poor black and affluent white adolescents. In terms of access to parental time and adult supervision, lower-class black young people are very clearly disadvantaged compared with their upper-class white counterparts. Whereas 73 percent of lower-class blacks grew up in a single-parent household and 3 percent came of age in a household with no parent at all, the respective figures for upper-class whites were only 14 percent and 1 percent. If investment of parental time is a critical resource in human development, poor African Americans clearly get less of it.

The gap in access to material resources is equally stark, with upper-class white adolescents enjoying a family income of around $87,100 per year and lower-class blacks one of just $9,300. Thus poor black adolescents, on average, receive just 11 percent of the material investment that upper-class white adolescents do. Similarly, whereas 76 percent of upper-class white adolescents enjoyed full access to health insurance, only 53 percent of lower-class blacks did. In terms of symbolic resources, the average occupational prestige of upper-class white parents stood at 47.2, compared with 27.4 for lower-class black parents. Finally, whereas 72 percent of upper-class white adolescents had at least one parent with a college degree, only 30 percent of lower-class black adolescents did.

We also observe significant differences in the family emotional environment. Whereas 13 percent of black adolescents experienced the death of an immediate family member while growing up, only 4 percent of upper-class whites did so; and whereas 21 percent of lower-class blacks reported a father going to prison or jail, only 8 percent of whites did. Upper-class whites also experienced a sterner family emotional environment than lower-class blacks, though the difference was rather small at just 5.3 percent (a sternness score of 16.75 versus 15.91). Emotional sternness is a mixed bag developmentally. Although a stern emotional style within families is associated with the attainment of fewer cognitive skills (see chapter 6), it generally yields benefits with respect to other outcomes, lowering the likelihood of an early sexual debut and unwed parenthood (chapter 4), reducing the incidence of risky health behaviors to yield better health outcomes (chapter 5), and reducing the likelihood of criminal involvement (chapter 7). On the whole, a stern disciplinary style probably carries more benefits than costs, especially for adolescents growing up in disadvantaged neighborhood, school, and peer environments.

The only family emotional resource for which lower-class blacks displayed an apparent advantage was mentorship. Whereas 37 percent of poor blacks reported having a family mentor other than a parent, just 28 percent of afflu-

Table 9.1   Social Ecologies

Ecological Spheres and Conditions	Lower-Class Blacks	Upper-Class Whites
Family composition		
Biological and stepparent	0.053	0.086
One biological parent	0.730	0.137
No biological parent	0.026	0.009
Family material resources		
Household income ($000)	9.301	87.115
Health insurance coverage less than a year	0.157	0.146
Health insurance coverage a year or more	0.529	0.759
Family symbolic resources		
Parental occupational prestige	27.425	47.234
Parent a college graduate	0.295	0.722
Family emotional resources		
Experienced family death	0.129	0.041
Family sternness	15.907	16.754
Father incarcerated	0.206	0.079
Family mentor	0.372	0.276
Neighborhood circumstances		
Material disadvantage	1.918	0.462
Social inefficacy	4.257	3.319
Scarcity of males	0.914	0.889
Neighborhood mentor	0.075	0.048
School circumstances		
School disadvantage	23.775	18.350
School inefficacy	12.645	12.609
School disorder	9.040	8.379
School mentor	0.113	0.229
Religious circumstances		
Religiosity	13.760	12.254
Religious involvement	6.040	5.618
Religious mentor	0.019	0.037
Peer circumstances		
Peer violence	2.635	1.388
Suicidal friend	0.039	0.089
Peer mentor	0.159	0.215
Interactive disadvantage index	36.901	27.579

Source: Authors' calculations based on data set described in Harris and Udry (2008).

ent whites did, but having a family mentor does not counterbalance the absence of a live-in father. The material circumstances of the neighborhood, not surprisingly, greatly favored upper-class whites. The average index of neighborhood disadvantage stood at just 0.36 for upper-class whites, versus 1.92 for lower-class blacks, implying a 4:1 differential in exposure to material disadvantage within neighborhoods. Lower-class black adolescents also grow up in less socially efficacious neighborhoods, with an inefficacy index of 4.26 compared with 3.32 for upper-class whites, a 28 percent difference. Males are also relatively scarcer in lower-class black neighborhoods, a ratio of unwed young females to males of 0.91, versus one of 0.89 in upper-class white neighborhoods. Unlike the circumstances in the family sphere, these neighborhood material and emotional disadvantages are not really offset by greater access to mentors. The share of lower-class black adolescents who report having a mentor in the neighborhood stood at just 7.5 percent, versus 5 percent of upper-class whites. Neighborhood mentors were generally unimportant as a source of support for either race-class group.

These contrasts in neighborhood circumstances are paralleled by differences in the social ecology of education. In general, lower-class blacks attend more materially disadvantaged schools characterized by less social efficacy, more disorder, and access to fewer school-based mentors. The material disadvantage score, for example, was 23.8 for lower-class black schools and 18.4 for upper-class white. Thus poor blacks attend schools that are, on average, 30 percent more disadvantaged than those attended by affluent whites. Although average school inefficacy scores were similar for the two race-class groups (12.7 versus 12.6) and the disorder scores likewise were not particularly different (9.0 versus 8.4), we observe a rather substantial difference in access to school mentors. Whereas 23 percent of upper-class whites reported having a school-based mentor, only 11 percent of lower-class blacks did so. Recall that school-based mentors, not surprisingly, are particularly important in predicting cognitive and educational attainments (see chapter 6).

Turning to the religious sphere, lower-class blacks display higher levels of religiosity than upper-class whites (13.8 versus 12.3, a difference of 12 percent) as well greater levels of religious involvement (6.0 versus 5.6, a 7 percent difference); but they are slightly less likely to report having a religious mentor (1.9 percent versus 3.7 percent). Finally, within the peer setting, lower-class blacks are exposed to considerably more violence than upper-class whites are. The peer violence index was 2.6 for lower-class blacks but only 1.4 for upper-class whites. When it comes to suicidal friends, however, upper-class whites were more disadvantaged. Whereas 8.9 percent of affluent white adolescents reported having a suicidal friend, only 3.9 percent among lower-class blacks did, a more than 2:1 differential. Peer mentorship was more common for upper-class white adolescents, however, 22 percent reporting a peer mentor compared with only 16 percent of lower-class blacks.

All in all, then, the social ecology experienced by the average lower-class black adolescent is considerably more disadvantaged than that faced by upper-class whites growing up in the United States: 36.9 versus 27.6. Because the index is logarithmic, the spread of 9.3 points indicates a substantial difference in cumulative disadvantage across social spheres.

Reproductive Outcomes

We undertake our counterfactual analysis by inserting the foregoing average ecological conditions into the series of equations estimated to predict reproductive, health, educational, criminal, and economic outcomes and assume the person in question is eighteen years old and not of immigrant origin. We then generate predicted values for the two contrasting social ecologies. We move through the equations in the order that they appear in the various chapters. Whenever a variable predicted in an earlier equation appears in a later equation, we insert the predicted value into the later equation. In chapter 3, for example, we assume ecological circumstances to predict the likelihood of sexual debut and then insert that prediction into the next equation to predict the likelihood that first intercourse occurred without contraception. We then use ecological indicators to generate predicted probabilities of marriage and cohabitation. Finally, we combine predicted values for the likelihood of marriage, cohabitation, and not using contraception with ecological indicators to predict the likelihood of unwed parenthood and teen motherhood, which are then brought forward and used as inputs for the equations in chapter 4.

Figure 9.1 presents the result of this sequential operation for female reproductive outcomes. It is immediately evident that shifting from a disadvantaged to an advantaged ecology clearly has strong effects on most of the reproductive outcomes, generally moving poor black women in a direction likely to enhance future socioeconomic welfare. Under the more advantaged

Figure 9.1   Lower-Class Black Reproduction

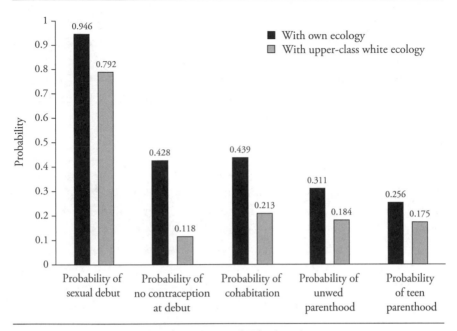

Source: Authors' compilation based on Harris and Udry (2008).

white ecology, for example, the probability of experiencing first intercourse by Wave 3 would drop from 0.95 to 0.79. Of course, this reduction in exposure to early sexual intercourse would by itself reduce the likelihood of an unwanted birth; in addition, however, the more advantaged upper-class white ecology also reduces the likelihood that first sex was unprotected. Whereas the probability of not using contraception at sexual debut stood at 0.43 for poor black women given their ecology, it would fall to 0.12 if they experienced that of upper-class women. Cohabitation with a sexual partner is also obviously a risk factor in predicting nonmarital childbearing, and the probability of cohabitation likewise drops substantially when a privileged white ecology is substituted for a poor black one. Given their own social ecology, 44 percent of lower-class black adolescents would be expected to have cohabited by Wave 3, compared with just 21 percent under the ecological circumstances typical for upper-class whites.

For lower-class black women, the reduced likelihood of sexual debut and lower probability of cohabitation, when combined with the more advantaged ecological circumstances of upper-class whites, dramatically reduces the odds of unwed and teenage childbearing. The observed social ecology for poor black adolescent females would normally predict a 0.31 probability of unwed childbearing and a 0.26 probability of teen childbearing by Wave 3. Under the upper-class white ecology, these figures drop to 0.18 and 0.175, respectively, yielding corresponding reductions of 41 percent and 32 percent in the likelihood of risky reproduction.

Health Outcomes

When it comes to health-related behaviors, we found that race-class patterns do not always correspond to common stereotypes. In particular, the social ecology of upper-class whites turned out to be more conducive to alcohol and drug abuse than that of lower-class blacks. Even after controlling for ecological circumstances, alcohol and drug abuse are more common among upper-class whites than other groups. In the case of these two health-related behaviors, therefore, shifting from a lower-class black social ecology to an upper-class white ecology is expected to increase the likelihood of deleterious behavior. That is precisely what we observe in figure 9.2. Given their social ecology, lower-class black adolescents are predicted to have a 0.29 probability of abusing alcohol and a 0.02 probability of abusing hard drugs, but, given the social ecology of upper-class whites, these figures rise to 0.68 and 0.06.

Even though blacks display a lower likelihood of smoking than whites irrespective of ecological circumstances, if lower-class black adolescents were to experience the more advantaged social ecology of upper-class white counterparts, their rate of smoking would be even lower. According to the estimates presented in figure 9.2, the probability of regularly smoking cigarettes was 0.39 for lower-class blacks given their ecology, but 0.21 given that of upper-class whites. The likelihood of engaging in risky sex (paid sex or sex with a known drug user) does not seem to be context dependent, being roughly 0.14 for lower-class blacks whatever their ecological circumstances. The likelihood of having a physical limitation, being obese (body mass index, or BMI, of 30 or greater), or having a sexually transmitted disease all appear to be quite sensitive to ecological conditions, however. Within their ecology, lower-class blacks have a predicted probability of physical limita-

Figure 9.2   Lower-Class Black Health Behaviors and Outcomes

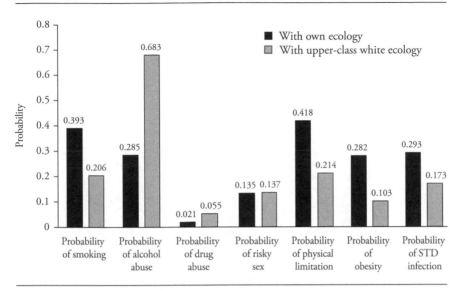

Source: Authors' compilation based on Harris and Udry (2008).

tion of 0.42, a probability of obesity of 0.28, and a probability of sexually transmitted disease (STD) infection of 0.29. Shifting to an upper-class white ecology, these figures drop to 0.21, 0.10 and 0.17, respectively, yielding reductions of 50 percent, 64 percent, and 41 percent in these deleterious health conditions.

Figure 9.3 considers the effect of these behaviors and the social ecological conditions that predict them on respondents' own subjective health ratings. As can be seen, the indices of poor health and depression do not change very much when the average social ecology of lower-class blacks is replaced by that of upper-class whites. The poor health index drops marginally from 2.37 to 2.19 and the depression index falls from 8.06 to 7.84. The perceived likelihood of an early death, however, displays a rather robust response to changing ecological circumstances. The scale measuring the degree to which poor black respondents expect not to survive into later adulthood drops from 4.69 to 2.84 if they assume the ecological circumstances of upper-class whites, a decline of 39 percent. Clearly, coming of age in an advantaged social ecology produces a brighter outlook on life and more hopeful expectations for the future.

Figure 9.3   Lower-Class Black Subjective Health Ratings

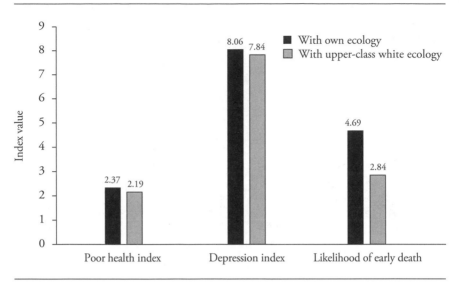

Source: Authors' compilation based on Harris and Udry (2008).

Human Capital Formation

Among the most critical dimensions of human development in postindustrial societies are those related to cognition and education, which are particularly sensitive to inputs of environmental resources. Figure 9.4 thus presents measures of various cognitive and educational outcomes predicted for lower-class blacks under their social ecology versus that of typical upper-class whites. As one would expect, shifting from a disadvantaged to an advantaged social ecology improves cognitive and educational outcomes. It reduces attention deficit by 13 percent, lowering the attention deficit and hyperactivity disorder (ADHD) score from 15.6 to 13.6. At the same time, it raises verbal skills by 10 percent, increasing the score on the Picture Vocabulary Test (PVT) from 85.5 to 93.1. In terms of academic achievement, high school grade point average (GPA) is projected to rise by 38 percent from 2.08 to 2.88, and the proportion of failed courses would be cut in half, going from 21.3 percent to 10.4 percent, ultimately yielding a 9 percent increase in the rate of high school graduation, from 87 percent to 95 percent.

Figure 9.4   Lower-Class Black Human Capital Formation

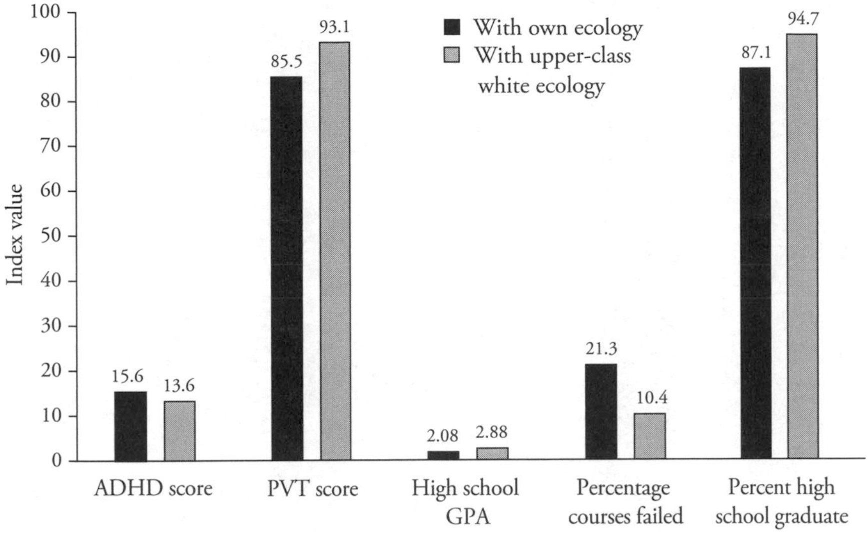

Source: Authors' compilation based on Harris and Udry (2008).

Crime and Delinquency

The final intermediate outcomes we consider are those related to crime and delinquency, which we assess in terms of three involvement indices: nonviolent crime, violent crime, and criminal justice. Predicted values for these outcomes are shown for lower-class black adolescents in figure 9.5 for the two ecological scenarios. Recall from chapter 7 that involvement in nonviolent crime generally rose with social class, whereas involvement in violent crime tended to decrease. As a result, exposing lower-class blacks to the more advantaged ecology of upper-class whites would increase their nonviolent criminal involvement and decrease their violent criminality. Given a lower-class black ecology, the predicted index of nonviolent crime is 0.76 and the predicted index of violent crime 0.69, whereas assuming an upper-class white ecology yields a predicted value of 1.29 for nonviolent criminal involvement (an increase of 70 percent) and 0.5 for violent criminal involvement (a decrease of 28 percent).

Given that violent crime is more likely to be prosecuted and punished

Figure 9.5   Lower-Class Black Crime and Delinquency

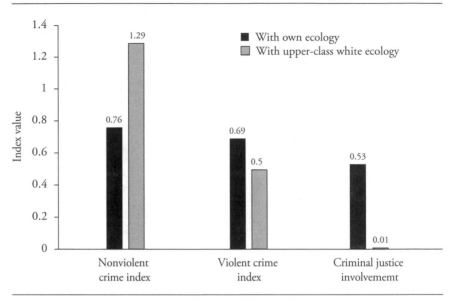

Source: Authors' compilation based on Harris and Udry (2008).

than nonviolent crime, the positive effect of the reduction in violent crime is likely to outweigh the negative influence of the increase to generate an overall improvement in well-being, in material if not moral terms. This interpretation is strengthened by the final bar graph in the figure, which shows the extent of criminal justice involvement under the two ecological scenarios. Shifting from a lower-class black social ecology to an upper-class white social ecology virtually eliminates criminal justice involvement for low-income blacks, reducing the index from 0.53 to effectively zero. To the extent that participation in violent crime and contact with the criminal justice system undermine life chances, therefore, improving the social ecology of lower-class blacks could produce big dividends (see Western 2006; Pager 2007).

Economic Independence

In general, figures 9.1 through 9.5 suggest that were the favorable social ecology experienced by upper-class white Americans accessible to lower-class African Americans, outcomes would be much improved along a variety of developmental dimensions: significantly lower rates of nonmarital childbearing, better outcomes on many health-related behaviors, a markedly more optimistic outlook on life, improved attention, greater verbal ability, better grades, higher rates of school completion, lower rates of violent criminality, and much lower levels of involvement with the criminal justice system. Ecological circumstances were measured during the late 1990s and intermediate outcomes in 2001 and 2003. We now consider their implications for the transition to adulthood, as measured by the achievement of economic independence by 2007 and 2008, when respondents were twenty-four to thirty-two years old.

The social benefits to be had by improving ecological circumstances for disadvantaged minorities are suggested by the bar graphs in figure 9.6. In particular, shifting from a lower-class black social ecology to an upper-class white one would dramatically raise the rate of college graduation, increasing the rate among poor blacks from around 8 percent to 73 percent. Likewise, the attainment of a graduate degree would rise from around 2 percent to 6

Figure 9.6   Lower-Class Black Transition to Adulthood

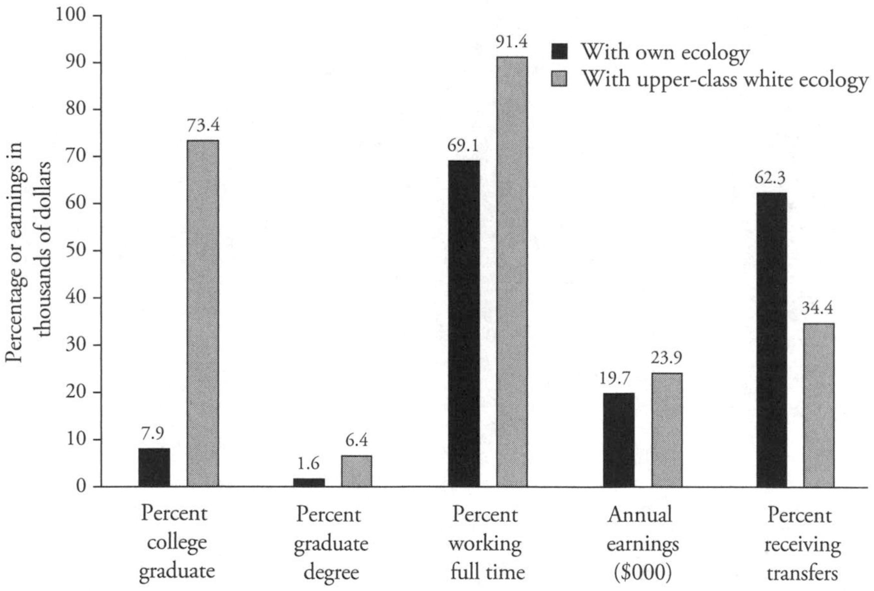

Source: Authors' compilation based on Harris and Udry (2008).

percent and these advances in education, in combination with the more advantaged ecological conditions, would sharply increase employment, with the proportion working full time rising from 69 percent to 91 percent. For poor black workers, moreover, the earnings premium would be 21 percent, raising annual earnings from around $19,700 to $23,900. In the end, the rate of dependency would be almost cut in half, the share receiving public transfers dropping from 62 percent to 34 percent.

WHAT IF UPPER-CLASS WHITES EXPERIENCED THE SOCIAL ECOLOGY OF LOWER-CLASS BLACKS?

The foregoing counterfactual estimates show what would happen in terms of human development and the attainment of adult economic independence if the social environments of lower-class blacks and upper-class whites were equalized, in this case, by giving the poor blacks access to the same advantaged spheres of social influence customarily enjoyed by affluent whites. Another way of showing the effect of equalizing ecologies, however, is to hypothetically assign upper-class whites the disadvantaged spheres of influence experienced by lower-class blacks in the United States—the counterfactual exercise to which we now turn.

Reproductive Outcomes

Whereas in the prior section, we saw that giving lower-class blacks the advantaged ecology of upper-class whites would generally improve their welfare on a variety of dimensions, giving upper-class whites the disadvantaged ecology of lower-class blacks can generally be expected to have the opposite effect. Figure 9.7 tests this hypothesis by presenting bar graphs of predicted reproductive outcomes for upper-class whites given their ecology and then that of lower-class blacks. As can be seen, upper-class females experience a 0.85 probability of sexual debut by Wave 3 given their ecology, a 0.28 likelihood of not using contraception during first intercourse, and a 0.34 probability of cohabitation. Assuming the social ecology of blacks, however, raises the probability of sexual debut to 0.96, of not using contraception to 0.68, and of cohabitation to 0.60. Despite the greatly increased exposure to the risk of unwanted pregnancy, however, probabilities of unwed and teenage childbearing do not rise that much. Shifting ecologies only increases the probability of unwed motherhood from 0.03 to 0.05 and the probability of teen mother-

Figure 9.7   Upper-Class White Reproduction

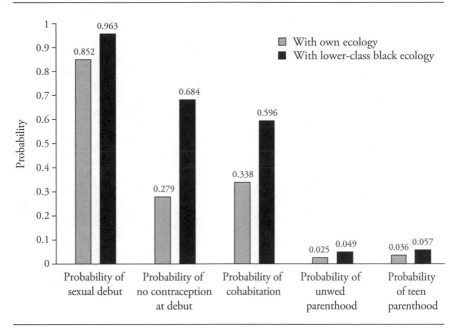

Source: Authors' compilation based on Harris and Udry (2008).

hood from 0.04 to 0.06 (in contrast to values of 0.31 and 0.26 for poor blacks under a lower-class black ecology). Thus, when it comes to reproduction, something distinctive is occurring in the poor black community that is not fully captured by differences in social ecology, at least as we have measured them here.

Health Outcomes

Figure 9.8 similarly shows how health-related behaviors would change if upper-class whites were compelled to grow up under the ecological circumstances of lower-class blacks. As we would expect given our earlier results, the probability of alcohol abuse and drug use would drop substantially, because these maladies are far more common in upper-class white families and advantaged neighborhoods and school environments. Thus the likelihood of alcohol abuse for upper-class whites falls from 0.82 under their ecology to 0.46 given a lower-class black ecology, and that of drug abuse from 0.20 to 0.09.

Figure 9.8   Upper-Class White Health Behaviors and Outcomes

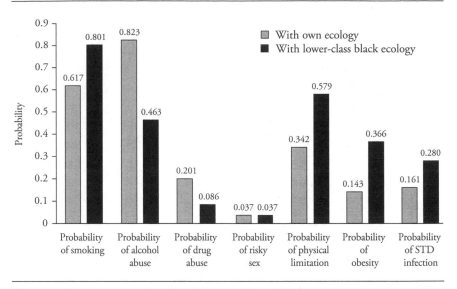

Source: Authors' compilation based on Harris and Udry (2008).

As before, the likelihood of engaging in risky sex is not affected by social context. All of the other health behaviors, however, move in a deleterious direction when upper-class whites are subjected to lower-class black circumstances. Thus the probability of smoking rises from 0.62 to 0.80, of reporting a physical limitation from 0.34 to 0.58, of obesity from 0.14 to 0.37, and of STD infection from 0.16 to 0.28.

Figure 9.9 shows the effect of ecological circumstances on respondents' overall assessments of their health, taking the foregoing health-related behaviors as predetermined and represented by the foregoing predicted values. As can be seen, the poor health index rises from 2.48 when an upper-class white ecology is assumed to 2.77 when a lower-class black one is, corresponding to a deterioration in general health of around 12 percent. Likewise, the depression index increases from 6.97 to 7.71, an increase of about 6 percent. The greatest contrast, however, is once again observed for the subjective likelihood of early death. Upper-class whites generally perceive a low likelihood of early death, but given the social ecology of poor blacks would be far more pessimistic. Thus expectation of an early death rises from an index value of

Figure 9.9   Upper-Class White Subjective Health Ratings

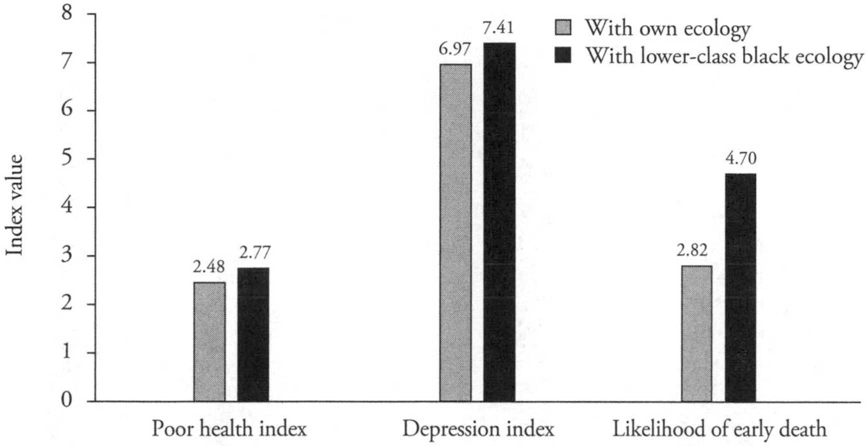

Source: Authors' compilation based on Harris and Udry (2008).

2.82 to 4.70, increasing the degree of pessimism about life chances by about 67 percent.

Human Capital Formation

The disadvantaged social ecology, higher rates of risky reproduction, and related poor health outcomes of lower-class blacks also undermine human capital formation, as shown in figure 9.10. In terms of cognitive potential, substituting the lower-class black ecology would increase the ADHD index for upper-class whites from 15.6 to 17.9 and reduce the PVT score from 103.8 to 97.1, shifts of 15 percent and 6 percent, respectively. The substitution of ecologies would also lower the expected GPA by 27 percent (from 2.97 to 2.17), increase the share of failed courses by 134 percent (from 8.2 percent to 19.2 percent), and reduce the likelihood of high school graduation by 4 percent (from 97.1 percent to 92.8 percent).

Crime and Delinquency

As with drug and alcohol abuse, the social ecology of upper-class whites is more conducive to participation in nonviolent crime than that of lower-class blacks, so substituting the latter for the former actually reduces nonvio-

Figure 9.10 Upper-Class White Human Capital Formation

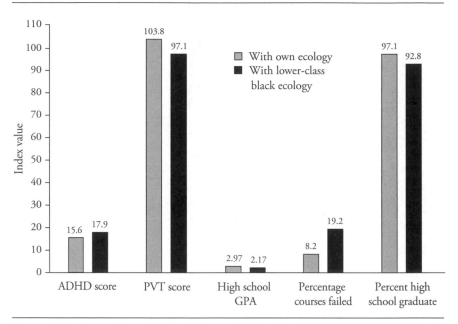

Source: Authors' compilation based on Harris and Udry (2008).

lent criminal involvement. As shown in figure 9.11, the index of nonviolent criminal involvement was 0.99 for upper-class whites under their ecology, but 0.46 under a lower-class black one. In contrast, the index of violent crime and especially criminal justice involvement rise substantially when lower-class black ecological conditions are substituted. Normally, for example, upper-class whites evince a violent crime index of 0.41 and a criminal justice involvement index of 0.47. Giving them lower-class black circumstances raises the former index to 0.57 (a 40 percent increase) and the latter to 1.13 (a 143 percent increase). If upper-class whites experienced the same social ecology as lower-class blacks, in other words, they would have far higher rates of violent criminality and much greater criminal justice involvement.

Transition to Economic Independence
The final stage of our counterfactual analysis considers what would happen in the transition to adult economic independence if upper-class whites faced the

Figure 9.11   Upper-Class White Crime and Delinquency

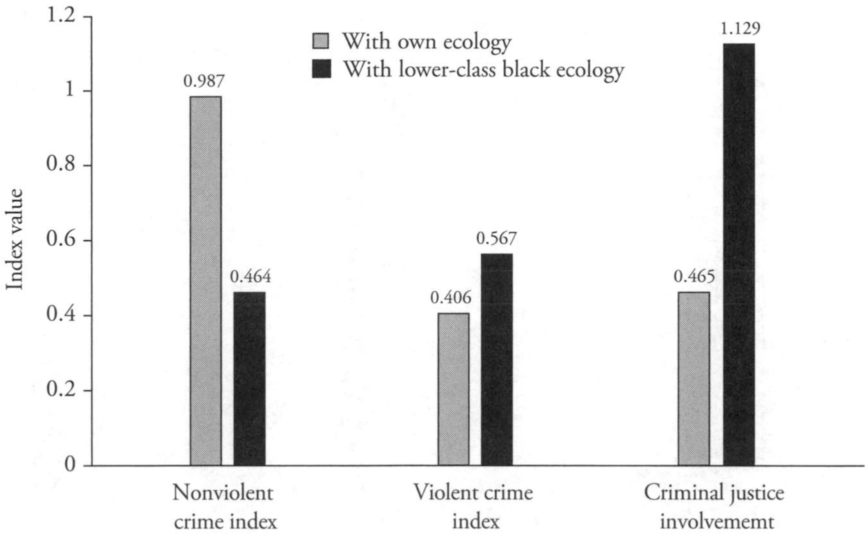

Source: Authors' compilation based on Harris and Udry (2008).

same disadvantaged ecology as lower-class blacks. Figure 9.12 thus predicts educational and employment outcomes for upper-class whites under the two contrasting scenarios. If upper-class whites grew up in the family, neighborhood, school, peer, and religious environment typical for lower-class blacks, their rates of college graduation would plummet dramatically, the rate of degree completion dropping from 60 percent to just 4 percent. Likewise, the predicted percentage obtaining a graduate degree would fall from 8 percent to around 2 percent.

Given these and prior shifts in human capital formation, it is hardly surprising to see rates of employment and earnings also drop significantly when a lower-class black ecology is assumed. Upper-class whites are typically predicted to exhibit a full-time employment rate of 90 percent. Under lower-class black circumstances, their predicted rate is just 67 percent. Among those working, furthermore, annual earnings decline by 16 percent (from $36,400 to $30,600). Not surprisingly given these predictions, the rate of expected dependency more than doubles, with the share receiving public transfers rising from 15 percent to around 34 percent.

Figure 9.12   Upper-Class White Transition to Adulthood

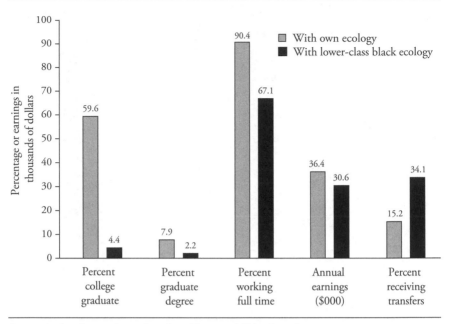

Source: Authors' compilation based on Harris and Udry (2008).

RACE-CLASS DIFFERENCES IN ECOLOGICAL PERSPECTIVE

As noted at the outset of this chapter, lower-class blacks have historically oc-cupied the bottom rungs of the social ladder in the United States and upper-class whites the top positions. Although recent trends in immigration and stratification have complicated this contrast by pushing Asians upward and Hispanics downward (see Massey 2007), the overall contrast in the well-being of affluent whites and poor blacks remains huge, and the two groups continue to occupy opposite ends of the socioeconomic spectrum. This stark contrast implies pronounced differences in access to critical material, sym-bolic, and emotional resources within social spheres central to human devel-opment. Our argument has been that differential access to a great extent ac-count for persistent differences in well-being by race and class in the United States today.

To demonstrate the relative influence of social ecology in determining life chances, we considered what would happen to lower-class blacks and upper-class whites under each other's ecologies. We generally found that reproductive outcomes, health, education, and antisocial behaviors such as crime and delinquency were strongly conditioned by circumstances prevailing in family, neighborhood, school, peer, and religious environments. As a result, when poor blacks were assigned the ecology of affluent whites, their welfare improved substantially, and when affluent whites were assigned that of poor blacks, theirs deteriorated.

We conclude this chapter by assessing the degree to which contrasting social ecologies can account for observed gaps between lower-class blacks and upper-class whites. We do so by considering outcomes predicted for the two race-class groups under three scenarios: each group is given its observed social ecology; lower-class blacks are given the upper-class white ecology; and upper-class whites are given the lower-class black ecology. We then computed black-white ratios for interim developmental outcomes and adult economic outcomes predicted from each set of assumptions. The results are plotted in figure 9.13, where the various outcomes are arrayed along the horizontal axis and the black-white ratio on the vertical axis. The solid black line shows the black-white gap under conditions that currently prevail for each race-class group and the dashed line shows what happens when lower-class blacks are given the social ecology of upper-class whites. To the extent that social ecology accounts for the black-white gap, the dashed line should track at or below 1.0. The dotted line shows what happens to upper-class whites when they are exposed to the social ecology of lower-class blacks. To the extent that social ecology explains the racial gap, the dotted line should track close to or above the solid line.

Following the solid line from left to right quickly reveals which outcomes display the largest racial gap. Pronounced departures from equality are indicated by spikes above or below the solid line corresponding to 1.0. As can be seen, compared with upper-class whites, lower-class blacks experience much higher probabilities of not using contraception at first intercourse (a ratio of 1.5), risky sex (3.6), obesity (2.0), STD infection (1.8), expectation of early death (1.7), failed courses (2.6), violent crime (1.7), and receipt of public transfers (4.1). On these outcomes, the dashed line falls close to or below the level of 1.0 in all cases except the probabilities of risky sex (3.7) and of receiving public transfers (2.6). The dotted line, meanwhile, equals or exceeds the solid line in all cases except the receipt of transfers (2.2). The solid line indicates that low-income blacks experience lower likelihoods of smoking than

Figure 9.13   Racial Differentials in Outcomes

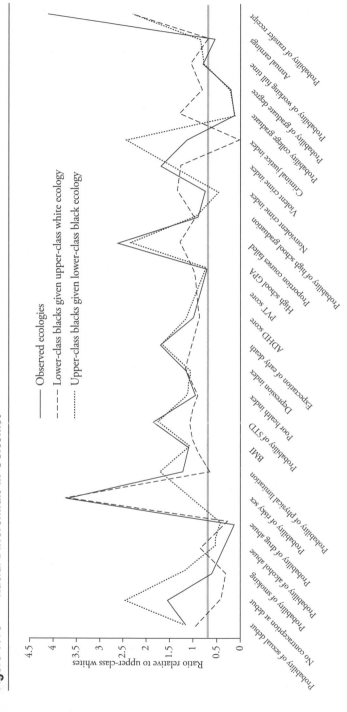

Source: Authors' compilation based on Harris and Udry (2008).

high income whites (a ratio of 0.6), as well as lower levels of alcohol abuse (0.3), hard drug use (0.1), college graduation (0.1), a graduate degree (0.2), working full time (0.8), GPA (0.7), PVT (0.8), and annual earnings (0.5). On these outcomes, the dashed line rises to or above 1.0 in all cases except smoking (0.3) and drug abuse (0.4). The dotted line moves toward the solid line in all cases.

These results mean that gaps between lower-class blacks and upper-class whites are substantially attributable to the contrasting ecological circumstances they experience, with the main exceptions being the likelihood of engaging in risky sex, receiving transfers, smoking, and using hard drugs. Two outcomes were not included in figure 9.13, however, because the solid line put them so off the scale compared with the other outcomes being plotted. These outcomes are the probability of unwed and teenage motherhood, which are graphed separately in figure 9.14. The solid black bar shows the observed ratio between lower-class blacks and upper-class whites to reveal that the likelihood of unwed motherhood is 12.4 times more likely among poor blacks and the likelihood of teenage motherhood is 7.1 times greater.

In contrast to most other outcomes, moreover, equalizing social ecologies

Figure 9.14   Racial Differentials in Unwed and Teenage Childbearing

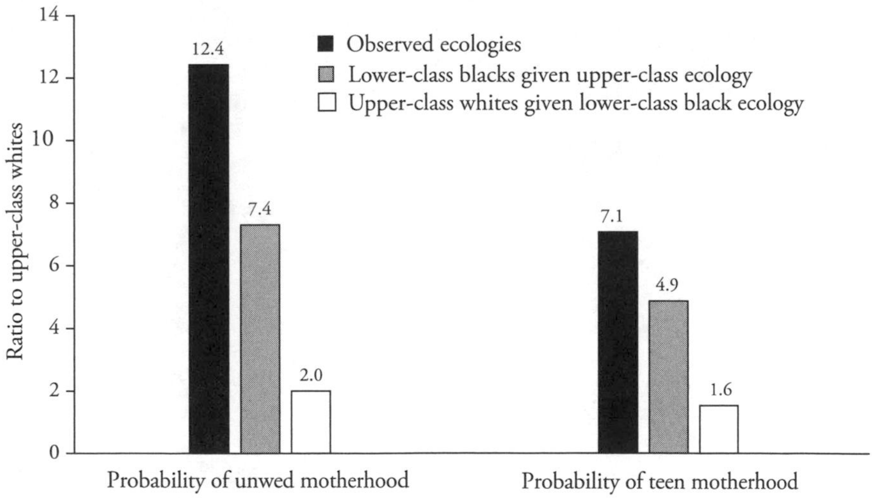

Source: Authors' compilation based on Harris and Udry (2008).

reduces the differential but it does not come close to eliminating it. Thus, assigning low-class blacks the ecological circumstances of affluent whites reduces the black-white ratio from 12.4 to 7.4, but the black rate of unwed childbearing nonetheless still remains more than seven times greater than the white rate. Similarly, assigning upper-income whites the ecological circumstances of low-income blacks yields a ratio of 2.0, not even close to the observed ratio of 12.4. Even if upper-class whites were to experience the deprived ecology of lower-class blacks, they would not display the same elevated rate of unwed childbearing. Similar results prevail with respect to the likelihood of teenage motherhood. Assigning low-class blacks the ecology of upper-class whites reduces the gap from 7.1 to 4.9, and giving upper-class whites the ecological conditions of lower-class blacks yields a ratio of 1.6, but the observed gap is in neither case close to accounted for by ecological circumstances.

In sum, although contrasting ecological circumstances go a long way toward explaining observed gaps in human development and socioeconomic achievement, they cannot readily explain differences in the likelihood of either nonmarital and teenage childbearing or of risky sex. Risky reproductive behaviors are thus a key nexus for the transmission of socioeconomic disadvantage among African Americans that cannot be attributed to differing ecological circumstances. Moreover, although diverging social ecologies may substantially reduce the black-white gap in dependency, they do not eliminate the differential propensity to receive public transfers. We return to consider these points in greater detail in the concluding chapter.

CHAPTER 10

The Ecology of Inequality

We wrote this book with both theoretical and substantive goals in mind. Theoretically, we sought to update, elaborate, and extend an ecological model of human growth and development introduced some time ago, but which, in our opinion, has received too little attention and has been unproductively relegated to a marginalized corner of social research. We also sought to underscore the importance and ubiquity of race-class interactions in contemporary American society, in terms of both how people are exposed to contrasting ecological advantages and disadvantages and how they respond to these divergent social ecologies in their development, behavior, and actions. Substantively, we sought to understand the ecological roots of socioeconomic disadvantage in the United States today by documenting the lack of access to resources in key social spheres. We also sought to identify the particular ecological mechanisms by which race-class inequalities are produced in contemporary American society, pinpointing the social spheres within which inequality is disproportionately generated, along with the factors within those spheres most responsible for effects. Finally, we also sought to apply the foregoing theoretical and substantive knowledge to identify concrete public actions that might mitigate the social ecology of inequality that has taken root in American society at the dawn of the twenty-first century.

THE ECOLOGICAL MODEL

Although prior studies have examined different facets of ecological stratification in the United States separately—focusing one by one on the social influence of families, schools, neighborhoods, or peers—to our knowledge no study has yet undertaken a comprehensive assessment encompassing all ecological spheres simultaneously even though Urie Bronfenbrenner (1979) laid out the basic framework of social ecology more than thirty years ago. Moreover, research to date has generally paid short shrift to the religious sphere and its role in the social ecology of human development, a sphere of social influence that is voluntary, to be sure, but one in which many people spend considerable amounts of time and energy, especially in the United States.

We also sought to move social research away from a view of people as fully rational actors in control of the world around them, and toward a perspective that views human beings as organisms embedded in and responding to a set of environmental influences that shape them. Although humans may indeed be "rational" after a fashion, research in the cognitive sciences increasingly indicates that human rationality is constrained in fundamental ways. First, human rationality is less Boolean than categorical. Rather than applying strict rules of arithmetic logic to maximize whatever for the moment we might perceive as "utility," our brains are wired to create categorical structures of thought that divide the world around us into discrete mental boxes, which through learning and experience come to be paired with attributes, meanings, and scripts. Although some of us are capable of breaking down and analyzing the world logically to arrive at an optimal outcome given certain constraints, we far more often fall back in daily life on cognitive heuristics, mental shortcuts that allow us to negotiate familiar environments well enough to survive with a minimum of cognitive effort, but which may lead to behavior that is not strictly logical or even self-interested (Ariely 2009; Kahneman 2011).

Not only is human cognition not strictly rational in the mathematical or deductive sense, it also operates under the powerful influence of emotion (LeDoux 1996). In reality, the human brain is composed of two interrelated cognitive systems: one emotional, older, and common to all mammals and rooted in interior organs of the brain; and another rational, more recently evolved, and rooted in the outer layers of the brain, notably the prefrontal cortex—that area that allows people to plan, organize, and anticipate based on categorical understandings of the past (Damasio 1994; LeDoux 2002). The two systems operate in parallel and are closely interconnected, but the number and rapidity of the neural connections running from the emotional to the rational brain is greater than vice versa, so that often the emotional brain tells the rational brain what to do. In a very real way, our desires and wants, likes and dislikes, arise in the emotional brain, typically though unconscious channels, and the rational brain simply rationalizes and acts based on these more deeply rooted feelings and pre-rational sentiments (Damasio 1999). Indeed, the emotional brain can often hijack the rational brain to suggest outcomes that are manifestly not in the material interests of the actor.

Moreover, the categorical schemas the human brain is programmed to construct are invariably paired with emotions acquired through interaction with the environment. These pairings develop through spontaneous conditioning from experiences in the empirical world as well as through deliberate conditioning by social others. To the extent that we understand the conceptual organization of human cognition and the meanings and emotions that are paired with conceptual categories, we are in a better position to understand human behavior—hence our emphasis here on emotional resources, in addition to material and symbolic resources, as essential to understanding human development and social action.

As with other animals, the actions and decisions of humans are also subject to environmental constraints that both limit the range of information and experience accessible to actors and determine the quantity of resources available for growth and development. In the case of human beings, however, the relevant environments are social rather than physical. Variations in social organization and culture enable human beings to exist in any physical setting. Although the long-term survival of the human race may depend on the ecological sustainability of the macro-social structures and ways of thinking that we have evolved in adapting to the global environment, the immediate survival of any individual human being depends more on daily interactions with micro-social environments in specific societies.

To grow and develop into well-functioning adults, and then to survive and prosper as mature beings, humans must gain access to adequate material, symbolic, and emotional resources from the micro-social environments they progressively inhabit as they move through life. We argue that in postindustrial societies such as the United States, the fundamental social spheres that people inhabit are families, neighborhoods, schools, and peer groups, supplemented in some cases by religious settings. As in the physical environment, resources are unevenly distributed across these environments, such that families, schools, neighborhoods, peers, and religions offer notably different degrees of access to material, symbolic, and emotional resources, yielding varying levels of constraint on development while growing up and varying limits to action and decision-making as adults.

In recent decades, social science has placed a great deal of emphasis on theories of rational action undertaken by autonomous individuals and has paid less attention to the constraints and contingencies imposed by heuristics, emotions, and context. The lack of attention to constraint and context is misleading enough when applied to adults, but is doubly flawed when applied to young people in the process of growth and development, who lack full agency, and are not in a position to choose the social environments they occupy, much less the resources they contain. For infants, children, and adolescents in postindustrial societies, the character of the social environment and the resources it offers are determined by the accident of birth.

As pointed out at the beginning of this book, the imperative to situate people in their environments has acquired a new urgency in recent years with the emergence of the field of epigenetics, or the study of gene-environment interactions. It has now been scientifically established that genes are not invariably expressed no matter the environment an organism occupies, but are actually turned on and off through interactions with the environment. Identical genomes may be expressed in entirely different ways depending on the environmental conditions they encounter. To understand human behavior fully, therefore, scientists need not only characterize a person's genetic endowment, but also comprehend and the environments that people inhabit at different stages in the life cycle. Because the relevant environments for human beings are social rather than physical, a full understanding of social ecology thus becomes essential.

RACE-CLASS INTERACTIONS

In the United States, two structural dimensions of social organization have played an outsized role in determining access to resources within the social world: race and class. Historically race was the master status, and nonwhite origins relegated people to decidedly less advantageous social environments. In the social construction of race, moreover, the most salient categorical distinction was that between those of African and European origin, at least in the United States. Within American society, people were systematically allocated to less desirable social spheres on the basis of visible African ancestry (Fredrickson 2002). Of course, unequal allocations to social spheres were also made on the basis of class—the position of one's parents in the socioeconomic hierarchy—but discrepancies in access to resources based on class were generally less stark and less durable than those based on race, especially from 1945 to 1975 (Massey 2007).

In the decades immediately following World War II, the United States was characterized by an egalitarian form of capitalism in which income and wealth were redistributed to achieve greater equity and markets were managed to achieve stability, avoid failures, and ensure transparency (Kenworthy 2004). Although the political economy was designed to produce greater equality, it was only for white people, given that the New Deal programs and policies that created it were thoroughly racialized to exclude blacks and other minorities (Katznelson 2005). The great era of white egalitarian capitalism was accompanied by rigid discrimination and segregation on the basis of race, de jure in the South and de facto elsewhere, but discrimination and segregation just the same. As a result, from 1940 to 1975 inequalities of wealth and income steadily eroded, opportunities proliferated, and the socioeconomic distribution generally widened in the middle while shrinking at the extremes to produce a genuinely middle-class society, at least for whites (Massey 2007). The major gaps in income and wealth were less on the basis of class than along the lines of race and ethnicity. White America formed a grand political coalition to support the maintenance of an open, affluent society as long as blacks, Hispanics, and Asians were largely excluded from it.

The civil rights movement of the 1960s upset this political balance. Civil rights acts passed in 1964, 1965, 1968, 1974, and 1977 progressively outlawed discrimination in consumer markets, labor markets, voting, housing markets, credit markets, and mortgage lending while a new War on Poverty sought to enfranchise minorities historically excluded from the New Deal and provide them with the resources they needed to catch up with white America (Quadagno 1996). These reforms were instigated by liberal Democrats in alliance with moderate Republicans, but this coalition proved unstable and short lived. The embrace of civil rights by the Democratic Party and its pursuit of racial redistribution alienated blue-collar ethnics in the North and socially conservative whites in the South, who increasingly threw their support to Republicans (Massey 2007). After a political realignment to Republican hegemony, the egalitarian political economy of the New Deal was steadily dismantled after 1980 to create a new laissez-faire system that abandoned the redistributive functions of government, cut taxes, reduced social spending, and most important, halted the racial redistribution launched by liberal Democrats.

The simultaneous granting of formal civil rights to minorities and the restructuring of the political economy in favor of the rich brought about a slow moderation of discrimination and racial segregation combined with a sharp increase in inequality, moving the American stratification system away from an additive allocation of people to social spheres on the basis of strong racial effects and weak class effects, and toward a new one that allocated people to spheres on the basis of an interaction between still potent racial effects and increasingly powerful class effects. As a result, in the United States today we observe steadily fewer pure race and class effects but a growing kaleidoscope of race-class interactions.

In terms of exposure to ecological advantages and disadvantages, the one distribution that remains closest to a pure class effect is (not surprisingly) income. When average household income is computed by race and class to yield sixteen race-class means, we find that the lower quadrant of the distribution is made up entirely of lower-class members of each racial group, the upper quadrant is composed entirely of upper-class members of each group, and the two middle quadrants are composed of the lower-middle-class and upper-middle-class members of each group, respectively (see figure 2.2). Even within this emblematic class distribution, however, we observe some variation by race, especially in the upper class, where Hispanic incomes average $97,000 per year and black incomes just $82,000. In other words, upper-class status affords Hispanics access to considerably more in the way of material resources than it does African Americans.

Perhaps the closest purely racial distribution of resources is the allocation of material disadvantages across neighborhoods, but even here departures from a strictly racial allocation of people to categories are clear. Across the sixteen race-class groups, the most disadvantaged quadrant of neighborhoods is indeed occupied only by blacks and is separated from the others by a quantum shift in the level of spatial deprivation (see figure 3.1). The other three quadrants are occupied by mixtures of whites, Asians, and Hispanics of different classes. Although whites and Asians tend cluster in the lowest quadrants of disadvantage, and Asians and Hispanics in the middle quadrants, no rigid allocation of people to quadrants on the basis of race applies.

For most other material, symbolic, and emotional resources, race and class interact in complicated ways to allocate advantages and disadvantages across social spheres. No single class effect comes into play on the propensity to smoke cigarettes, for example (see figure 5.1). Among whites, cigarette smoking declines with rising class standing, whereas among Hispanics it increases;

among Asians and blacks, we observe no class gradient at all. Similarly, no systematic effect of race related to health (see figure 5.10). Health differences between whites, Asians, Hispanics, and blacks are small and nonsignificant in the upper class, at least in the young ages observed here, but among those in the lower class, intergroup differences are pronounced.

William Julius Wilson (1978) long ago alerted social scientists to the declining significance of race in the United States; and although it took researchers a bit longer to appreciate the size and permanence of the increase in class stratification (Levy 1988), the foundations for a new interaction between race and class have now been in place for several decades. Nonetheless race and class continue mostly to be treated as main effects in simple additive models. We thus hope that our work here encourages future scholars to routinely consider race and class as interactive effects rather than as simple main effects in behavioral models.

THE ECOLOGICAL ROOTS OF DISADVANTAGE

In adopting an ecological model of human development that considers race-class interactions across multiple social spheres simultaneously, we sought to shed light on those resources and spheres especially critical in promoting healthy human development and a successful transition to independent adulthood. We considered five social spheres and used data available from the Adolescent Health Survey to measure, to the best of our ability, the relative access of individuals in different race-class groups to material, symbolic, and emotional resources among families, schools, neighborhoods, peers, and religious settings.

The material resources we considered included income and access to health insurance within the family sphere and indicators of socioeconomic disadvantage within the neighborhood and school spheres. Examination of these variables reveals huge discrepancies in access to material resources among adolescents. With respect to average income, the range of access extended from just $9,300 per year among lower-class blacks to $97,000 per year among upper-class Hispanics, a tenfold gap from top to bottom. Given the high cost of health care, the lack of government health insurance, and the ever-present possibility of illness or injury, access to health insurance constitutes a second critical resource in the United States. Once again, access to this material benefit varies widely by race and class. Whereas 80 percent of upper-class Asians were fully covered by health insurance, only 46 percent of lower-class Hispanics were, a 1.7 ratio. The range in access to material resources was just as great in the school and neighborhood spheres. Our factor scale of neighborhood disadvantage ranged from a high of 1.92 for lower-class blacks to a low of 0.46 for upper-class whites, a 4.2 ratio. The index of school disadvantage ranged more narrowly, from 13.7 for upper-class blacks and Hispanics to 11 among lower- and upper-middle-class Asians, a ratio of 1.5.

In addition to these material resources, we also examined two symbolic resources in the family sphere: the status derived from parents' occupational and educational achievements. Average parental occupational status ranged from 47.2 SEI points among upper-class whites to a low of 26.1 among lower-class Hispanics, a ratio of 1.8. The share with a college-educated parent ranged from 72 percent to 15 percent between the same two groups, a ratio of 4.8. Owing to limitations of the Add Health data, we were unable to develop other measures of access to symbolic resources, leaving the social status of neighborhoods, schools, peer networks, and religious settings unmeasured. An important task for future research is to develop better indicators of symbolic resources in these social spheres. Nonetheless, the data are sufficient to confirm that American society is characterized by a huge range in the degree of access to material and symbolic resources and that these differences in access are largely structured along race and class lines.

Owing to the richness of the Adolescent Health Survey, we were able to develop several measures of access to emotional resources. Within the family sphere, we found huge differences in access to adult time and attention, which were mostly determined by the presence or absence of a biological father within the family. Whereas 76 percent of low-income blacks had no father present, only 12 percent among upper-middle-class Asians did, a ratio of 6.3. These contrasting frequencies of father presence produce corresponding child-adult ratios of 1.54 and 0.92, meaning that adolescents in the most advantaged group had access to 60 percent more adult time and attention than the least advantaged.

Although unwed childbearing and union dissolution account for most father absence, mortality and incarceration also play an important role and these emotional burdens are quite unevenly distributed among families. Whereas 14.3 percent of lower-middle-class blacks experienced the death of an immediate family member and 27 percent experienced paternal incarceration, the corresponding figures for upper-middle-class Asians were just 1.1 percent and 1.5 percent, yielding huge ratios of 13:1 and 18:1. For some, these inequalities were offset by access to a family mentor, which we defined as a trusted adult confidant who was not a parent. Some 37 percent of lower-class blacks reported access to a family mentor, but only 15 percent for upper-middle-class Asians did, a ratio of more than 2.

We also found widespread differences in the family sternness—the degree to which adults in the family were perceived to care about respondents, express love and warmth for them, communicate with them, and understand them. High scores indicated a colder and more remote emotional style and low scores a warmer and more accepting one. On this index, we observe a range from 19.9 for low-income Asians to 15.9 for low-income blacks, a ratio of 1.3. We also sought to measure degree of access to emotional resources within neighborhoods, focusing on social efficacy, which we defined as the degree to which people know their neighbors, interact with them, expect them to look out for one another, and feel safe and happy in their presence. We constructed the scale so that higher values indicated less efficacy, or greater inefficacy within neighborhoods. This scale revealed substantial variation in exposure to neighborhood inefficacy by race and class, from to a high of 5.59 for lower-class Asians to a low of 3.32 for upper-class whites, a ratio of 1.7.

Owing to high levels of unemployment, high rates of incarceration, and excess mortality, low-income neighborhoods are often characterized by a relative scarcity of what William Julius Wilson has called "marriageable males"—young men in a position to get married and support a family. To assess variation in this emotional resource, we computed the ratio of unmarried females age twenty to twenty-four to unmarried males age twenty to twenty-four. As expected, the relative scarcity of young men within neighborhoods was greatest for African Americans, the highest index of 0.944 observed for lower-middle-class blacks and the lowest value of 0.822 for lower-class whites, yielding a ratio of 1.1. As a final indicator of access to emotional resources within neighborhoods, we assessed whether respondents reported an adult neighbor as their mentor. We found significant variation, from 15.3 percent for upper-class blacks to 3.7 percent for upper-class Asians, a ratio of 4.1.

Turning to the educational sphere, we computed measures of social inefficacy and social disorder within schools. Social efficacy was assessed as the degree to which teachers and other actors at school were perceived to care about them, treat them well, and make them feel happy and integrated in the school community. We defined social disorder as the degree to which students felt unsafe and insecure at school and perceived issues such as drugs, harassment, vandalism, and stress to be problems. The range of school inefficacy scores was rather narrow, from a high of 13.7 points among upper-class blacks to a low of 11 among lower-class Asians , a ratio of just 1.2. We also observed a rather narrow range of school disorder, from 9.92 among lower-class Asians to 8.28 among upper-class whites, another 1.2 ratio. Degree of access to a school mentor varied more widely, from 30 percent among lower-class Asians to 10 percent among lower-class Hispanics.

The last two spheres of influence we considered with respect to emotional resources were peer groups and religious settings. Among peers, we measured the emotional burden of exposure to violence by assessing the degree to which respondents witnessed or were involved in violent acts such as verbal harassment, physical assaults, fights, stabbings, gunplay, and shootings. The resulting index ranged from 2.81 for lower-class Hispanics to 1.18 for upper-class Asians, a ratio of 2.4. We also assessed the degree of emotional turmoil in a person's friendship network by measuring the relative frequency with which respondents reported the attempted suicide of a friend. Whereas only 1.5 percent of lower-middle-class Asians reported such an attempt, 13.6 percent of upper-class Hispanics did, yielding a ratio of 9.1. To some extent, these emotional burdens were offset by access to adult friends or acquaintances as mentors. Where 26.7 percent of upper-middle-class Asians reported a peer mentor, only 13.4 percent of upper-middle-class blacks did, producing a ratio of 2.0.

Religiosity refers to the extent to which respondents believe in God, report that religion is important to them, believe that scripture is the word of God, and pray frequently. It might be considered a form of "spiritual capital," a resource of solace and support that people might use to overcome adversity (Capaldi and Malloch 2012). The religiosity scale ranged from a high of 14.6 for lower-middle-class blacks to a low of 10.8 for lower-class Asians, a modest ratio of 1.4. Our scale of religious involvement captures the frequency of service attendance and youth group participation and ranged from 7.1 among lower-middle-class blacks to 4.4 among lower-class whites, a ratio of 1.6. Finally, access to a religious mentor ranged from 5.6 percent among upper-middle-class Asians to just 1 percent among lower-middle-class Hispanics, a ratio of 5.6.

The foregoing ranges in the degree of access to material, symbolic, and emotional resources succinctly capture the degree of inequality that exists within the social ecology of the United States and signal which resources in which spheres display the most inequality and hence the greatest potential for stratifying young people on the basis of race and class. Figure 10.1 summa-

Figure 10.1   Ecological Indicators

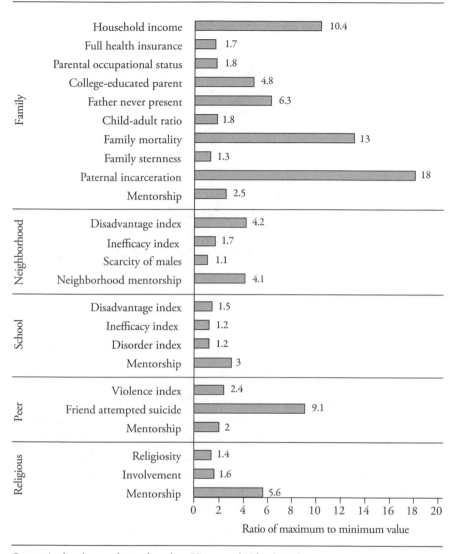

Source: Authors' compilation based on Harris and Udry (2008).

rizes the ranges just discussed in the form of a bar chart that shows ratios of the highest to the lowest race-class average for each resource in each social sphere. The ratios range from 1.1 to 18, but if we consider only those with ratios of 2.0 or above we can narrow the list of potentially important pathways of stratification.

In the family sphere, the most unequally distributed resources appear to be household income (a ratio of 10.4), parental education (4.8), father absence (6.3), mortality (13), and paternal incarceration (18). Among neighborhoods material disadvantage (4.2) and mentorship (4.1) stand out, whereas in the school sphere mentorship appears to be the key resource (3). All three peer indicators display a significant range from top to bottom, the violence index standing at 2.4, mentorship at 2.0, and peer suicide at 9.1. In the religious sphere, the greatest range is observed in access to mentors, a ratio of 5.6. In a sense, the uneven distribution of these resources across these spheres constitute prime exemplars of what Jonathan Kozol (1991) has called the "savage inequalities" of American society.

MECHANISMS OF ECOLOGICAL INEQUALITY

Although the ecological mechanisms that generate race-class inequality in the United States are many and complex, certain spheres appear to be relatively more important than others and some resource variables appear over and over to influence relative disadvantage on multiple outcomes. In earlier chapters, we summarized ecological effects in the form of tables that included ecological variables grouped by sphere down the side and specific outcomes arrayed across the top and coded the relative significance and direction of effects within the body of the table.

Here we step back even further to consider the overall significance of ecological factors on mediating stratification outcomes—those related to reproduction, health, human capital formation, and expressions of deviance in the form of crime and delinquency. To visualize the effects, we draw upon the aforementioned tables to build summary indices of relative significance. Specifically, moving down the tables row by row, we add the number of pluses or minuses in each cell moving left to right. This operation yields a composite index of the number and size of effects corresponding to each ecological variable with respect reproduction, health, human capital, and delinquency, which we then standardize by expressing as a ratio of the maximum possible index achievable for each set of outcomes (the sum that would result if all effects were significant at $p < 0.001$). The resulting measures of relative significance for the ecological factors are depicted in the bar chart shown in figure 10.2, in which factors are grouped by social sphere.

In the family sphere, what is perhaps most interesting is what is not important in determining key intermediate outcomes. Traditional explanatory

Figure 10.2   Determining Mediating Outcomes

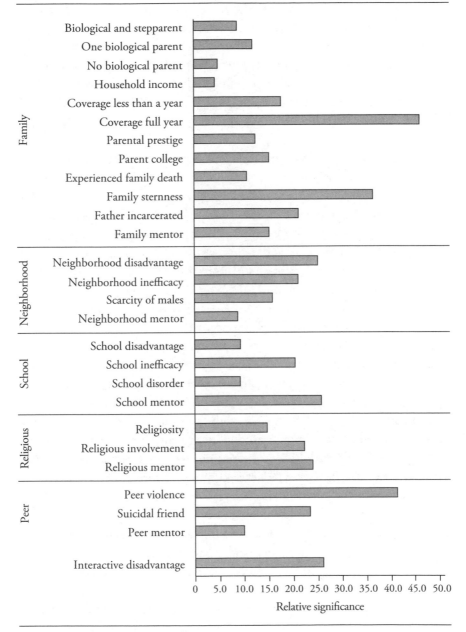

Source: Authors' compilation based on Harris and Udry (2008).

variables such as household income, family structure, and parental prestige appear to matter relatively little in the end. What matters most in determining outcomes with respect to reproduction, health, human capital, and crime delinquency are, in descending order, access to health insurance, family sternness, and paternal incarceration, followed by parental college education and access to a family mentor. Within families, therefore, the only material resource that matters is access to health insurance, and intermediate behavioral outcomes are generally more strongly connected to emotional and symbolic resources.

Material resources matter more when it comes to neighborhoods, where relative significance is greatest for neighborhood disadvantage followed by neighborhood social inefficacy and a scarcity of marriageable males. Within the educational sphere, exposure to social efficacy and access to a school-based mentor appear to be the key ecological factors in determining reproductive, health, educational, and delinquent behaviors. Although religiosity is by no means insignificant in and of itself, intermediate stratification outcomes appear to be more significantly determined by religious involvement and access to a religious mentor. In the peer environment, exposure to violence is highly significant in determining mediating outcomes, second only to access to insurance in the family sphere. Having a suicidal friend also plays an important role, but access to a peer mentor is of minor significance. Finally, the accumulation of disadvantages across spheres has a rather strong cumulative interactive effect on mediating behaviors and outcomes.

Although figure 10.2 provides a rough assessment of the relative significance of different factors in determining intermediate outcomes that condition the transition to adulthood, it does not reveal which variables operate through which spheres. The next two figures therefore indicate relative significance separately for different sets of mediating variables. Figure 10.3 shows the relative significance of ecological variables in determining reproductive and health-related outcomes. Figure 10.4 does the same for outcomes related to human capital formation and crime-delinquency.

The bar charts in figure 10.3 reveal that reproductive outcomes are most strongly related to exposure to multiple disadvantages across spheres, followed by peer violence, family sternness, religiosity, access to a religious mentor, family mortality, school inefficacy, religious involvement, and a scarcity of males. Thus the mediation of reproductive behaviors has little to do with material conditions in any sphere, but follow preponderantly from emotional

Figure 10.3   Determining Health and Reproductive Outcomes

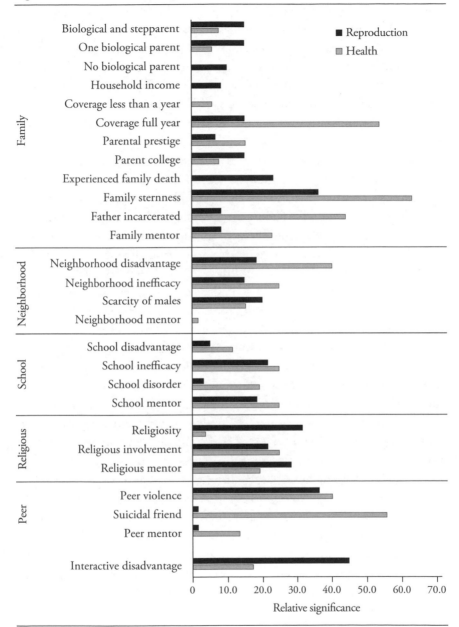

Source: Authors' compilation based on Harris and Udry (2008).

circumstances, most notably sternness and mortality in the family sphere, violence in the peer network, and religiosity, and participation and mentorship in the religious sphere. Access to health insurance surprisingly is not very important when it comes to reproduction. Instead, coming from a stern family, experiencing the death of a close relative, and religious involvement, belief, and mentorship all act powerfully to lower the likelihood of early sexual intercourse, cohabitation, and risky sexual behavior to reduce the odds of unwed fertility. In contrast, exposure to peer violence increases the likelihood of these outcomes.

When it comes to health outcomes and behaviors, the leading determinants appear to be family sternness, having a suicidal friend, access to health insurance, paternal incarceration, neighborhood disadvantage, and exposure to peer violence. Within the family, a stern emotional style and full insurance coverage reduce the likelihood of risky reproductive behaviors and improve health outcomes, whereas paternal incarceration generally increases the health and behavioral risks. Aside from health insurance, the only other material condition really to make a difference in determining health is neighborhood disadvantage, which generally undermines self-assessed health. Within the peer setting, having a suicidal friend and exposure to violence also increase risky health behaviors and compromise health outcomes.

Turning to figure 10.4, we see that a variety of factors are significant in determining human capital formation. Within the family sphere, the most important are access to health insurance, parental education, growing up in a single-parent family, parental prestige, family sternness, and access to a family member. Access to health insurance is by far the most important, indeed the most significant single effect across all spheres of influence. As one would expect, having a prestigious, college-educated parent, and access to insurance and a family mentor act to boost cognitive skills and high school academic achievement, whereas originating in a single-parent family reduces academic achievement and a stern family background lowers cognitive skills. After health insurance, the next most important are exposure to peer violence, which has a strong negative effect, followed by access to a school mentor, access to a religious mentor, and then religious and religious involvement, all of which have positive effects.

When we originally developed the index of sternness, we expected it to have a detrimental effect on many outcomes, in line with work coming out of developmental psychology, which generally found that warmth, comfort, and

Figure 10.4   Determining Human Capital Formation, Crime, and Delinquency

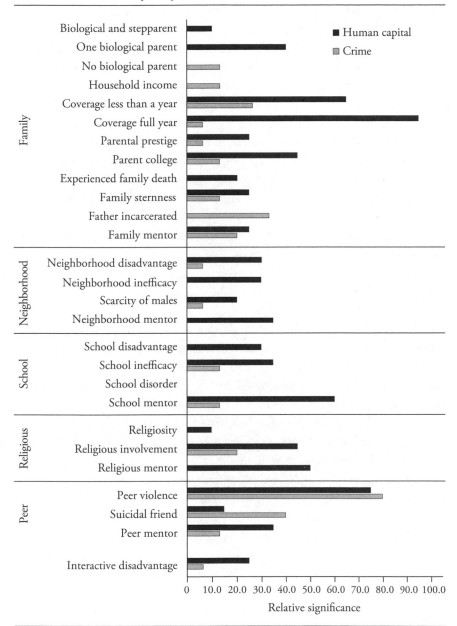

Source: Authors' compilation based on Harris and Udry (2008).

caring were important in producing healthy adults. Instead, we found that emotional sternness, at least as measured here, mostly had beneficial effects, and that a reduction in verbal ability among those exposed to a stern up-bringing was the only detectable downside. In contrast, sternness offers a va-riety of benefits in generating better outcomes with respect to reproduction, health, and crime that in most cases outweigh the negative effects on cogni-tive skills in making the transition to adulthood. For an upper-class family living in a safe and affluent neighborhood and sending children to privileged schools with privileged students, a warmer, more caring, and engaged style of child rearing makes sense and is ultimately beneficial. For a lower-class family living in a dangerous, disadvantaged neighborhood, and sending children to poorly performing schools where their children are exposed to delinquent and often violent peers, however, a lax style of child rearing probably does more harm than good.

Few ecological factors have much significance in determining criminal and delinquent outcomes, but four stand out. Greater exposure to peer violence, association with a suicidal friend, and paternal incarceration all tend to in-crease criminality and criminal justice involvement. Access to health insur-ance, however, tends to reduce it. Crime and delinquency are unrelated or weakly related to composition of the family of origin, parental attainments, school conditions, neighborhood conditions, or religious circumstances.

This discussion has focused on intermediate outcomes experienced in late adolescence and early adulthood. To conclude we turn to the transition to adult economic independence. Figure 10.5 applies the same procedures used to construct the prior figures to indicate the relative significance of ecological factors in determining the transition to economic independence, along with the intermediate outcomes just discussed. Even controlling for mediating re-productive, health, human capital, and delinquency outcomes, access to health insurance while growing up emerges as the strongest single influence on the transition to adulthood, even though these intermediate outcomes were themselves strongly influenced by access to health insurance. In con-trast, after controlling for intermediate outcomes, other material indicators and family circumstances matter little. Family composition, household in-come, family sternness, and family mortality have no direct effect on eco-nomic independence, whereas the effects of parental prestige, parental educa-tion, family mentors, and school disadvantage are small.

Among material indicators, only neighborhood disadvantage has even a modest effect on the transition to adulthood. Among the remaining factors,

Figure 10.5   Conditioning the Transition to Adulthood

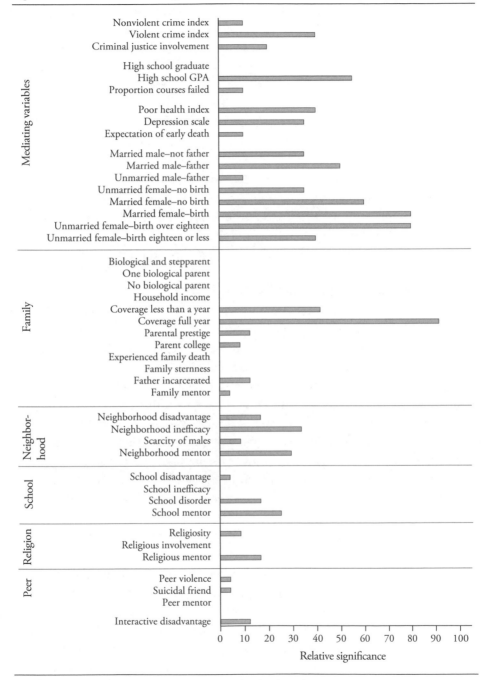

Source: Authors' compilation based on Harris and Udry (2008).

the most significant are neighborhood inefficacy, neighborhood mentors, school mentors, and religious mentors, yet even these are generally small by comparison with the effects of mediating variables. To the extent that they affect the transition to adulthood, therefore, ecological variables tend to do so more indirectly than directly, through their influence on intervening outcomes. Among intervening outcomes, clearly the most important is family status. Specifically, early entry into childbearing and to a lesser extent marriage have highly significant effects on the transition to adulthood, generally working to undermine attainments in higher education, employment, and earnings and to increase the likelihood of dependency. Apart from family status, other important outcomes mediating the transition to adult independence are grade point average in high school, which emerges as far more significant in predicting a successful transition to adulthood than either graduation or course failure, as well as degree of involvement in violent crime, poor health, and depression, all of which tend to inhibit a successful transition.

AN ECOLOGICAL PERSPECTIVE ON POLICY

As with most social science research, this study has its methodological weaknesses and epistemological limitations. Although we took care to sort out the timing of events under analysis by measuring spheres of advantage and disadvantage between 1994 and 2000, intermediate outcomes in 2001 and 2002, and the transition to adulthood in 2007 and 2008 (see figure 1.1), the order in which we considered the intermediate outcomes themselves—reproduction, health, education, crime, and delinquency—was determined by assumption, and even the successive staging of spheres, intermediate outcomes, and adult achievements does not ensure a clean causal interpretation.

As a result, the usual caveats pertain to our results and conclusions given potential biases stemming from the classic epistemological problems of endogeneity, selectivity, and unmeasured heterogeneity. Although we have generally spoken in the language of unidirectional determinism between independent and dependent variables, endogeneity refers to the ever-present possibility of reverse causality, mutual causal influence, or joint determination by a third variable to produce a spurious correlation. Selectivity refers to the fact that the social world systematically selects people to occupy different social categories, which in fact was the point of the entire study. Although we have sought to identify and model critical selective processes, our models may in fact be incorrect or incomplete. As a result, when we attribute an effect to a variable such as access to health insurance, the apparent effect may actually reflect existing differences between those with and without insurance rather than any effect of the insurance itself. Finally, although Add Health is a remarkably comprehensive data set, it is impossible to measure everything. Key determinants of certain outcomes may be unmeasured to exacerbate threats from selectivity.

Bearing these threats to validity in mind, two policy arenas stand out for the extent of their influence on the production and reproduction of disadvantage in the United States. The first is access to health insurance. Compared with other developed nations, the United States has had a decidedly spotty and imperfect health-care system that leaves many people uninsured and uncovered, a pattern exacerbated by the Great Recession of 2008. In our models, access to health insurance is one of the strongest and most consistent predictors of welfare on a variety of key dimensions.

Whether the Patient Protection and Affordable Care Act signed into law by President Obama in 2010 actually functions to alleviate inequities in access to health insurance remains to be seen. For the sake of illustration, however, suppose all American families had full access to health insurance. In the reproductive realm, far more young people would use contraception and fewer would cohabit before marriage, thus lowering the likelihood of early childbearing. With respect to health, fewer would smoke or use hard drugs, and many fewer would come to experience physical limitations, poor physical health, depression, or fatalism about life chances. More human capital would be formed as attention deficit order would be reduced and verbal intelligence would rise, accompanied by rising grade point averages and graduation rates. Even controlling for these intermediate outcomes, full access to health care in adolescence would greatly enhance college admittance, full employment, and earnings in adulthood to dramatically lower rates of public dependency.

Although it is too soon to know exactly how effectively health-care reform will be implemented, our analysis clearly suggests that improving health-care coverage in the United States may well pay important dividends in reducing racial and class inequalities, overcoming persistent disadvantage, and generally enhancing the prospects for economic independence and prosperity. Although the precise causal connections between health insurance and the various outcomes are not always clear and remain to be elucidated, a growing body of research indicates that health insurance, or the lack of it, has strong effects on a remarkable range of outcomes relevant to human well-being beyond health itself (Hadley 2002; Wolman and Wilhelmine 2004; McWilliams 2009).

The second policy arena to stand out in our ecological analysis is the American criminal justice complex. Because of changes in drug laws and criminal procedures during the 1970s and 1980s, the United States came to exhibit the highest rate of incarceration of any nation in the world; the burdens of this mass incarceration fall disproportionately on the socially and economically marginalized, most notably African Americans (Alexander 2010). The irony, of course, is that our data reveal that African Americans living in poor neighborhoods and attending disadvantaged schools are least likely to abuse alcohol and drugs, and that demand for drugs and alcohol in the United States originates primarily among upper-class whites in affluent schools and neighborhoods, meaning that once again poor minorities pay the price for the vices of the elite.

Our work adds to the growing body of work generated by other social scientists to demonstrate the excessive societal costs of mass incarceration (Tonry 1996; Pattillo, Weiman, and Western 2004; Western 2006; Alexander 2010). According to our ecological analyses, reducing the rate of paternal incarceration in the United States would go a long way toward increasing the age of first intercourse, reducing the odds of cohabitation, lowering cigarette consumption, mitigating alcohol abuse, reducing hard drug use, lowering rates of obesity, reducing crime rates, increasing rates of college graduation, and ultimately lower rates of public dependency.

Finally, following earlier observers such as Daniel Patrick Moynihan (1965) and Sara McLanahan and Gary Sandefur (1994), our ecological study underscores the importance of the family as a crucible for generating—and therefore possibly ameliorating—racial and class inequality. As we have seen, the most important mediating variable conditioning the transition to independent adulthood is family status, and unwed and teenage childbearing are a severe drag on attainment among young adults. Increasing insurance coverage and reducing incarceration can be expected to help reduce unwed childbearing and marital disruption, of course, but family sternness, religiosity, and religious participation also appear to be important, along with exposure to peer violence, neighborhood disadvantage, a lack of marriageable males, and social inefficacy within schools and neighborhoods.

Although public policy makers are in no position to advocate religious beliefs or practices or tell families how to raise their children, and whereas disadvantage and inefficacy with neighborhoods are structural features of American society that will be difficult to change in the short run, the work of Frank Furstenberg and colleagues (1999) suggests that one reason stern, religious families are more successful in raising their children to be productive adults is that they insulate them from the deleterious influences of their ecological surroundings through close supervision and control. Given the inability of many poor parents to provide this sort of supervision and control given the multiple challenges and problems they themselves face, a possible alternative is for society to provide the insulation from disadvantaged neighborhoods, peers, and even families by extending the school day, cutting back on the length of summer vacations, expanding day care, and increasing afterschool care. Abundant evidence suggests that the more that poor, disadvantaged young people can be insulated from the deleterious social ecologies that surround them, the better they do in school and therefore in life (Entwisle and Alexander 1982; Entwisle, Alexander, and Olson 1997).

APPENDIX A

Data from the Adolescent Health Survey

The Adolescent Health Survey (Add Health) was launched in the 1994–1995 school year by investigators at the University of North Carolina in Chapel Hill. Using a comprehensive list of high schools in the United States, they created a stratified sample to select eighty schools that were representative of the nation's adolescents with respect to region, metropolitan status, school size, school type, race, and ethnicity. To be eligible for inclusion, a school had to contain an eleventh grade and enroll a total of more than thirty students. The response rate by schools selected for participation was around 70 percent. The survey was longitudinal and unfolded in a series of waves.

ADD HEALTH WAVE 1

After agreeing to participate, officials in each high school were asked to identify feeder schools, defined as those containing a seventh grade, and sending at least five students to the school. Investigators then randomly selected one of these feeder schools with a probability proportional to the number of students it sent to the high school. If the selected school declined to participate, a replacement was selected using the same probability-proportional-to-size method. The final sample included eighty high schools and fifty-two feeder schools, for a total of 132 schools. Twenty-eight of the high schools also included grades seven through twelve and thus did not require sampling additional feeder schools.

All students attending the selected schools were asked to complete a self-administered survey during a specific forty-five- to sixty-minute class period between September 1994 and April 1995. Although make-up surveys were not offered to absent students, parents were notified of the survey date in advance and more than ninety thousand students ultimately completed the questionnaire, which gathered information on students' social and demographic characteristics, household composition, education and occupation of parents, and future expectations, self-esteem, health status, friendships, and extracurricular activities.

Those students who completed the in-school survey were then stratified by grade and sex and a subset of 12,105 respondents were randomly selected for an in-home interview, with over-sampling on the basis of race, ethnicity, and physical disability yielding an additional 471 students with disabilities, 1,038 black students having a parent with a college degree, 334 Chinese students, 450 Cuban students, and 437 Puerto Rican students. The core sample itself included more than 1,500 students of Mexican origin. To undertake detailed studies of social networks, all students in a subset of sixteen schools were selected to participate in the in-home survey, yielding another 2,559 adolescents. For detailed studies of inherited traits and behaviors, a genetic subsample of adolescents residing together was compiled that included 1,981 twins, 1,186 full siblings, 783 half siblings, 415 unrelated adolescents, and 162 siblings of twins, for a total of 4,527. In all, some 21,921 adolescents were interviewed in the first wave survey.

The in-home survey lasted one to two hours and was administered as a computer-assisted personal interview between April and December of 1995. The survey compiled detailed data on the respondent's health status, health service use, nutrition, peer networks, decision processes, family dynamics, educational aspirations, employment experience, romantic partnerships, sexual behavior, substance use, and criminal activities. Respondents also completed an abridged version of the Peabody Picture Vocabulary Test (PVT) and interviewers took down the street address or captured the latitude and longitude of the domicile using a global positioning system (GPS) device, thus enabling complete geocoding of 98 percent of all cases. With appropriate weighting, the Wave 1 sample is representative of adolescents attending grades seven through twelve in the United States during the 1994–1995 school year, when most respondents were age twelve to eighteen.

In addition to interviewing students in the home, Add Health researchers also interviewed a parent (usually the mother) to ask about inheritable health conditions, marriages and partnerships, neighborhood characteristics, organizational involvements, health-related behaviors, educational attainment, employment, income, and transfers, as well as patterns of communication and interaction with the adolescent and familiarity with his or her friends and their families. Administrators from each school were also asked to complete a self-administered questionnaire covering school policies, teacher characteristics, health services, and student body characteristics.

ADD HEALTH WAVE 2

During the following year, Add Health investigators sought to re-interview all respondents who completed the baseline survey, with the exception of former twelfth-graders who had graduated and the disabled sample. The Wave 2 survey took place in respondents' homes from April through August of 1996. In addition to questions asked on the first wave, additional items recorded information on sun exposure, nutrition, and current height and weight. Although parents were not re-interviewed in 1996, school administrators were contacted by telephone and asked to update information from the first year as well as to provide new information on school dress codes and security measures.

ADD HEALTH WAVE 3

From August of 2001 through April of 2002, interviewers sought to interview all respondents to the Wave 1 survey who could be located, including those in correctional facilities but excluding those currently residing abroad. In the end, 15,170 interviews were completed for a follow-up rate of around 69 percent. At the time of the Wave 3 interview, the vast majority of respondents were between the ages of nineteen and twenty-six years and had graduated from high school; many others had graduated from college; and a large share had entered the labor force, either as high school or college graduates. In addition to updating information from Wave 1, the Wave 3 questionnaire compiled histories of relationships, marriages, childbearing, education, and labor force participation and other topics relevant to young adults such as delinquency and violence, criminal justice involvement, use of tobacco, alcohol, and drugs, mistreatment by adults, civic participation, and an accounting of daily activities.

ADD HEALTH WAVE 4

Investigators at the University of North Carolina conducted a fourth in-home interview in 2007 and 2008 with as many of the original Wave 1 respondents who could be located agreed to be interviewed. Wave 4 administered a comprehensive personal interview that collected physical measurements and bio-specimens as well as asking detailed questions about social outcomes and behavior. At the time of the Wave 4 interview, participants were twenty-four to thirty-two years old and most had made the transition to young adulthood. As with prior waves of the survey, investigators obtained longitudinal data on the social, economic, psychological, and health circumstances of respondents as well as longitudinal geographic data.

By the time of Wave 4, the sample had become geographically dispersed, with respondents located in all fifty states. Investigators successfully located 92.5 percent of the Wave 1 sample and interviewed 80.3 percent of eligible sample members through a computer-assisted personal interview that lasted around ninety minutes, which was followed by a thirty-minute session in which interviewers took physical measurements and collected biological specimens. In the end, 15,701 respondents were interviewed for the fourth wave.

CREATION OF WORKING DATA FILES

In this analysis, we seek to draw on the unusually rich data available from the Add Health Survey to assess a respondent's relative access to material, symbolic, and emotional resources in four key ecological settings—families, neighborhoods, schools, and peers—and to measure how advantages and disadvantages experienced in adolescence condition developmental outcomes observed in young adulthood. In terms of the survey's design, we thus seek to measure ecological circumstances experienced by respondents at Wave 1, when they were age twelve to eighteen, or average circumstances they experienced between Waves 1 and 3 as they aged from twelve to eighteen to nineteen to twenty-six, and then to estimate the effect of these ecological exposures to specific outcomes observed at Wave 3, focusing on the domains of social reproduction, health and well-being, cognition and education, criminal justice, and employment.

To compile comprehensive measures of each ecological settings we draw not only on the surveys of adolescents at Waves 1 and 3, but also census tract files derived from the geocodings logged at each survey, the Wave 1 parental survey, the Wave 1 and Wave 2 school-administered surveys. Each survey has its own response rate and missing data, such that the creation of data files built on information from multiple surveys and waves inevitably reduces the final sample size through list-wise deletion of cases. For critical variables such as household income, which always in survey work is plagued by missing data problems, we used multiple imputation to derive estimates so as to maintain a reasonable sample size. When all was said and done, the final working file created by combining data from the adolescent, parent, and administrator surveys, the three waves of the basic adolescent survey, and the geocoded census tract files associated with each wave yielded a working data set with 8,998 cases. Because of item nonresponse and other sources of missing data for specific variables, the total number of cases available for multivariate analyses will generally fall below this maximum.

Although this is quite a large sample overall, when it is broken down into race-class categories, some of the resulting cells can be quite small. Given their numerical dominance in the population, cell sizes for whites are generally sufficient. When the sample's 5,039 whites are classified by quartile in the overall income distribution, for example, the resulting cell sizes are 925 for the lower class, 1,149 for the lower middle class, 1,148 for the upper middle class, and 1,537 for the upper class. Given their status as the nation's two largest minorities, the subdivision of 1,894 black and 1,482 Hispanic respondents by class also yields reasonably large cell sizes. Among blacks, we get 739 in the lower class, 443 in the lower middle class, 361 in the upper middle class, and 303 in the upper class, and among Hispanics the corresponding cell sizes are 568, 411, 304, and 199.

The most limited cell sizes naturally occur for Asians, who constitute a relatively small proportion of the student population, only one of whose constituent groups was oversampled. Subdividing Add Health's 629 Asians by class yields more problematic cell sizes of 83, 147, 164, and 235, respectively, moving from lower to upper class. Thus we expect to observe the greatest sampling variability in computing class-specific indicators for Asians and the greatest stability in computing these indicators for whites, calculations for Hispanics and African Americans generally falling between the two in terms of reliability.

In the final analytic chapter, we draw on information from Wave 4 to assess how adolescent social ecology and the intermediate conditions attained in Wave 3 conditioned the final transition to adulthood. The accumulated attrition of the sample from both unit and item nonresponse across the four waves yielded a final panel of 7,866 respondents with completed interviews across all the survey waves, including 4,527 whites, 395 Asians, 1,234 Hispanics, and 1,610 blacks, though again in specific model estimations these numbers will tend to be reduced because of item nonresponse. Obviously the reductions between Waves 3 and 4 exacerbate the sample size difficulties noted earlier, especially with respect to Asians. Means, standard deviations, and ranges for all variables used in the analyses are presented in table A1.

Table A.1   Means, Standard Deviations, and Ranges of Principal Variables

Variable	Mean	SD	Minimum	Maximum
Independent variables				
Age at Wave 3	21.45	1.67	18	27
Parent foreign born	0.148	0.355	0	1
Married male–not father	0.025	0.157	0	1
Married male–father	0.030	0.170	0	1
Unmarried male–father	0.048	0.215	0	1
Unmarried female–no birth	0.317	0.215	0	1
Married female–no birth	0.041	0.198	0	1
Married female–mother	0.057	0.231	0	1
Unmarried female-birth over eighteen	0.059	0.236	0	1
Unmarried female-birth eighteen or younger	0.024	0.154	0	1
Living with stepparent at Wave 1	0.083	0.276	0	1
Living with single parent at Wave 1	0.313	0.464	0	1
Living with no parent at Wave 1	0.013	0.113	0	1
Household income ($000)	40.58	23.30	0	80
Had health insurance less than a year	0.180	0.384	0	1
Had health insurance full year	0.625	0.484	0	1
Parental occupational status	39.41	19.20	0	78
Parent college educated	0.497	0.500	0	1
Death in family	0.070	0.256	0	1
Family sternness scale	76.17	15.33	1	101
Father incarcerated	0.141	0.348	0	1

Table A.1   (continued)

Variable	Mean	SD	Minimum	Maximum
Had family mentor	0.267	0.442	0	1
Neighborhood disadvantage index	0.782	0.643	0.077	4.047
Neighborhood inefficacy index	3.775	2.990	0	16
Ratio never married women to men	0.863	0.285	0	11.533
Had neighborhood mentor	0.072	0.285	0	1
School disadvantage index	20.36	7.391	3	42
School inefficacy index	12.78	6.530	0	40
School disorder index	8.612	2.928	0	19
Had school mentor	0.812	0.386	0	1
Religiosity scale	12.34	5.560	0	18
Religious involvement index	5.442	4.017	0	12
Had religious mentor	0.026	0.161	0	1
Peer violence index	1.847	2.744	0	20
Friend attempted suicide	0.081	0.273	0	1
Had peer mentor	0.213	0.409	0	1
Logged interactive index	32.90	5.448	14.697	51.166
Dependent variables				
Chapter 4				
Ever had intercourse	0.861	0.346	0	1
Age at first intercourse	16.33	2.21	10	25
Unprotected first intercourse	0.360	0.480	0	1
Parenthood outside or inside marriage	0.305	0.620	0	2
Parenthood below or above age eighteen	0.403	0.764	0	2
Ever married	0.171	0.377	0	1
Ever pregnant	0.060	0.238	0	1
Chapter 5				
Ever smoked cigarettes regularly	0.429	0.495	0	1
Age began smoking	16.27	2.39	5	25
Drunk more than once a month	0.531	0.499	0	1
Used hard drugs (not marijuana)	0.206	0.404	0	1
Ate fast food during past week	0.823	0.382	0	1
Ever had sex for pay or with drug user	0.057	0.232	0	1
Body mass index	26.59	6.41	14.31	62.41

Table A.1   (continued)

Variable	Mean	SD	Minimum	Maximum
Obesity	0.237	0.425	0	1
Has limitation on activity	0.259	0.438	0	1
Ever diagnosed with STD	0.081	0.273	0	1
Poor health index	2.01	0.869	1	5
Depression scale	4.54	4.05	0	25
Scale of likelihood of early death	2.51	2.30	0	15
Chapter 6				
ADHD score	14.46	10.94	0	144
Picture vocabulary score	99.45	14.78	7	122
GPA	2.48	0.867	0.001	4
Proportion courses failed	0.093	0.170	0	1
Graduated high school	0.799	0.401	0	1
Chapter 7				
Nonviolent crime index	0.557	1.570	0	21
Violent crime index	0.515	1.459	0	21
Index of criminal justice involvement				
Chapter 8				
College graduate	0.303	0.016	0	1
Graduate degree	0.062	0.004	0	1
Part-time worker	0.110	0.003	0	1
Full-time worker	0.717	0.011	0	1

Source: Authors' calculations based on data set described in Harris and Udry (2008).

APPENDIX B

Construction of Indices

Table B.1   Indices

	Min	Max
Family mortality		
Wave 1 adolescent in-home interview		
Nonresidential biological mother died before age eighteen (yes or no)	0	1
Nonresidential biological father died before age eighteen (yes or no)	0	1
Wave 3 adolescent in-home interview		
Sibling died before age eighteen (yes or no)	0	1
Residential mother died before age eighteen (yes or no)	0	1
Residential father died before age eighteen (yes or no)	0	1
Scale range (dichotomy, 1 if experienced any of above events, 0 otherwise)	0	1
Family sternness		
Wave 1 adolescent in-home interview		
How much adults care about R (very much–not at all)	0	4
How much parents care about R (very much–not at all)	0	4
How much family members understand R (very much–not at all)	0	4
How much R feels like wants to leave home (not at all–very much)	0	4
How much family has fun together (very much–not at all)	0	4
How much family pays attention to R (very much–not at all)	0	4
Mother is warm and loving (strongly agree–strongly disagree)	0	4
Mother talks to understand what is wrong (strongly agree–strongly disagree)	0	4
Satisfaction with communication with mother (strongly agree–strongly disagree)	0	4

Table B.1   (*continued*)

	Min	Max
Satisfaction with relationship with mother (strongly agree-strongly disagree)	0	4
Wave 2 adolescent in-home interview		
How much adults care about R (very much-not at all)	0	4
How much parents care about R (very much-not at all)	0	4
How much family members understand R (very much-not at all)	0	4
How much R feels like wants to leave home (not at all-very much)	0	4
How much family has fun together (very much-not at all)	0	4
How much family pays attention to R (very much-not at all)	0	4
Mother is warm and loving (strongly agree-strongly disagree)	0	4
Mother talks to understand what is wrong (strongly agree-strongly disagree)	0	4
Satisfaction with communication with mother (strongly agree-strongly disagree)	0	4
Satisfaction with relationship with mother (strongly agree-strongly disagree)	0	4
Scale range (sum)	0	80
Cronbach's alpha		0.896
Neighborhood disadvantage		
Wave 1 census tract file		
Percentage receiving welfare	0	100
Percentage in poverty	0	100
Percentage unemployed	0	100
Percentage female-headed households	0	100
Percentage African American	0	100
Wave 3 census tract file		
Percentage receiving welfare	0	100
Percentage in poverty	0	100
Percentage unemployed	0	100
Percentage female-headed households	0	100
Percentage African American	0	100
Scale range (weighted factor score)	0.36	19.70
Cronbach's alpha		0.828
Neighborhood inefficacy		
Wave 1 adolescent in-home interview		
R knows most people in neighborhood (yes or no)	0	1
In past month R stopped to talk to neighbor on street (yes or no)	0	1
People in neighborhood look out for one another (yes or no)	0	1

Table B.1   (continued)

	Min	Max
R usually feels safe in neighborhood (yes or no)	0	1
Happiness with life in neighborhood (very much-not at all)	0	4
Wave 2 adolescent in-home interview		
R knows most people in neighborhood (yes or no)	0	1
In past month R stopped to talk to neighbor on street (yes or no)	0	1
People in neighborhood look out for one another (yes or no)	0	1
R usually feels safe in neighborhood (yes or no)	0	1
Happiness with life in neighborhood (very much-not at all)	0	4
Scale range (Sum)	0	16
Cronbach's alpha		0.697
School disadvantage		
Wave 1 school administrator questionnaire		
Average daily attendance (five categories, >=95 percent to 75–79 percent)	0	4
Average class size (eight categories, ten to thirteen to thirty-eight to forty-one)	0	8
Percent teachers at school five years or more (eight categories, 0–12.5 to 87.5–100)	0	8
Percent teachers with a master's or higher (eight categories, 0–12.5 to 87.5–100)	0	8
Percentage dropping out during year (six categories, 0–16.7 to 83.3–100)	0	6
Percentage of students testing below grade level (four categories, 0–24 to 75–100)	0	4
Athletic physical and non-athletic physical services provided or referred (yes or no)	0	1
Wave 1 in-school adolescent questionnaire		
Percentage students nonwhite (four categories, 0–24 to 75–100)	0	4
Percentage students not in clubs, organizations, teams (four categories, 0–19 to 30–40)	0	4
Scale range (sum)	0	47
Cronbach's alpha		0.687
School inefficacy		
Wave 1 adolescent in-home interview		
How much teachers care about R (very much-not at all)	0	4
R feels close to people at school (strongly agree-strongly disagree)	0	4
R feels part of school (strongly agree-strongly disagree)	0	4
R is happy to be at school (strongly agree-strongly disagree)	0	4
Teachers treat students fairly (strongly agree-strongly disagree)	0	4

Table B.1   (continued)

	Min	Max
Wave 2 adolescent in-home interview		
How much teachers care about R (very much-not at all)	0	4
R feels close to people at school (strongly agree-strongly disagree)	0	4
R feels part of school (strongly agree-strongly disagree)	0	4
R is happy to be at school (strongly agree-strongly disagree)	0	4
Teachers treat students fairly (strongly agree-strongly disagree)	0	4
Scale range (sum)	0	40
Cronbach's alpha		0.814
School disorder		
Wave 1 adolescent in-home interview		
R feels safe at school (strongly agree-strongly disagree)	0	4
Wave 2 adolescent in-home interview		
R feels safe at school (strongly agree-strongly disagree)	0	4
Wave 2 school administrator questionnaire		
Security or police officer on duty (no or yes)	0	1
Other security or safety features (no or yes)	0	1
How big a problem is smoking (no problem-big problem)	0	2
How big a problem is drug use (no problem-big problem)	0	2
How big a problem is sexual harassment (no problem-big problem)	0	2
How big a problem is vandalism (no problem-big problem)	0	2
How big a problem is stress or pressure (no problem-big problem)	0	2
Scale range (sum)	0	20
Cronbach's alpha		0.602
Peer violence		
Wave 1 adolescent in-home interview		
In past 12 months R saw shooting or stabbing (never-once-more than once)	0	2
In past 12 months someone pulled a gun or knife on R (never-once-more than once)	0	2
In past 12 months someone cut or stabbed R (never-once-more than once)	0	2
In past 12 months R got into a physical fight (never-once-more than once)	0	2
In past 12 months R was jumped (never-once-more than once)	0	2
Wave 2 adolescent in-home interview		
In past 12 months R saw shooting or stabbing (never-once-more than once)	0	2

Table B.1 (continued)

	Min	Max
In past 12 months someone pulled a gun or knife on R (never-once-more than once)	0	2
In past 12 months someone cut or stabbed R (never-once-more than once)	0	2
In past 12 months was in a serious fight (never-once-more than once)	0	2
In past 12 months R was jumped (never-once-more than once)	0	2
Did any romantic partner call R names, insulted, or treated disrespectfully (no or yes)	0	1
Did any romantic partner swear at R (no or yes)	0	1
Did any romantic partner threaten R with violence (no or yes)	0	1
Did any romantic partner push or shove R (no or yes)	0	1
Did any romantic partners throw something that could hurt R (no or yes)	0	1
Scale Range (sum)	0	25
Cronbach's alpha		0.778

Index of cumulative disadvantage
   Family context
      Income deprivation   [1- (R's Income/90th Percentile Income)]*100 + 1
      Status deprivation   [1- (SEI of R's Parent /Maximum SEI)]*100 + 1
      Human capital deprivation   [1 if No Parent Attended College, 0 Otherwise]*100 + 1
      Paternal deprivation   [1 if Father Never Present, 0 Otherwise]*100 + 1
      Family mortality   [1 if Family Member Died, 0 Otherwise]*100 + 1
      Family sternness   [R's Sternness Index /Maximum Sternness Index]*100 + 1
   Neighborhood context
      Material disadvantage   [R's Disadvantage Index/Max. Disadvantage Index]*100 + 1
      Social inefficacy   [R's Inefficacy Index/Maximum Inefficacy Index]*100 + 1
   School context
      Material disadvantage   [R's Disadvantage Index/Max. Disadvantage Index]*100 + 1
      Social inefficacy   [R's Inefficacy Index/Maximum Inefficacy Index]*100 + 1
      Social disorder   [R's Disorder Index/Maximum Disorder Index]*100 + 1
   Peer context
      Interpersonal violence [R's Violence Index/Maximum Violence Index]*100 + 1

Religiosity scale
   Wave 1 adolescent in-home interview

	Min	Max
R reports having a religion	0	1
R agrees that scripture is word of God	0	1

Table B.1   (continued)

	Min	Max
Importance of religion to R (not important–very important)	0	4
How often R prays (never–at least once a day)	0	5
Wave 2 adolescent in-home interview		
R reports having a religion	0	1
R agrees that scripture is word of God	0	1
Importance of religion to R (not important–very important)	0	4
How often R prays (never–at least once a day)	0	5
Scale range (sum)	0	22
Cronbach's alpha		0.838
Religious involvement scale		
Wave 1 adolescent in-home interview		
Frequency of service attendance (never–once a week or more)	0	4
Frequency of participation in youth activities (never–once a week or more)	0	4
Wave 2 adolescent in-home interview		
Frequency of service attendance (never–once a week or more)	0	4
Frequency of participation in youth activities (never–once a week or more)	0	4
Scale range	0	16
Cronbach's alpha		0.854
Depression index		
Wave 3 adolescent in-home interview		
How often health or emotional problem caused R to miss day of school (never–every day)	0	4
How often health or emotional problem caused R to miss social activity (never–every day)	0	4
How often last week R bothered by things that usually don't bother (never–all the time)	0	3
How often last week R didn't feel like eating (never–all the time)	0	3
How often last week R could not shake off the blues (never–all the time)	0	3
How often last week R felt that just as good as other people (all the time–never)	0	3
How often last week R had trouble keeping mind on what was doing (never–all the time)	0	3
How often last week R felt depressed (never–all the time)	0	3
How often last week R felt that too tired to do things (never–all the time)	0	3
How often last week R felt hopeful about the future (never–all the time)	0	3

Table B.1   (continued)

	Min	Max
How often last week R thought life had been a failure (never-all the time)	0	3
How often last week R felt fearful (never-all the time)	0	3
How often last week R felt happy (all the time-rarely)	0	3
How often last week R talked less than usual (never-all the time)	0	3
How often last week R felt lonely (never-all the time)	0	3
How often last week people unfriendly to R (all the time-never)	0	3
How often last week R enjoyed life (all the time-never)	0	3
How often last week R felt sad (never-all the time)	0	3
How often last week felt people disliked R (never-all the time)	0	3
How often last week R felt hard to get started (never-all the time)	0	3
How often last week R felt life not worth living (never-all the time)	0	3
Scale range (sum)	0	65
Cronbach's alpha		0.801
Likelihood of early death index		
Wave 1 adolescent in-home interview		
Chances of living to age thirty-five (almost certain-almost no chance)	0	4
Chances of being killed by age twenty-one (almost no chance-almost certain)	0	4
Wave 2 adolescent in-home interview		
Chances of living to age thirty-five (almost certain-almost no chance)	0	4
Chances of being killed by age twenty-one (almost no chance-almost certain)	0	4
Scale range	0	16
Cronbach's alpha		0.647
Nonviolent crime index		
Wave 3 adolescent in-home interview		
How often deliberately damaged property (never, 1–2, 3–4, 5 or more)	0	3
How often stole something worth less than $50 (never, 1–2, 3–4, 5 or more)	0	3
How often stole something worth more than $50 (never, 1–2, 3–4, 5 or more)	0	3
How often went into house or building to steal something (never, 1–2, 3–4, 5 or more)	0	3
How often bought, sold, or held stolen property (never, 1–2, 3–4, 5 or more)	0	3

Table B.1   (continued)

	Min	Max
How often used someone else's credit card, bank card, or ATM	0	3
How often sold marijuana or other drugs (never, 1–2, 3–4, 5 or more)	0	3
Scale range	0	21
Cronbach's alpha		0.693
Violent crime index		
Wave 3 adolescent in-home interview		
How often use or threaten to use a weapon to get something (never, 1–2, 3–4, 5 or more)	0	3
How often used a weapon in a fight (never, 1–2, 3–4, 5 or more)	0	3
How often carry a handgun to school or work (never, 1–2, 3–4, 5 or more)	0	3
Number of handguns owned (none, 1, 2, 2–4, 5+)	0	4
How often got badly injured in a fight (none, 1, 2, 3–4, 5 or more)	0	4
How often hurt someone badly in a fight (never, 1–2, 3–4, 5 or more)	0	4
How often took part in a fight between friends and another group (0, 1, 2, 3 or more)	0	3
Scale range	0	24
Cronbach's alpha		0.670
Criminal justice involvement index		
Wave 3 adolescent in-home interview		
How often stopped by police for questioning (0–4)	0	4
How many times arrested before eighteen (never, 1–2, 3–4, 5 or more)	0	4
Number of convictions and guilty pleas (none, 1–2, 3–4, 5 or more)	0	4
Total duration of time spent in detention or probation (0, 1–2, 3–4, 5+ months)	0	4
Ever in jail or prison	0	1
Scale range	0	17
Cronbach's alpha		20.575

Source: Authors' calculations based on data set described in Harris and Udry (2008).

APPENDIX C

Table C.1   Comparison of Race-Class Group Effects in Full and Reduced Samples

	Full Sample		Reduced Sample	
	B	SE	B	SE
Chapter 4				
Predicting first female intercourse				
	N=4,718		N=3,738	
White lower	0.957***	0.248	1.117***	0.245
White lower middle	0.334+	0.174	0.172	0.197
White upper middle	0.131	0.185	0.149	0.191
White upper	—	—	—	—
Asian lower	0.786	0.644	1.037	0.764
Asian lower middle	−0.474	0.409	−0.365	0.468
Asian upper middle	−0.767+	0.450	−0.662	0.453
Asian upper	−0.626	0.411	−0.715+	0.445
Hispanic lower	−0.109	0.187	−0.113	0.214
Hispanic lower middle	0.141	0.374	0.094	0.424
Hispanic upper middle	−0.317	0.376	−0.383	0.407
Hispanic upper	1.596**	0.538	1.216	0.544
Black lower	1.039**	0.324	1.163***	0.325
Black lower middle	1.292***	0.361	1.256**	0.419
Black upper middle	0.842**	0.316	0.486	0.329
Black upper	0.427	0.383	0.232	0.400
Predicting age at first female intercourse				
	N=4,072		N=3,204	
White lower	−0.691***	0.152	−0.623***	0.191
White lower middle	−0.599***	0.155	−0.555***	0.166

Table C.1   (continued)

	Full Sample		Reduced Sample	
	B	SE	B	SE
White upper middle	−0.269	0.177	−0.308+	0.173
White upper	—	—	—	—
Asian lower	1.009*	0.500	0.924+	0.534
Asian lower middle	1.677*	0.563	1.699*	0.742
Asian upper middle	−0.339	0.830	−0.216	0.895
Asian upper	0.578+	0.336	0.716	0.430
Hispanic lower	0.267	0.456	0.233	0.449
Hispanic lower middle	0.006	0.422	−0.159	0.417
Hispanic upper middle	−0.091	0.374	−0.256	0.426
Hispanic upper	0.019	0.435	0.531	0.542
Black lower	−0.637***	0.175	−0.653***	0.187
Black lower middle	−0.713***	0.209	−0.722**	0.261
Black upper middle	−0.243	0.293	−0.458+	0.271
Black upper	−0.461	0.313	−0.339	0.329

Predicting first male intercourse

	N=4,192		N=3,390	
White lower	0.341	0.215	0.496*	0.252
White lower middle	0.350+	0.204	0.240	0.218
White upper middle	0.049	0.201	0.040	0.223
White upper	—	—	—	—
Asian lower	−1.587**	0.599	−2.268***	0.676
Asian lower middle	−0.326	0.435	−0.747+	0.454
Asian upper middle	−0.854+	0.464	−0.802	0.504
Asian upper	−0.332	0.330	−0.544	0.372
Hispanic lower	0.322	0.346	0.084	0.331
Hispanic lower middle	0.901*	0.391	1.160**	0.383
Hispanic upper middle	0.187	0.433	0.322	0.435
Hispanic upper	0.474	0.442	0.500	0.487
Black lower	0.371	0.239	0.642*	0.283
Black lower middle	0.691+	0.390	0.859+	0.452
Black upper middle	0.356	0.412	0.306	0.416
Black upper	0.308	0.403	0.142	0.405

Predicting age of first male intercourse

	N=3,542		N=2,846	
White lower	−0.480**	0.168	−0.293	0.185
White lower middle	−0.320+	0.171	−0.250	0.178

Table C.1   (continued)

	Full Sample		Reduced Sample	
	B	SE	B	SE
White upper middle	0.163	0.151	0.215	0.149
White upper	—	—	—	—
Asian lower	0.792	0.644	1.571***	0.351
Asian lower middle	0.875*	0.404	0.621	0.445
Asian upper middle	0.484	0.441	0.329	0.505
Asian upper	1.011*	0.465	0.375	0.407
Hispanic lower	−0.604*	0.283	−0.413	0.299
Hispanic lower middle	−0.869**	0.294	−1.004***	0.291
Hispanic upper middle	−0.528	0.483	−0.446	0.471
Hispanic upper	−0.476	0.304	−0.591	0.390
Black lower	−1.324***	0.276	−1.487***	0.295
Black lower middle	−1.240***	0.263	−1.297***	0.319
Black upper middle	−1.223***	0.296	−0.754**	0.284
Black upper	−1.105**	0.344	−0.907**	0.351

Predicting likelihood of first female intercourse without contraception

	N=4,034		N=3,167	
White lower	0.467**	0.164	0.540***	0.164
White lower middle	0.285+	0.163	0.284	0.185
White upper middle	0.186	0.155	0.206	0.161
White upper	—	—	—	—
Asian lower	0.095	0.523	0.226	0.548
Asian lower middle	0.335	0.429	0.394	0.483
Asian upper middle	0.193	0.605	0.310	0.613
Asian upper	0.202	0.307	0.068	0.388
Hispanic lower	0.378	0.264	0.473+	0.291
Hispanic lower middle	0.566*	0.248	0.661*	0.307
Hispanic upper middle	0.335	0.312	0.229	0.344
Hispanic upper	0.383	0.314	0.269	0.424
Black lower	0.046	0.179	−0.020	0.195
Black lower middle	−0.068	0.232	−0.097	0.294
Black upper middle	0.055	0.231	0.102	0.289
Black upper	−0.190	0.309	−0.195	0.315

Predicting likelihood of first male intercourse without contraception

	N=3,479		N=2,793	
White lower	0.234	0.163	0.186	0.178
White lower middle	−0.174	0.174	−0.212	0.201

Table C.1   (continued)

	Full Sample		Reduced Sample	
	B	SE	B	SE
White upper middle	0.090	0.135	0.122	0.143
White upper	—	—	—	—
Asian lower	−2.517***	0.657	−1.956**	0.628
Asian lower middle	−0.253	0.585	−0.459	0.576
Asian upper middle	−0.094	0.447	−0.002	0.505
Asian upper	−0.028	0.332	0.092	0.386
Hispanic lower	0.323	0.262	0.345	0.262
Hispanic lower middle	0.109	0.253	0.009	0.333
Hispanic upper middle	−0.078	0.318	−0.056	0.350
Hispanic upper	0.239	0.377	0.383	0.390
Black lower	−0.271	0.205	−0.174	0.246
Black lower middle	−0.144	0.254	0.115	0.273
Black upper middle	−0.144	0.297	−0.028	0.337
Black upper	0.250	0.382	0.164	0.391

	Marriage	Cohabitation	Marriage	Cohabitation
	B	B	B	B

Predicting likelihood of female marriage and cohabitation (standard errors not shown)

	N=4,755		N=3,733	
White lower	0.498***	0.584***	0.483**	0.589***
White lower middle	0.403***	0.353***	0.377**	0.347***
White upper middle	0.224**	0.108	0.246*	0.105
White upper	—	—	—	—
Asian lower	0.316	−0.294	0.389	−0.180
Asian lower middle	0.032	−0.471	0.207	−0.262
Asian upper middle	0.147	−0.253	0.302	−0.059
Asian upper	0.132	−0.600**	0.126	−0.846***
Hispanic lower	0.506*	0.081	0.439**	0.158
Hispanic lower middle	0.382**	0.053	0.397*	0.064
Hispanic upper middle	0.192	0.067	0.189	0.029
Hispanic upper	−0.216	0.066	−0.141	−0.067
Black lower	−0.141	0.216*	−0.142	0.239*
Black lower middle	−0.029	0.154	0.025	0.110
Black upper middle	−0.149	−0.318*	−0.209	−0.318*
Black upper	−0.560**	−0.122	−0.816***	−0.137

Table C.1   (*continued*)

	Full Sample		Reduced Sample	
	B	SE	B	SE

Predicting likelihood of male marriage and cohabitation (standard errors not shown)

	N=4,219		N=3,384	
White lower	0.280*	0.532***	0.313*	0.607***
White lower middle	0.209	0.290***	0.249	0.393***
White upper middle	0.191	0.139	0.231*	0.162+
White upper	—	—	—	—
Asian lower	−0.064	−0.441	−1.066**	−0.215
Asian lower middle	−0.773*	−0.417	−1.375***	−0.745+
Asian upper middle	−0.133	−0.129	−0.098	−0.099
Asian upper	0.137	−0.350+	0.192	−0.264
Hispanic lower	0.571***	0.280+	0.684***	0.227
Hispanic lower middle	0.432**	0.257+	0.547**	0.364*
Hispanic upper middle	0.349+	0.052	0.511**	−0.035
Hispanic upper	0.042	−0.259	0.197	−0.332+
Black lower	0.103	0.376*	0.021	0.344*
Black lower middle	0.045	0.002	0.116	0.393*
Black upper middle	0.080	0.305	0.108	0.038
Black upper	−0.461	−0.570***	−0.317	0.277

	Nonmarital	Marital	Nonmarital	Marital
	B	B	B	B

Predicting likelihood of motherhood inside and outside marriage (standard errors not shown)

	N=4,767		N=3,860	
White lower	1.562***	1.229***	1.615***	1.099***
White lower middle	0.846**	0.938***	0.769**	0.923**
White upper middle	0.570*	0.520	0.629*	0.569*
White upper	—	—	—	—
Asian lower	−2.534***	−0.103	−2.708**	0.013
Asian lower middle	−0.031	0.767	0.410	1.121*
Asian upper middle	−0.926	−2.347**	−0.590	−2.099*
Asian upper	−1.131	0.730	−2.610***	0.864
Hispanic lower	1.250***	1.227***	1.492***	0.965**
Hispanic lower middle	1.616***	1.381***	1.707***	1.406***
Hispanic upper middle	1.243**	0.766+	1.366**	0.549
Hispanic upper	1.111*	−1.926**	0.533	−2.749***

Table C.1   (continued)

	Full Sample		Reduced Sample	
	B	SE	B	SE
Black lower	2.112***	0.614*	2.229***	0.664+
Black lower middle	1.974***	0.458	2.247***	0.671
Black upper middle	1.314***	0.676	1.399***	0.508
Black upper	1.379***	−0.325	1.665***	−1.489*

Predicting likelihood of fatherhood inside and outside of marriage (standard errors not shown)

	N=4,230		N=3,298	
White lower	0.971***	0.734*	0.682*	0.766*
White lower middle	0.680*	0.456	0.596+	0.578
White upper middle	−0.028	0.438	−0.149	0.419
White upper	—	—	—	—
Asian lower	−2.816**	−2.140*	−3.195**	2.153*
Asian lower middle	−2.427***	−35.797***	−2.235***	−29.765***
Asian upper middle	−0.599	−0.229	−0.508	−0.551
Asian upper	−4.007***	0.979	−3.838***	1.008
Hispanic lower	1.420***	1.395***	1.242***	1.330***
Hispanic lower middle	1.219**	1.157**	1.389***	1.242*
Hispanic upper middle	1.499***	0.597	1.521***	0.871
Hispanic upper	−0.194	0.506	−0.033	0.766
Black lower	1.458***	−0.165	1.575***	−0.647
Black lower middle	1.269***	0.412	0.881*	0.331
Black upper middle	1.378***	0.707	1.482***	0.573
Black upper	1.962***	−0.147	1.877***	0.143

	Nonmarital	Marital	Nonmarital	Marital
	B	SE	B	SE

Predicting likelihood of motherhood before age eighteen

	N=4,763		N=3,678	
White lower	1.102***	0.299	0.889**	0.312
White lower middle	0.745*	0.381	0.387	0.402
White upper middle	0.049	0.354	−0.224	0.368
White upper	—	—	—	—
Asian lower	−3.208**	1.110	−3.194**	1.120
Asian lower middle	−0.545	0.922	−0.413	0.951
Asian upper middle	−2.291***	0.592	−2.460**	0.885
Asian upper	−3.023***	0.728	−2.803***	0.708

Table C.1   (continued)

	Full Sample		Reduced Sample	
	B	SE	B	SE
Hispanic lower	1.009*	0.436	0.813	0.521
Hispanic lower middle	1.377*	0.542	1.255*	0.540
Hispanic upper middle	0.638	0.508	0.157	0.618
Hispanic upper	0.897+	0.536	−0.010	0.904
Black lower	1.404***	0.179	1.379***	0.349
Black lower middle	1.129**	0.382	1.175***	0.379
Black upper middle	1.364**	0.428	1.323**	0.458
Black upper	1.171*	.572	1.125+	0.613

Chapter 5
Predicting regular smoking

	N=8,981		N=7,169	
White lower	0.387***	0.109	0.327**	0.122
White lower middle	0.334***	0.100	0.312**	0.110
White upper middle	0.147	0.092	0.175	0.096
White upper	—	—	—	—
Asian lower	−0.644	0.468	−0.793	0.525
Asian lower middle	−0.709+	0.394	−0.585	0.420
Asian upper middle	−0.435	0.350	−0.262	0.382
Asian upper	−0.671***	0.241	−0.613*	0.249
Hispanic lower	−0.562***	0.155	−0.738***	0.181
Hispanic lower middle	−0.546*	0.215	−0.440+	0.237
Hispanic upper middle	−0.281	0.233	−0.247	0.233
Hispanic upper	−0.290	0.293	−0.277	0.302
Black lower	−0.933***	0.170	−0.877***	0.155
Black lower middle	−0.644**	0.239	−0.526+	0.292
Black upper middle	−1.435***	0.221	−1.443***	0.226
Black upper	−0.816**	0.281	−0.829**	0.327

Predicting age when regular smoking began

	N=3,378		N=2,670	
White lower	−0.890***	0.167	−0.985***	0.184
White lower middle	−0.509***	0.138	−0.464**	0.151
White upper middle	−0.248	0.158	−0.128	0.165
White upper	—	—	—	—
Asian lower	−0.698	0.867	−0.964	1.135
Asian lower middle	0.387	0.520	0.485	0.609

Table C.1   (continued)

	Full Sample		Reduced Sample	
	B	SE	B	SE
Asian upper middle	1.297***	0.367	1.230***	0.371
Asian upper	1.092***	0.319	0.898**	0.350
Hispanic lower	0.272	0.269	0.539+	0.282
Hispanic lower middle	−0.840*	0.392	−1.004*	0.404
Hispanic upper middle	0.516	0.510	0.780	0.517
Hispanic upper	−0.164	0.339	−0.497	0.449
Black lower	0.493+	0.268	0.399	0.328
Black lower middle	0.784*	0.362	0.847*	0.423
Black upper middle	1.161**	0.385	1.434***	0.450
Black upper	0.736*	0.295	0.432	0.483
Predicting alcohol abuse				
	N=8,949		N=7,146	
White lower	−1.024***	0.122	−1.047***	0.144
White lower middle	−0.578***	0.105	−0.601***	0.119
White upper middle	−0.509***	0.111	−0.482***	0.112
White upper	—	—	—	—
Asian lower	−1.746***	0.476	−1.977***	0.539
Asian lower middle	−1.441***	0.296	−1.061***	0.325
Asian upper middle	−1.167***	0.289	−1.143***	0.329
Asian upper	−1.131***	0.227	−1.109***	0.258
Hispanic lower	−1.294***	0.141	−1.284***	0.169
Hispanic lower middle	−1.199***	0.151	−1.311***	0.187
Hispanic upper middle	−0.790***	0.188	−0.884***	0.200
Hispanic upper	−0.727**	0.232	−0.487*	0.229
Black lower	−2.034***	0.165	−1.999***	0.162
Black lower middle	−1.376***	0.152	−1.466***	0.191
Black upper middle	−1.749***	0.187	−1.666***	0.191
Black upper	−1.418***	0.175	−1.543***	0.206
Predicting hard drug use				
	N=8,996		N=7,147	
White lower	−0.375***	0.136	−0.314*	0.159
White lower middle	−0.218+	0.129	−0.201	0.146
White upper middle	−0.298*	0.126	−0.284*	0.127
White upper	—	—	—	—
Asian lower	−1.068*	0.540	−1.194*	0.590
Asian lower middle	−0.796+	0.484	−0.474	0.544

Table C.1 (continued)

	Full Sample		Reduced Sample	
	B	SE	B	SE
Asian upper middle	−0.474	0.373	−0.280	0.369
Asian upper	−0.795*	0.348	−0.891*	0.418
Hispanic lower	−0.507**	0.174	−0.393+	0.208
Hispanic lower middle	−0.546*	0.227	−0.479*	0.244
Hispanic upper middle	−0.479+	0.246	−0.560*	0.259
Hispanic upper	−0.162	0.301	0.032	0.317
Black lower	−2.049***	0.259	−1.884***	0.276
Black lower middle	−1.174***	0.268	−1.058***	0.308
Black upper middle	−2.288***	0.479	−2.279***	0.571
Black upper	−1.770***	0.339	−1.606***	0.357

Predicting consumption of fast food

	N=8,995		N=7,173	
White lower	0.581***	0.144	0.551***	0.164
White lower middle	0.408***	0.112	0.465***	0.131
White upper middle	0.197	0.121	0.161	0.130
White upper	—	—	—	—
Asian lower	0.129	0.418	−0.095	0.436
Asian lower middle	0.272	0.390	0.698	0.401
Asian upper middle	−0.245	0.360	−0.193	0.379
Asian upper	−0.117	0.266	−0.226	0.323
Hispanic lower	0.734***	0.221	0.847***	0.240
Hispanic lower middle	0.876***	0.217	0.951***	0.286
Hispanic upper middle	0.383	0.276	0.321	0.299
Hispanic upper	0.103	0.295	0.214	0.305
Black lower	0.568***	0.164	0.863***	0.214
Black lower middle	0.636**	0.210	0.954***	0.263
Black upper middle	0.790**	0.260	1.019***	0.244
Black upper	0.711+	0.416	0.891*	0.429

Predicting engaging in risky sex (paid or with drug dealer)

	N=8,969		N=7,164	
White lower	0.577***	0.255	0.372	0.311
White lower middle	0.608**	0.236	0.550*	0.268
White upper middle	0.399	0.112	0.387	0.287
White upper	—	—	—	—
Asian lower	−3.228***	0.985	−3.060**	0.994
Asian lower middle	1.183*	0.584	1.477*	0.624

Table C.1   (continued)

	Full Sample		Reduced Sample	
	B	SE	B	SE
Asian upper middle	−0.953	0.937	−0.844	0.929
Asian upper	0.388	0.524	0.600	0.528
Hispanic lower	0.659+	0.363	0.595	0.471
Hispanic lower middle	0.930**	0.339	0.924**	0.341
Hispanic upper middle	0.876*	0.418	0.647	0.439
Hispanic upper	0.415	0.499	0.529	0.429
Black lower	1.608***	0.219	1.425***	0.261
Black lower middle	1.265***	0.350	1.352***	0.373
Black upper middle	1.463***	0.284	1.267***	0.328
Black upper	1.043*	0.410	1.021*	0.482

Predicting limitation on physical activity

	N=8,831		N=6,844	
White lower	0.447***	0.101	0.431**	0.140
White lower middle	0.226*	0.123	0.330*	0.136
White upper middle	0.193+	0.107	0.195	0.121
White upper	—	—	—	—
Asian lower	0.869*	0.366	1.100**	0.400
Asian lower middle	0.046	0.315	0.382	0.370
Asian upper middle	−0.296	0.252	−0.524+	0.290
Asian upper	0.169	0.207	0.325	0.263
Hispanic lower	0.200	0.165	0.419*	0.183
Hispanic lower middle	−0.043	0.195	0.097	0.214
Hispanic upper middle	0.214	0.263	0.068	0.276
Hispanic upper	−0.148	0.369	−0.235	0.329
Black lower	0.101	0.168	0.080	0.189
Black lower middle	−0.064	0.207	0.025	0.264
Black upper middle	−0.152	0.225	−0.398	0.257
Black upper	−0.002	0.249	−0.041	0.245

Predicting body mass index

	N=8,575		N=7,226	
White lower	1.246**	0.397	1.100*	0.461
White lower middle	1.146***	0.199	1.209***	0.326
White upper middle	0.101	0.326	0.096	0.347
White upper	—	—	—	—
Asian lower	−1.969*	0.937	−2.992***	0.834
Asian lower middle	0.076	0.883	0.677	0.952

Table C.1 (continued)

	Full Sample		Reduced Sample	
	B	SE	B	SE
Asian upper middle	0.211	1.019	0.140	1.001
Asian upper	−1.694*	0.649	−1.506*	0.701
Hispanic lower	1.253**	0.424	1.377**	0.501
Hispanic lower middle	2.493***	0.549	2.395***	0.750
Hispanic upper middle	0.810	0.567	1.138+	0.648
Hispanic upper	1.446*	0.736	1.693*	0.856
Black lower	1.623***	0.443	1.498**	0.481
Black lower middle	2.362***	0.671	2.352**	0.856
Black upper middle	2.212***	0.679	2.158**	0.671
Black upper	1.712	1.137	1.849	1.162
Predicting obesity				
	N=8,575		N=7,686	
White lower	0.459**	0.147	0.536***	0.165
White lower middle	0.421***	0.112	0.450***	0.128
White upper middle	0.137	0.140	0.185	0.140
White upper	—	—	—	—
Asian lower	−0.652	0.679	−1.105	0.984
Asian lower middle	0.290	0.380	0.396	0.385
Asian upper middle	0.086	0.395	0.093	0.445
Asian upper	−0.385	0.312	−0.339	0.375
Hispanic lower	0.393*	0.182	0.446*	0.225
Hispanic lower middle	0.632**	0.201	0.592*	0.245
Hispanic upper middle	0.238	0.246	0.424+	0.256
Hispanic upper	0.492+	0.273	0.580*	0.292
Black lower	0.618***	0.146	0.653***	0.169
Black lower middle	0.581**	0.225	0.594*	0.274
Black upper middle	0.733***	0.220	0.722***	0.220
Black upper	0.645+	0.353	0.726*	0.351
Predicting STD diagnosis				
	N=8,947		N=6,954	
White lower	−0.094	0.189	−0.095	0.225
White lower middle	−0.320	0.199	−0.454*	0.226
White upper middle	−0.040	0.175	−0.160	0.194
White upper	—	—	—	—
Asian lower	−0.309	1.007	−0.103	1.015
Asian lower middle	−2.031**	0.698	−1.777**	0.674

Table C.1   (continued)

	Full Sample		Reduced Sample	
	B	SE	B	SE
Asian upper middle	−0.089	0.544	0.058	0.577
Asian upper	−0.642	0.556	−0.777	0.629
Hispanic lower	0.147	0.245	0.151	0.327
Hispanic lower middle	0.206	0.276	0.020	0.371
Hispanic upper middle	−0.559	0.443	−0.464	0.499
Hispanic upper	−0.583	0.432	−1.127*	0.519
Black lower	0.710***	0.191	0.789***	0.199
Black lower middle	1.168***	0.229	1.240***	0.275
Black upper middle	0.920***	0.240	1.091***	0.281
Black upper	1.237***	0.224	1.298***	0.258
Predicting poor overall health				
	N=8,996		N=6,549	
White lower	0.192***	0.043	0.186***	0.054
White lower middle	0.134**	0.048	0.153**	0.060
White upper middle	0.051	0.034	0.054	0.040
White upper	—	—	—	—
Asian lower	0.532*	0.216	0.523*	0.258
Asian lower middle	0.393*	0.142	0.580**	0.183
Asian upper middle	0.194*	0.087	0.220*	0.094
Asian upper	0.058	0.087	0.012	0.080
Hispanic lower	0.158*	0.065	0.164+	0.086
Hispanic lower middle	0.120+	0.067	0.115+	0.071
Hispanic upper middle	0.032	0.088	−0.030	0.087
Hispanic upper	0.139	0.116	0.109	0.088
Black lower	0.068	0.060	0.079	0.062
Black lower middle	0.154*	0.070	0.188*	0.095
Black upper middle	−0.049	0.065	0.016	0.076
Black upper	0.123	0.104	0.060	0.110
Predicting depression score				
	N=8,936		N=6,525	
White lower	0.646**	0.227	0.734**	0.243
White lower middle	0.329	0.221	0.506*	0.243
White upper middle	0.240	0.208	0.330	0.221
White upper	—	—	—	—
Asian lower	1.861**	0.707	2.653***	0.799
Asian lower middle	0.698	0.562	1.395*	0.658

Table C.1   (continued)

	Full Sample		Reduced Sample	
	B	SE	B	SE
Asian upper middle	0.707+	0.376	1.034*	0.429
Asian upper	1.624**	0.555	1.290*	0.460
Hispanic lower	1.559***	0.332	1.601***	0.394
Hispanic lower middle	0.621	0.387	0.916*	0.435
Hispanic upper middle	2.234***	0.447	2.007**	0.659
Hispanic upper	−0.207	0.418	−0.115	0.479
Black lower	1.298***	0.307	1.402***	0.332
Black lower middle	1.374***	0.377	1.337***	0.404
Black upper middle	0.823+	0.427	0.856+	0.493
Black upper	0.808*	0.372	0.873+	0.475
Predicting perceived likelihood of early death				
	N=8,996		N=6,550	
White lower	0.512***	0.114	0.433***	0.133
White lower middle	0.339**	0.117	0.453***	0.125
White upper middle	0.222*	0.101	0.207*	0.098
White upper	—	—	—	—
Asian lower	0.560+	0.347	0.529+	0.319
Asian lower middle	0.850*	0.382	1.238**	0.422
Asian upper middle	0.370	0.310	0.388	0.275
Asian upper	0.124	0.262	0.114	0.325
Hispanic lower	1.732***	0.230	1.867***	0.220
Hispanic lower middle	0.895***	0.238	0.890***	0.243
Hispanic upper middle	0.912***	0.251	0.923***	0.274
Hispanic upper	0.680*	0.279	0.882**	0.303
Black lower	1.422***	0.143	1.597***	0.173
Black lower middle	1.318***	0.184	1.414***	0.252
Black upper middle	0.855***	0.203	0.889***	0.253
Black upper	0.935***	0.236	0.840**	0.288
Chapter 6				
Predicting ADHD score				
	N=8,996		N=7,138	
White lower	2.031***	0.564	1.894**	0.681
White lower middle	1.383**	0.501	1.445*	0.493
White upper middle	0.278	0.527	0.365	0.602
White upper	—	—	—	—

Table C.1 (continued)

	Full Sample		Reduced Sample	
	B	SE	B	SE
Asian lower	−0.342	1.108	−0.011	1.273
Asian lower middle	−1.929	1.207	−1.326	1.221
Asian upper middle	−2.274**	0.856	−1.846+	0.973
Asian upper	−0.582	0.839	−0.463	0.787
Hispanic lower	1.861*	0.959	0.630	0.718
Hispanic lower middle	−0.832	0.811	−0.897	0.808
Hispanic upper middle	−1.706*	0.799	−1.486+	0.912
Hispanic upper	1.416	1.707	−0.535	0.941
Black lower	0.762	0.969	−0.478	0.647
Black lower middle	0.029	0.946	−0.421	0.784
Black upper middle	−1.439+	0.721	−2.606***	0.729
Black upper	−1.652*	0.721	−1.485*	0.738

Predicting Picture Vocabulary Score

	N=8,669		N=6,897	
White lower	−5.337***	0.831	−5.384***	0.886
White lower middle	−3.644***	0.696	−3.547***	0.761
White upper middle	−2.109***	0.509	−1.789***	0.510
White upper	—	—	—	—
Asian lower	−12.656***	2.621	−13.284***	2.991
Asian lower middle	−12.588**	4.103	−11.183**	4.111
Asian upper middle	−2.107	1.990	−2.525	2.098
Asian upper	−5.090**	1.864	−4.869*	2.055
Hispanic lower	−13.759***	1.335	−14.285***	1.353
Hispanic lower middle	−10.607***	1.329	−10.514***	1.324
Hispanic upper middle	−9.191***	1.846	−9.554***	2.186
Hispanic upper	−4.418**	1.508	−2.976*	1.374
Black lower	−20.163***	1.712	−19.104***	1.571
Black lower middle	−13.493***	1.458	−11.683***	1.215
Black upper middle	−13.493***	1.458	−11.494***	1.459
Black upper	−8.645***	1.929	−8.519***	2.111

Predicting high school GPA

	N=7,277		N=5,653	
White lower	−0.504***	0.056	−0.558***	0.063
White lower middle	−0.341***	0.047	−0.319***	0.055
White upper middle	−0.124**	0.041	−0.123**	0.044
White upper	—	—	—	—

Table C.1   (*continued*)

	Full Sample		Reduced Sample	
	B	SE	B	SE
Asian lower	−0.099	0.203	−0.097	0.212
Asian lower middle	−0.109	0.180	−0.074	0.127
Asian upper middle	0.015	0.110	−0.029	0.121
Asian upper	0.180*	0.081	0.159+	0.087
Hispanic lower	−0.678***	0.097	−0.690***	0.106
Hispanic lower middle	−0.697***	0.088	−0.751***	0.089
Hispanic upper middle	−0.524***	0.088	−0.580***	0.094
Hispanic upper	−0.287***	0.073	−0.259***	0.077
Black lower	−0.922***	0.089	−0.943***	0.113
Black lower middle	−0.795***	0.097	−0.755***	0.113
Black upper middle	−0.536***	0.106	−0.464***	0.108
Black upper	−0.437***	0.131	−0.445**	0.143

Predicting proportion of courses failed

	N=7,277		N=5,653	
White lower	0.071***	0.011	0.078***	0.012
White lower middle	0.050***	0.009	0.046***	0.009
White upper middle	0.013*	0.006	0.011	0.007
White upper	—	—	—	—
Asian lower	0.008	0.024	0.019	0.028
Asian lower middle	0.040	0.040	0.014	0.019
Asian upper middle	0.014	0.015	0.022	0.017
Asian upper	−0.003	0.013	−0.003	0.015
Hispanic lower	0.121***	0.021	0.118***	0.020
Hispanic lower middle	0.125***	0.024	0.130***	0.026
Hispanic upper middle	0.081***	0.022	0.085***	0.024
Hispanic upper	0.026*	0.013	0.019	0.014
Black lower	0.137***	0.019	0.138***	0.025
Black lower middle	0.121***	0.021	0.108***	0.023
Black upper middle	0.071*	0.028	0.056*	0.024
Black upper	0.051+	0.029	0.048	0.031

Predicting high school graduation

	N=8,990		N=5,652	
White lower	−1.556***	0.167	−1.627***	0.232
White lower middle	−1.122***	0.158	−1.196***	0.230
White upper middle	−0.584***	0.165	−0.579*	0.245
White upper	—	—	—	—

Table C.1   (*continued*)

	Full Sample		Reduced Sample	
	B	SE	B	SE
Asian lower	−0.100	0.673	−0.670	0.824
Asian lower middle	−0.432	0.536	−0.904	0.574
Asian upper middle	0.064	0.560	−0.820	0.559
Asian upper	0.500	0.494	0.109	0.743
Hispanic lower	−1.858***	0.188	−2.041***	0.251
Hispanic lower middle	−1.506***	0.202	−0.182***	0.272
Hispanic upper middle	−1.009***	0.263	−1.264***	0.352
Hispanic upper	−0.815*	0.376	0.047	0.520
Black lower	−1.380***	0.190	−1.636***	0.287
Black lower middle	−1.206***	0.221	−1.228***	0.308
Black upper middle	−0.693**	0.264	−0.910*	0.401
Black upper	−0.361	0.388	−0.353	0.581

Chapter 7
Predicting involvement in nonviolent crime

	N=8,837		N=5,597	
White lower	−0.333***	0.082	−0.353**	0.109
White lower middle	−0.150	0.097	−0.172	0.116
White upper middle	−0.170*	0.087	−0.190+	0.112
White upper	—	—	—	—
Asian lower	−0.566***	0.104	−0.670***	0.105
Asian lower middle	−0.477***	0.105	−0.543***	0.126
Asian upper middle	−0.205	0.188	−0.310+	0.181
Asian upper	−0.330**	0.106	−0.376**	0.128
Hispanic lower	−0.162	0.104	−0.176	0.149
Hispanic lower middle	−0.253*	0.121	−0.287*	0.119
Hispanic upper middle	−0.092	0.164	−0.321*	0.161
Hispanic upper	−0.268*	0.115	−0.208	0.165
Black lower	0.227*	0.097	−0.280*	0.120
Black lower middle	0.076	0.234	0.175	0.425
Black upper middle	−0.157	0.133	−0.159	0.181
Black upper	0.020	0.165	−0.113	0.240

Predicting involvement in violent crime

	N=8,767		N=5,578	
White lower	−0.052	0.078	−0.022	0.095
White lower middle	−0.080	0.072	−0.091	0.082
White upper middle	−0.107	0.069	−0.126+	0.072
White upper	—	—	—	—

Table C.1   (*continued*)

	Full Sample		Reduced Sample	
	B	SE	B	SE
Asian lower	0.034	0.480	0.109	0.595
Asian lower middle	−0.347**	0.111	−0.363**	0.141
Asian upper middle	−0.277*	0.181	−0.253+	0.135
Asian upper	−0.327***	0.084	−0.314*	0.125
Hispanic lower	0.024	0.079	−0.085	0.084
Hispanic lower middle	−0.157+	0.092	−0.133	0.104
Hispanic upper middle	0.215	0.205	0.039	0.239
Hispanic upper	−0.032	0.163	−0.055	0.207
Black lower	0.263+	0.141	0.202	0.169
Black lower middle	0.481*	0.209	0.540	0.335
Black upper middle	0.035	0.129	0.092	0.197
Black upper	0.202	0.203	0.130	0.275
Predicting criminal justice involvement				
	N=8,827		N=5,488	
White lower	−0.034	0.064	−0.103	0.096
White lower middle	0.007	0.065	−0.100	0.074
White upper middle	−0.080	0.059	−0.114	0.073
White upper	—	—	—	—
Asian lower	−0.270*	0.134	−0.403***	0.101
Asian lower middle	−0.173	0.146	−0.100	0.196
Asian upper middle	0.021	0.144	0.131	0.198
Asian upper	−0.002	0.139	0.178	0.204
Hispanic lower	−0.055	0.100	−0.132	0.111
Hispanic lower middle	−0.130	0.084	−0.046	0.120
Hispanic upper middle	0.137	0.178	−0.131	0.146
Hispanic upper	0.080	0.148	−0.076	0.153
Black lower	−0.032	0.086	−0.205	0.092
Black lower middle	0.193	0.165	0.275	0.293
Black upper middle	−0.142	0.094	−0.053	0.157
Black upper	−0.028	0.104	−0.018	0.145
Chapter 8				
Predicting receipt of college degree by Wave 4				
	N=7,851		N=5,013	
White lower	−1.901***	0.178	−1.679***	0.184
White lower middle	−1.235***	0.112	−1.150***	0.126
White upper middle	−0.724***	0.114	−0.697***	0.121
White upper	—	—	—	—

Table C.1 (continued)

	Full Sample		Reduced Sample	
	B	SE	B	SE
Asian lower	−1.393*	1.269	−1.279*	0.607
Asian lower middle	−0.453	0.344	−0.531+	0.392
Asian upper middle	0.407	0.301	0.080	0.399
Asian upper	0.394	0.273	0.427	0.309
Hispanic lower	−1.648***	0.238	−1.534***	0.284
Hispanic lower middle	−2.019***	0.282	−1.753***	0.300
Hispanic upper middle	−0.722**	0.228	−0.551*	0.252
Hispanic upper	−1.097***	0.259	−0.650*	0.284
Black lower	−1.812***	0.247	−1.709***	0.243
Black lower middle	−1.432***	0.232	−1.176***	0.273
Black upper middle	−0.856***	0.243	−0.738**	0.684
Black upper	−0.432	0.311	−0.421	0.331

Predicting receipt of graduate degree by Wave 4

	N=7,851		N=5,013	
White lower	−1.827***	0.318	−1.477***	0.362
White lower middle	−0.877***	0.168	−0.733***	0.201
White upper middle	−0.772***	0.180	−0.675***	0.186
White upper	—	—	—	—
Asian lower	−0.996	0.955	−0.889	0.976
Asian lower middle	−0.135	0.387	−0.566	0.505
Asian upper middle	−0.294	0.422	−0.279	0.451
Asian upper	0.128	0.433	−0.120	0.476
Hispanic lower	−1.334***	0.390	−1.252**	0.468
Hispanic lower middle	−1.729***	0.518	−1.245*	0.525
Hispanic upper middle	−1.127**	0.417	−0.908*	0.459
Hispanic upper	−0.855	0.545	−0.399	0.568
Black lower	−1.627***	0.378	−1.392***	0.392
Black lower middle	−1.473***	0.328	−1.206**	0.429
Black upper middle	−0.683*	0.340	−0.413	0.369
Black upper	−0.150	0.404	−0.224	0.480

Predicting part-time employment at Wave 4

	N=7,821		N=5,005	
White lower	−0.565***	0.276	−0.564*	0.279
White lower middle	−0.184	0.193	−0.106	0.232
White upper middle	−0.945	0.198	−0.060	0.234
White upper	—	—	—	—

Table C.1   (continued)

	Full Sample		Reduced Sample	
	B	SE	B	SE
Asian lower	−0.718	1.111	−0.461	1.345
Asian lower middle	0.097	0.604	−0.082	0.617
Asian upper middle	0.394	0.504	0.417	0.589
Asian upper	−0.177	0.462	0.136	1.001
Hispanic lower	−1.189***	0.316	−1.066***	0.319
Hispanic lower middle	−0.550+	0.331	−0.015	0.423
Hispanic upper middle	0.625	0.565	0.037	0.726
Hispanic upper	−0.472	0.513	−0.413	0.700
Black lower	−0.548*	0.264	−0.599+	0.348
Black lower middle	−0.128	0.302	0.157	0.407
Black upper middle	−0.265	0.471	0.068	0.433
Black upper	−0.818**	0.325	−0.586	0.472

Predicting full-time employment at Wave 4

	N=7,821		N=5,005	
White lower	−0.792***	0.189	−0.804***	0.245
White lower middle	−0.363*	0.154	−0.341*	0.169
White upper middle	−0.143	0.146	−0.196	0.200
White upper	—	—	—	—
Asian lower	−0.301	0.754	−0.262	0.995
Asian lower middle	−0.168	0.410	−0.466	0.466
Asian upper middle	−0.382	0.410	−0.848	0.501
Asian upper	−0.031	0.426	0.383	0.841
Hispanic lower	−0.439	0.279	−0.662**	0.252
Hispanic lower middle	−0.370	0.224	−0.303	0.366
Hispanic upper middle	0.594	0.414	0.411	0.457
Hispanic upper	−0.458	0.396	−0.076	0.437
Black lower	−0.875***	0.205	−0.890***	0.224
Black lower middle	−0.476+	0.258	−0.786**	0.306
Black upper middle	−0.499	0.413	−0.193	0.350
Black upper	−0.757**	0.262	−0.813*	0.340

Predicting annual earnings at Wave 4

	N=6,093		N=4,020	
White lower	−0.425***	0.079	−0.309***	0.067
White lower middle	−0.268***	0.046	−0.234***	0.049
White upper middle	−0.146**	0.045	−0.162***	0.048

Table C.1   *(continued)*

	Full Sample		Reduced Sample	
	B	SE	B	SE
White upper	—	—	—	—
Asian lower	−0.306	0.234	−0.331	0.271
Asian lower middle	0.080	0.127	0.138	0.138
Asian upper middle	−0.132	0.228	−0.019	0.123
Asian upper	0.223*	0.093	0.224	0.078
Hispanic lower	−0.213**	0.067	−0.304***	0.082
Hispanic lower middle	−0.242*	0.117	−0.257*	0.104
Hispanic upper middle	−0.056	0.082	0.057	0.090
Hispanic upper	−0.031	0.107	0.039	0.125
Black lower	−0.577***	0.081	−0.611***	0.117
Black lower middle	−0.424***	0.082	−0.351***	0.088
Black upper middle	−0.341***	0.079	−0.225**	0.084
Black upper	−0.109	0.106	−0.130	0.111
Predicting TANF receipt at Wave 4				
	N=7,839		N=5,001	
White lower	1.466***	0.150	1.304***	0.182
White lower middle	0.700***	0.134	0.612***	0.162
White upper middle	0.264+	0.142	0.192	0.171
White upper	—	—	—	—
Asian lower	0.324	0.783	0.062	1.044
Asian lower middle	−0.390	0.726	−0.107	0.771
Asian upper middle	−0.979+	0.535	−1.234	0.881
Asian upper	−0.886+	0.504	−1.027+	0.592
Hispanic lower	0.800***	0.217	0.873***	0.253
Hispanic lower middle	0.825***	0.239	0.948**	0.328
Hispanic upper middle	0.696**	0.258	0.604+	0.325
Hispanic upper	0.162	0.300	−0.170	0.390
Black lower	1.802***	0.170	1.907***	0.552
Black lower middle	1.111***	0.247	0.891**	0.329
Black upper middle	1.371***	0.268	1.106***	0.278
Black upper	0.756**	0.277	0.575+	0.330

Source: Authors' calculations based on data set described in Harris and Udry (2008).

REFERENCES

Aaronson, Daniel. 1998. "Using Sibling Data to Estimate the Impact of Neighborhoods on Children's Educational Outcomes." *Journal of Human Resources* 33(4): 915–46.

Aber, J. Lawrence, Neil G. Bennett, Dalton C. Conley, and Jiali Li. 1997. "The Effects of Poverty on Child Health and Development." *Annual Review of Public Health* 18: 463–83.

Adler, Nancy E., and David H. Rehkopf. 2008. "U.S. Disparities in Health: Descriptions, Causes, and Mechanisms." *Annual Review of Public Health* 29: 235–52.

Agid, O., B. Shapira, J. Zislin, M. Ritsner, B. Hanin, H. Murad, T. Troudart, M. Bloch, U. Heresco-Levy, and B. Lerer. 1999. "Environment and Vulnerability to Major Psychiatric Illness: A Case Control Study of Early Parental Loss in Major Depression, Bipolar Disorder, and Schizophrenia." *Molecular Psychiatry* 4(2): 163–72.

Akers, Ronald L., Marvin D. Krohn, Lonn Lanza-Kaduce, Marcia Radosevich. 1979. "Social Learning and Deviant Behavior: A Specific Test of a General Theory." *American Sociological Review* 44(4): 636–55.

Akresh, Ilana Redstone. 2007. "Dietary Assimilation and Health Among Hispanic Immigrants to the United States." *Journal of Health and Social Behavior* 48(4): 404–17.

———. 2008. "Overweight and Obesity Among Foreign-Born and U.S.-Born Hispanics." *Biodemography and Social Biology* 54(2): 183–99.

Alexander, Karl L., Doris R. Entwisle, and Linda S. Olson. 2001. "Schools, Achievement, and Inequality." *American Educational Research Association* 23(2): 171–91.

———. 2007. "Lasting Consequences of the Summer Learning Gap." *American Sociological Review* 72(2): 167–80.

Alexander, Michelle. 2010. *The New Jim Crow: Mass Incarceration in the Age of Colorblindness*. New York: New Press.

Allis, C. David, Thomas Jenuwein, Danny Reinberg, and Marie-Laure Caparros. 2007. *Epigenetics*. Cold Spring Harbor, N.Y.: Cold Spring Harbor Laboratory Press.

Anderson, Elijah. 1999. *Code of the Street: Decency, Violence, and the Moral Life of the Inner City*. New York: W. W. Norton.

Antonovsky, Aaron. 1967. "Social Class Life Expectancy and Overall Mortality." *Milbank Memorial Fund Quarterly* 45(2): 31–73.

Ariely, Dan. 2009. *Predictably Irrational: The Hidden Forces That Shape Our Decisions*. New York: Harper.

Aries, Philippe. 1965. *Centuries of Childhood: A Social History of Family Life*. New York: Vintage.

Armour, Stacey, and Dana L. Haynie. 2007. "Sexual Debut and Delinquency." *Journal of Youth and Adolescence* 36(2): 141–52.

Arnett, Jeffrey J. 2010. *Adolescence and Emerging Adulthood: A Cultural Approach*, 4th ed. Boston, Mass.: Prentice Hall.

Astone, Nan M., and Sara McLanahan. 1991. "Family Structure, Parental Practices, and High School Completion." *American Sociological Review* 56(3): 309–20.

Baker, Wayne E. 2004. *America's Crisis of Values: Perception and Reality*. Princeton, N.J.: Princeton University Press.

Bartels, Larry M. 2008. *Unequal Democracy: The Political Economy of the New Gilded Age*. Princeton, N.J.: Princeton University Press.

Bean, Frank D., Cynthia Feliciano, Jennifer Lee, and Jennifer Van Hook. 2009. "The New U.S. Immigrants: How Do They Affect Our Understanding of the African American Experience?" *Annals of the American Academy of Political and Social Science* 621(1): 202–20.

Becker, Gary S. 1994. *Human Capital: A Theoretical and Empirical Analysis with Special Reference to Education*, 3rd ed. Chicago: University of Chicago Press.

Berger, Peter. 1999. *The Desecularization of the World: Resurgent Religion and World Politics*. Grand Rapids, Mich.: Eerdmans Publishing.

Berkman, Lisa F. 2009. "Social Epidemiology: Social Determinants of Health in the United States: Are We Losing Ground?" *Annual Review of Public Health* 30: 27–41.

Bianchi, Suzanne M. 2000. "Maternal Employment and Time with Children: Dramatic Change or Surprising Continuity?" *Demography* 37(4): 401–14.

Bianchi, Suzanne M., John P. Robinson, and Melissa A. Milkie. 2006. *Changing Rhythms of American Family Life*. New York: Russell Sage Foundation.

Biblarz, Timothy J., and Adrian E. Raftery. 1993. "The Effects of Family Disruption on Social Mobility." *American Sociological Review* 58(1): 97–107.

Bittman, Michael, Paula England, Liana Sayer, Nancy Folbre, and George Matheson. 2003. "When Does Gender Trump Money?: Bargaining and Time in Household Work." *American Journal of Sociology* 109(1): 186–214.

Black, Sir Douglas, et al. 1980. "Inequalities in Health: Report of a Research Working Group." London: Her Majesty's Printing Office.

Blackburn, Elizabeth H. 2006. "A History of Telomere Biology." In *Telomeres*, 2nd ed., edited by Titia de Lang, Vicki Lundblad, and Elizabeth Blackburn. Cold Spring Harbor, N.Y.: Cold Spring Harbor Laboratory Press.

Blau, Peter M., and Otis Duncan. 1967. *The American Occupational Structure*. New York: John Wiley & Sons.

Boas, Franz. 1940. *Race, Language, and Culture*. Chicago: University of Chicago Press.

Bobo, Lawrence D. 1989. "Keeping the Linchpin in Place: Testing the Multiple Sources of Opposition to Residential Integration." *International Review of Social Psychology* 2(3): 305–23.

Bobo, Lawrence D., and Camille Z. Charles. 2009. "Race in the American Mind: From the Moynihan Report to the Obama Candidacy." *Annals of the American Academy of Political and Social Science* 621(4): 243–59.

Booth, Alan, and D. Wayne Osgood. 1993. "The Influence of Testosterone on Deviance in Adulthood: Assessing and Explaining the Relationship." *Criminology* 31(1): 93–117.

Bourdieu, Pierre. 1986. "The Forms of Capital." In *Handbook of Theory and Research for the Sociology of Education*, edited by John G. Richardson. New York: Greenwood Press.

Bourdieu, Pierre, and Jean Claude Passeron. 1990. *Reproduction in Education, Society and Culture*. Thousand Oaks, Calif.: Sage Publications.

Bowles, Samuel, and Herbert Gintis. 1976. *Schooling in Capitalist America: Educational Reform and the Contradiction of Economic Life*. New York: Basic Books.

Bradley, Robert H., and Robert F. Corwyn. 2002. "Socioeconomic Status and Child Development." *Annual Review of Psychology* 53: 371–99.

Brescia, Raymond H. 2009. "Subprime Communities: Reverse Redlining, the Fair Housing Act, and Emerging Issues in Litigation Regarding the Subprime Mortgage Crisis." *Albany Government Law Review* 2(164): 164–216.

Bronfenbrenner, Urie. 1973. "The Social Ecology of Human Development: A Retrospective Conclusion." In *Brain and Intelligence: The Ecology of Child Development*, edited by Frederick Richardson. Hyattsville, Md.: National Educational Press.

———. 1979. *The Ecology of Human Development: Experiments by Nature and Design*. Cambridge, Mass.: Harvard University Press.

———. 2001. "The Bioecological Theory of Human Development." In *International Encyclopedia of the Social and Behavioral Sciences*, edited by Neil J. Smelser and Paul B. Baltes. New York: Elsevier.

Browning, Christopher R., Seth L. Feinberg, and Robert D. Dietz. 2004. "The Paradox of Social Organization: Networks, Collective Efficacy, and Violent Crime in Urban Neighborhoods." *Social Forces* 83(2): 503–34.

Burgess, Ernest W. 1925. "The Growth of the City: An Introduction to a Research Project." In *The City*, edited by Robert E. Park and Ernest W. Burgess. Chicago: University of Chicago Press.

Capaldi, Nicholas N., and Theodore Roosevelt Malloch. 2012. *America's Spiritual Capital*. South Bend, Ind.: St. Augustine's Press.

Card, David, and Alan B. Krueger. 1996. "School Resources of Student Outcomes: A Review of the Literature and New Evidence from North and South Carolina." *Journal of Economic Perspectives* 10(1): 31–50.

Card, David, and Thomas Lemieux. 2001. "Can Falling Supply Explain the Rising Return to College for Younger Men? A Cohort-Based Analysis." *Quarterly Journal of Economics* 116(2): 705–46.

Carlson, Marcia J., and Mary E. Corcoran. 2001. "Family Structure and Children's Behavioral and Cognitive Outcomes." *Journal of Marriage and Family* 63(9): 779–92.

Carroll, Annemaree, Stephen Houghton, Kevin Durkin, and John A. Hattie. 2008. *Adolescent Reputations and Risk: Developmental Trajectories to Delinquency*. New York: Springer.

Casper, Lynne, and Suzanne Bianchi. 2001. *Continuity and Change in the American Family*. Thousand Oaks, Calif.: Sage Publications.

Cavalli-Sforza, L. Luca, Paolo Menozzi, and Alberto Piazza. 1994. *The History and Geography of Human Genes*. Princeton, N.J.: Princeton University Press.

Cavanagh, Shannon E. 2004. "The Sexual Debut of Girls in Early Adolescence: The Intersection of Race, Pubertal Timing, and Friendship Group Characteristics." *Journal of Research on Adolescence* 14(3): 285–312.

Cavazos-Rehg, Patricia A., Melissa J. Krauss, Edward L. Spitznagel, Mario Schootman, Kathleen K. Bucholz, Jeffrey F. Peipert, Vetta Sanders-Thompson, Linda B. Colter, and Laura Jean Beirut. 2009. "Age of Sexual Debut Among U.S. Adolescents." *Contraception* 80(2): 159–62.

Cavazos-Rehg, Patricia A., Edward L. Spitznagel, Kathleen K. Bucholz, John Nurnberger Jr., Howard J. Edenberg, John R. Kramer, Samuel Kuperman, Victor Hesselbrock, and Laur Jean Bierut. 2010. "Predictors of Sexual Debut at Age 16 or Younger." *Archives of Sexual Behavior* 39(3): 664–73.

Ceci, Stephen J., and Wendy M. Williams, eds. 2000. *The Nature-Nurture Debate: The Essential Readings*. New York: Blackwell.

Champagne, Frances A. 2012. "Interplay Between Social Experiences and the Genome: Epigenetic Consequences for Behavior." *Advances in Genetics* 77: 33–57.

Chandler, Tetrius, and Gerald Fox. 1974. *3000 Years of Urban Growth*. New York: Academic Press.

Charles, Camille Z. 2003. "The Dynamics of Racial Residential Segregation." *Annual Review of Sociology* 29: 167–207.

Chase-Lansdale, P. Lindsay, R. Gordon, K. Brooks-Gunn, P. K. Klebanov. 1997. "Neighborhood and Family Influences on the Intellectual and Behavioral Competence of Preschool and Early School-Age Children." In *Neighborhood Poverty*, vol. 1, *Context and Consequences for Children*, edited by Jeanne Brooks-Gunn, Greg J. Duncan, and Lawrence A. Aber. New York: Russell Sage Foundation.

Chatters, Linda M., Robert Joseph Taylor, and Rukmalie Jayakody. 1994. "Fictive Kinship Relations in Black Extended Families." *Journal of Comparative Family Studies* 25(3): 297–312.

Chen, Edith, Sheldon Cohen, and Gregory E. Miller. 2010. "How Low Socioeconomic Status Affects 2-Year Hormonal Trajectories in Children." *Psychological Science* 21(1): 31–37.

Chen, Edith, and Laurel Q. Paterson. 2006. "Neighborhood, Family, and Subjective Socioeconomic Status: How Do They Relate to Adolescent Health?" *Health Psychology* 25(6): 704–14.

Choi, Seok J., Jon Ondrich, and John Yinger. 2005. "Do Rental Agents Discriminate Against Minority Customers? Evidence from the 2000 Housing Discrimination Study." *Journal of Housing Economics* 14(1): 1–25.

Christakis, Nicholas A., and James H. Fowler. 2009. *Connected: The Surprising Power of Our Social Networks and How They Shape Our Lives — How Your Friends' Friends' Friends Affect Everything You Feel, Think, and Do*. Boston, Mass.: Little, Brown.

Chumlea, William Cameron, Christine M. Schubert, Alex F. Roche, Howard E. Kulin, Peter A. Lee, John H. Himes, and Shumei S. Sun. 2003. "Age at Menarche and Racial Comparisons in U.S. Girls." *Pediatrics* 111(1): 110–13.

Clampet-Lundquist, Susan, and Douglas S. Massey. 2008. "Neighborhood Effects on Economic Self-Sufficiency: A Reconsideration of the Moving to Opportunity Experiment." *American Journal of Sociology* 114(1): 107–43.

Coleman, James S. 1963. *The Adolescent Society*. New York: Free Press.

———. 1966. *Equality of Educational Opportunity*. Washington: U.S. Department of Health, Education, and Welfare, Office of Education.

Collins, Chiquita A., and David R. Williams. 1999. "Segregation and Mortality: The Deadly Effects of Racism." *Sociological Forum* 14(3): 495–523.

Costa, Lucio G., and David L. Eaton, eds. 2006. *Gene-Environment Interactions: Fundamentals of Ecogenetics*. New York: Wiley-Liss.

Croizeta, Jean-Claude, and Marion Dutreacutevisa. 2004. "Socioeconomic Status and Intelligence: Why Test Scores Do Not Equal Merit." *Journal of Poverty* 8(3): 91–107.

Crowder, Kyle, and Scott J. South. 2003. "Neighborhood Distress and School Drop-out: The Variable Significance of Community Context." *Social Science Research* 32(4): 659–98.

———. 2005. "Race, Class, and Changing Migration Patterns Between Poor and Nonpoor Neighborhoods." *American Journal of Sociology* 110(6): 1715–63.

Crowder, Kyle, Scott J. South, and Erick Chavez. 2006. "Wealth, Race, and Inter-Neighborhood Migration." *American Sociological Review* 71(1): 72–94.

Cuddy, Amy J. C., Susan T. Fiske, Virginia S. Y. Kwan, Peter Glick, Stephanie De-moulin, Jacques-Philippe Leyens, Michael Harris Bond, Jean-Claude Croizet, Naomi Ellemers, Ed Sleebos, Tin Tin Htun, Hyun-Jeong Kim, Greg Maio, Judi Perry, Kristina Petkova, Valery Todorov, Rosa Rodríguez-Bailón, Elena Morales, Miguel Moya, Marisol Palacios, Vanessa Smith, Rolando Pérez, Jorge Vala, and Rene Ziegler. 2009. "Stereotype Content Model Across Cultures: Towards Universal Similarities and Some Differences." *British Journal of Social Psychology* 48(1): 1–33.

Cunha, Flavio, and James J. Heckman. 2009. "The Economics and Psychology of Inequality and Human Development." *Journal of the European Economic Association* 7(2–3): 320–64.

Cunha, Flavio, James J. Heckman, Lance Lochner, and Dimitriy Masterov. 2006. "Interpreting the Evidence on Life Cycle Skill Formation." In *Handbook of the Economics of Education*, edited by Eric Hanushek and Finis Welch. Amsterdam: North Holland.

Dabbs, James M., Timothy S. Carr, Robert L. Frady, and Jasmin K. Riad. 1995. "Testosterone, Crime, and Misbehavior Among 692 Male Prison Inmates." *Personality and Individual Differences* 18(5): 627–33.

Dabbs, James M., Barry Ruback, Robert L. Frady, Charles H. Hopper, and Demetrios S. Sgoutas. 1988. "Saliva Testosterone and Criminal Violence Among Women." *Personality and Individual Differences* 9(2): 269–75.

Damasio, Antonio R. 1994. *Descartes' Error: Emotion, Reason, and the Human Brain*. New York: Putnam.

———. 1999. *The Feeling of What Happens: Body and Emotion in the Making of Consciousness*. New York: Houghton Mifflin Harcourt.

Darling-Hammond, Linda. 1999. *Teacher Quality and Student Achievement: A Review of State Policy Evidence*. Seattle: Center for the Study of Teaching and Policy, University of Washington.

Darwin, Charles. 1859. *On the Origin of Species*. London: John Murray.

Davis, Phyllis. 1999. *The Power of Touch: The Basis for Survival, Health, Intimacy, and Emotional Well-Being*. New York: Hay House.

Davis-Kean, Pamela E. 2005. "The Influence of Parent Education and Family Income on Child Achievement: The Indirect Role of Parental Expectations and the Home Environment." *Journal of Family Psychology* 19(2): 294–304.

Denton, Nancy A., and Douglas S. Massey. 1989. "Racial Identity Among Caribbean Hispanics: The Effect of Double Minority Status on Residential Segregation." *American Sociological Review* 54(5): 790–808.

Devlin, Bernie, Stephen E. Fienberg, Daniel P. Resnick, and Kathryn Roeder. 1997. *Intelligence, Genes, and Success: Scientists Respond to The Bell Curve*. New York: Springer.

Diamond, Jared. 2012. *The World Until Yesterday: What Can We Learn from Traditional Societies?* New York: Viking.

DiPrete, Thomas A., and Gregory A. Eirich. 2006. "Cumulative Advantage as a Mechanism for Inequality: A Review of Theoretical and Empirical Developments." *Annual Review of Sociology* 32: 271–97.

Doyle, Orla, Colm P. Harmon, James J. Heckman, and Richard Tremblay. 2009. "Investing in Early Human Development: Timing and Economic Efficiency." *Economics and Human Biology* 7(1): 1–6.

Dressler, William W., Kathryn S. Ochs, and Clarence C. Gravlee. 2005. "Race and Ethnicity in Public Health Research: Models to Explain Health Disparities." *Annual Review of Anthropology* 34: 231–52.

Duncan, Greg J., and Jeanne Brooks-Gunn. 1997. "The Effects of Poverty on Children." *The Future of Children* 7(2): 55–71.

Duncan, Greg J., and Stephen W. Raudenbush. 1999. "Assessing the Effects of Context in Studies of Child and Youth Development." *Educational Psychologist* 34(1): 29–41.

Duncan, Otis D. 1961. "A Socioeconomic Index for All Occupations." In *Occupations and Social Status*, edited by Albert J. Reiss Jr. New York: Free Press.

Duncan, Otis D., David L. Featherman, and Beverly Duncan. 1972. *Socioeconomic Background and Achievement.* New York: Seminar Press.

Earls, Felton, and Mary Carlson. 2001. "The Social Ecology of Child Health and Well-being." *Annual Review of Public Health* 22:143–66.

Edin, Kathryn, Timothy J. Nelson, and Rechell Paranal. 2004. "Fatherhood and Incarceration as Potential Turning Points in the Criminal Careers of Unskilled Men." In *Imprisoning America: The Social Effects of Mass Incarceration*, edited by Mary Pattillo, David Weiman, and Bruce Western. New York: Russell Sage Foundation.

Eliot, Lise. 1999. *What's Going on in There? How the Brain and Mind Develop in the First Five Years of Life.* New York: Bantam.

Elo, Irma T. 2009. "Social Class Differentials in Health and Mortality: Patterns and Explanations in Comparative Perspective." *Annual Review of Sociology* 35: 535–72.

Emerson, Michael O., and Christian Smith. 2000. *Divided by Faith: Evangelical Religion and the Problem of Race in America.* New York: Oxford University Press.

England, Paula, and Emily Fitzgibbons Shafer. 2009. "Everyday Gender Conflicts in Low-Income Couples." In *Unmarried Couples with Children*, edited by Paula England and Kathryn Edin. New York: Russell Sage Foundation.

Entwisle, Doris R., and Karl L. Alexander. 1982. "Summer Setback: Race, Poverty, School Composition, and Mathematics Achievement in the First Two Years of School." *American Sociological Review* 57(1): 72–84.

Entwisle, Doris R., Karl L. Alexander, and Linda S. Olson. 1997. *Children, Schools, and Inequality.* Boulder, Colo.: Westview Press.

Epel, Elissa S., Elizabeth H. Blackburn, Jue Lin, Firdaus S. Dhabhar, Nancy E. Adler, Jason D. Morrow, and Richard M. Cawthon. 2004. "Accelerated Telomere Shortening in Response to Life Stress." *Proceedings of the National Academy of Sciences* 101(49): 17312–15.

Estes, Richard. 1991. *The Behavior Guide to African Mammals.* Berkeley: University of California Press.

Evans, Gary W. 2006. "Child Development and the Physical Environment." *Annual Review of Psychology* 57: 423–51.

Evans, Gary W., and Elyse Kantrowitz. 2002. "Socioeconomic Status and Health: The Potential Role of Environmental Risk Exposure." *Annual Review of Public Health* 23: 303–31.

Farley, Reynolds, and William H. Frey. 1994. "Changes in the Segregation of Whites from Blacks during the 1980s: Small Steps Toward a More Integrated Society." *American Sociological Review* 59(1): 23–45.

Fergusson, David, Nicola Swain-Campbell, and John Horwood. 2004. "How Does Childhood Economic Disadvantage Lead to Crime?" *Journal of Child Psychology and Psychiatry* 45(5): 956–66.

Finn, Jeremy D., and Charles M. Achilles. 1999. "Tennessee's Class Size Study: Findings, Implications, Misconceptions." *Educational Evaluation and Policy Analysis* 21(2): 97–109.

Fischer, Claude S. 1982. *To Dwell Among Friends: Personal Networks in Town and City*. Chicago: University of Chicago Press.

Fischer, Claude S., Martin Sanchez Jankowski, Samuel R. Lucas, Ann Swidler, and Kim Voss. 1996. *Inequality by Design: Cracking the Bell Curve Myth*. Princeton, N.J.: Princeton University Press.

Fischer, Claude S., Gretchen Stockmayer, Jon Stiles, and Michael Hout. 2004. "Distinguishing the Geographic Levels and Social Dimensions of U.S. Metropolitan Segregation, 1960–2000." *Demography* 41(1): 37–59.

Fischer, Mary J., and Douglas S. Massey. 2004. "The Social Ecology of Racial Discrimination." *City and Community* 3(3): 221–43.

Fiske, Susan T., Amy J. C. Cuddy, Peter Glick, and Jun Xu. 2002. "A Model of (Often Mixed) Stereotype Content: Competence and Warmth Respectively Follow from Perceived Status and Competition." *Journal of Personality and Social Psychology* 82(6): 878–902.

Flynn, James R. 1987. "Massive IQ Gains in 14 Nations: What IQ Tests Really Measure." *Psychological Bulletin* 101(2): 171–91.

———. 2007. *What Is Intelligence?: Beyond the Flynn Effect*. New York: Cambridge University Press.

Foster, Michael, and Sara McLanahan. 1996. "An Illustration of the Use of Instrumental Variables: Do Neighborhood Conditions Affect a Young Person's Chance of Finishing High School?" *Psychological Methods* 3(1): 249–60.

Fox, Robin 1984. *Kinship and Marriage: An Anthropological Perspective*. New York: Cambridge University Press.

Frank, Robert. 2007a. *Falling Behind: How Rising Inequality Harms the Middle Class*. Berkeley: University of California Press.

———. 2007b. *Richistan: A Journey Through the American Wealth Boom and the Lives of the New Rich*. New York: Crown Publishers.

Franke, Todd M. 2000. "Adolescent Violent Behavior: An Analysis Across and Within Racial/Ethnic Groups." *Journal of Multicultural Social Work* 8(1): 47–70.

Fredrickson, George M. 2002. *Racism: A Short History*. Princeton, N.J.: Princeton University Press.

Friedman, Samantha, and Gregory D. Squires. 2005. "Does the Community Reinvestment Act Help Minorities Access Traditionally Inaccessible Neighborhoods?" *Social Problems* 52(2): 209–31.

Furstenberg, Frank F., Jr. 2009. "If Moynihan Had Only Known: Race, Class, and Family Change in the Late 20th Century." *Annals of the American Academy of Political and Social Science* 621: 94–110.

Furstenberg, Frank F., Jr., Thomas Cook, Jacqueline Eccles, and Glenn Elder. 1999. *Managing to Make It: Urban Families and Adolescent Success*. Chicago: University of Chicago Press.

Galton, Francis. 1869. *Hereditary Genius: An Inquiry into Its Laws and Its Consequences*. London: MacMillan.

Gamble, Clive. 1999. *The Paleolithic Societies of Europe*. Cambridge: Cambridge University Press.

Ganzeboom, Harry B. G., and Donald J. Treiman. 1996. "Internationally Comparable Measures of Occupational Status for the 1988 International Standard Classification of Occupations." *Social Science Research* 25(3): 201–39.

Garner, Catherine L., and Stephen W. Raudenbush. 1991. "Neighborhood Effects on Educational Attainment: A "Multi-level Analysis." *Sociology of Education* 64(4): 251–62.

Geller, Amanda, Irwin Garfinkle, Carey E. Cooper, and Ronald B. Mincy. 2009. "Parental Incarceration and Child Well Being: Implications for Urban Families." *Social Science Quarterly* 90(5): 1186–1202.

Geronimus, Arlene T. 2001. "Understanding and Eliminating Racial Inequalities in Women's Health in the United States: The Role of the Weathering Conceptual Framework." *Journal of the American Medical Women's Association* 56(4):133–36.

Geronimus, Arline T., Margaret Hicken, Danya Keene, and John Bound. 2006. "'Weathering' and Age Patterns of Allostatic Load Scores Among Blacks and Whites in the United States." *American Journal of Public Health* 96(5): 826–33.

Gilens, Martin. 2012. *Affluence and Influence: Economic Inequality and Political Power in America*. Princeton, N.J.: Princeton University Press.

Goerge, Robert M., Allen Harden, and Bong Joo Lee. 2008. "Consequences of Teen Childbearing for Child Abuse, Neglect, and Foster Care Placement." In *Kids Having Kids: Economic Costs and Social Consequences of Teen Pregnancy*, edited by Saul D. Hoffman and Rebecca A. Maynard. Washington, D.C.: Urban Institute Press.

Goldin, Claudia, and Lawrence F. Katz. 1999. "The Returns to Skill in the United

States Across the Twentieth Century." *NBER* working paper no. 7126. Cambridge, Mass.: National Bureau of Economic Research.

———. 2008. *The Race Between Education and Technology.* Cambridge, Mass.: Harvard University Press.

Goldsheider, Calvin, and Peter Uhlenberg. 1969. "Minority Group Status and Fertility." *American Journal of Sociology* 74(4): 361–72.

Goodwin Paula Y., William D. Mosher, and Anjani Chandra. 2010. "Marriage and Cohabitation in the United States: A Statistical Portrait Based on Cycle 6 (2002) of the National Survey of Family Growth." *Vital Health Statistics* 23(28): 1–45.

Gould, Stephen J. 1981. *The Mismeasure of Man.* New York: W. W. Norton.

Gray, Alistair M. 1982. "Inequalities in Health: The Black Report—A Summary and Comment." *International Journal of Health Services* 12(3): 349–80.

Grogger, Jeffrey. 2008. "Consequences of Teen Childbearing for Incarceration Among Adult Children: Approach and Estimates through 1991." In *Kids Having Kids: Economic Costs and Social Consequences of Teen Pregnancy*, edited by Saul D. Hoffman and Rebecca A. Maynard. Washington, D.C.: Urban Institute Press.

Guilford, J. P. 1967. *The Nature of Human Intelligence.* Englewood Cliffs, N.J.: McGraw-Hill.

Hadley, Jack. 2002. *Sicker and Poorer: The Consequences of Being Uninsured—Executive Summary.* Menlo Park, Calif.: Henry J. Kaiser Family Foundation. Available at: http://kff.org/uninsured/report/sicker-and-poorer-the-consequences-of-being (accessed February 13, 2014).

Halle, Tamara. 2002. *Charting Parenthood: A Statistical Portrait of Fathers and Mothers in America.* Washington, D.C.: Child Trends.

Hammen, Constance. 2005. "Stress and Depression." *Annual Review of Clinical Psychology* 1: 293–319.

Harding, David G. 2003. "Counterfactual Models of Neighborhood Effects: The Effect of Neighborhood Poverty on High School Dropout and Teenage Pregnancy." *American Journal of Sociology* 109(3): 676–719.

Harding, David J. 2010. *Living the Drama: Community, Conflict, and Culture Among Inner-City Boys.* Chicago: University of Chicago Press.

Harlow, Harry F. 1964. "Early Social Deprivation and Later Behavior in the Monkey." In *Unfinished Tasks in the Behavioral Sciences*, edited by Arnold Abrams, Harry H. H. Gurner, and James E. P. Tomal. Baltimore, Md.: Williams & Wilkins.

Harlow, Harry F., and Clara M. Harlow. 1986. *From Learning to Love: The Selected Papers of H. F. Harlow.* New York: Praeger.

Harmon, Colm, Ian Walker, and Niels Westergard-Nielsen. 2001. *Education and Earnings in Europe: A Cross Country Analysis of the Returns to Education.* London: Edward Elgar.

Harris, Judith R. 1998. *The Nurture Assumption: Why Children Turn Out the Way They Do*. New York: Free Press.

Harris, Kathleen Mullan, and J. Richard Udry. 2008. *National Longitudinal Study of Adolescent Health (Add Health), 1994–2008*. ICPSR21600-v14. Chapel Hill: Carolina Population Center, University of North Carolina-Chapel Hill. doi:10.3886 /ICPSR21600.v14. Available at: http://www.icpsr.umich.edu/icpsrweb/ICPSR /studies/21600 (accessed February 27, 2014).

Harris, Maxine. 1995. *The Loss That Is Forever: The Lifelong Impact of the Early Death of a Mother or Father*. Boston, Mass.: E. P. Dutton.

Haskins, Ron. 2009. "Moynihan Was Right: Now What?" *Annals of the American Academy of Political and Social Science* 621: 111–31.

Hauser, Robert M., and David L. Featherman. 1977. *The Process of Stratification: Trends and Analyses*. New York: Academic Press.

Hauser, Robert M., and John Robert Warren. 1997. "Socioeconomic Indexes for Occupations: A Review, Update, and Critique." *Sociological Methodology* 27(1): 177–298.

Haveman, Robert, Barbara Wolfe, and Elaine Peterson. 2008. "Consequences of Teen Childbearing for the Life Chances of Children 1968–88." In *Kids Having Kids: Economic Costs and Social Consequences of Teen Pregnancy*, edited by Saul D. Hoffman and Rebecca A. Maynard. Washington, D.C.: Urban Institute Press.

Haynes, Stephen R. 2012. *The Last Segregated Hour: The Memphis Kneel-Ins and the Campaign for Southern Church Desegregation*. Oxford: Oxford University Press.

Heckman, James J. 2006. "Skill Formation and the Economics of Investing in Disadvantaged Children." *Science* 312(5782): 1900–02.

———. 2007. "The Economics, Technology, and Neuroscience of Human Capability Formation." *Proceedings of the National Academy of Sciences* 104(33): 13250–55.

Heckman, James J., and Dimitriy V. Masterov. 2007. "The Productivity Argument for Investing in Young Children." *Review of Agricultural Economics* 29(3): 446–93.

Herrnstein, Richard, and Charles Murray. 1994. *The Bell Curve: Intelligence and Class Structure in American Life*. New York: Free Press.

Hertzman, Clyde, and Tom Boyce. 2010. "How Experience Gets Under the Skin to Create Gradients in Developmental Health." *Annual Review of Public Health* 21: 29–47.

Hoffman, Patricia. 2002. "The Impact of Delayed Parenting on Child Outcomes: Linear Relationship Between Maternal Age and Externalizing Problems." Presented at the annual meeting of the American Sociological Association. Philadelphia, Pa. (August 14, 2002).

Hoffman, Saul D. 2008. "Updated Estimates of the Consequences of Teen Child-bearing for Mothers." In *Kids Having Kids: Economic Costs and Social Consequences of Teen Pregnancy*, edited by Saul D. Hoffman and Rebecca A. Maynard. Washington, D.C.: Urban Institute Press.

Hoffman, Saul D., and Lauren Sue Scher. 2008. "Consequences of Teen Childbearing for the Life Chances of Children 1979–2002." In *Kids Having Kids: Economic Costs and Social Consequences of Teen Pregnancy*, edited by Saul D. Hoffman and Rebecca A. Maynard. Washington, D.C.: Urban Institute Press.

Holmes, T. H., and R. H. Rahe. 1967. "The Social Readjustment Rating Scale." *Journal of Psychosomatic Research* 11(2): 213–18.

Hotz, V. Joseph, Susan W. McElroy, and Seth G. Sanders. 2008. "Consequences of Teen Childbearing Through 1993." In *Kids Having Kids: Economic Costs and Social Consequences of Teen Pregnancy*, edited by Saul D. Hoffman and Rebecca A. Maynard. Washington, D.C.: Urban Institute Press.

Hunter, Albert. 1975. *Symbolic Communities: Study of the Persistence and Change of Chicago's Local Communities*. Chicago: University of Chicago Press.

Iannaccone, Lawrence R. 1990. "Religious Practice: A Human Capital Approach." *Journal for the Scientific Study of Religion* 29(3): 297–314.

Iceland, John, and Rima Wilkes. 2006. "Does Socioeconomic Status Matter? Race, Class, and Residential Segregation." *Social Problems* 53(2): 248–73.

Inglehart, Ronald. 1977. *The Silent Revolution: Changing Values and Political Styles Among Western Publics*. Princeton, N.J.: Princeton University Press.

Jargowsky, Paul A. 1997. *Poverty and Place: Ghettos, Barrios, and the American City*. New York: Russell Sage Foundation.

Jayakody, Rukmalie, Arland Thornton, and William Axinn. 2007. *International Family Change: Ideational Perspectives*. New York: Routledge.

Jencks, Christopher, and Susan E. Mayer. 1990. "The Social Consequences of Growing Up in a Poor Neighborhood." In *Inner-City Poverty in the United States*, edited by Laurence Lynn and Michael McGeary. Washington, D.C.: National Academy Press.

Jencks, Christopher, and Meredith Phillips. 1998. *The Black-White Test Score Gap*. Washington, D.C.: Brookings Institution Press.

Johnson, Byron R., Spencer DeLi, David B. Larson, and Michael McCullough. 2000. "A Systematic Review of the Religiosity and Delinquency Literature: A Research Note." *Journal of Contemporary Criminal Justice* 16(1): 32–52.

Johnson, Elizabeth I., and Jane Waldfogel. 2004. "Children of Incarcerated Parents: Multiple Risks and Children's Living Arrangements." In *Imprisoning America: The Social Effects of Mass Incarceration*, edited by Mary Pattillo, David Weiman, and Bruce Western. New York: Russell Sage Foundation.

Kaestle, Christien E., Carolyn T. Halpern, William C. Miller, and Carol A. Ford. 2005. "Early Sexual Debut and Sexually Transmitted Infections in Adolescents and Young Adults." *American Journal of Epidemiology* 161(8): 774–80.

Kaestner, Robert, Jay A. Pearson, Danya Keene, and Arline T. Geronimus. 2009. "Stress, Allostatic Load, and Health of Mexican Immigrants." *Social Science Quarterly* 90(5): 1089–101.

Kahneman, Daniel. 2011. *Thinking Fast and Slow*. New York: Farrar, Straus, and Giroux.

Katz, Michael, and Mark Stern. 2006. *One Nation Divisible: What America Was and What It Is Becoming*. New York: Russell Sage Foundation.

Katznelson, Ira. 2005. *When Affirmative Action Was White: An Untold History of Racial Inequality in the Twentieth Century*. New York: W. W. Norton.

Keister, Lisa A. 2000. *Wealth in America: Trends in Inequality*. New York: Cambridge University Press.

Kelly, Robert L. 1995. *The Foraging Spectrum: Diversity in Hunter-Gatherer Lifeways*. Washington, D.C.: Smithsonian Institution Press.

Kendig, Sarah M., and Suzanne M. Bianchi. 2008. "Single, Cohabiting, and Married Mothers' Time with Children." *Journal of Marriage and the Family* 70(5): 1228–40.

Kenworthy, Lane. 2004. *Egalitarian Capitalism: Jobs, Incomes, and Growth in Affluent Countries*. New York: Russell Sage Foundation.

Kitagawa, Evelyn M., and Phillip M. Hauser. 1973. *Differential Mortality in the United States: A Study in Socioeconomic Epidemiology*. Cambridge, Mass.: Harvard University Press.

Kohn, Melvin. 1989. *Class and Conformity: A Study in Values—With a Reassessment*. Chicago: University of Chicago Press.

Kosmin, Barry A., and Ariela Keysar. 2009a. *American Religious Identification Survey (ARIS 2008): Summary Report*. Hartford, Conn.: Trinity College Press.

———. 2009b. *American Nones: The Profile of the No Religion Population*. Hartford, Conn.: Trinity College Press.

Kozol, Jonathan. 1991. *Savage Inequalities: Children in America's Schools*. New York: Crown Publishers.

————. 2005. *The Shame of the Nation: The Restoration of Apartheid Schooling in America*. New York: Crown Publishers.

Krivo, Lauren J., and Ruth D. Peterson. 1996. "Extremely Disadvantaged Neighborhoods and Urban Crime." *Social Forces* 75(3): 619–50.

————. 2000. "The Structural Context of Homicide: Accounting for Racial Differences in Process." *American Sociological Review* 65(4): 547–59.

Krysan, Maria, and Amanda E. Lewis. 2004. *The Changing Terrain of Race and Ethnicity*. New York: Russell Sage Foundation.

Lamont, Michele. 2000. *The Dignity of Working Men: Morality and the Boundaries of Race, Class, and Immigration*. New York: Russell Sage Foundation.

Lareau, Annette. 2000. *Home Advantage: Social Class and Parental Intervention in Elementary Education*. Lanham, Md.: Rowman & Littlefield.

————. 2003. *Unequal Childhoods: Class, Race, and Family Life*. Berkeley: University of California Press.

Laslett, Peter. 1971. *The World We Have Lost*. London: Methuen.

LeDoux, Joseph. 1996. *The Emotional Brain: The Mysterious Underpinnings of Emotional Life*. New York: Simon & Schuster.

————. 2002. *Synaptic Self: How Our Brains Become Who We Are*. New York: Viking.

Lee, Jennifer, and Frank D. Bean. 2010. *The Diversity Paradox: Immigration and the Color Line in the 21st Century*. New York: Russell Sage Foundation.

Leventhal, Tama, and Jeanne Brooks-Gunn. 2000. "The Neighborhoods They Live in: The Effects of Neighborhood Residence on Child and Adolescent Outcomes." *Psychological Bulletin* 126(2): 309–37.

Levy, Frank. 1988. *Dollars and Dreams: The Changing American Income Distribution*. New York: W. W. Norton.

Levy, Marion J. 1972. *Modernization: Latecomers and Survivors*. New York: Basic Books.

Lillie-Blanton, Marsha, P. Ellen Parsons, Helene Gayle, and Anne Dievler. 1996. "Racial Differences in Health: Not Just Black and White But Shades of Gray." *Annual Review of Public Health* 17: 411–48.

Lin, Ann Chih, and David R. Harris. 2008. *The Colors of Poverty: Why Racial and Ethnic Disparities Persist*. New York: Russell Sage Foundation.

Link, Bruce G., Elmer Struening, Michael Rahav, Jo C. Phelan, and Larry Nuttbrock. 1997. "On Stigma and Its Consequences: Evidence for Longitudinal Study of Men with Dual Diagnoses of Mental Illness and Substance Abuse." *Journal of Health and Social Behavior* 38(2): 177–90.

Lomnitz, Larissa. 1977. *Networks and Marginality*. New York: Academic Press.

Lord, Richard. 2004. *American Nightmare: Predatory Lending and the Foreclosure of the American Dream*. Monroe, Me.: Common Courage Press.

Luecken, Linda J. 1998. "Childhood Attachment and Loss Experiences Affect Adult Cardiovascular and Cortisol Function." *Psychosomatic Medicine* 60(6): 765–72.

———. 2000. "Attachment and Loss Experiences During Childhood Are Associated with Adult Hostility, Depression, and Social Support." *Journal of Psychosomatic Research* 49(1): 85–91.

Macmillan, Ross. 2001. "Violence and the Life Course: The Consequences of Victimization for Personal and Social Development." *Annual Review of Sociology* 27: 1–22.

Maddison, Angus. 2001. *The World Economy: Historical Statistics*. Paris: Organization for Economic Cooperation and Development.

Manlove, Jennifer S., Elizabeth Terry-Humen, Lisa A. Miniceli, and Kristin A. Moore. 2008. "Outcomes for Children of Teen Mothers from Kindergarten Through Adolescence." In *Kids Having Kids: Economic Costs and Social Consequences of Teen Pregnancy*, edited by Saul D. Hoffman and Rebecca A. Maynard. Washington, D.C.: Urban Institute Press.

Mann, Jim, and Stewart Truswell. 1998. *Essentials of Human Nutrition*. New York: Oxford University Press.

Marmot, Michael G. 2004. *The Status Syndrome: How Social Standing Affects Our Health and Longevity*. New York: Henry Holt.

Marmot, Michael G., Manolis Kogevinas, and M. A. Elston. 1987. "Social/Economic Status and Disease." *Annual Review of Public Health* 8: 111–35.

Marmot, Michael G., Geoffrey Rose, M. J. Shipley, and P.J.S. Hamilton. 1978. "Employment Grade and Coronary Heart Disease in British Civil Servants." *Journal of Epidemiology and Community Health* 32(4): 244–49.

Marmot, Michael G., M. J. Shipley, and Geoffrey Rose. 1984. "Inequalities in Death: Specific Explanations of a General Pattern?" *Lancet* 323(8384): 1003–6.

Martin, John Levi. 2009. *Social Structures*. Princeton, N.J.: Princeton University Press.

Massey, Douglas S. 1985. "Ethnic Residential Segregation: A Theoretical Synthesis and Empirical Review." *Sociology and Social Research* 69(3): 315–50.

———. 2001. "The Prodigal Paradigm Returns: Ecology Comes Back to Sociology." In *Does It Take a Village? Community Effects on Children, Adolescents, and Families* edited by Alan Booth and Ann C. Crouter. Mahwah, N.J.: Lawrence Erlbaum Associates.

————. 2004. "Segregation and Stratification: A Biosocial Perspective." *DuBois Review: Social Science Research on Race* 1(1): 1–19.

————. 2005a. *Strangers in a Strange Land. Humans in an Urbanizing World*. New York: Norton.

————. 2005b. "Racial Discrimination in Housing: A Moving Target." *Social Problems* 52(2): 148–51.

————. 2007. *Categorically Unequal: The American Stratification System*. New York: Russell Sage Foundation.

Massey, Douglas S., Len Albright, Rebecca Casciano, Elizabeth Derickson, and David Kinsey. 2013. *Climbing Mount Laurel: The Struggle for Affordable Housing and Social Mobility in an American Suburb*. Princeton, N.J.: Princeton University Press.

Massey, Douglas S., and Brooks Bitterman. 1985. "Explaining the Paradox of Puerto Rican Segregation." *Social Forces* 64(2): 306–31.

Massey, Douglas S., Camille Z. Charles, Garvey F. Lundy, and Mary J. Fischer. 2003. *The Source of the River: The Social Origins of Freshmen at America's Selective Colleges and Universities*. Princeton, N.J.: Princeton University Press.

Massey, Douglas S., Gretchen A. Condron, and Nancy A. Denton. 1987. "The Effect of Residential Segregation on Black Social and Economic Well-being." *Social Forces* 66(1): 29–56.

Massey, Douglas S., and Nancy A. Denton. 1985. "Spatial Assimilation as a Socioeconomic Outcome." *American Sociological Review* 50(1): 94–105.

————. 1993. *American Apartheid: Segregation and the Making of the Underclass*. Cambridge, Mass.: Harvard University Press.

Massey, Douglas S., and Mitchell L. Eggers. 1990. "The Ecology of Inequality: Minorities and the Concentration of Poverty 1970–1980." *American Journal of Sociology* 95(5): 1153–88.

————. 1993. "The Spatial Concentration of Affluence and Poverty During the 1970s." *Urban Affairs Quarterly* 29(2): 299–315.

Massey, Douglas S., and Mary J. Fischer. 2003. "The Geography of Inequality in the United States 1950–2000." In *Brookings-Wharton Papers on Urban Affairs 2003*, edited by William G. Gale and Janet Rothenberg Pack. Washington, D.C.: Brookings Institution Press.

Massey, Douglas S., and Eric Fong. 1990. "Segregation and Neighborhood Quality: Blacks, Hispanics, and Asians in the San Francisco Metropolitan Area." *Social Forces* 69(1): 15–32.

Massey, Douglas S., Andrew B. Gross, and Kumiko Shibuya. 1994. "Migration, Segregation, and the Spatial Concentration of Poverty." *American Sociological Review* 59(3): 425–45.

Massey, Douglas S., and Garvey Lundy. 2001. "Use of Black English and Racial Discrimination in Urban Housing Markets: New Methods and Findings." *Urban Affairs Review* 36(4): 470–96.

Massey, Douglas S., and Brendan P. Mullan. 1984. "Processes of Hispanic and Black Spatial Assimilation." *American Journal of Sociology* 89(4): 836–73.

Massey, Douglas S., and LiErin Probasco. 2010. "Divergent Streams: Race-Gender Achievement Gaps at Selective Colleges and Universities." *The DuBois Review: Social Science Research on Race* 7(1): 219–46.

Massey, Douglas S., Jonathan Rothwell, and Thurston Domina. 2009. "Changing Bases of Segregation in the United States." *Annals of the American Academy of Political and Social Science* 626: 74–90.

Massey, Douglas S., and Robert J. Sampson. 2009. "Moynihan Redux: Legacies and Lessons." *Annals of the American Academy of Political and Social Science* 621: 6–27.

Mathews, T. J., and Brady E. Hamilton. 2009. "Delayed Childbearing: More Women Are Having Their First Child Later in Life." *NCHS Data Brief* 21. Atlanta, Ga.: Centers for Disease Control and Prevention.

Mayer, Susan E. 1997. *What Money Can't Buy: Family Income and Children's Life Chances*. Cambridge, Mass.: Harvard University Press.

McCarty, Nolan, Keith T. Poole, and Howard Rosenthal. 2006. *Polarized America: The Dance of Ideology and Unequal Riches*. Cambridge, Mass.: MIT Press.

McDade, Thomas W. 2005. "The Ecologies of Human Immune Function." *Annual Review of Anthropology* 34: 495–521.

McEwen, Bruce S. 1998. "Protective and Damaging Effects of Stress Mediators." *New England Journal of Medicine* 338(3): 171–79.

McEwen, Bruce, and Elizabeth N. Lasley. 2002. *The End of Stress as We Know It*. Washington, D.C.: Joseph Henry Press / Dana Press.

McLanahan, Sara. 1988. "Family Structure and Dependency: Early Transitions to Female Household Headship." *Demography* 25(1): 1–16.

———. 2004. "Diverging Destinies: How Children Are Faring Under the Second Demographic Transition." *Demography* 41(4): 607–27.

———. 2009. "Fragile Families and the Reproduction of Poverty." *Annals of the American Academy of Political and Social Science* 621: 111–31.

McLanahan, Sara, and Christine Percheski. 2008. "Family Structure and the Reproduction of Inequalities." *Annual Review of Sociology* 34: 257–76.

McLanahan, Sara, and Gary Sandefur. 1994. *Growing Up with a Single Parent: What Hurts, What Helps?* Cambridge, Mass.: Harvard University Press.

McLoyd, Vonnie C. 1998. "Socioeconomic Disadvantage and Child Development." *American Psychologist* 53(2): 185–204.

McPherson, Miller, Lynn Smith-Lovin, and James M Cook. 2001. "Birds of a Feather: Homophily in Social Networks." *Annual Review of Sociology* 27: 415–44.

McWilliams, J. Michael. 2009. "Health Consequences of Uninsurance Among Adults in the United States: Recent Evidence and Implications." *Milbank Quarterly* 87(2): 443–94.

Michael, Robert T., John H. Gagnon, Edward O. Laumann, and Gina Kolata. 1994. *Sex in America: A Definitive Survey.* Boston, Mass.: Little, Brown.

Miller, Gregory E., Edith Chen, Alexandra K. Fok, Hope Walker, Alvin Lim, Erin F. Nicholls, Steve Cole, and Michael S. Kobor. 2009. "Low Early-Life Social Class Leaves a Biological Residue Manifested by Decreasing Glucocorticoid and Increased Proinflamatory Signaling." *Proceedings of the National Academy of Sciences* 106(34): 14716–21.

Mincer, Jacob A. 1974. *Schooling, Experience, and Earnings.* New York: Columbia University Press.

Mintz, Steven, and Susan Kellogg. 1988. *Domestic Revolutions: A Social History of American Family Life.* New York: Collier Macmillan.

Monheit, Alan C. 1994. "Underinsured Americans: A Review." *Annual Review of Public Health* 15: 461–85.

Montague, Ashley. 1971. *Touching: The Human Significance of the Skin.* New York: Columbia University Press.

Moore, Mignon R. 2001. "Family Environment and Adolescent Sexual Debut in Alternative Household Structures." In *Social Awakening: Adolescents' Behavior as Adult Approaches*, edited by Robert T. Michael. New York: Russell Sage Foundation.

Morenoff, Jeffrey, Robert J. Sampson, and Stephen Raudenbush. 2001. "Neighborhood Inequality, Collective Efficacy, and the Spatial Dynamics of Urban Violence." *Criminology* 39(3): 517–60.

Moynihan, Daniel Patrick. 1965. *The Negro Family: The Case for National Action.* Washington: U.S. Department of Labor.

Musick, Kelly, and Robert D. Mare. 2004. "Family Structure, Intergenerational Mobility, and the Reproduction of Poverty: Evidence for Increasing Polarization?" *Demography* 41(4): 629–48.

————. 2006. "Recent Trends in the Inheritance of Poverty and Family Structure." *Social Science Research* 35(4): 471–99.

Naifeh, Mary. 1998. "Trap Door, Revolving Door? Or Both?" *Current Population Reports*, series P70, no. 63. Washington: U.S. Bureau of the Census. Available at: http://www.census.gov/prod/3/98pubs/p70-63.pdf (accessed February 13, 2014).

National Center for Education Statistics. 2009. *Digest of Education Statistics, 2008.* Washington: U.S. Department of Education.

National Center for Health Statistics. 2008. "Prevalence of Overweight, Obesity, and Extreme Obesity Among Adults: United States Trends 1976–80 Through 2005–2006." Available at: http://www.cdc.gov/nchs/data/hestat/overweight/overweight _adult.pdf (accessed August 9, 2010).

National Institute of Mental Health. 2010. "Attention Deficit Hyperactivity Disorder." Bethesda, Md.: U.S. Department of Health and Human Services. Available at: http://www.nimh.nih.gov/health/publications/attention-deficit-hyperactivity -disorder/adhd_booklet.pdf (accessed August 19, 2010).

National Research Council. 2003. *Hidden Costs, Value Lost: Uninsurance in America.* Washington, D.C.: National Academies Press.

Neckerman, Kathryn. 2004. *Social Inequality.* New York: Russell Sage Foundation.

Nestle, Marion. 2002. *Food Politics: How the Food Industry Influences Nutrition and Health.* Berkeley: University of California Press.

Nisbett, Richard E. 2009. *Intelligence and How to Get It: Why Schools and Cultures Count.* New York: W. W. Norton.

Norris, Pippa, and Ronald Inglehart. 2004. *Sacred and Secular: Religion and Politics Worldwide.* New York: Cambridge University Press.

Orfield, Gary, and Susan Eaton. 1996. *Dismantling Desegregation: The Quiet Reversal of Brown v. Board of Education.* New York: New Press.

Orfield, Myron. 2002. *American Metropolitics: The New Suburban Reality.* Washington, D.C.: Brookings Institution Press.

Pager, Devah. 2007. *Marked: Race, Crime, and Finding Work in an Era of Mass Incarceration.* Chicago: University of Chicago Press.

Pampel, Fred C., Patrick M. Krueger, and Justin T. Tenney. 2010. "Socioeconomic Disparities in Health Behaviors." *Annual Review of Sociology* 36: 349–70.

Park, Robert E. 1926. "The Urban Community as a Spatial Pattern and a Moral Order." In *The Urban Community*, edited by Ernest W. Burgess and Robert E. Park. Chicago: University of Chicago Press.

Parkin, Robert, and Linda Stone, eds. 2004. *Kinship and Family: An Anthropological Reader.* New York: Wiley.

Pattillo, Mary, David Weiman, and Bruce Western, eds. 2004. *Imprisoning America: The Social Effects of Mass Incarceration.* New York: Russell Sage Foundation.

Peterson, Ruth D., and Lauren J. Krivo. 2010. *Divergent Social Worlds: Neighborhood Crime and the Racial-Spatial Divide.* New York: Russell Sage Foundation.

Pettigrew, Thomas. 1979. "Racial Change and Social Policy." *Annals of the American Academy of Political and Social Science* 441: 114–31.

Phillips, Deborah, Kathleen McCartney, and Sandra Scarr. 1987. "Child-Care Quality and Children's Social Development." *Developmental Psychology* 23(4): 537–43.

Piketty, Thomas, and Emmanuel Saez. 2003. "Income Inequality in the United States, 1913–1998." *Quarterly Journal of Economics* 158(1): 1–16.

Polednak, Anthony P. 1997. *Segregation, Poverty, and Mortality in Urban African Americans.* New York: Oxford University Press.

Pong, Suet-Ling, and Lingxin Hao. 2007. "Neighborhood and School Factors in the School Performance of Immigrants' Children." *International Migration Review* 4(1): 206–41.

Preston, Samuel H. 1970. *Older Male Mortality and Cigarette Smoking.* Population monograph no. 7. Berkeley: University of California Press, Institute of International Studies.

Purnell, Thomas, William Idsardi, and John Baugh. 1999. "Perceptual and Phonetic Experiments on American English Dialect Identification." *Journal of Language and Social Psychology* 18(1): 10–30.

Quadagno, Jill. 1996. *The Color of Welfare: How Racism Undermined the War on Poverty.* New York: Oxford University Press.

Quillian, Lincoln. 2002. "Why Is Black-White Residential Segregation So Persistent? Evidence on Three Theories from Migration Data." *Social Science Research* 31(2): 197–229.

Rainwater, Lee, and William L. Yancey. 1967. *The Moynihan Report and the Politics of Controversy.* Cambridge, Mass.: MIT Press.

Reardon, Sean F., and Kendra Bischoff. 2011. "Income Inequality and Income Segregation." *American Journal of Sociology* 116(4): 1092–153.

Reimers, Fernando, ed. 2001. *Unequal Schools, Unequal Chances: The Challenges to Equal Opportunity in the Americas.* Cambridge, Mass.: Harvard University, Rockefeller Center for Latin American Studies.

Ridley, Matt. 2004. *The Agile Gene: How Nature Turns on Nurture.* New York: Harper.

Robert, Stephanie A., and James A. House. 2000. "Socioeconomic Inequalities in Health: An Enduring Sociological Problem." In *Handbook of Medical Sociology,* edited by Chloe E. Bird, Peter Conrad, and Alan M. Fremont. Upper Saddle River, N.J.: Prentice Hall.

Rosenfield, Sarah. 1997. "Labeling Mental Illness: The Effects of Received Services and Perceived Stigma on Life Satisfaction." *American Sociological Review* 62(4): 660–72.

Ross, Stephen L., and Margery A. Turner. 2004. "Other Things Being Equal: A Paired Testing Study of Discrimination in Mortgage Lending." *Journal of Urban Economics* 55(2): 278–97.

Ross, Stephen L., and John Yinger. 2002. *The Color of Credit: Mortgage Discrimination, Research Methodology, and Fair-Lending Enforcement*. Cambridge, Mass.: MIT Press.

Rothstein, Richard. 2004. *Class and Schools: Using Social, Economic, and Educational Reform to Close the Black-White Achievement Gap*. New York: Teacher's College Press.

Rothwell, Jonathan, and Douglas S. Massey. 2009. "The Effect of Density Zoning on Racial Segregation in U.S. Urban Areas." *Urban Affairs Review* 44(6): 799–806.

———. 2010. "Density Zoning and Class Segregation in U.S. Metropolitan Areas." *Social Science Quarterly* 91(5): 1123–43.

Rowe, David C., Kristen C. Jacobson, and Edwin J. C. G. van den Oord. 1999. "Genetic and Environmental Influences on Vocabulary IQ: Parental Education Level as Moderator." *Child Development* 70(5): 1151–62.

Rugh, Jacob S., and Douglas S. Massey. 2010. "Racial Segregation and the American Foreclosure Crisis." *American Sociological Review* 75(5): 629–51.

———. 2013. "Segregation in Post-Civil Rights America: Stalled Integration or End of the Segregated Century?" *The DuBois Review: Social Science Research on Race*. doi: 10.10170S1742058X13000180. Available at: http://journals.cambridge.org /download.php?file=%2FDBR%2FS1742058X13000180a.pdf&code=4723fe 5909453e0d0efbe7a12d05dd39 (accessed February 13, 2014).

Rushton, J. Phillipe. 1994. *Race, Evolution, and Behavior: A Life History Perspective*. New Brunswick, N.J.: Transaction Press.

Rutter, Michael. 2006. *Genes and Behavior: Nature-Nurture Interplay Explained*. New York: HarperCollins.

Sampson, Robert J. 2001. "How Do Communities Undergird or Undermine Human Development? Relevant Contexts and Social Mechanisms." In *Does It Take a Village? Community Effects on Children, Adolescents, and Families*, edited by Alan Booth and Nan Crouter. Mahwah, N.J.: Lawrence Erlbaum Associates.

————. 2003. "The Neighborhood Context of Well Being." *Perspectives in Biology and Medicine* 46(3): S53–S73.

————. 2004. "Neighborhood and Community: Collective Efficacy and Community Safety." *New Economy* 11(2): 106–13.

————. 2005. "Social Ecology and Collective Efficacy Theory." In *The Essential Criminology Reader*, edited by Stuart Henry and Mark Lanier. Boulder, Colo.: Westview.

————. 2006. "Collective Efficacy Theory: Lessons Learned and Directions for Future Inquiry." In *Advances in Criminological Theory, Taking Stock: The Status of Criminological Theory*, edited by Francis T. Cullen, John Paul Wright, and Kristie R. Blevins. New Brunswick: Transaction Publishers.

————. 2008. "Moving to Inequality: Neighborhood Effects and Experiments Meet Social Structure." *American Journal of Sociology* 114(1): 189–231.

————. 2012. *Great American City: Chicago and the Enduring Neighborhood Effect*. Chicago: University of Chicago Press.

Sampson, Robert J., and Corina Graef. 2009. "Neighborhood Social Capital as Differential Social Organization." *American Behavioral Scientist* 52(11): 1579–605.

Sampson, Robert J., and John H. Laub. 1993. *Crime in the Making: Pathways and Turning Points Through Life*. Cambridge, Mass.: Harvard University Press.

Sampson, Robert J., Doug McAdam, Heather MacIndoe, and Simón Weffer-Elizondo. 2005. "Civil Society Reconsidered: The Durable Nature and Community Structure of Collective Civic Action." *American Journal of Sociology* 111(3): 673–714.

Sampson, Robert J., and Jeffrey D. Morenoff. 2004. "Spatial (Dis)Advantage and Homicide in Chicago Neighborhoods." In *Spatially Integrated Social Science*, edited by Michael Goodchild and Donald Janelle. New York: Oxford University Press.

Sampson, Robert J., Jeffrey Morenoff, and Felton Earls. 1999. "Beyond Social Capital: Spatial Dynamics of Collective Efficacy for Children." *American Sociological Review* 64(5): 633–60.

Sampson, Robert J., Jeffrey D. Morenoff, and Thomas Gannon-Rowley. 2002. "Assessing Neighborhood Effects: Social Processes and New Directions in Research." *Annual Review of Sociology* 28: 443–78.

Sampson, Robert J., and Stephen W. Raudenbush. 1999. "Systematic Social Observation of Public Spaces: A New Look at Disorder in Urban Neighborhoods." *American Journal of Sociology* 105(3): 603–51.

————. 2004. "Seeing Disorder: Neighborhood Stigma and the Social Construction of Broken Windows." *Social Psychology Quarterly* 67(4): 319–42.

Sampson, Robert J., Stephen Raudenbush, and Felton Earls. 1997. "Neighborhoods and Violent Crime: A Multilevel Study of Collective Efficacy." *Science* 277(5328): 918–24.

Sampson, Robert J., and Patrick Sharkey. 2008. "Neighborhood Selection and the Social Reproduction of Concentrated Racial Inequality." *Demography* 45(1): 1–29.

Sampson, Robert J., Patrick Sharkey, and Stephen Raudenbush. 2008. "Durable Effects of Concentrated Disadvantage on Verbal Ability Among African-American Children." *Proceedings of the National Academy of Sciences* 105(3): 845–53.

Santibáñez, Lucrecia, Georges Vernez, and Paula Razquin. 2005. *Education in Mexico: Challenges and Opportunities*. Santa Monica, Calif.: RAND Corporation.

Sapolsky, Robert M. 2004. "Organismal Stress and Telomeric Aging: An Unexpected Connection." *Proceedings of the National Academy of Sciences* 101(50): 17323–24.

Scher, Lauren Sue, and Saul D. Hoffman. 2008. "Consequences of Teen Childbearing for Incarceration Among Adult Children: Updated Estimates Through 2002." In *Kids Having Kids: Economic Costs and Social Consequences of Teen Pregnancy*, edited by Saul D. Hoffman and Rebecca A. Maynard. Washington, D.C.: Urban Institute Press.

Schnittker, Jason, and Jane D. McLeod. 2005. "The Social Psychology of Health Disparities." *Annual Review of Sociology* 31: 75–103.

Schulz, P. C., C. Kirschbaum, J. Prüsser, and D. Hellhamer. 1998. "Increased Free Cortisol Secretion after Awakening in Chronically Stressed Individuals Due to Work Overload." *Stress Medicine* 14(1): 91–97.

Schultz, T. Paul. 2003. "Human Capital, Schooling, and Health." *Economics and Human Biology* 1(2): 207–21.

Schultz, Theodore W. 1963. *The Economic Value of Education*. New York: Columbia University Press.

Schuman, Howard, Charlotte Steeh, Lawrence D. Bobo, and Maria Krysan. 1998. *Racial Attitudes in America: Trends and Interpretations*. Cambridge, Mass.: Harvard University Press.

Schwadel, Philip. 2009. "Neighbors in the Pews: Social Status Diversity in Religious Congregations." *Interdisciplinary Journal of Research on Religion* 5(2): 1–24.

Seeman, T. E., Burton H. Singer, J. W. Rowe, R. I. Horwitz, and Bruce S. McEwen. 1997. "Price of Adaptation: Allostatic Load and Its Health Consequences." *Archives of Internal Medicine* 157(19): 2259–68.

Sellström, E., and S. Bremberg. 2006. "Is There a School Effect on Pupil Outcomes? A Review of Multilevel Studies." *Journal of Epidemiology and Community Health* 60(2): 149–55.

Shafii, Taraneh, Katherine Stovel, and King Holmes. 2007. "Association Between Condom Use at Sexual Debut and Subsequent Sexual Trajectories." *American Journal of Public Health* 97(6): 1090–95.

Sharkey, Patrick. 2013. *Stuck in Place: Urban Neighborhoods and the End of Progress Toward Racial Equality*. Chicago: University of Chicago Press.

Singh, Susheela, Deirdre Wulf, Renee Samara, and Yvette P. Cuca. 2000. "Gender Differences in the Timing of First Intercourse: Data from 14 Countries." *International Family Planning Perspectives* 26(1): 21–28.

Sjoberg, Gideon. 1960. *The Pre-Industrial City: Past and Present*. Glencoe, Ill.: Free Press.

Small, Mario. 2009. *Unanticipated Gains: Origins of Network Inequality in Everyday Life*. New York: Oxford University Press.

Small, Mario Luis, and Katherine Newman. 2001. "Urban Poverty After the Truly Disadvantaged: The Rediscovery of the Family, the Neighborhood, and Culture." *Annual Review of Sociology* 27: 23–45.

Smeeding, Timothy M. 2005. "Public Policy, Economic Inequality, and Poverty: The United States in Comparative Perspective." *Social Science Quarterly* 86(s1): 955–83.

Smilde, David. 2007. *Reason to Believe: Cultural Agency in Latin American Evangelicalism*. Berkeley: University of California Press.

Smith, Adam. 1904. *An Inquiry into the Nature and Causes of the Wealth of Nations*, 5th ed. London: Methuen.

Smith, Kirsten P., and Nicholas A. Christakis. 2008. "Social Networks and Health." *Annual Review of Sociology* 34: 405–29.

Smith, Robin, and Michelle DeLair. 1999. "New Evidence from Lender Testing: Discrimination at the Pre-application Stage." In *Mortgage Lending Discrimination: A Review of Existing Evidence*, edited by Margery A. Turner and Felicity Skidmore. Washington, D.C.: Urban Institute.

Snedker, Karen A., Jerald R. Herting, and Emily Walton. 2009. "Contextual Effects and Adolescent Substance Use: Exploring the Role of Neighborhoods." *Social Science Quarterly* 90(5): 1272–97.

South, Scott J., Kyle Crowder, and Erick Chavez. 2005. "Exiting and Entering High-Poverty Neighborhoods: Latinos, Blacks, and Anglos Compared." *Social Forces* 84(6): 873–900.

South, Scott J., Kyle Crowder, and Jeremy Pais. 2008. "Inter-Neighborhood Migration and Spatial Assimilation in a Multi-ethnic World: Comparing Latinos, Blacks, and Anglos." *Social Forces* 87(3): 415–43.

Spriggs, Aubrey L., and Carolyn T. Halpern. 2008. "Timing of Sexual Debut and Initiation of Postsecondary Education by Early Adulthood." *Perspectives on Sexual and Reproductive Health* 40(3): 152–61.

Squires, Gregory D. 1994. *Capital and Communities in Black and White: The Intersections of Race, Class, and Uneven Development.* Albany: State University of New York Press.

———. 2004. *Why the Poor Pay More: How to Stop Predatory Lending.* New York: Praeger.

Squires, Gregory D., and Jan Chadwick. 2006. "Linguistic Profiling: A Tradition of the Property Insurance Industry." *Urban Affairs Review* 41(3): 400–15.

Stark, Rodney. 2007. *Discovering God: The Origins of the Great Religions and the Evolution of Belief.* New York: Harper.

Stark, Rodney, and William S. Bainbridge. 1987. *A Theory of Religion.* New York: Peter Lang.

Stark, Rodney, and Roger Finke. 2000. *Acts of Faith: Explaining the Human Side of Religion.* Berkeley: University of California Press.

Steffensmeier, Darrell, and Emilie A. Allan. 1996. "Gender and Crime: Toward a Gendered Theory of Criminal Offending." *Annual Review of Sociology* 22: 450–87.

Steffensmeier, Darrell, Emilie A. Allan, Miles D. Harer, and Cathy Streifel. 1989. "Age and the Distribution of Crime." *American Journal of Sociology* 94(4): 803–31.

Sterling, Peter, and Joseph Eyer. 1988. "Allostasis: A New Paradigm to Explain Arousal Pathology." In *Handbook of Life Stress, Cognition, and Health*, edited by Shirley Fischer and James Reason. New York: John Wiley and Sons.

Stützle W., T. Gasser, L. Molinari, R. H. Largo, and P. J. Huber. 1980. "Shape-Invariant Modeling of Human Growth." *Annals of Human Biology* 7(6): 507–28.

Sullivan, Teresa A., Elizabeth Warren, and Jay L. Westbrook. 1989. *As We Forgive Our Debtors: Bankruptcy and Consumer Credit in America.* New York: Oxford University Press.

———. 2000. *The Fragile Middle Class: Americans in Debt.* New Haven, Conn.: Yale University Press.

Suttles, Gerald. 1968. *The Social Order of the Slum: Ethnicity and Territory in the Inner City.* Chicago: University of Chicago Press.

Surgeon General's Advisory Committee on Smoking and Health. 1964. *Smoking and Health.* Public Health Service publication no. 1103. Washington: U.S. Department of Health and Human Services, Office of the Surgeon General.

Suzuki, Miho M., and Adrian Bird. 2008. "DNA Methylation Landscapes: Provocative Insights from Epigenomics." *Nature Reviews Genetics* 9(6): 465–76.

Taylor, Shelley E., Rena L. Repetti, and Teresa Seeman. 1997. "Health Psychology: What is an Unhealthy Environment and How Does It Get Under the Skin?" *Annual Review of Psychology* 48: 411–47.

Telles, Edward E., and Vilma Ortiz. 2008. *Generations of Exclusion: Mexican Americans, Assimilation, and Race.* New York: Russell Sage Foundation.

Thomas, Adam, and Isabel Sawhill. 2002. "For Richer or for Poorer: Marriage as an Antipoverty Strategy." *Journal of Policy Analysis and Management* 21(4): 587–99.

Thompson, Derek. 2012. "A Giant Statistical Round-Up of the Income Inequality Crisis in 16 Charts." *The Atlantic.* Available at: http://www.theatlantic.com/busi ness/archive/2012/12/a-giant-statistical-round-up-of-the-income-inequality -crisis-in-16-charts/266074 (accessed July 31, 2013).

Thornton, Arland, William G. Axinn, and Yu Xie. 2007. *Marriage and Cohabitation.* Chicago: University of Chicago Press.

Tiemeier, H., R. K. Lenroot, D. K. Greenstein, L. Tran, R. Pierson, and J. N. Giedd. 2009. "Cerebellum Development During Childhood and Adolescence: A Longitudinal Morphometric MRI Study." *Neuroimage* 49(1): 63–70.

Todaro, Michael P., and Stephen P. Smith. 2008. *Economic Development,* 10th ed. Reading, Mass.: Addison-Wesley.

Tonry, Michael. 1996. *Malign Neglect: Race, Crime, and Punishment in America.* New York: Oxford University Press.

Turner, Margery A., Fred Freiberg, Eerin B. Godfrey, Carla Herbig, Diane K. Levy, and Robert E. Smith. 2002. *All Other Things Being Equal: A Paired Testing Study of Mortgage Lending Institution.* Washington: U.S. Department of Housing and Urban Development.

U.S. Census Bureau. 2009. *Historical Income Inequality Tables.* Washington: U.S. Bureau of the Census. Available at: http://www.census.gov/hhes/www/income /histinc/ineqtoc.html (accessed February 13, 2014).

———. 2010. "Estimated Median Age at First Marriage, by Sex: 1890 to the Present." Available at: http://www.census.gov/population/socdemo/hh-fam/ms2.pdf (accessed February 13, 2014).

United Nations. 1980. *Patterns of Urban and Rural Population Growth.* New York: United Nations Department of International Economic and Social Affairs.

———. 2010. *World Urbanization Prospects: The 2010 Revision.* New York: United Nations.

Visscher, Tommy L. S., and Jacob C. Seidell. 2001. "The Public Health Impact of Obesity." *Annual Review of Public Health* 22: 335–75.

Wagstaff, Adam, and Eddy van Doorslaer. 2000. "Income Inequality and Health: What Does the Literature Tell Us?" *Annual Review of Public Health* 21: 543–67.

Walsemann, Katrina M., Gilbert C. Gee, and Arline Geronimus. 2009. "Ethnic Differences in Trajectories of Depressive Symptoms." *Journal of Health and Social Behavior* 50(1): 82–98.

Walsemann, Katrina M., Arline T. Geronimus, and Gilbert C. Gee. 2008. "Accumulating Disadvantage Over the Life Course: Evidence from a Longitudinal Study Investigating the Relationship Between Educational Advantage in Youth and Health in Middle Age." *Research on Aging* 30(2): 169–99.

Warner, R. Stephen. 1993. "Work in Progress Toward a New Paradigm for the Sociological Study of Religion in the United States." *American Journal of Sociology* 98(5): 1044–93.

Western, Bruce. 2006. *Punishment and Inequality in America*. New York: Russell Sage Foundation.

Western, Bruce, Leonard M. Lopoo, and Sara McLanahan. 2004. "Incarceration and the Bonds Between Parents in Fragile Families." In *Imprisoning America: The Social Effects of Mass Incarceration*, edited by Mary Pattillo, David Weiman, and Bruce Western. New York: Russell Sage Foundation.

Wilkes, Rima, and John Iceland. 2004. "Hypersegregation in the Twenty-First Century: An Update and Analysis." *Demography* 41(1): 23–36.

Wilkinson, Ian A. G., John A. Hattie, Judy M. Parr, Michael A. R. Townsend, Irene Fung, Charlotte Ussher, Martin Thrupp, Hugh Lauder, and Tony Robinson. 2000. *Influence of Peer Effects on Learning Outcomes: A Review of the Literature*. Auckland: New Zealand Ministry of Education.

Williams, David R., and Chiquita Collins. 2001. "Racial Residential Segregation: A Fundamental Cause of Racial Disparities in Health." *Public Health Reports* 116(5): 404–16.

Williams, Richard, Reynold Nesiba, and Eileen Diaz McConnell. 2005. "The Changing Face of Inequality in Home Mortgage Lending." *Social Problems* 52(2): 181–208.

Willis, Paul E. 1977. *Learning to Labour: How Working-Class Kids Get Working-Class Jobs*. Farnborough, U.K.: Saxon House.

Wilson, James Q. 2009. "Pat Moynihan Talks About Families." *Annals of the American Academy of Political and Social Science* 621: 28–34.

Wilson, William J. 1978. *The Declining Significance of Race: Blacks and Changing American Institutions*. Chicago: University of Chicago Press.

———. 1987. *The Truly Disadvantaged: The Inner City, the Underclass, and Public Policy*. Chicago: University of Chicago Press.

Windle, Michael. 1992. "Temperament and Social Support in Adolescence: Interrelations with Depressive Symptoms and Delinquent Behaviors." *Journal of Youth and Adolescence* 21(1): 1–21.

Wolfe, Barbara, and Emilie McHugh Rivers. 2008. "Children's Health and Health Care." In *Kids Having Kids: Economic Costs and Social Consequences of Teen Pregnancy*, edited by Saul D. Hoffman and Rebecca A. Maynard. Washington, D.C.: Urban Institute Press.

Wolff, Edward N. 2002. *Top Heavy: The Increasing Inequality of Wealth in America and What Can Be Done About It*. New York: New Press.

Wolfgang, Marvin E., Robert M. Figlio, and Thorsten Sellin. 1972. *Delinquency in a Birth Cohort*. Chicago: University of Chicago Press.

Wolman, Dianne Miller, and Mille Wilhelmine. 2004. "The Consequences of Uninsurance for Individuals, Families, Communities, and the Nation." *Journal of Law, Medicine, and Ethics* 32(3): 397–403.

Wright, Erik O. 1997. *Class Counts: Comparative Studies in Class Analysis*. New York: Cambridge University Press.

Wright, Robert. 2009. *The Evolution of God*. Boston, Mass.: Little, Brown.

Wu, Lawrence L. 1996. "Effects of Family Instability, Income, and Income Instability on the Risk of a Premarital Birth." *American Sociological Review* 61(3): 386–406.

Yen, Irene H., and S. Leonard Syme. 1999. "The Social Environment and Health: A Discussion of the Epidemiologic Literature." *Annual Review of Public Health* 20: 287–308.

Yinger, John. 1995. *Closed Doors, Opportunities Lost: The Continuing Costs of Housing Discrimination*. New York: Russell Sage Foundation.

Zittoun, Tania. 2006. *Transitions: Symbolic Resources in Development*. Charlotte, N.C.: Information Age Publishing.

INDEX

Boldface numbers refer to figures and tables.